LAW AND PSYCHOLOGICAL PRACTICE

LAW AND PSYCHOLOGICAL PRACTICE

Robert L. Schwitzgebel
Claremont Graduate School
R. Kirkland Schwitzgebel
California Lutheran College

JOHN WILEY & SONS
NEW YORK   CHICHESTER   BRISBANE   TORONTO

Cover Design by Kevin J. Murphy

Library of Congress Cataloging in Publication Data:

Schwitzgebel, Robert L
    Law and psychological practice.

    Includes index.
    1. Law—Psychology. 2. Psychologists—Legal
status, laws, etc. 3. Psychology, Forensic.
4. Mental health laws. I. Schwitzgebel, Ralph K.,
1934–   joint author. II. Title.
K487.P75S38   340.1'9   79–20112
ISBN 0–471–76694–1

Printed in the United States of America

10 9 8 7 6 5 4 3 2 1

This publication is designed to provide accurate and authoritative information with regard to the subject matter covered. It is sold with the understanding that the publisher is not engaged in rendering legal or other professional services. If legal advice or other expert assistance is required, the services of a competent professional should be sought.
    —from a Declaration of Principles jointly adopted by a Committee of the American Bar Association and a Committee of Publishers and Associations.

Acknowledgments

We wish to acknowledge the very valuable assistance of Jeffrey D. Ross, J.D., who, as a research assistant and undergraduate student at Claremont Mens College, composed the first draft of most of the chapters of this book. His work was not only distinguished for its quality but also by the fact that his writing did not extinguish even in the face of numerous revisions, continual editing, and other forms of "intellectual brutality" on the part of his employer. The hours spent working with Mr. Ross on this project were among the most pleasant of the entire endeavor.

Our appreciation goes also to David Helgeson whose erudition was not constrained by compelled attention to detail.

R.L.S.
R.K.S.

Contents

Appendixes

Introduction

Television-show lawyers are to law what Emily Post is to a barroom brawl. Neither accurately reflects the day-to-day reality of professional and social life. The domain of law is formidable in scope, but concealed (as are most professions) by an esoteric vocabulary and by informal routines of practice that are necessary to deal with daily obligations.

The law does not solve legal problems—it creates them. It systematically restructures social or interpersonal conflicts into a particular, logical matrix. Thus, for example, many lawyers find it very exasperating to obtain *legally* relevant material in a divorce case because the parties involved see the situation from an emotional rather than a logical perspective. Such restructuring may have a socially useful function in one situation but a destructive result in another. Perhaps there are some matters that should *not* be the law's business. Some mental health specialists feel this way about the intrusion of recent court decisions that set certain standards for psychotherapeutic practice.[1] But on the other hand, this same legal process, by means of case and statutory law, grants various professional licenses that reduce competition (presumably from quacks) and increases the professional's income.

The purpose of this book is to lead human service professionals and interested clients through unfamiliar territory. In a way, the book may be conceived as a "guide dog" for the "legally blind." But first, a warning to the uninitiated is necessary: For your own happiness, stay as far from the law as possible (without actually becoming a criminal). As a beginner, you are likely to be plunged into a fog

1

of complex detail where semantic traps have been set by adversaries. Whether your introduction comes as patient, administrator, expert witness, or just a casual reader, you will probably experience confusion, boredom, anxiety, or anger. Formal law takes shape on paper in the form of statutes, cases, procedural rules, and regulations. (See Appendix A.) The 1978 *Federal Register* contained 61,261 pages of proposed or adopted rules and regulations. A single malpractice case can produce 15 pounds of court records.[2]

Although litigation takes up only a small proportion of the total legal endeavor, the threat of a negative outcome in court is the ultimate sanction that lawyers and their clients work to avoid. The adversary method of obtaining "facts" is itself a dignified but stressful procedure. Psychologist Edwin Thorndike found, according to his criteria, that the "goodness of a city" was *inversely* correlated with the number of lawyers.[3] The greater the number of lawyers, presumably the more litigious the community. The number of court cases has risen drastically in the past decade (as has the number of lawyers)—perhaps to the point of "legal pollution."[4]

Lawyers should not be blamed for all this apparent lack of goodness. The law has a rightful place among human endeavors, not because it has produced elaborate rules, or even "justice," but because it is the primary formal means by which civilized societies attempt to prevent and resolve conflict. It is better to have an injured person go to court to try to collect monetary compensation or compel someone to keep a promise than for that person to take direct and violent revenge, because innocent onlookers may get hurt. Few would argue with the proposition that the expansion of law into an effective world court is preferable to war as a way of solving international disputes. (Litigation is obviously not the only peaceful means of resolving conflict; grievance procedures, negotiation, and arbitration are practical alternatives.[5])

The conflict-resolution function of law relies heavily on the community-at-large believing that the procedures and judgments of courts are "fair"—even though what is seen as "fair" or "just" at one time or in one community may be quite different at another time or in another place. The content of a decision is secondary to the process: "It is more important for society that the dispute be settled peaceably than that it be settled in any particular way."[6] To keep things from becoming too fickle, considerable weight is placed on precedent and the doctrine of *stare decisis* ("let the decision stand"). Also juries and expert witnesses, though expensive and cumbersome, are very useful in "sharing the blame" if a decision proves unpopular.

Another function of the law, in addition to resolving conflict by compensating an injured party, is to change the behavior of wrongdoers. Although a traditional and widely accepted goal of criminal law has been to deter the criminal and others from similar, unwanted behavior in the future, civil law (which deals with noncriminal disputes between private citizens) has focused on finding a remedy for injuries. A "behavior-modification" model of civil law would seek not only to compensate the victim but to deter wrongdoers. If injured parties cannot be found, the wrongdoers would still be made to pay.[7] The behavior modification function of law should also include positive reinforcement procedures. Obvious examples are tax rebates for charitable contributions and insurance reimbursements to qualified health service providers.

Much of this book consists simply of references to legally applied consequences and contingencies (e.g., award of child custody based on psychological tests, minimum wage for patient labor, withdrawal of practitioner's license for "poor moral character"). The reader may wonder why so little reference is made to professional ethics in this book. The answer is simple: Most ethical codes are vaguely formulated and rarely enforced. Therefore they provide almost no specific and tangible guidance to either practitioners or clients.

Associate U.S. Supreme Court Justice Oliver Wendell Holmes advised that if you want to know the law, you must look at it as does a bad man who cares only for material consequences and not about the "vaguer sanctions of conscience."[8] He will want to avoid paying money and keep out of jail if he can. The law talks about "rights," "duties," "malice," "intent," and so forth. Nothing is easier than to take these words in their subjective moral sense and so fall into a semantic fallacy. These concepts are nothing but a prediction that if a person does, or fails to do, certain things, he or she will be made to suffer by the judgment of the court.

This volume gives the reader a limited number of legal definitions, sources, standards, and procedures relevant to resolving conflicts or avoiding litigation in the areas of mental health, criminal justice, and social welfare. It is almost inevitable that an introductory book that seeks to be practical will present some of the lowest and most mundane aspects of the legal craft—what in juisprudence is disparagingly and appropriately referred to as "black-letter law" (i.e., ritualized rules, procedures, and precedents devoid of creative solutions). Because of the diversity and sometimes rapid change in local case and statutory law, it is impossible to make a general statement about legal requirements applicable in all jurisdictions. No claim is made therefore as to the current validity or accuracy of particular citations or interpretations of law. What we have tried to do is to provide a summary that reflects general patterns of law and practice. Each reader will have to evaluate this summary statement in terms of his/her own legal and professional situation.

The long-term general consequences of increased legal intervention in mental health matters are still a matter of speculation. Many individuals have undoubtedly been helped, and have been spared the institutionalized destruction of their lives. But it must also be realized that others may have been harmed by a denial of protective institutionalization. It is no advance to trade authoritarian treatment for authoritarian nontreatment, to move people with problems from back wards to back alleys.[9] Prior to making major, precedent-setting decisions or statutory enactments, it might be desirable to make a systems analysis of the consequences of various options. Or at least some arrangement for data feedback might be instituted so that the mandated change becomes something of a quasi-experiment instead of mere political manipulation. Some policies act in a counter-intuitive manner (e.g., giving a very severe penalty for drug usage *reduces* the total time offenders spend in prison on this charge because judges and juries hesitate to impose the penalty, and plea bargaining for a lesser charge increases).

Unfortunately, the courts and legislatures often lack the capacity to obtain relevant information about technical issues. The parties at litigation are primarily interested in winning, not in going beyond the needs of the immediate situation and solving a cluster of complex, collateral problems.[10] In terms of overall impact, legislative lawmaking has now been largely delegated to administrative agencies because legislators seldom have the time or technical competence equivalent to that of experts employed on administrative staffs in such areas as public utilities, medicine, or communications.

Law is our best-articulated plan of social management. Yet there remains a tenacious suspicion that our wisest words are little more than illusory afterthoughts to profound and only partially controlled physical events—to incredible complexities, barely sensed, that exceed any present human symbol system. The law operates almost exclusively in the mediums of the spoken and written word. To this extent, lawyers are more similar to philosophers, journalists, or poets than to musicians, architects, or physicians. Perhaps some intuition of a yet-undeveloped structure of nonverbal wisdom prompted Justice Holmes in 1913 to report a futuristic vision:[11]

> I think it probable that civilization somehow will last as long as I care to look ahead—perhaps with smaller numbers, but perhaps also bred to greatness and splendor by science. I think it not improbable that man, like the grub that prepares a chamber for the winged thing it never has seen but is to be—that man may have cosmic destinies that he does not understand.... The other day a dream was pictured to my mind. It was evening. I was walking homeward on Pennsylvania Avenue near the Treasury, and as I looked beyond Sherman's statue to the west, the sky was aflame with scarlet and crimson from the setting sun. But, like the note of downfall in Wagner's opera, below the skyline there came from little globes the pallid discord of the electric lights. And I thought to myself the Götterdämmerung will end, and from those globes clustered like evil eggs will come the new masters of the sky.... Then I remembered the faith that I partly have expressed. Faith in a universe not measured by our fears, a universe that has thought to myself the Gotterdämmerung will end, and from those globes clustered like the electric lights, there shown the stars.

NOTES

1. Stone, A. A. The *Tarasoff* decisions: Suing psychotherapists to safeguard society. 90 *Harvard Law Review* 358 (1976).

2. A case presenting an apparently frivolous claim against a psychoanalyst settled out of court for $2000 as reported in Slawson, P. F. Psychiatric malpractice: A regional incidence study. 126 *American Journal of Psychiatry* 1302, 1305 (March 1970).

3. Thorndike, E. L. *Your city.* New York: Harcourt Brace Jovanovich, 1939, p. 32.

4. "We suffer from legal pollution . . . the courts are looked at as the arbitrators of all sorts of social problems that were never thought to be within the judicial province." Hager, P. Legal pollution seen by law dean. *Los Angeles Times,* Part II, p. 6, January 5, 1975, quoting Thomas Ehrlich, dean of Stanford Law School. Filings in federal courts of appeal increased over 250 percent in the last decade. Howard, J. W., Jr. Law enforcement in an urban society. 29 *American Psychologist* 223 (April 1974).

5. *See,* Law Enforcement Assistance Administration, *Citizen dispute settlement* (The Night Prosecutor Program of Columbus, Ohio). Washington, D.C.: National Institute of Law Enforcement and Criminal Justice, 1974; American Arbitration Association, *Commercial arbitration rules.* New York: American Arbitration Assoc., 1973.

6. Scott, K. E. Two models of the civil process. 27 *Stanford Law Review* 937 (1975). This quotation is Professor Scott's characterization of the "conflict-resolution" model. He also makes a cogent analysis of the "behavior modification" model that he believes deserves wider acceptance.

7. Illustrating the conflict-resolution model is Eisen v. Carlisle & Jacquelin, 479 F.2d 1005 (2d Cir. 1973), *vac. & remand.,* 417 U.S. 156 (1974), in which the court refused to "disgorge" from two New York Stock Exchange firms an estimated $120 million, that they had accumulated from small commission overcharges, because most of the six million clients over the four-year period could not be identified. Illustrating the behavior-modification model is Daar v. Yellow Cab Co., 67 Cal. 2d 695, 433 P.2d 732 (1967) in which the Los Angeles cab company was required to lower its fares for eight years to meet the equivalent of the $1.4 million (less $200,000 in attorneys' fees) it overcharged passengers by stepping up its meters over a previous four-year period. *Cf.* Scott, *id.* at 937.

8. This paragraph paraphrases the views of Justice Holmes in his *Collected Legal Papers* (New York: Harcourt Brace Jovanovich, 1921), pp. 169–173.

9. Slovenko, R., and Luby, E. D. On the emancipation of mental patients. 3 *The Journal of Psychiatry and Law* 191 (Summer 1975). Similarly, Sedgwic, P. Illness—mental and otherwise. 1 *The Hastings Center Studies* 19, 39 (1973): "[Anti-psychiatry theorists] can expose the hypocrisies and annotate the tragedies of official psychiatry, but the concepts which they have developed enable them to engage in no public action which is grander than that of wringing their hands."

10. Law professor Arthur S. Miller has asserted: "The adversary system, in sum, is based on two premises: first, that the lawyers and judges are competent in the matters dealt with, and second, that the system can provide enough of the right type of data to make viable decisions. Neither idea is valid." Miller, A. S. Drawing the indictment. 51 *Saturday Review* 39, 40 (1968).

11. Holmes, O. W. *Collected legal papers.* New York: Harcourt Brace Jovanovich, 1921, pp. 296–297; reprint of speech to Harvard Law School Association of New York, Feb. 15, 1913.

1

Civil Commitment Procedures

The governments of most civilized countries have assumed a duty to protect their citizens from being harmed by others or by themselves. In the United States, all 50 states and the District of Columbia have statutes that provide for the custody and restraint of persons displaying certain aberrant behaviors that may be dangerous or harmful either to themselves or others.

The restraint of socially deviant persons is usually accomplished in one of two ways: (a) by the application of *criminal sanctions* (e.g., incarceration) for behaviors judged to be felonies or misdemeanors, or (b) by the application of *civil procedures* (e.g., compulsory commitment or treatment) for behaviors related to "mental illness." Sometimes a mentally ill person who commits a crime will be institutionalized under special criminal laws such as those for "mentally disordered sex offenders." This chapter deals only with the *civil* (noncriminal) commitment of mentally disabled persons.

COMMITMENT WITHOUT JUDICIAL ORDER

Many, if not most, mental patients are initially admitted to a hospital without judicial order.[1] The procedures and terminology vary from state to state, but detention is customarily permitted under an emergency or temporary commitment statute. A police officer, a mental health professional, or in some states any citizen, may initiate the involuntary detention of another person by alleging certain facts about

6

the person that would make him/her an appropriate patient. Usually the alleged facts will include some past or predicted harmful behavior. The harm may be deliberate or unintentional. It may be directed toward others or against oneself (e.g., self-mutilation or suicide). Often, the harm to oneself involves an inability to provide for basic personal needs such as food, clothing, or shelter. Those persons who are unable to provide such needs for themselves are typically termed "gravely disabled."

Following an examination by one or two physicians[2] or the director of a mental health receiving facility,[3] the individual may be involuntarily detained for a limited time. The necessary examination and certification for emergency detention may be done, in most states, by private-practice physicians in the community or physicians employed by the receiving facility. A well-known, controversial case was that of retired Major General Edwin Walker, arrested during an integration disturbance at the University of Mississippi in 1962. Before he could post bail, he was flown in a Border Patrol plane to a federal psychiatric center. The necessary affidavit stating that Walker's behavior "may be indicative of an underlying mental disturbance" was signed by the Chief Psychiatrist of the Federal Bureau of Prisons who relied on newspaper clippings and old medical records but did not conduct a personal examination.[4]

A few states require some judicial approval prior to emergency detention—for example, Alabama (hearing), Indiana (endorsement by a judicial officer), Texas (warrant from a magistrate), Virginia (judicial order although the presence of the person is not required if inconvenient). Some states require higher standards for the commitment of an individual who is being treated by prayer or under the care of a "religious person"—for example, Idaho and Missouri.

The permissible duration of an emergency admission varies widely among the states, from 24 hours in Texas to 20 days in New Jersey.[5] One federal district court held that "the maximum period which a person may be detained without a preliminary hearing is 48 hours."[6] The preliminary hearing is to determine whether there is probable cause for the continued detention of the person. Prior to the hearing, the patient must be given notice of his/her rights. In some states, the mental health personnel must show by a "preponderance of the evidence" or even "beyond a reasonable doubt" that probable cause exists for the patient's detention.[7] The patient has a right to counsel, but other details of the hearing procedure (e.g., the person's presence at the hearing, the right to refuse medication prior to the hearing, the right to present witnesses) are not uniformly established. The hearing may be conducted informally in the judge's chambers, and use data based only on documents submitted by the hospital and by the patient or his/her counsel.

Another type of admission involves a situation in which the person volunteers to enter the institution with or without a written application. This voluntary or nonprotested admission is technically not a "commitment" at all because there is no order for detainment by civil authority. As in a general hospital, the person is free to leave at any time. However, a patient may be required to sign out "against medical advice" or to notify the hospital a few days before the leaving date. During that time, the hospital may instigate commitment proceedings to challenge and delay the release.[8] In actual practice, "voluntary" admission is seldom as benign as the formalities make it appear. Usually there is considerable pressure from relatives, civil authorities, and mental health personnel who are becoming worried or angry about the person's deviant behavior. One hospital survey reportedly found that 40 percent of the persons voluntarily admitted to a large, public mental hospital in Chicago were threatened with involuntary commitment by police officers who brought them to the institution.[9]

COMMITMENT BY ORDER OF THE COURT

An important legal-social issue is when and under what conditions a court may order (or forbid) treatment. The primary purpose of a judicial hearing is to determine whether the individual meets the criteria for commitment specified by statute and whether treatment is desirable.

The criteria necessary to obtain a formal civil commitment vary considerably from state to state. Typical statutes require that the person be mentally ill *and* meet at least one of the conditions listed below. Mental illness alone is not a sufficient condition for involuntary civil commitment. Some typical additional conditions required by various states are the following:

- The person must be dangerous to himself or others if allowed to remain at liberty.
- The person must present a likelihood of serious harm to himself or others.
- The person must be gravely disabled so as to be unable to provide for his/her basic physical needs.
- The person must be lacking sufficient insight or capacity to make responsible decisions concerning hospitalization.
- The person must be in need of care and treatment in a hospital.

The prerequisite condition, that of being mentally ill, is of primary importance. Without such proof, a formal commitment may not be made even if the other conditions listed above are present.

Recent statutory developments suggest a trend toward limiting involuntary civil commitment to mentally ill persons who are dangerous to themselves or others or are likely to cause harm to themselves or others. Twenty states use a "dangerousness" criterion for commitment, and 28 states use a "likelihood of serious harm" criterion. The criterion of "needing treatment" can be found in 23 states. This criterion, once very common, has come under legal attack because of its vagueness, and is seldom used in new commitment statutes. Table 1.1 (at the end of this chapter) shows the criteria used for the judicial commitment of the mentally ill.

The process of formal commitment usually begins when a concerned person, who is not the patient, petitions the court for an examination of a supposedly ill person. The alleged mentally ill person then receives a copy of this petition. After a psychiatric examination, a formal court hearing is held to determine whether the individual should be committed. These procedures are discussed in more detail below, using the California statute for illustrative purposes. See also Figure 1.1.

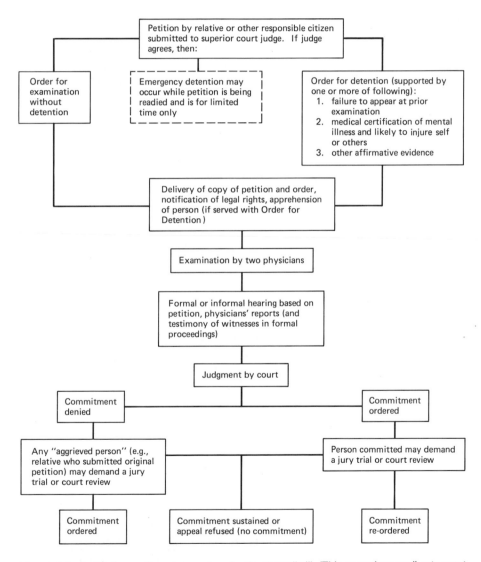

Figure 1.1. Judicial commitment procedure for the mentally ill. (This procedure applies to most states, but jurisdictional variations are likely to invalidate portions of it.)

This statute reflects fairly well typical statutory requirements and major current trends in civil commitment.

Petition for Examination

Under usual circumstances, a relative or a friend will act as petitioner, although it is legally possible for police officers, welfare officials, probation officers, and similar persons to file a petition if there is no relative or friend available or willing to do so. Often a family physician will be the petitioner, although the physician cannot also then conduct the required mental examination. The only residence requirement for a person being committed is that the person be physically in the county when the petition is signed. Furthermore, the petitioner need not be a resident of the county where s/he signs the petition.

There is no age minimum required for a person to be legally committed to an institution. Minors, except those who are wards of the juvenile court, can be adjudged as mentally ill and committed via the same procedure used for adults. In many jurisdictions, minors can also be "voluntarily" admitted on the parents' "signature," but this is being questioned on due-process grounds.[10]

After the petition for examination has been filed (see Box 1-1), it is then presented to a superior court magistrate. The magistrate has two options if s/he is satisfied that the person is "mentally ill, and in need of supervision, treatment, care or restraint."[11] The magistrate's first option is to order the person to remain at home pending examination by two medical examiners. This is known as an "order for

---

BOX   1-1

IN THE COURT OF THE COUNTY JUDGE,
IN AND FOR _____Pinellas_____ COUNTY,
STATE OF FLORIDA.

INQUISITION OF INCOMPETENCY

__Kenneth Donaldson_____   (Petition by member of family
                                         or next of kin)

TO _____Hon. Jack F. White_____ , COUNTY JUDGE IN AND FOR THE

COUNTY AFORESAID:

Your petitioner respectfully represents unto your Honor that _____ *he is the*
_____father_____ *of* _____Kenneth Donaldson_____ , *who is* _____50_____

years of age, and whose address is _____Belleaire Village Trailer Court, Largo (A St.)_____ ,

Florida. The said _____Kenneth Donaldson_____ *is believed to be incompetent within*

the intent and meaning of Section 394.20, Florida Statutes, 1941, as amended by Chapter 23157, Laws of 1945, and the nature of h___is___ disability is Persecution complex, increasing signs of paranoid delusions, petitioner believes him to be potentially dangerous.

The members of the family of the said ____Kenneth Donaldson____ *with their addresses, are as follows:*

Members of Family	*Relationship*	*Addresses*
William T. Donaldson	Father	Belleaire Village
		Trailer Court,
Marjorie K. Donaldson	Mother	A Street, Largo, Florida

   WHEREFORE, your petitioners pray that an examination be made as to the mental and physical condition, or both, of the said ____Kenneth Donaldson____ *, as provided by law, and that an order be entered adjudging the said* ____Kenneth Donaldson____ *to be incompetent, if* _____ *he is so found.*

                                        /s/ William T. Donaldson

STATE OF FLORIDA
COUNTY OF _____Pinellas_____

____William T. Donaldson____ *being sworn by me, the undersigned officer, says on oath that the statements contained in the foregoing petition are true, to the best of h___is___ knowledge and belief.*

                                        /s/ William T. Donaldson

Sworn to and subscribed before me at Clearwater, Fla., this 10th day of December A.D. *19* 56 .

                        (Notarial Seal)
                        /s/ Ruby W. Breaker
                        _____

                        Notary Public, State of Florida
                        at large. My commission expires
                        Jan. 18, 1960. Bonded by
                        American Surety Co. of N.Y.

                                        Filed Dec. 10, 1956
                                        Jack F. White, County Judge
                                        By R. W. Breaker, Clerk.

Source: Donaldson, K. *Insanity Inside Out.* New York: Crown, 1976, p. 14.

examination.'' The second option is to issue an ''order for detention,'' whereby the person is placed in institutional custody. The detention order may be issued if one of the following conditions apply: (a) in the opinion of a physician or of the County Mental Health Director or a designee the person is mentally ill and likely to injure himself or others if not immediately detained,[12] (b) the person had been allowed previously to remain at home pending examination and failed to appear for the examination, or (c) there is some other reason, such as protection of the disturbed person from hostile relatives, that detention is needed.[13] But note again that legally a person may be involuntarily detained in protective custody for only a limited time prior to a preliminary or formal hearing.[14]

Delivery of Petition and Order

A police officer or mental health counselor must personally serve the individual with a copy of the relative's petition for examination, along with the judge's order for examination or detention. In addition, the person's nearest relative must be served with a copy of the petition unless, of course, the relative filed the original petition. If there is no relative in the same county, then a friend or a companion must be served with the copy. These copies must be delivered no less than one day before the scheduled examination.[15] The person must be advised of his/her legal rights, which include a personal appearance before the court (along with witnesses and legal counsel) following the examination.

A person may be served with a judge's order of detention at any time of the night or day, and the officer serving the order has the authorization to apprehend the person and take him/her to the designated place of detention. The officer is obligated to safeguard the person's personal property if there are no relatives or guardians.

Examination

After the alleged mentally ill person has received a copy of the petition, an order for examination, and a notice of his/her legal rights, s/he is then required to submit to an examination by two professionally qualified persons (at least one of whom must be a licensed physician but not necessarily a psychiatrist).[16] These examiners are sup- posed to act in ''good faith'' and to see or hear the person's abnormal behavior for themselves (not simply take a relative's word for it). The examiners should spend some time (preferably alone) with the patient; observe the patient while s/he is not under the influence of drugs or take into account the influence of drugs if they are necessary; administer a physical examination; and record verbatim statements made by the patient. It is legally important that the examiners distinguish between what others tell them about the patient and what they personally observe. Specifically, the examiners should check for general appearance and for clarity of mind and memory. Any delusions or hallucinations should be noted as well as the patient's understanding of the complaints against him/her. The examiners may also obtain information regarding the person's use of alcohol or other drugs, employment status, intelligence, and prior mental health or criminal history. Their diagnostic conclusion about the patient should be reached independently rather than by collaboration.

In jurisdictions where a nonpsychiatric physician or psychologist may sign a commitment order on an emergency basis, s/he should take care to: provide correct transportation (in most states only the police, not an ambulance service may legally transport a patient against his/her will), know in advance that the assigned facility offers appropriate treatment, avoid conflicts of interest (e.g., being a relative), avoid subterfuge, and consult with a psychiatrist if possible.

The Hearing

In some states a formal court hearing will be held only if the alleged mentally ill person files a request within a limited period (e.g., four days) following receipt of the examination or detention orders from the court. In other states, formal hearing is mandatory.[17] The court may subpoena its own witnesses. The alleged mentally disabled person has the right to counsel, and in many jurisdictions is entitled to listen to the testimony, to cross-examine, to have an independent expert examination, and to refuse to testify.[18]

Informal "hearings" have traditionally been conducted casually in the judge's chambers without the prospective patient being present. The judge's decision may be based on the physicians' certificates and on a report from the hospital if the person has been detained on an emergency basis. Commitment hearings customarily occupy only a very small portion of a crowded court calendar. One study found that hearings for institutionalized retarded adults usually lasted between five and ten minutes.[19]

The procedures of a formal hearing vary greatly from jurisdiction to jurisdiction. A complete hearing under Oregon statutes, for example, would involve the judge's recitation to the patient of his/her rights, including his/her right to remain silent.[20] The judge must also advise the patient of his/her right to subpena witnesses, to cross-examine witnesses and experts or to move to have them excluded from the hearing. The patient or his/her counsel may present evidence such as the results of psychiatric examinations, police reports, and hospital records.[21] The patient may suggest placements that are less restrictive than commitment, and the court may be required to consider these alternatives.[22] Finally, if the patient does not have funds to obtain legal counsel, and wants counsel, the court will appoint one without cost. Legal counsel may also be requested from the court by the patient's relatives or friends.

If the person is hospitalized by a judge or designated hearing panel, s/he may later request a jury review.[23] When a commitment order has *not* been issued, some jurisdictions allow "any person aggrieved thereby" to similarly demand a jury trial.[24] When the option of a jury trial is not specifically provided by statute, case law suggests that the patient probably does not have such a right.[25] Nonetheless, at least a perfunctory review by the court could be initiated by the patient or his/her counsel by a Writ of Habeas Corpus. A jury, of course, may sustain or deny the appeal.

A mentally disabled person is not the only type of individual who may be involuntarily committed to a state or county hospital. Mentally retarded persons, drug addicts, epileptics, alcoholics, and others may be committed through the use of procedures quite similar or identical to those outlined here.

RELEASE FROM CONFINEMENT

A patient may be released from involuntary confinement in one of three ways: leaves of absence, discharge, or Writ of Habeas Corpus. Leaves of absence (conditional releases or trial visits) are typically granted by the superintendent of the committing institution. A common form of leave involves the placement of the patient in a certified private home, with the state's central health agency sharing part of the cost. Conditional releases often impose additional requirements on both the patient and the institution. Typical requirements are that the patient must make a satisfactory adjustment to his/her new environment, that s/he must report regularly (perhaps weekly) to a local clinic, and that the institution examine the patient at least once per year. If the patient complies with the conditions of the leave, his/her case will usually be reviewed periodically to determine what future treatment, if any, is necessary.

The law related to standards for conditional release is not well established. Conditional release may, in fact, be mandated by the U.S. Constitution when outpatient facilities are available that the patient requires.[26]

A leave may be revoked at any time, thereby requiring the person to return to the institution. The revocation should not be arbitrary or based upon false information. A provision of a Pennsylvania statute that permitted summary revocation of a patient's leave was found unconstitutional because the hospital made no verification of the information upon which the decision was based and because there was inadequate proof of medical need for hospital confinement.[27]

Most states allow the superintendent of the committing institution or an official of the department of mental health to order a discharge, or unconditional release, of a patient. Although the courts commit the patient, hospital personnel presumably have sufficient contact with the patient to determine whether release is advisable. In most states, the decision for an unconditional release is primarily a decision of the hospital or central health agency officials, although notification of a court may be required prior to release.

Approximately one-third of the states also allow release of a mental patient by court order. Generally, patients may file a petition with the local court which will then order an examination of the patient and conduct a hearing if the examination indicates there is no need for further confinement. Again, as a last resort, the patient may petition the federal district court for a Writ of Habeas Corpus if there appears to be a violation of federal constitutional protections under Article I, Section 9 (see Chapter 16 and Appendix *D*).

COMMENTARY

In recent years, federal courts have become more actively involved in setting standards and procedures for commitment. In principle, constitutional doctrines delineated by the courts simply provide the outer limits within which local jurisdictions are free to vary. Thus, a local practice or rule would violate the Constitution only if it is beyond a rather broad and sometimes vague area of local discretion typically permitted by the courts.

The Constitution's Fourth Amendment establishes an individual's right against unreasonable *searches and seizures*. If a person is dangerous, then his/her apprehension is usually not considered unreasonable. The state may restrain a person in a manner necessary and essential to assure public safety. The apprehension of a nondangerous person who is only suspected of being mentally disabled presents a more difficult problem.

The concepts of "mental illness" and "dangerousness" have been used during the past century in America to achieve a variety of ill-defined and sometimes legally suspect objectives. Because mental illness and dangerousness are not clearly defined in behavioral terms, the concepts can be used to describe nearly any socially undesirable action. For example, the wreckless spending of the savings of a family[28] and the writing of bad checks[29] have been labeled as "dangerous." In another case, a 19-year-old woman was committed to the Arizona State Hospital for 59 years (from 1912 to 1971) for being dangerous.[30] The official records reportedly showed that the major "symptoms" that led to her commitment were laughter, singing, and a willingness to talk to anyone. These "symptoms" are not unlike those of a teenage girl who has, as the saying goes, "fallen in love." (Being "in love" is usually a desirable and benign psychotic state—and that is not yet a crime in our country nor sufficiently dangerous to require institutionalization.)

On the other hand, the concepts of mental illness and dangerousness have undoubtedly allowed brief, civil confinement of persons who otherwise would have inflicted serious bodily harm on themselves or others. Consider, for example, the criminal career of Edmund Kemper III who at age 15 fatally shot his grandparents to "see how it would feel." After six years of hospitalization, he was set free; three years later he reportedly confessed to dismembering six young girls and murdering his mother with a hammer.[31] *Criminal* proceedings for confinement can usually be initiated only after the harm has been done. However, *civil* proceedings are available in all states whereby the state can confine a person for anticipated harm. If a man is loading a machine gun in his back yard and aiming it toward a local sorority house, the state can intervene. It does not need to wait until the first round is fired. But it is precisely this preventative authority of the state which, when combined with the vagaries of "mental illness" and "dangerousness," can result in abuses of civil liberty.

There is a clear tendency for physicians and officials to overpredict the dangerousness of patients seen by them. Studies suggest that perhaps only five to ten percent of those persons committed to mental institutions as dangerous to other people would, in fact, be involved in subsequent offenses against others if released.[32] Because of a strong and unfavorable public reaction when an ex-patient or parolee becomes involved in a violent act, and because the assessment of dangerousness is very difficult, this tendency to over-predict is understandable.[33] It is, nonetheless, still biased.

The potential for abuse might be sharply limited if dangerous behavior could be accurately defined and measured. Traditionally, the central focus of legal definitions of dangerousness has been upon the individual actor. The origin of dangerous conduct was assumed to lie primarily within the individual. This fit well with the old view in psychology of "traits" or "psychodynamic mechanisms." This view is still reflected in serveral well-known psychological scales used to assess sociopathic personality. More recently, a view has been emerging that focuses upon the interaction of a person and the particular social situation. In this view, there must be a behavior, a social context in which the behavior occurs, and an observer who is in some position of power or influence to label the behavior.[34] Some persons may be dangerous only in particular situations (e.g., barrooms), under particular conditions such as intoxication, and in particular interpersonal contexts (e.g., threats to self-esteem by authority figures). Too often, enduring personality dispositions are inferred from actions which are in fact responses to specific situations. Thus, factors in the environment that may elicit or maintain deviant behaviors are overlooked.

When the term "dangerousness" (or the phrase "likelihood of serious harm") is used as a criterion for civil commitment, it is functioning as both a scientific and a legal concept. It involves a mixed issue of epistomology and jurisprudence. Behavioral explanation and prediction is the special area of expertise of the mental health professional or behavioral scientist. The personal and social importance of these predictions are matters of law, to be determined by the judge or jury. The mixed nature of the "dangerousness" construct has been explicitly recognized by some courts: "The likelihood of future conduct, the type of misconduct to be expected, and its probable frequency are questions of fact; whether the expected harm, and its apparent likelihood, are sufficiently great to warrant coercive intervention under our statutes are questions of law."[35]

The role of the mental health professional is to provide the court with "facts" rather than to reach conclusions of law. It is not surprising therefore that courts become upset when data are inadequate, irrelevant, or even concealed from the court. In one case, a psychiatric resident diagnosed a patient as "recovered" although subsequent testimony revealed that during a visit to the hospital by his wife, prior to release, the patient threatened to kill her.[36] An employee of the hospital was notified of the threat. The court, however, was not told of the threat nor of the basis for the recommended discharge. Two months later, the patient shot and killed his wife. The hospital was found negligent.

As the scientific study of dangerousness shifts from a focus on personality traits to an examination of person-environment interactions, the information presented to courts will change. Perhaps the social environments of a prospective patient should be examined as thoroughly as the prospective patient. The alleged deviant behavior should be reliably assessed as to its history, frequency, duration, intensity, and so forth.[37] If the deviant behavior is not too generalized, specific environments might be "quarantined" or made off-limits rather than (or in addition to) the person's being institutionalized. This means, in effect, that courts might ultimately begin to set more precise conditions for release to be met by both the patient and persons associated with the patient.

The current emphasis upon environmental factors in dangerousness also fits well with the emerging legal principle of the "least restrictive alternative." In two well-known cases, *Lake* v. *Cameron*[38] and *Lessard* v. *Schmidt*[39], the state was required to show that alternatives to involuntary full-time commitment were not suitable. This doctrine asserts that the state's police power is appropriately restricted when the same basic purpose can be accomplished with fewer deprivations imposed on the individual. Many of the newer commitment statutes expressly require the court to consider alternatives that are less restrictive than hospitalization.[40] In some states, the individual may be "committed," but the commitment may be to a group home or a community program. The least restrictive alternative principle may also be applied to placements within a hospital.[41]

A legal requirement to use the least restrictive alternative has little practical value if no alternatives exist or if such are unknown to the courts. Often the placement of a prospective patient will depend upon the skill and knowledge of the person's attorney because judges do not have time to explore alternatives.[42] An attorney working with a knowledgeable social worker might find alternatives suitable to the court. If the commitment statute or case law in the state does not expressly allow less restrictive alternatives, the attorney may persuade the judge to "adjourn" or "continue" the case without a finding for a specified period of time (e.g., six months). This continuance might be conditioned upon the prospective patient's participation in certain commitment alternatives such as taking medication, seeing a therapist, or living with a responsible relative.[43] Of course, the development of these more benign control strategies opens up the possibility that bothersome but less dangerous people, who would not now be committed, might then be required to submit to treatment.

In many areas of mental health practice, formal constitutional law is one of the least important factors determining actual practice. Everything written about formal law, therefore, must be followed by a caveat that such requirements may be ignored in local practice. It comes as quite a surprise to persons naive in the ways of the law to learn that many pronouncments of the Supreme Court are ignored or circumvented in practice. Two other sources of law are statutory law and administrative law. Rules and precedents established from these sources may have equal or more impact on local practice than Supreme Court decisions. For example, the standard of care required of an examining practitioner may be determined by contractual or fiduciary relationships established by statute, case law, and customary practice. Failure to meet this standard of care while examining a patient may become an element in a malpractice action against the practitioner (see Chapter 15).

Civil commitment involves a complex process of balancing important personal, professional, and social interests. It should, therefore, be conducted with thoughtful concern for the lives of those persons inevitably affected: patient, potential victim, family, and practitioner.

NOTES

1. Ennis, B. and Siegel, L. *The rights of mental patients*. New York: Avon Books, 1973, p. 17. They state that "In New York City, for example, about 99 percent of all involuntary patients are hospitalized, initially, under the emergency procedure." Conversely, in the District of Columbia, emergency admissions have ranged from 12 to 58 percent according to data published in *Hearings on Constitutional Rights of the Mentally Ill,* U.S. Senate Committee on the Judiciary, 91st Congress, 1969–70, Table V. The number of admissions to state and county mental hospitals in 1972 was: voluntary 196,364; nonprotesting 23,095; and involuntary 169,032, as reported in Stone, A. A. *Mental health and law: A system in transition.* Rockville, Md.: Center for Studies of Crime and Delinquency, NIMH, 1975, p. 44, citing unpublished material by Taube as source.
2. *Cf.* New York Mental Hygiene Law, sec. 31.27 (1976). Some states, such as West Virginia, permit certification for involuntary hospitalization by one physician and one psychologist. In Idaho, a "designated examiner" for certification may be a physician or a clinical psychologist.
3. *Cf., e.g.,* California Welfare and Institutions Code, sec. 5150 (1976).
4. The purpose of the examination was to determine if Walker was competent to stand trial. One week later, a U.S. District Court judge found that there was reasonable cause to seek the order for psychiatric tests but that, on the basis of testimony by Walker's own psychiatrist, Walker was "functioning currently at the superior level." 60 *Newsweek* (Dec. 3, 1962), p. 35. For statistics on commitment and alleged abuse of emergency hospitalization under the New York Mental Hygiene Law, see Zusman, J. and Shaffer, S. Emergency psychiatric hospitalization via court order: A critique. 130 *American Journal of Psychiatry* 1323 (1973).
5. Texas Rev. Civil Statutes Ann., article 547–27 (Supp. 1973) (24 hours); District of Columbia Code Ann. 21–523 (1973) (72 hours); New Jersey Statutes Ann., sec. 30:4–37 (1975) (20 days).

6. *Lessard v. Schmidt,* 349 F. Supp. 1078 (E.D. Wisc. 1972), *vacated and remanded on other grounds,* 94 S. Ct. 713 (1974), *reinstated* 413 F. Supp. 1318 (E.D. Wisc. 1976). In fiscal year 1973 in Michigan, approximately 4000 of 10,000 hospitalized persons were committed under a temporary commitment law requiring a court order based only on certification of two physicians that detention was "necessary and essential." A three-judge federal panel concluded that "dangerous to self or others" should be the basis of commitment and that the 120 days of temporary commitment allowed in Michigan prior to a preliminary hearing should be approximately five days. *Bell v. Wayne County General Hospital,* 348 F. Supp. 1085 (Mich. 1974).

7. Preponderance of the evidence is required by the Washington Rev. Code Ann. 71.05.240 (1976). The person also has the right to remain silent and must be informed that any statement he/she makes may be used against him/her. The person can present evidence, cross-examine witnesses, and refuse medication 24 hours prior to the hearing (71.05.200). For long-term commitment in Washington state, the standard of proof is "clear, cogent, and convincing" (71.05.310). This reflects the trend of requiring either a "beyond a reasonable doubt" standard or a "clear and convincing" standard. See Wexler, D.B. Current currents in institutionalization. 14 *Arizona Law Review* 979, 981–986 (1977).

8. Most voluntary admission statutes contain provisions permitting a brief delay (from 48 hours to 10 days)—for example, Connecticut Gen. Stat. Ann., sec. 17–187(a) (Supp. 1977); D.C. Code Ann., sec. 21–512 (1973).

9. Gilboy, J. A. and Schmidt, J. R. "Voluntary" hospitalization of the mentally ill. 66 *Northwestern University Law Review* 429, 433, 438–439 (1971). Monahan, J. and Wexler, D. B. A definite maybe: Proof and probability in civil commitment. 2 *Law and Human Behavior* 37 (1978). The Supreme Court is considering a case that may have wide impact on the standard of proof required—Addington v. Texas, U.S. Supreme Ct., Oct. term, 1978, No. 77-5992.

10. Adversary proceedings not required before or after commitment of a minor by a parent to a state facility. Parham v. J.R. 99 S. Ct. 2493 (1979).

11. California Welfare and Institutions Code, sec. 5050.

12. *Id.,* or similarly, Oregon Rev. Stat., sec. 426.070(3),(5) (1976).

13. Aitken, J. Commitment proceedings. *California Family Lawyer.* (Calif. Continuing Education of the Bar), 1973, Ch. 12, p. 420.

14. See *supra* note 5.

15. California Welfare and Institutions Code, secs. 5206, 5208 (1977). However, statutory provision for notice is vague or nonexistent in most states.

16. Oregon Rev. Stat., sec. 426.110 (1976): California Welfare and Institutions Code, sec. 5251 (1977). Basic guidelines for examination by nonpsychiatric physicians appears in Chayet, N. Should you sign that commitment order? 48 *Medical Economics* 31 (Nov. 22, 1971).

17. *E.g.,* New Jersey State. Ann. 30:4–37 (1976), and Pennsylvania Act 143, sec. 304 (1976) (formal hearing required); California Welfare and Institutions Code, secs. 5252.1, 5302, 5303 (1977) (formal hearing only on request for 14-day treatment but required for subsequent 90-day treatment).

18. *E.g.,* Pennsylvania Act 143, sec. 304 (1976).

19. Kay, R. Legal planning for the mentally retarded: The California experience. 60 *California Law Review* 438 (1972).

20. Summarized from Mutnick, J. S. Involuntary commitment proceeding. 2 *Willamette Law Journal* 315 (1975). Oregon S.B. 480 (eff. Oct. 4, 1977) (amending Oregon Rev. Stat. 426.100). *See also* similar extensive rights given to patients in Ohio Rev. Code Ann., sec. 5122.15 (1977).

21. In a civil proceeding, in contrast to a criminal proceeding, the patient might attempt to exclude certain medical records as evidence by asserting a doctor-patient privileged communication. If the commitment procedure is viewed as a quasi-criminal process, one can argue that a *Miranda* warning prior to examination is necessary in order to avoid self-incrimination. *See generally,* Note, Developments in the law—Civil commitment of the mentally ill. 87 *Harvard Law Review* 1190 (1974).

22. See Lessard v. Schmidt, *supra* note 6.

23. Alaska Statutes, sec. 47.30.070 (1977); D.C. Code Ann., sec. 21-545(a) (1973): Michigan Comp. Laws Ann., sec. 330,1458 (1977). About one-quarter of the jurisdictions make a jury trial available at the request of the patient.

24. California Welfare and Institutions Code, sec. 5129.

25. Few, if any, cases have directly tested the issue of whether a jury is a required element of due process in civil commitment, as it is in adult criminal cases. In juvenile criminal proceedings, McKeiver v. Penn., 403 U.S. 528 (1971), held that a jury was not required. In view of the potential cost in time, money, and complexity of decision-making, it is unlikely that many courts will find denial of a jury in adult or juvenile civil commitment cases unreasonable—if other procedural safeguards are followed (e.g., access to counsel).

26. U.S. v. McNeil, 434 F.2d 502 (D.C. Cir. 1970).

27. Meisel v. Kremens, 405 F. Supp. 1253 (E.D. Pa. 1975).

28. U.S. v. Charnizon, 232 A.2d 586 (D.C. Ct. App. 1967).

29. Overholser v. Russell, 283 F.2d 195 (1960).

30. Wexler, D. B., Scoville, S. E. *et. al.* Administration of psychiatric justice: Theory and practice in Arizona. 13 *Arizona Law Review* (entire issue) 1–2 (1971).

31. "How to tell who will kill." 81 *Newsweek* (June 4, 1973), p. 69.

32. Steadman, H. J., and Keveles, R. The community adjustment and criminal activity of the Baxstrom patients: 1966–1970. 129 *American Journal of Psychiatry* 129 (1972), 304–310. Note, *HEW News* (Alcohol, Drug Abuse, and Mental Health Administration news release based on a symposium sponsored by the NIMH Center for Studies of Crime and Delinquency), August 8, 1974, at p. 2.

33. Decision-making bias was dramatically demonstrated in a study cited by Scheff, T. J. Decision rules, types of error, and their consequences on medical diagnosis. 8 *Behavioral Science* 79 (1963). One thousand school children were sequentially examined by four independent groups of physicians asked to make a judgment regarding the advisability of tonsillectomy. Of an initial group of 1000 children, 389 still had their tonsils and were submitted to the second group of physicians. Of these, 174 children were selected for tonsillectomy. The remaining 215 children apparently had normal tonsils. Another group of physicians was then asked to examine these 215 children; 99 were recommended for tonsillectomy. The 116 children, who had now survived two screenings, were then submitted to still another group of physicians. Again, approximately one-half were judged to need the operation.

A review of 4000 young offenders in California allegedly showed that "for every 20 people diagnosed as dangerous, there were 19 errors." Monahan, J. In defense of civil liberty—despite fear of violence. *Los Angeles Times,* Part 6, p. 3, Feb. 3, 1974.

See also, generally, Bohmer, C. Judicial use of psychiatric reports in sentencing sex offenders. 1 *Journal of Psychiatry and Law* 223 (1973); Rosenhan, D. L. On being sane in insne places. 179 *Science* 250 (Jan. 19, 1973), and critiques in 84 *Journal of Abnormal Psychology* 433 (1975); Ennis, B. J., and Litwack, T. R. Psychiatry and the presumption of expertise: Flipping coins in the courtroom. 62 *California Law Review* 693 (1974).

34. Shah, S. A. Dangerousness: A paradigm for exploring some issues in law and psychology. 33 *American Psychologist* 224 (1978). *Also* generally, Livermore, J. M., Malmquist, C. P., and Meehl, P. E. On the justifications for civil commitment, 117 *University of Pennsylvania Law Review* 75 (November 1968).

35. Dixon v. Jacobs, 427 F.2d 589, 595, n. 17 (D.C. Cir. 1970) (Chief Judge Bazelon).

36. Hicks v. U.S., 511 F.2d 407 (D.C. Cir. 1975) ($90,000 awarded to plaintiffs under Federal Tort Claims Act).

37. There is increasing emphasis on the requirement of a past overt act, attempt, or threat to inflict harm instead of a prediction about future behavior based on inferred personality characteristics. Some commitment statutes require such an overt act, attempt, or threat for certain categories of commitment—*e.g.,* Alabama (act/long-term), Arizona (act/long-term), California (act/long-term), New York (act/emergency admission for harm to others), Washington (threat or act/long-term). *See also Harvard Law Review, supra* note 21, at 1205–6; Lessard v. Schmidt, *supra* note 6; State of Oregon v. O'Neill, 545 P.2d 97 (Ore. 1976); *but see* United States ex rel. Matthew v. Nelson, No. 72-C-2104 (N.D. Ill., Aug. 18, 1978) as cited in 1 *Mental Disability Law Reporter* 1 (January 1976).

38. Lake v. Cameron, 364 F.2d. 657 (D.C. Cir. 1966).

39. Lessard v. Schmidt, *supra* note 6. *See also, Lynch v. Baxley,* 386 F. Supp. 378 (M.D. Ala. 1974); Morales v. Terman, 383 F. Supp. 53 (E.D. Tex. 1974), *rev'd.* 535 F. 2d 864 (5th Cir. 1976), *reinstated* 430 U.S. 322 (1977).

40. *See e.g.,* Alabama, Delaware, Hawaii, Illinois, Kansas (reasonable alternatives), Kentucky, Louisiana, Maine, Maryland, Minnesota (no suitable alternative), Nebraska, New Mexico, Oklahoma, Rhode Island (alternatives deemed unsuitable), Tennessee (less drastic alternatives), Utah, Virginia, West Virginia.

41. *See e.g.,* Covington v. Harris, 419 F.2d 617 (D.C. Cir. 1969); Dixon v. Weinberger, 405 F. Supp. 974 (D.D.C. 1975).

42. Examples of working with the court to provide alternative placements for retarded persons are provided in Soskin, R.M. The least restrictive alternative: In principle and in application. 2 *Amicus* 28 (1977). In one instance, a judge ordered the development and funding of a supervised community apartment facility with a behavior modification program [In the Interest of Stephanie L. No. J-184924 Juv. Div. (C.C.D. Phila. County 1977)].

43. Brooks, A. D. Alternatives to involuntary commitment. *Law, psychiatry and the mental health system* Boston: Little, Brown, 1974, pp. 727–734.

Table 1.1 Criteria for the Judicial Commitment of the Mentally Ill*

State	Mental Illness or Disability	Danger to Self	Danger to Others	Harm to Self	Harm to Others	Gravely Disabled	In Need of Treatment	Other	Notes and Comments
Alabama Act 1226 (Reg. ses. 1975), Act 670 (Reg. ses. 1977)	X			(X)	(X)			X[1,2,3]	[1]Threat of substantial harm must be evidenced by a recent overt act. [2]Treatment must be available or confinement must be necessary. [3]Commitment must be the least restrictive alternative necessary and available.
Alaska Stat. §47.30.070 (1977)	X	(X)	(X)				(X)[1]		[1]and "because of his illness, lacks sufficient insight or capacity to make responsible decisions concerning hospitalization" §.070(i)
Arizona Rev. State Ann. §36-501,540 (1974)	X	(X)	(X)			(X)	X[1]		[1]This criterion of need of treatment is required for the commitment of a person presenting a danger to himself or to others, not for the commitment of a person gravely disabled.

Arkansas Stat. Ann. §59-408 (1971)	X	(X)	(X)[1]		(X)[2]
California Welf. & Inst'ns. Code §§5008, 5260, 5264, 5300, 5304, 5350-58 (West Supp. 1970, Supp. 1977)	X		(X)[1]	(X)[2]	(X)[3]
Colorado Rev. Stat. Ann. §27-10-109 (1975)	X	(X)	(X)		
Connecticut Public Act 77-595, §§1,3 (1977)	X	(X)	(X)		

Arkansas

[1] "dangerous to himself or to society." The Commissioner of Mental Health Services interprets this to mean danger to others. Pers. corresp. 10/17/77

[2] "best interest of the patient"

California

[1] Involuntary treatment is time limited. Conservatorship may be used to continue treatment. Conservatee may be placed in an inpatient facility or required to undergo outpatient treatment. §§5260, 5264, 5358.

[2] Person must have threatened, attempted or inflicted physical harm upon the person of another after taken into custody or have attempted or inflicted physical harm prior to custody. Person must also present an imminent threat of physical harm. §5304

[3] Conservatorship may be used to continue treatment. §§5254, 5358.

Table 1.1 Continued

State	Mental Illness or Disability	Danger to — Self	Danger to — Others	Harm to — Self	Harm to — Others	Gravely Disabled	In Need of Treatment	Other	Notes and Comments
Delaware Tit. 16 §§5001, 5010, 5012 (Supp. 1976)	X[1]			(X)	(X)		(X)[1]	(X)[2]	[1]The court must find that the patient is a "mentally ill person." §5010. The definition of a "mentally ill person" includes a person who requires treatment and who must either be unable to make responsible decisions with respect to hospitalization or must pose a real and present threat of harm to himself, others, or property. §5010 [2]Harm to property is included. See note above. The court must also consider "all available alternatives" and order disposition "as imposes the least restraint." §5010
District of Columbia Code Ann. §21-545 (1965)	X			(X)	(X)				
Florida Stat. Ann. §394, 467 (1977)	X			(X)	(X)		(X)[1]		[1]"and lacks sufficient capacity to make a responsible application on his own behalf." 394-467 (b)

State						
Georgia Code Ann. §§88-507 (1970)	X			(X)	(X)	(X)[1]
Hawaii Rev. Stat. §§334-1, 60 (1976)	X[1]	(X)	(X)		(X)[2]	X[3] (X)[4]
Idaho Code §66-329,337 (1977)	X			(X)	(X)	
Illinois Mental Health Code §§1-11, 9-5 (1975)	X			(X)	(X)	X[1]

[1] Incapable of caring for his physical health and safety. §507.3 (h)

[1] Or suffering from substance abuse 334-60 (b) (1) (A)

[2] The definition of "dangerous to self" includes physical injury evidenced by "neglect or refusal to take necessary care for one's own physical health and safety together with incompetence to determine whether treatment for mental illness or substance abuse is appropriate." §334-1

[3] and there is no suitable less restrictive alternative §334-60 (b) (1) (c)

[4] Dangerous to property §334-60 (b) (1) (B)

[1] The definition of a "person in need of mental treatment" includes one who is reasonably expected to "intentionally or unintentionally physically injure himself or other persons, or is unable to care for himself so as to guard himself from physical injury or to provide for his own physical needs." §1-11

Table 1.1 *Continued*

State	Mental Illness or Disability	Danger to		Harm to		Gravely Disabled	In Need of Treatment	Other	Notes and Comments
		Self	Others	Self	Others				
Indiana Code §16-14-9.1-1,10 (1976)	X	(X)	(X)			(X)	X		
Iowa Code §229 (1977)	X[1]			(X)	(X)		X	X[2]	[1]The definition of "seriously mentally impaired" includes a person who is afflicted with mental illness, lacks sufficient judgment to make responsible decisions with respect to hospitalization or treatment, and who is likely to physically injure self or others or is likely to inflict serious emotional injury on family members or others. §229.1(2) [2]likely to benefit from treatment, and lack of judgment about treatment. §229.14(2)
Kansas Stat. Ann. §§59-2902,2917 (1977)	X[1]	(X)	(X)				X	X[2]	[1]The definition of a mentally ill person includes a person who is in need of treatment, is dangerous to self or others, and lacks sufficient understanding about the need for treatment or refuses to seek treatment. §59-2902

26

State					
Kentucky Rev. Stat. Ann. §§202A.010, 080 (1976)	X	(X)	(X)		X[1]
Louisiana SB658 §§2.55 (Reg. ses. 1977)	X	(X)[1]	(X)	(X)	X[2]
Maine Rev. Stat. Ann. tit. 34 §§2251, 2334 (1977)	X		(X)[1]	(X)	(X)[2]	X[3]

[1] "the least restrictive alternative mode of treatment requires hospitalization and . . . that treatment which can reasonably benefit the respondent is available in the hospital." 202A.080(6)

[2] The court must make a careful consideration of reasonable alternatives to inpatient treatment. §59-2917

[1] The definition of "dangerous to self" includes both physical and emotional harm to self. §2(4)

[2] Commitment for dangerousness or mental disability is to be in a facility least restrictive of liberty. §55(E)

[1] The definition of "likelihood of serious harm" includes a substantial risk of physical harm to the person himself or others and a determination that community resources for care and treatment are not available.

[2] Inability to avoid or protect self from severe physical or mental impairment or injury and a consideration of less restrictive treatment settings and modalities. §2251(7)(C)

Table 1.1 Continued

State	Mental Illness or Disability	Danger to		Harm to		Gravely Disabled	In Need of Treatment	Other	Notes and Comments
		Self	Others	Self	Others				
									[3]"Inpatient hospitalization is the means best available for treatment of the patient" and the court is "satisfied with the individual treatment plan offered by the hospital." §2334(5)(A)(2),(3)
Maryland Art. 59 §12 (1974)	X[1]						X[2]	X[3]	[1]The definition of mental illness includes a consideration of the safety of the persons or property of others. [2]"For the protection of himself or others, needs inpatient medical care or treatment." §12(a)(2) See also, the petition for release with a similar criterion for mental illness. §15(d) [3]"Is unable or unwilling to be voluntarily admitted." §12(a)(3)
Massachusetts Gen. Laws Ann. c. 123 §§1,7,8 (1977)	X			(X)[1]	(X)	(X)[2]			[1]Although the section of the statute requiring a judicial finding uses the term "dangerous persons," in its caption, these persons are defined in terms of likelihood of serious harm to self or others. The

state courts customarily use the substantive criterion of harm as intended by the person drafting the statute. Pers. comm., statute draftsperson, Jan. 15, 1978.

[2]The term gravely disabled is not used. The concept of gravely disabled may be inferred from the definition of "likelihood of serious harm" which includes "a very substantial risk of physical impairment or injury to the person himself as manifested by evidence that such person's judgment is so affected that he is unable to protect himself in the community and that reasonable provision for his protection is not available in the community." §1

[1]The definition of a "person requiring treatment" includes (1) a person who can reasonably be expected to seriously physically injure himself or another person and who has engaged in acts or threats supportive of that expectation, or (2) a person unable to attend to his basic physical needs and who has demonstrated that inability, or (3) a person who is unable to understand his need for treatment and whose continued behavior can reasonably be expected to result in significant physical harm to himself or others. §330.1401

| Michigan Comp. Laws Ann. §§330.1401, 1468 (1977) | X | (X) | (X) | (X) | X[1] |

Table 1.1 *Continued*

State	Mental Illness or Disability	Danger to — Self	Danger to — Others	Harm to — Self	Harm to — Others	Gravely Disabled	In Need of Treatment	Other	Notes and Comments
Minnesota Stat. Ann. §§253A.02, 07 (1976)	X	(X)[1]		(X)	(X)	(X)[2]		X[3]	[1]"A mentally ill person may be committed if he has (1) attempted to harm himself or others physically, or (2) has failed to protect himself from exploitation, or (3) has failed to care for his own needs, and (4) no suitable alternatives can be found to hospitalization, and (5) he is dangerous to the public." §.07(17)(a),(c) [2]There must be evidence that the person has "failed to protect himself from exploitation from others" or "failed to care for his own needs for food, clothing, shelter, safety or medical care." §.07(17)(a)(1)(ii),(iii) [3]No suitable alternative to involuntary hospitalization available. §.07(17)(a)(2) The general intent of the commitment criteria is the "welfare" of the mentally ill person and the "protection of society." §.07(17)(a)(1)

State (citation)					
Mississippi Code Ann. §§41-21-61, 83 (1976)	X	(X)	(X)	X[1]	
Missouri Ann. Stat. §202.807 (1977)	X		X	X[1]	
Montana SB413 §38-1302, 1306 (1977)	X[1]	(X)	(X)	(X)	
Nebraska LB 806 §§9, 47, 48, 51 (1976)	X[1]	(X)	(X)	(X)[2]	X[3]

[1] A "person in need of mental treatment" includes a person afflicted with mental illness who is reasonably expected to "intentionally or unintentionally physically injure himself or other persons, or is unable to care for himself so as to guard himself from physical injury, or to provide for his own physical needs." §41-21-61(c)

[1] and "because of his mental condition, lacks sufficient insight or capacity to make responsible decisions with respect to his hospitalization." §807(5)

[1] "'Seriously mentally ill' means suffering from a mental disorder which has resulted in self-inflicted injury or injury to others, or the imminent threat thereof, or which has deprived the person afflicted of the ability to protect his life or health." §38-1302(14)

[1] The subject must be found to be a "mentally ill dangerous person" defined as a mentally ill person who presents "(1) A substantial risk of serious harm to another person or persons within the near future . . . or (2) a substantial risk of serious harm to himself within the near future . . ." §§9, 47.

31

Table 1.1 *Continued*

State	Mental Illness or Disability	Danger to Self	Danger to Others	Harm to Self	Harm to Others	Gravely Disabled	In Need of Treatment	Other	Notes and Comments
Nevada Rev. Stat. §§433, 194, 433A, 310 (1975)	X[1]			(X)	(X)	(X)			[2]Harm to the person himself may be evidenced by his "inability to provide for his basic human needs, including food, clothing, shelter, essential medical care, or personal safety." §9(2) [3]Neither voluntary hospitalization nor less restrictive treatment alternatives must be available or sufficient to prevent harm. §§47, 48 [1]The definition of a "mentally ill person" includes the presentation of a "clear and present danger to himself or others," but danger is not included as a required finding of the court. §194(2)
New Hampshire Rev. Stat. Ann. §135-B:26 (1973)	X	(X)	(X)						

State						
New Jersey Stat. Ann. §30:4-36,37,38 (1976)	X	(X)[1]	(X)			
New Mexico H.B. 472 as amend. (1st ses. 1977)	X			(X)	(X)	X[1]
New York Mental Hygiene Law §§31.01,27,33,37,39 (1976)	X					X[1]
North Carolina Gen. Stat. §122.58.2,.8 (1976)	X	(X)	(X)		(X)[1]	

[1] "The court shall enter a judgment of commitment to an appropriate institution if it finds from the evidence presented at the hearing that the institutionalization of the patient is required by reason of his being a danger to himself or the community if he is not so confined and treated." N.J. Supreme Court Rule 4:74-7(f)

[1] Extended treatment must be likely to improve the person's condition and the commitment must be consistent with the "least drastic means principle." §11(c)

[1] The court determines that the patient "requires continued retention for care and treatment or transfer and continued retention." §31.33(b) The criteria for involuntary admission have been constitutionally challenged and one court has interpreted the statute to incorporate a dangerousness criterion. Pers. comm., Deputy Counsel, Dep't. Mental Hygiene, Nov. 1977.

[1] The 1974 law abandoned the concept of gravely disabled as a separate commitment criterion, but the phrase "dangerous to himself" is now defined to include persons who are "unable to provide for their basic needs for food, clothing, or shelter." 58.2(1)

Table 1.1 Continued

State	Mental Illness or Disability	Danger to		Harm to		Gravely Disabled	In Need of Treatment	Other	Notes and Comments
		Self	Others	Self	Others				
North Dakota S.B. 2164, §§1(11), 20, (45th Legis. Assembly, 1977)	X			(X)	(X)	(X)	X[1]		[1]The definition of a "person requiring treatment" includes a person who can be reasonably expected "to intentionally or unintentionally seriously physically harm himself or another person" or one who is unable to attend to his basic physical needs, such as food, clothing, or shelter and has demonstrated this inability by failing to meet these needs. §1(11)(a),(b)
Ohio Rev. Code Ann. §5122.01,.15 (1977)	X[1]			(X)	(X)	(X)[2]		(X)[3]	[1]A "mentally ill person subject to hospitalization by court order" means a mentally ill person who represents a substantial risk of physical harm to himself or others. §.01(B)(1),(2) [2]A person subject to hospitalization is one who "represents a substantial and immediate risk of serious physical impairment or injury to himself as manifested by evidence that he is unable to provide for and is not providing for his basic physical needs because of his mental

illness and that appropriate provision for such needs cannot be made immediately available in the community." §.01(B)(3)

[3]The person "would benefit from treatment in a hospital for his mental illness and is in need of such treatment as manifested by evidence of behavior that creates a grave and imminent risk to substantial rights of others or himself." §5122.01(B)(4)

Oklahoma
Stat. Ann. tit.
43A, §§3,54.1
(Supp. 1977)

X[1]   (X)   (X)   (X)[2]   X   X[3]

[1]A "person requiring treatment" is defined as either: "(1) A person who has a demonstrable mental illness and who as a result of that mental illness can be expected within the near future to intentionally or unintentionally seriously and physically injure himself or another person; or (2) A person who has a demonstrable mental illness and who as a result of that mental illness is unable to attend to those of his basic physical needs such as food, clothing or shelter that must be attended to in order for him to avoid serious harm in the near future and who has demonstrated such inability by failing to attend to those basic physical needs in the recent past." §3(S)(1),(2)

[2]See definition above.

[3]The court shall select the least restrictive alternative for treatment which is appropriate. §54.1(F)

Table 1.1 *Continued*

State	Mental Illness or Disability	Danger to		Harm to		Gravely Disabled	In Need of Treatment	Other	Notes and Comments
		Self	Others	Self	Others				
Oregon Rev. Stat. §§426.005,.130, .301,.303 (1976)	X[1]	(X)	(X)			(X)[2]			[1] A mentally ill person is defined as one "who, because of a mental disorder, is either: (a) dangerous to himself or others; or (b) unable to provide for his basic personal needs and is not receiving such care as is necessary for his health or safety." §426.005(2)(b) [2] See definition above.
Pennsylvania Act 143, §301(a), 304,305 (ses. 1976)	X[1]	(X)	(X)			(X)[2]	X		[1] Persons subject to involuntary treatment are those who are severely mentally disabled and in need of treatment. "A person is severely mentally disabled when, as a result of mental illness, his capacity to exercise self-control, judgment and discretion in the conduct of his affairs and social relations or to care for his own personal needs is so lessened that he poses a clear and present danger of harm to others or to himself." §301(a) See also §§304(f), 305. [2] Danger to self includes behavior indicating that the person "would be unable, without

36

care, supervision and the continued assistance of others, to satisfy his need for nourishment, personal or medical care, shelter, or self-protection and safety," and there must be reasonable probability that death, serious bodily injury or serious physical debilitation would ensue within 30 days. §301(b)(2)(i) Attempted suicide or self mutilation may also be used to establish danger to self. §301(b)(2)(ii), (iii)

Rhode Island Gen. Laws Ann. §§ 40.1-5-2, -8,-11 (1977)	X[1]	(X)	(X)	(X)	X	X[2]
South Carolina Code Ann. §§32-911, 966 (1977)	X	(X)	(X)	(X)[1]	X	(X)[2]

[1]"Mental disability" is defined as a "mental disorder in which the capacity of a person to exercise self-control or judgment in the conduct of his affairs and social relations or to care for his own personal needs is significantly impaired" §40.1-5-2(13).

[2]"All alternatives to certification have been investigated and deemed unsuitable." 40.1-5-8(10) (Some errors occurred in the 1977 published compilations. Pers. comm., Director, Dep't. Mental Health, Retardation and Hospitals, July '77.)

[1]The definition of "likelihood of serious harm" includes "a very substantial risk of physical impairment or injury to the person himself as manifested by evidence that such

Table 1.1 *Continued*

State	Mental Illness or Disability	Danger to Self	Danger to Others	Harm to Self	Harm to Others	Gravely Disabled	In Need of Treatment	Other	Notes and Comments
									person's judgment is so affected that he is unable to protect himself in the community and that reasonable provision for his protection is not available in the community." §32-911(2)(3) ²The person "lacks sufficient insight or capacity to make responsible decisions with respect to his treatment." §32-966(1)
South Dakota Comp. Laws Ann. §§27A-1-1,-2, 27A-9-18 (1977)	X¹	(X)	(X)			(X)²	X		¹The definition of a mentally ill person includes a person "whose mental condition is such that his behavior establishes one or more of the following: (1) He lacks sufficient understanding or capacity to make responsible decisions concerning his person so as to interfere grossly with his capacity to meet the ordinary demands of life; or (2) He is a danger to himself or others." §27A-1-1 ²See definition above.

State						
Tennessee Code Ann. §33-604 (1977)	X	(X)	(X)	(X)[1]		X[2]
Texas Rev. Civ. Stat. Ann. art. 5547-52 (1977)	X				X[1]	
Utah Code Ann. §64-7-36 (1975)	X	(X)[1]	(X)	(X)[2]	(X)[3]	X[4]

Tennessee Code Ann. §33-604 (1977)

[1] "The definition of "likelihood of serious harm" includes a "reasonable certainty that severe impairment or injury will result to the person alleged to be mentally ill as manifested by his inability to avoid or protect himself from such impairment or injury and suitable community resources for his care are unavailable." §33-604(a)

[2] "All available less drastic alternatives to commitment to a mental hospital or treatment resource" must be unsuitable. §33-604(d)

Texas Rev. Civ. Stat. Ann. art. 5547-52 (1977)

[1] "If the court or the jury, as the case may be, finds that the proposed patient is mentally ill and requires hospitalization in a mental hospital for his own welfare and protection or the protection of others, the court shall order that the mentally ill person be committed as a patient to a mental hospital for an indefinite period." Art. 5547-52

Utah Code Ann. §64-7-36 (1975)

[1] "An immediate danger that the proposed patient will injure himself, herself or others" §64-7-36(6)(b)

[2] See lack of capacity to provide self with basic necessities of life indicating that the patient is in need of treatment, note 3 infra.

39

Table 1.1 Continued

State	Mental Illness or Disability	Danger to		Harm to		Gravely Disabled	In Need of Treatment	Other	Notes and Comments
		Self	Others	Self	Others				
									[3]Patient needs care or treatment and either "lacks sufficient insight to make responsible decisions as to the need for care and treatment . . . or lacks sufficient capacity to provide himself or herself with the basic necessities of life." §64-7-36(c)(i), (ii)
									[4]There must be "no appropriate less restrictive alternative" to hospitalization and the court must determine that the hospital or facility "can provide the individual with treatment that is adequate and appropriate to the individual's conditions and needs." §64-7-36 (6)(d)
Vermont Stat. Ann. tit. 18, §§7101(11), 7607 (1976)	X			(X)	(X)		(X)[1]		[1]This need for treatment must be accompanied by a lack of insight or capacity for decision making concerning his mental condition. §7607(2)(B)

State (Citation)						Notes
Virginia Code Ann. §§37.1-1, 67.3 (1976)	X[1]	(X)	(X)		(X)[2]	X[3]	[1] A mentally ill person is defined as "any person afflicted with mental disease to such an extent that for his own welfare or the welfare of others he requires care and treatment." § 37.1-1(15) Care and treatment is not, however, a specific finding that the court must make to commit a person. [2] The person has been "proven to be so seriously mentally ill as to be substantially unable to care for himself." §37.1-67.3 [3] Alternatives must be investigated and "no less restrictive alternative to institutional confinement and treatment" found suitable. §37.1-67.3
Washington Rev. Code Ann. §§71.05.020,.280, .320 (1976)	X	(X)	(X)	(X)		(X)[1]	[1] Person is in custody because he has committed acts constituting a felony and "as a result of mental disorder presents a substantial likelihood of repeating similar acts." §320(2)(c) See also §280(3)
West Virginia Code Ann. §§27-1-2,12;27-5-4 (1977)	X	(X)	(X)	(X)		X[1,2]	[1] Person must be a resident or patient at a facility in the county of the hearing. §27-5-4(d) [2] A finding must also be made as to whether there is a "less restrictive alternative than commitment appropriate for the individual" 27-5-4(d)

41

Table 1.1 *Continued*

State	Mental Illness or Disability	Danger to		Harm to		Gravely Disabled	In Need of Treatment	Other	Notes and Comments
		Self	Others	Self	Others				
Wisconsin Stat. §§ 51.01(12), 51.20 (1977)	X	(X)[1]	(X)			(X)[2]		X[3]	[1]"The person is considered ''dangerous'' because of ''a substantial probability of physical harm'' to himself or ''a substantial probability of physical harm'' to other individuals. §51.20(1)(a)(2) [2]The person ''evidences such impaired judgment, manifested by evidence of a pattern of recent acts or omissions, that there is a very substantial probability of physical impairment or injury to himself or herself.'' §51.20(1)(a)(2) [3]The person must be a ''proper subject for treatment.'' §51.20(1)(a)(1)
Wyoming Stat. Ann. §25-60(j) (1977)	X			(X)	(X)		(X)[1]		[1]"and, because of his illness, lacks sufficient capacity to make responsible decisions with respect to his hospitalization.'' §25-60(j) (iii)

*To read this table, X's without parentheses should be interpreted as "generally required" criteria for the long-term, judicial commitment of residents of that particular state. In most states, there will also be X's in parentheses. These (X)'s indicate "alternative" criteria that may be used to commit certain persons—in addition to the required criteria indicated by X's. For example, in Alaska, a person must be mentally ill *and either* (a) likely to harm himself or others, *or* (b) be in need of treatment. If the person is in need of treatment, he must also lack sufficient insight or capacity to make responsible decisions concerning hospitalization. At least one alternative criterion is required for commitment in those states showing both "generally required" and "alternative" criteria.

Sources and limitations of data: From a methodological point of view, the process of accurately coding state statutes for commitment critieria is complex and inevitably subject to some error. One problem is the delay in translating legislative action into official state records and into out-of-state sources of information. This results in difficulty in setting a precise cutoff date for a study because new information sometimes arrives changing information already coded prior to the cutoff date. To help solve the problem of delay, informal sources of information and enacted legislation have been used.

Another problem is the interpretation or understanding of the statute. For example, an intermediate appellate court has interpreted a provision of the New York code as including, by incorporation, a dangerousness criterion even though the statute appears to require only "in need of care and treatment" and "in need of retention and treatment" (N.Y. Mental Hygiene Law §§31.01,31.31). This statute has not been coded here in terms of dangerousness, however, because persons working in the system apparently do not yet recognize or use this judicial interpretation. Thus, a major source of variance lies in the interpretation of statutes.

A large source of ambiguity also lies in the definition of mental illness in statutes, particularly when that definition is not compatible with, or broader than, the formal judicial findings required of the court for commitment. In this table, formally required judicial findings are used and supplemented by statutory definitions. In some instances, a statute incorporates a definition from such findings, as in Illinois where a "person in need of mental treatment" is defined as one who is reasonably expected to "intentionally or unintentionally physically injure himself or other persons, or is unable to care for himself so as to guard himself from physical injury or to provide for his own physical needs" (Ill. Mental Health Code §§1-11, 9-5). This statute is coded to include the criteria of mental illness, need of treatment, likelihood of serious harm, and gravely disabled. On the other hand, a definition of mental illness could include the need for treatment, but this need for treatment might not be specifically mentioned in the statute annotations as a judicial requirement for commitment. In such situations, the need for treatment would generally *not* be coded as a required criterion unless this criterion could be inferred from secondary sources as being commonly used in the jurisdiction. These secondary sources would typically be departmental regulations and legal cases.

In summary, a table of this type is subject to methodological problems that preclude complete accuracy or interpretive agreement. For general statistical purposes, however, this table should be suitable. For specific information about commitment in a particular state, the sources suggested in the table as well as local attorneys should be consulted.

43

CHAPTER 2

Patients' Rights

The basic rights of mentally disabled people in institutions have often been ignored or abused. In the well-known *Wyatt* v. *Stickney* case, for example, it was revealed that in Alabama state mental facilities there was only one physician available for every 2000 patients.[1] Under these conditions, adequate medical care was impossible.

In the past, the courts have been reluctant to consider cases brought by institutionalized patients because their care and their treatment were considered matters beyond the scope of judicial competence. Such matters were assumed to lie within the special expertise of hospital administrators and treatment personnel. However, as abuses became increasingly apparent, the courts began taking a more active role in defining and protecting patients' rights.

In legal terms, a "right" is more than just a privilege or a moral imperative. It is a power or capacity, authorized by the state, that a person can use to compel another person to act or not to act. A right on the part of one individual implies that another individual has a duty. Therefore, if committed patients have a legal right to adequate medical care—which they do—then hospital administrators and staff have a duty to provide such care. (The right to treatment of *voluntary* mental patients, while it should be the same as for *involuntary* patients, has seldom, if ever, been directly litigated. The court is apparently less concerned with voluntary patients because it assumes that they have the option of leaving the institution.)

The reader is cautioned again that many of the legal rights of case law spelled out in this chapter may not be reflected in day-to-day treatment. The reasons, both valid and invalid, are numerous—for example, the cited cases may not be controlling within the institution's jurisdiction, the cost of implementing the rights may be too great, or the staff might be ignorant of requirements or unwilling to make changes. It is the old and continuing problem of translating theory into practice.

Several states have established, by case law or statute, standards for the care of persons in institutions.[2] Administrative guidelines have been promulgated by federal agencies, but these are usually less detailed than those of private accrediting groups such as the Joint Commission on Accreditation of Hospitals (JCAH).[3] The JCAH has been particularly active in formulating standards for residential facilities for the mentally retarded. The stringent JCAH standards are in themselves without the force of law, but nonetheless are complied with by hospitals wishing to remain or to become accreditied. Summarized below are some emerging legal doctrines relevant to various aspects of patient care.

Individualized Treatment

Wyatt v. *Stickney* held that persons involuntarily institutionalized "have a constitutional right to receive such individual treatment as will give each of them a realistic opportunity to be cured or to improve his or her mental condition."[4] Accordingly, the court ruled that each patient shall have an individualized treatment plan developed by "qualified mental health professionals." The treatment plan should contain:

- A statement of the nature of the specific problems and specific needs of the patient.
- A statement of the least restrictive treatment conditions necessary to achieve the purposes of commitment.
- A description of intermediate and long-range treatment goals, with a projected timetable for their attainment.
- A statement and rationale for the plan of treatment for achieving these intermediate and long-range goals.
- A specification of staff responsibility and a description of proposed staff involvement with the patient in order to attain these treatment goals.
- Criteria for release to less restrictive treatment conditions, and criteria for discharge.
- A notation of any therapeutic tasks and labor to be performed by the patient. . . .[5]

A "qualified mental health professional" was defined as "(1) a psychiatrist with three years of residency training in psychiatry; (2) a psychologist with a doctoral degree from an accredited program; (3) a social worker with a master's degree from an accredited program and two years of clinical experience under the supervision of a Qualified Mental Health Professional; or (4) a registered nurse with a graduate degree in psychiatric nursing and two years of clinical experience under the supervision of a Qualified Mental Health Professional.''[6]

Physical Environment

Standards have been enumerated for the day rooms, dining facilities, resident units, toilets, lavatories, and shower areas of hospitals. For example, day rooms are to be adequately furnished with reading lamps, tables, chairs, television, and other recreational facilities. Comfortable chairs and tables with hard, washable surfaces are to be provided in dining facilities. (The JCAH requires dining areas to be designed to promote maximum self-development, social interaction and pleasure.[7]) No patient can be made to share a resident unit with more than five other persons. Curtains or screens are to be provided for privacy, and a comfortable bed, closet or locker, chair, and bedside table are to be furnished. One toilet (in a separate stall to insure privacy) may be required for eight persons; one tub or shower for 15 persons. Minimal floor areas per patient have also been specified.[8]

Personal Clothing

The *Wyatt* guidelines accord each patient the right to wear his/her own clothing unless such clothing is determined by a qualified mental health professional to be dangerous or otherwise inappropriate to the treatment program. If a patient has no suitable clothing, the hospital is obligated to supply an adequate allowance of ''various types of neat, clean, and seasonable clothing'' from which the patient shall be able to select.[9]

Personal Activities

Patients have the right to physically exercise several times per week, and hospitals must provide facilities and equipment for such exercise. Presuming his/her treatment plan allows outdoor activity, patients have the right to be outdoors regularly and frequently.[10] In Pennsylvania, patients have the right to be employed at a useful occupation and to market items (keeping the proceeds) which are products of his/her skill or labor.[11] Regarding social intercourse, institutions are to provide, with adequate supervision, suitable opportunities for the patient's interaction with members of the opposite sex.[12]

As guaranteed by the First Amendment of the Constitution, patients have the right to free exercise of religion. Both case law[13] and state statute[14] have recognized that provisions for worship must be made available to all patients on a nondiscriminatory basis.

Patient Labor

The fundamental constitutional guideline regarding patient labor is the Thirteenth Amendment's prohibition of slavery and involuntary servitude. *Jobsen* v. *Henne*[15] held that mandatory patient work programs that supply institutional needs (e.g., floor scrubbing or wall painting), *as well as provide therapy,* are constitutional. However, where no compensation *and* no therapeutic purpose is served, a violation of the Thirteenth Amendment has been found.[16] *Wyatt* strictly limited involuntary labor by holding that even if there is therapeutic value, no patient "shall be required to perform labor which involves the operation and maintenance of the hospital or for which the hospital is under contract with an outside organization."[17] The *Wyatt* court did not explain why the mere fact that labor is beneficial to the institution should cause it to be prohibited, although institutions might understandably tend to be overly enthusiastic about budget-saving assignments. The court's prohibition is possibly too broad.

In situations where hospital operation and maintenance are *not* involved, involuntary labor can perhaps be required only when specific tasks are (a) approved as a therapeutic activity by a qualified mental health professional and integrated into the patient's individualized treatment plan, and (b) supervised by a staff member to oversee the therapeutic aspects of the aspects of the activity.[18]

How much must patients be paid? In a landmark 1973 case, *Souder* v. *Brennan,*[19] a federal district court ruled that residents of institutions that provide care for the aged, mentally ill, or the retarded, must meet the minimum wage of the Fair Labor Standards Act for services that economically benefit the institution. The *Souder* opinion, however, relied on an earlier Supreme Court case which the Court subsequently overruled.[20] Therefore, the applicability of the federal minimum wage standard is dubious, and state statutes and regulations, if any, are applicable.

Voluntary labor, including institutional maintenance, is permitted by patients sufficiently competent to give informed consent.[21]

Mechanical Restraints and Isolation

Mechanical restraits have sometimes been used to control destructive patients, to punish problem patients, or to help an undermanned hospital staff. The latter two uses are rarely approved, and their effectiveness might be matched by other treatments such as tranquilizing drugs. A provision of the Kansas regulation requires that "seclusion and other mechanical restraints used for the sole or principle purpose of controlling behavior which is the result of mental illness shall be instituted only when part of an individual treatment plan or in the event of an emergency situation."[22] Seclusion and restraint may be used only on order of a licensed physician; and in an emergency situation where no treatment plan exists, the seclusion or restraint must be reviewed, confirmed, and documented by a physician at least every 72 hours.

The JCAH has specified that restraint shall not be employed as punishment merely for the convenience of staff or as a substitute for a treatment program.[23] Time limitations are set for restraint (12 hours), as are time minimums for the opportunity to exercise (ten minutes per two hours of restraint). *Wyatt* also prohibited physical restraint of mental patients except for emergency situations which explain the rationale for such action. If restraint is employed, the patient must have bathroom privileges every hour and must be bathed every 12 hours.[24]

Wyatt set similar conditions for the isolation of patients. JCAH standards permit the use of "time-out devices" if a resident is not placed alone in a locked room.[25] In a case involving a mentally ill inmate in a correctional institution, a federal court ordered that restraint or seclusion should be used only in emergencies to prevent serious injury, that the person be released every two hours, and unless the person makes overt gestures threatening serious injury, or a physician certifies in writing that release would be harmful, seclusion cannot be reimposed.[26] After 48 hours, a psychiatrist not employed by the hospital must certify in writing the need for continued seclusion or restraint. It should be noted that behavior modification or other treatments using brief isolation are not affected by such a ruling because "time-out" procedures involve minutes rather than hours of isolation.

Long-term isolation of mental patients might be analogous to the solitary confinement of prisoners. The Eighth Amendment has been cited in numerous cases which have held that certain conditions accompanying the solitary confinement of prisoners constituted cruel and unusual punishment.[27] However, no court has yet held that solitary confinement itself, reasonably used, is a violation of the Eighth Amendment. The extention, by analogy, of correctional case law to the area of mental health should be done with great caution. Prisoners are generally regarded as having a status of diminished civil liberty. Some authorities, for whom the analogy between prisoners in solitary confinement and patients in seclusion is strong, speculate that hospital seclusion may not meet the constitutional test.[28]

Nonetheless, institutions are generally under an obligation to protect their patients from harm, including harm from themselves or other patients. This may necessitate the temporary restraint or isolation of some patients. If this is necessary, the procedure used should be that which is the least restrictive alternative necessary for protection and safety. Long-term restraint or isolation may require prior review by persons other than the treatment staff. The periodic review by an institutional human rights group regarding treatment options generally available for those patients believed to be dangerous may also be required.

Experimental Research and Hazardous Treatment

Experimental research and hazardous treatment procedures should comply with guidelines established by organizations such as the American Federation for Clinical Research, the National Commission for Protection of Human Subjects of Biomedical and Behavioral Research, the American Psychological Association, the U.S. Department of Health, Education, and Welfare, and the World Medical Association.[29] The *Wyatt* court confirmed that patients should not be subjected to research or hazardous treatment without their expressed and informed consent and the consent of next of kin[30] (see Chapter 11).

Communications and Visitations

The majority of states have statutory provisions on the subject of patient correspondence and visitation. Ambiguities exist, however, regarding the right to correspondence and visitation in those states that have no relevant statutes. An inherent right to communicate seemingly exists only to the extent that communications allow the correction of a wrongful confinement. Typically, these communications are directed to attorneys and public officials.

The British Royal Commission on Mental Illness recommended that outgoing letters should not be subject to censorship except when addressees request that communications be scrutinized or withheld.[31] An even broader recommendation in *Wyatt* suggested that patients are unqualifiedly allowed to send sealed mail to anyone and to receive sealed mail from public officials, private physicians, and attorneys.[32] A problem exists, however, when patients send obscene, threatening, or libelous materials through the mail. At minimum, sending such materials may violate postal regulations. Some hospitals forbid the mailing of letters that contain names of other patients, obscene materials, or threats. Alternatively, some hospitals insert a small printed notice in all outgoing mail to the effect that the writer is a hospital resident and that communication should be regarded accordingly.[33] A similar problem exists regarding potentially harmful information or material contained in incoming mail. Statutes seldom differentiate between outgoing and incoming mail when regulating patient communication.

Typically, and according to an NIMH Draft Act,[34] institution supervisors have discretionary powers to control visitation. Attorneys, physicians, and clergymen may have, by statute,[35] special visitation privileges.

Medication

According to *Wyatt,* no medication may be administered without a written order of a physician.[36] Medication may not be used as punishment or as a substitute for a treatment program. It may not be used merely for the convenience of the hospital staff nor may it interfere with a patient's treatment program. Unnecessary or excessive medication is not to be administered.

A patient's right to refuse medication has received considerable attention. In *Winters* v. *Miller,*[37] a Christian Scientist was administered medication against her religious beliefs. The court held that, absent a finding of "special incompetence" (mere mental illness was not considered a special incompetence), a mental patient retains the right to refuse medication on First Amendment grounds.[38] The *Winters* court implied that procedural due process (Fifth Amendment) may also provide a constitutional safeguard against unwanted medication or treatment:

> While it may be true that the state could validly undertake to treat Miss Winters if it did stand in a *parens patriae* relationship to her and such a relationship may be created if and when a person is found *legally* incompetent, there was never any effort on the part of the appellees to secure such a judicial determination of incompetency before proceeding to treat Miss Winters. . . . Under our Constitution there is no procedural right more fundamental than the right of the citizen, except in exceptional circumstances, to tell his side of the story to an impartial tribunal.[39]

Similarly, in *Scott* v. *Plante*,[40] a patient was administered psychotropic medication without his consent. [Apparently] the patient had *not* been found legally incompetent to consent to (or to refuse) treatment. The Court concluded, in part, that the patient (or someone standing *in loco parentis* to him/her) should be given, in the absence of an emergency, the opportunity for a judicial hearing before being subjected to such treatment without his/her consent.

Medication may be viewed as an "intrusive" mode of treatment, somewhat similar to psychosurgery or ETC, therefore requiring not only patient consent but also some demonstration on the part of the institution that less intrusive forms of treatment have been considered[41] (see Chapter 5).

The issue of refusing medication is a thorny one. If a person is judged so mentally ill that s/he has to be institutionalized, how can this person be able to make a judgment regarding taking or not taking certain drugs? At this point, the distinctions between voluntary and involuntary admission, plus a determination of specific incompetencies, may be appropriate.

Dignity and Privacy

Wyatt not only promulgated the patient's right to dignity[42] but also emphasized the constitutional right of privacy established in *Griswold* v. *Connecticut*.[43] These two cases, however, have left the interpretation of these "rights" open to debate. One group of concerned citizens has interpreted these cases as requiring that hospitals should provide a safe, clean, and wholesome environment, and should inform the patient of civil rights and treatment procedures.[44] The patient's knowledge of relevant aspects of his treatment is presumably necessary for the maintenance of his physical and psychological integrity[45] and is vital to the patient's capacity to give informed consent. Informed consent is required for most forms of treatment that are not of an emergency nature.

Right to Treatment

"Treatment" may be defined as a course of planned intervention designed to change behaviors that are considered (by some standard) aberrant, disordered, or dangerous. Treatment may include a wide range of psychological, sociological, and medical procedures. Psychological and sociological procedures commonly involve psychoanalysis, client-centered counseling, behavior therapy, sociodrama, sensitivity training, occupational therapy, existential analysis, and so forth. These procedures may be integrated at the direction of a physician with specifically medical techniques such as chemotherapy, shock therapy, or psychosurgery.

The "right to treatment" refers to the right of involuntarily committed patients to receive adequate treatment during their confinement in mental institutions.[46] The right is based upon the notion that a fundamental purpose of involuntary civil commitment of nondangerous persons is treatment[47]—therefore, treatment should in fact be provided. Merely labeling normal staff-patient interaction as "milieu therapy" is not adequate.[48] The right to treatment applies to both mentally ill and mentally retarded persons,[49] whether the commitment has been through civil or criminal procedures.

One traditional grounding for this treatment doctrine can be found in the local statutes or mental health regulations of various jurisdictions. In the landmark case of *Rouse* v. *Cameron*,[50] the plaintiff-patient was charged with a misdemeanor, but was found "not guilty by reason of insanity." After four years of confinement during which he had received little or no psychiatric treatment, the plaintiff submitted a petition of habeas corpus to the Court of Appeals. The court held that a right to treatment was cognizable under the D.C. Code,[51] stating: "The purpose of involuntary hospitalization is treatment, not punishment. . . . Absent treatment, the hospital is transform[ed] . . . into a penitentiary where one could be held indefinitely for no convicted offense."[52] There has been considerable legal recognition of a right to treatment in both case law and statutes.[53]

The right to treatment doctrine has been argued on three constitutional grounds: cruel and unusual punishment, equal protection, and due process. Cruel and unusual punishment has been occasionally argued successfully when an involuntary patient received no treatment,[54] but the equal protection clause has been more prominent.[55] The Massachusetts Supreme Judicial Court in 1968 warned: "If such treatment is not available on a reasonable, nondiscriminatory basis, there is substantial risk that constitutional requirements of equal protection of the laws will not be satisfied. Differences in treatment may be justified by differences in particular cases but should be reasonably related to the varying circumstances."[56]

The third constitutional ground, due process, has received the most attention.[57] "To deprive any citizen of his or her liberty upon the altruistic theory that the confinement is for humane therapeutic reasons and then fail to provide adequate treatment violates the very fundamentals of due process."[58] The only Supreme Court right-to-treatment case[59] was decided primarily on due process grounds. The Court, in *O'Connor* v. *Donaldson,* acknowledged that a nondangerous civilly committed mental patient has a constitutional right to be released if he is not dangerous to himself or others, is capable of surviving in the community with help, and is receiving only custodial care. This landmark case is limited because it did not deal with (a) dangerous, civilly committed mental patients; (b) patients who are receiving treatment but who nonetheless insist on release; (c) patients who have committed crimes and are residing in mental institutions indefinitely; or (d) the criteria by which the standards of treatment are to be judged. Interpreted in a narrow and practical manner, *O'Connor*[60] probably gives nondangerous, civilly committed patients access to release (as opposed to the creation of treatment where none exists) but may not provide them, when entering an institution, a very effective authority for demanding treatment.[61]

There still remains the practical problem of determining when treatment that is provided meets judicially acceptable standards. The terms "adequate," "appropriate," and "suitable" have been used by the courts to describe the legally required standards of treatment. But treatment is not likely to be adequate, appropriate, or suitable if it is not also "effective" in achieving a primary goal of the commitment process: namely, the restoration of the patient to normal mental functioning and his/her return to satisfactory living in the community. A provision of the Florida commitment code expressly addresses the required quality and objective of treatment: "Each patient in a facility shall receive treatment suited to his needs, which shall be administered skillfully, safely, and humanly with respect for his dignity and personal integrity. Each patient shall receive such medical, vocational, social, educational, and rehabilitative services as his condition requires to bring about an early return to his community."[62] The overall quality of treatment in a mental health facility should not differ substantially from the quality of treatment in general medical facilities, at least in principle. There has been already a dramatic increase in the cost of residential psychiatric patient care.[63] In the past, some right-to-treatment cases have drawn criticism from medical organizations because the courts (being comprised of nonmedical personnel) are presumably not as competent as hospital staff to make treatment decisions.[64] Nonetheless, it should be clear that the translation of legal or ethical principles into day-to-day practice involves difficult political and economic decisions that fall into the domain of courts and legislatures as well as medicine and related disciplines.

Right to Refuse Treatment

Where a right-to-treatment doctrine is established, a right-to-*refuse*-treatment cannot be far behind.[65] It should be noted that the right to *obtain* treatment does not impose an obligation upon a patient to *accept* treatment. The right-to-treatment doctrine seeks to make adequate (effective) treatment programs available for those patients who want to participate in treatment. The patient does not normally have a duty to exercise the right to treatment. (Similarly, the right to vote does not impose an obligation to vote.)

The concept of the right to refuse treatment is a complex one. The relevant law is in a period of development and flux. Among some obvious legal problems are: (a) the patient's competency to decide whether or not to refuse treatment, (b) procedures for obtaining *informed* consent of a severely disturbed but legally competent person, (c) handling objections on religious grounds, (d) the potential civil liability of a practitioner if a patient who has refused treatment injures himself or others, and (e) the increased cost to taxpayers of patients who refuse less expensive treatments and insist on more expensive ones (e.g., individual psychotherapy instead of group therapy or medication).[66]

Perhaps a few emerging conceptual trends in the law should be noted. A voluntary, competent patient may generally refuse treatment. If, however, the patient presents an emergency in which there is a likelihood beyond a reasonable doubt of substantial physical injury to others or himself by suicide or self-mutilation, for example, emergency commitment procedures may be initiated as provided by state law. (All states provide for such procedures by statute.) Treatment should probably not be forced upon a committed but legally competent mental patient who refuses treatment unless there has been a prior judicial review. The commitment of a patient to a mental health facility does not of itself mean that the person is legally incompetent with respect to all decisions or rights. A judicial hearing is usually required to establish a patient's specific areas of competency and incompetency.

Persons are sometimes placed in mental hospitals for "observation" prior to a judicial hearing on involuntary commitment, competency to stand trial, need for guardianship or related matters involving the person's mental status. Treatment should generally not be imposed, except in a clear emergency, until there has been a judicial determination of his mental status and his ability to consent to treatment. "Restraint" (not "treatment") is usually permitted in emergency situations.

Although acceptance or refusal of treatment should be, as far as possible, a voluntary choice by the patient, the fact that involuntary commitment is coercive does not necessarily mean that all choices made within that context are impermissibly coerced.[67] Many decisions, whether inside or outside a hospital, are an alternative between two undesirable choices, but are nonetheless voluntary. A competent patient who refuses treatment (particularly if it is non-intrusive) that would facilitate his/her release from the institution cannot later claim that s/he should be released because treatment is inadequate.[68]

Concern is often expressed about legally incompetent patients who lack the mental competency to give informed consent for treatment, the problem is one of protecting legally incompetent persons from excessively intrusive treatment while at the same time allowing such persons to benefit from necessary therapy. Precedent exists for administering intrusive forms of treatment to an incompetent nonconsenting patient following an adversary proceeding in which the patient has a guardian *ad litem*.[69] In such a proceeding, the court would weigh the patient's need for treatment against the intrusiveness of the treatment by considering factors such as the changes in behavior and mental activity to be produced by the treatment, possible aversive side effects, the acceptance of the procedure by the medical community, or its experimental nature, intrusion into the patient's body and the pain involved, and the patient's ability to determine for him/herself the desirability of the treatment.[70] Current trends suggest that the legally incompetent patient should, at minimum, be provided with a due process hearing at which the patient has legal counsel, an independent psychiatrist or psychologist to assist him, and access to medical records. State statutes often specify the conditions under which treatment may be imposed or refused.

Civil Rights and Privileges

Because of the value placed on individual civil liberties, being a mental patient cannot in itself be the sole reason for deeming a person incompetent "to manage his affairs, to contract, to hold professional or occupational or vehicle operator's licenses, to marry and obtain a divorce, to register and vote, or to make a will."[71] As mentioned previously with respect to refusing treatment, an affirmative finding of special incompetence is usually necessary to restrict civil liberties. An Arizona statute not only forbids denial of "any civil right" or discrimination with regard to employment or obtaining licences, but also states that applications for positions, licenses and housing shall contain no requests for information which encourages such discriminations."[72] Many states require mental health facilities to inform patients of their rights by means of printed announcement.[73]

Least Restrictive Alternative

The doctrine of the least restrictive alternative applies not only to the consideration of alternatives to commitment but also to the alternatives for treatment available within an institution.[74] This would seem to be particularly applicable when treatment is imposed upon incompetent patients. The doctrine as it is developing may also apply to treatment alternatives allowing gradual release into the community, such as transferring patients from larger to smaller living units and then from segregated living into a community-based halfway house. The court in *Wyatt* suggested that individualized treatment plans are necessary for an "effective treatment program" in public institutions, and it subsequently required that each treatment plan contain "a statement of the least restrictive treatment conditions necessary to achieve the purposes of commitment."[75]

Some state statutes explicitly require least restrictive conditions.[76] Courts will sometimes interpret commitment statutes as requiring the least restrictive treatment conditions when the statute provides for the "care and treatment" of patients.[77]

To implement the least restrictive alternatives doctrine, one writer has suggested the following administrative steps:[78] (1) Determine the alternatives within the system. (2) Remove artificial barriers that would otherwise make an alternative unsuitable. (3) Examine what other institutions offer and fill in the gaps by procedures such as contracting for services or sharing services. (4) Evaluate the effectiveness of the treatment alternatives. (5) Establish machinery for the efficient transfer of patients from one alternative to another. (6) Place patients in the least restrictive alternative appropriate to their needs. (7) Document why any less restrictive alternative would not be suitable. (8) Evaluate patient progress annually, or more often. (9) Change placement when treatment is not meeting stated objectives or progress indicates a transfer to a less restrictive alternative can be made. (10) When patients are ready to move out of your jurisdiction into another setting, continue services until the new placement begins.

Contractual Agreements about Treatment

As noted earlier, patients retain most of their basic rights following commitment. Many personal services can be provided on a contractual basis including medical care and psychotherapy. A patient typically consents to medical treatment (thus allowing the physician to touch the patient's body), and also agrees to follow instructions and to pay a reasonable fee. This agreement is a contract. If the patient fails to pay, s/he may be sued for breach of contract. The contract does not need to be a written one. It may be an oral agreement or an implicit understanding. Similarly, private patient psychotherapy involves both consent and a contract.

Two illustrative contracts can be found in Appendixes F and G. The contract in Appendix F specifies, in detail, the goal of the treatment program, procedures, and expected outcome.[79] Measurement of treatment objectives is clearly described, and one-third of the therapist's fee is payable only after achievement of the stated objectives. This contingent fee arrangement is rather unusual, but it is one that some psychologists use when they are quite sure that their treatment techniques are effective. The sample contract in Appendix G also requires express agreement regarding the goals of treatment.[80] It contains standard provisions regarding payment, renegotiation of the contract, and the confidentiality of information communicated during treatment. (These contracts are presented for illustrative purposes only. Care should be exercised in adopting them for one's own use because the details and context of practices differ. Particular caution is necessary in making broad promises about the confidentiality of information. See Chapter 12).

Contracts are also possible within an institutional setting. The contract could be a simple one stating that the therapist or institution agrees to provide treatment that is "customary and usual in the profession." A simple written agreement such as this might reduce the likelihood of a patient being neglected or of his/her being given treatment of an obviously inferior quality. Failture to provide customary and usual treatment would constitute a breach of contract.[81]

Contracts can also encourage a more open discussion of privileges and responsibilities between the patient and therapist. A contract could clarify, for example, matters such as visitation privileges, control of personal property, the behavioral accomplishments necessary for release, leave revocation procedures, obligations with regard to participation in therapy and medication regimens, and so forth.

Finally, the use of contracts allows the patient and therapist to negotiate privileges and responsibilities particularly suited to the needs of the patient and his/her particular life situation. This enhances individual choice. At the same time, it allows supervision and control by responsible agencies, professional organizations, or institutional review panels in much the same way that written individualized treatment plans provide one means of documenting and monitoring the quality of patient care.

NOTES

1. Wyatt v. Stickney, 325 F. Supp. 781 (M.D. Ala. 1971), *enforced in* 334 F. Supp. 1341 (M.D. Ala. 1971), 344 F. Supp. 373, 379 (M.D. Ala. 1972), *aff'd sub nom* Wyatt v. Aderholt, 503 F.2d 1305 (5th Cir. 1974).
2. New York Mental Hygiene Law, sec. 29.13 (1976) (written treatment plans required for persons in Dept. of Mental Hygiene programs); Ohio Rev. Code Ann., sec. 5119.10 (1977) (Dept. of Mental Health and Mental Retardation institutions must comply with JCAH standards for program and staffing). To compare statutes with detailed specifications of patient rights, *see, e.g.*, Arizona Rev. Stat. Ann., secs. 36-506 to 514 (1974); Michigan Comp. Laws Ann., ch. 7 (1977); New Jersey Stat. Ann., sec. 30:4–24.2 (1976); Wisconsin Stat., sec. 51.61 (1977).
3. Accreditation Council for Services for Mentally Retarded and Other Developmentally Disabled Persons (Joint Commission on Accreditation of Hospitals), *Standards for residential facilities for the mentally retarded*. May 5, 1971 (mimeo.). For a sample of federal guidelines, *see* HEW regulations for Medicaid residents in nursing-homes in the *Federal Register* (March 29, 1976). *See also,* Commission on Accreditation of Rehabilitation Facilities, *Standards manual for rehabilitation facilities*. Chicago, 1973.
4. Wyatt, 344 F. Supp. at 374. The value of this case as precedent may be somewhat diminished by a narrower ruling in O'Connor v. Donaldson, 422 U.S. 563 (1975) negating some earlier Fifth Circuit court opinion. *But see,* Welsch v. Likins, 373 F. Supp. 487 (D. Minn. 1976). It is not unusual for recent commitment statutes to contain provisions for a right to treatment, *see, e.g.,* Arizona, Florida, Georgia, Hawaii, Illinois, Kansas, Nebraska, New Hampshire, New Jersey, New Mexico, New York, North Dakota, Ohio, Oklahoma, Pennsylvania, Rhode Island, Utah, Vermont, Washington, and Wisconsin.
5. Wyatt, 344 F. Supp. at 384.
6. A "qualified mental health professional" is defined in the appendix to Wyatt, 344 F. Supp. at 379.

7. Standards (JCAH), *supra* note 3, at section 2.2.3.2.4.
8. Wyatt, 344 F. Supp. at 381–382: 3.72 sq. meters (40 sq. ft.) for day room, .93 sq. meters (10 sq. ft.) for dining room, 7.43 sq. meters (80 sq. ft.) for patients' room, etc. Toilet facilities recommended in Levering, S. *Patients' rights: Manual for nurses* (mimeo.) at p. 12, Philadelphia: Mental Patients Civil Liberties Project, 1975.
9. Wyatt, 344 F. Supp. at sections 11, 12.
10. Bartley v. Kremens, 402 F. Supp. 1039 (E.D. Pa. 1975), *rev'd.* 431 U.S. 119 (1977); J.L. & J. R. v. Parham, 412 F. Supp. 112 (M.D. Ga. 1976, 431 U.S. 936 (1977).
11. Pennsylvania Mental Health and Mental Retardation Act of 1976, sec. 423.
12. Wyatt, 344 F. Supp. 373 at sec. 17. *See also,* New Jersey Stat. Ann., sec. 30:4–24.2(e)(10)(1976).; Ohio Rev. Code Ann., sec. 5122.29(J)(1977); Kansas Stat. Ann., sec. 59-2929 (1977)(conjugal visits if facilities are available).
13. Wyatt, 344 F. Supp. 373; *see also* Winters v. Miller, 466 F.2d 65 (2d Cir. 1971).
14. *E.g.,* Nebraska LB806, sec. 76(6) (1976)(includes both religious and political activity).
15. Jobsen v. Henne, 355 F.2d 129 (2d Cir. 1966).
16. Weidenfeller v. Kidulis, 380 F. Supp. 445 (E.D. Wisc. 1974). *See generally,* Friedman, P. The mentally handicapped citizen and institutional labor, 87 *Harvard Law Review* 567 (1974).
17. Wyatt, 344 F. Supp. 373 at sec. 18A.
18. Wyatt, 344 F. Supp. 373 at sec. 18B1.
19. Souder v. Brennan, 367 F. Supp. 808 (D.D.C. 1973).
20. Souder relied upon Maryland v. Wirtz, 392 U.S. 183 (1968) upholding the application of the 1966 Amendments of the Fair Labor Standards Act, 29 U.S.C. section 206, subjecting state institutions to the minimum wage. The Supreme Court reversed itself, overruling Maryland v. Wirtz, in National League of Cities v. Usery, 96 S. Ct. 2465 (1976). The Court had previously held that federal courts are barred, under the 11th Amendment, from granting relief under the Fair Labor Standards Act to a consenting state. Employees of the Dept. of Public Health and Welfare v. Missouri, 411 U.S. 279 (1973). Some states expressly apply the Fair Labor Standards Act, as amended, to patient labor policies—for example, Nebraska LB 806, sec. 76(7)(1976).
21. Dale v. State, 355 N.Y.S. 2d 485 (Sup. Ct. N.Y., App. Div., May 1974).
22. Kansas Department for Human Resources, 902 *Kansas Administrative Register* 12:020, sec. 10 (1977).
23. Standards (JCAH), *supra* note 3, at sec. 2.1.8.6.
24. Wyatt, 344 F. Supp. 373 at Sec. 7.
25. Standards (JCAH), *supra* note 3, at secs. 2.1.8.5 and 2.1.8.9.
26. Negron v. Ward, 74 Civ. 1480 (S.D. N.Y. July 13, 1976) as reported in 1 *Mental Disability Law Reporter* 191 (1976). *See also* Welsch v. Likins, 373 F. Supp. 487 (D. Minn. 1974) (resident in seclusion must be checked every half hour); and Morales v. Turman, 383 F. Supp. 53 (E.D. Tex. 1974), *rev'd* 535 F.2d 864 (5th Cir. 1976), *reinstated* 430 U.S. 322 (1977) (juvenile inmates may be placed in time-out or isolation for treatment purposes not exceeding one hour.).
27. *See* Wright v. McNann, 387 F.2d 519 (2d Cir. 1967) (prisoner was forced to remain nude and exposed to the winter cold); Sinclair v. Henderson, 331 F. Supp. 1123 (E.D. La. 1971) (prisoner was confined for long periods without regular outdoor exercise). Reported in Ferleger, D. Loosing the chains: In-hospital civil liberties of mental patients, 13 *Santa Clara Lawyer* 447 (1973).

28. Ferleger, *id.*

29. Position statement of the American Federation for Clinical Research on the DHEW proposed rules, 23 *Clinical Research* 53 (Feb. 1975); American Psychological Association, Ethical principles in the conduct of research with human participants (1973); National Institutes of Health, *Institutional guide to DHEW policy on protection of human subjects,* DHEW Publication No. 72-102, 1972, as updated in 45 *Code of Federal Regulations,* part 46 (Jan. 1978) implementing National Research Act, Public Law 93-348 (July 1974); Code of ethics on human experimentation. 38 *American Journal of Orthopsychiatry* 589 (1968). *See also* Association for the Advancement of Behavior Therapy, Ethical issues for human services (1977). Many states have statutory provisions or health department regulations related to research with mental patients. These sources should be consulted.

30. Wyatt, 344 F. Supp. 373 at secs. 8, 9.

31. Royal Commission on the Law Relating to Mental Illness and Mental Deficiency, 1954–57, Cmnd., No. 169, sec. 299, at 103, cited in J. S. Brakel and R. S. Rock (Eds.), *The mentally disabled and the law.* Chicago: Univ. of Chicago Press, 1971, at p. 157.

32. Failure to forward letters to attorneys has been held as an unreasonable restraint on the patient's right of habeas corpus. Hoff v. State, 279 N.Y. 490, 18 N.E.2d 671 (1939); Stowers v. Ardmore Acres Hospital, 172 N.W.2d 497 (1969), *aff'd* 191 N.W.2d 335 (1971); *see generally,* Note, The committed mentally ill and their right to communicate, 7 *Wake Forest Law Review* 297 (1971).

33. One hospital administrator reported that a 70-year-old patient wrote to her 10-year-old granddaughter at school stating: "Your mother is a whore. She sent me away to get rid of me so she could entertain men at home. She will do the same to you unless you send her away." The child was brutally shocked by the letter. Nonetheless, this administrator believes that fewer than one out of 150 patients needs to be restricted from sending letters or making phone calls. Davidson, H. Mental hospitals and the civil liberties dilemma. 51 *Mental Hygiene* 374, 376 (1967).

34. National Institutes of Mental Health, *A draft act governing hospitalization of the mentally ill.* (Public Health Service Publication No. 51). Washington, D.C.: Government Printing Office, 1952.

35. In 1971, 30 states had enacted relevant statutes, eight of which allowed unrestricted visits from clergymen, according to Brakel and Rock, *supra* note 31 at p. 158. *See* illustrative current statutes as per *supra* note 12.

36. Wyatt, 344 F. Supp. 373, at section 1.

37. Winters v. Miller, 446 F.2d 65 (2d Cir. 1971), *cert. denied* 404 U.S. 985 (1971). *But see* Whitree v. State, 56 Misc. 2d 693, 290 N.Y.S.2d 489 (Ct. Cl. 1968) (dicta) (liability for *failure* to treat patient, including use of tranquilizing drugs which patient refused on religious grounds).

38. Ferleger, *supra* note 27, at 475, interpreting *Winters, id.* Ferleger (p. 475) notes that the Supreme Court has held that to restrict recognition of conscientious objection to military service *only* to persons professing *traditional* religious belief is unconstitutional. U.S. v. Seeger, 380 U.S. 163 (1965).

39. Winters v. Miller, 446 F.2d 65, 71 (2d Cir. 1971).

40. Scott v. Plante, 532 F.2d 939 (3rd Cir. 1976).

41. *Re* Cleo F. Lundquist, No. 150151 (Probate Ct., Ramsey County, Minn., Apr. 30, 1976) (refusal of Prolixin upheld, citing Price v. Sheppard, 239 N.W.2d 905 [Minn. 1976] wherein ECT refused) as reported in 1 *Mental Disability Law Reporter* 190 (1976).

42. Wyatt, 344 F. Supp. 373, at Appendix A, sec. II.

43. Griswold v. Connecticut, 381 U.S. 479 (1965).

44. Mental Patients Civil Liberties Project, Philadelphia, Pa. For addresses of various interest groups and organizations, *see* Appendix 00.

45. "No right is held more sacred, or is more carefully guarded, by the common law, than the right of every individual to the possession and control of his own person, free from all restraint or interference of others, unless by clear and unquestionable authority of law." Union Pacific Ry v. Botsford, 141 U.S. 250, 251 (1891), as reported in Ferleger, *supra* note 27, at 471.

46. *See generally,* D. S. Burris (Ed.), *The right to treatment: A symposium.* New York: Springer Publishing Company, 1969 (reprinted from 57 *Georgetown Law Journal* (March 1969); Schwitzgebel, R. K. The right to effective mental treatment. 62 *California Law Review* 936 (May 1974); Schwitzgebel, R. K., Implementing a right to effective treatment. 1 *Law and Psychology Review* 117 (Spring 1975). The right to treatment was publicly suggested first by Birnbaum and Kittrie: *See* Birnbaum, M. The right to treatment. 46 *American Bar Association Journal* 499 (1960); Kittrie, N. Compulsory mental treatment and the requirements of "due process." 21 *Ohio State Law Journal* 28, 51 (1960).

47. ". . . where a nondangerous patient is involuntarily civilly committed to a state mental hospital, the only constitutionally permissible purpose of confinement is to provide treatment . . . and that such a patient has a constitutional right to such treatment as will help him to be cured or to improve his mental condition." Donaldson v. O'Connor, 493 F.2d 504, 527 (5th Cir. 1974), *aff'd. in part sub nom.* O'Connor v. Donaldson, 422 U.S. 563 (1975).

48. Morales, *supra* note 26. Of similar opinion: "If society confines a man for the benevolent purpose of helping him—'for his own good,' in the standard phrase—then its right to do so withhold his freedom depends entirely upon whether help is in fact provided." Bazelon, D. L., Implementing the right to treatment. In G. H. Morris (Ed.), *The mentally ill and the right to treatment.* Springfield, Ill.: Charles C Thomas, 1970, p. 102.

49. ". . . When a state institutionalizes individuals because they are retarded, the U.S. Constitution (8th and 14th Amendments) . . . require the state to provide such minimally adequate habilitation as will afford a reasonable opportunity for them to acquire and maintain such life skills as are necessary to enable them to cope as effectively as their capacities permit." Terri Lee Halderman, et al. v. Pennhurst State School and Hospital, *et al.*, C.A. No. 74-1345 (E.D. Pa. March 17, 1978) as reported in 2 *Mental Disability Law Reporter* 200, 213. *See generally,* Steinbock, E. A. *et al.* Civil rights of the mentally retarded: An overview. 1 *Law and Psychology Review* 152 (Spring 1975).

50. Rouse v. Cameron, 373 F.2d 451 (D.C. Cir. 1966).

51. D.C. Code, sec. 21-562 (Supp. V, 1966).

52. Rouse, 373 F.2d 451, 453 (D.C. Cir. 1966).

53. *See supra* note 4 for statutes. For judicial application of a mental health code to affirm a right to treatment, see Woe v. Mathews, 408 F. Supp. 419 (E.D. N.Y. 1976) as well as Halderman, *supra* note 49 at p. 213.

54. *See, e.g.,* People *ex rel.* Kaganovitch v. Wilkins, 23 App. Div. 2d 178, 259 N.Y.S.2d

462 (4th Dep't 1965); Wolfersdorf v. Johnson, 317 F. Supp. 66 (S.D.N.Y. 1970); Martarella v. Kelley, 349 F. Supp. 575 (S.D.N.Y. 1972), enforced 359 F. Supp. 479 (S.D.N.Y. 1973). *But see* Note, Civil commitment of the mentally ill. 87 *Harvard Law Review* 1330–1333 (1973).

55. *See, e.g.,* Nason v. Superintendent of Bridgewater State Hospital, 353 Mass. 604, 233 N.E.2d 908 (1968); People v. Mancuse, 274 N.Y.S.2d 477 (Sup. Ct., App. Div. 1966).

56. Nason, 353 Mass. at 604, 233 N.E.2d at 908; *see also, In re* Anonymous, 69 Misc. 2d 181, 329 N.Y.S.2d 542 (Sup. Ct. 1972).

57. *See, e.g.,* Harvin v. United States, 445 F.2d 675 (D.C. Cir. 1971) (*en banc*); *In re* Maddox, 351 Mich. 358, 88 N.W.2d 470 (1968); *In re* Anonymous, 69 Misc. 2d 181, 329 N.Y.S.2d 542 (Sup. Ct. 1972).

58. Wyatt, 325 F. Supp. 781, 785 (M.D. Ala. 1975).

59. Donaldson, *supra* note 47.

60. O'Connor, 422 U.S. 563, 572 (1975).

61. Lattman, M. S. Whatever happened to Kenneth Donaldson? 1 *Mental Disability Law Reporter* 288 (1977).

62. Florida Stat. Ann., sec. 394.459(4) (1977). It can be argued that when government action infringes upon the protected interests of a person, the means chosen by the government should be reasonably related to the government's purpose that justifies the infringement. In discussing this principle, Friedman commented: "Thus, a mental patient or prisoner may use this legal principle to attack behavioral procedures for which there is no evidence of effectiveness. This legal attack would be available for many treatments now in use, ranging from group therapy to milieu therapy." Friedman, P. R. Legal regulation of applied behavior analysis in mental institutions and prisons. 17 *Arizona Law Review* 39, 72 n. 168. *See* Jackson v. Indiana, 406 U.S. 715, 738 (1972); Clevand Bd. of Educ. v. LaFleur, 414 U.S. 632, 643 (1974). *See also,* Schwitzgebel, R. K. Right to treatment for the mentally disabled: The need for realistic standards and objective criteria. 8 *Harvard Civil Rights - Civil Liberties Law Review* 513 (1973); Schwitzgebel, *supra* note 46; Stone, *infra* note 66, at pp. 67–68. There may be, of course, some dangerous patients for whom no effective treatment presently exists. In these cases, the situation should be made explicit and then, ideally, a court or jury (rather than a mental health professional) should make the decision about the need and legal justification for the continued retention of this person if s/he is imminently dangerous.

63. Three-year increase at Willowbrook State School (N.Y.) following court order (*cf.* NYARC v. Carey, *infra* note 74) from $4600 to $26,300 per resident. Harvard Law Review, Mental health litigation: Implementing institutional reform. 2 *Mental Disability Law Reporter,* 221, 223 n. 31. State of N.J. in the Interest of D.F., 145 N.J. Super. 381, (N.J. App. 1976) (order vacated to send juvenile delinquent to state facility costing $40,000 per year per resident due to cost). *See also* Roth, L. H. Involuntary civil commitment: The right to treatment and the right to refuse treatment. 7 *Psychiatric Annals* 50, 68 (May 1977).

64. The American Psychiatric Association argued that "the definition of treatment and the appraisal of its adequacy are matters for medical determination." It chastised legal formulations of the right to treatment because "some courts, attorneys, statutes, and judicial formulations reiterate, almost ritualistically, that hospitalization without treatment equates with punishment. This is not the case." American Psychiatric Association,

A position statement on the question of adequacy of treatment. 123 *American Journal of Psychiatry* 1459 (May 1967). However, a later position paper of the APA Task Force on the Right to Treatment stated that "the American Psychiatric Association, whose membership has always implicitly recognized and worked to implement the right to adequate care and treatment, now joins and endorses efforts toward this goal by its explicit support of this right" (p. 1, June 8, 1975 draft). The report also stresses that to assure this right without society fulfilling a corresponding duty to provide adequate funding places "an unfair and unjust burden" on psychiatrists (p. 4).

65. A useful, state-by-state summary of right-to-refuse-treatment statutes can be found in 2 *Mental Disability Law Reporter* 240 (1977) and 390 (1978) (New Mexico amend.) *See also* Rennie v. Klein, 462 F. Supp. 1131 (D. N.J. 1978); Szasz, T. S. The right to health, 57 *Georgetown Law Journal* 323 (March 1969); Schwitzgebel, R. K. *Legal aspects of the enforced treatment of offenders*. Rockville, Md.: Center for Studies of Crime and Delinquency, NIMH, DHEW publication, 1980.

66. Stone, A. A. The right to refuse treatment. *Mental health and law: A system in transition*. Rockville, Md.: Center for Studies of Crime and Delinquency, HIMH, DHEW Publication No. 75-176 (1975). For discussion of some problems with right-to-refuse-treatment, *see* Zusman, J. Again the fifth to refuse treatment. 1 *Advocacy Now* 8 (1979).

67. "If involuntary confinement itself creates coercion, administering any therapy to the patient violates his right *not* to be treated without free consent—which obviously vitiates entirely the right *to* treatment. "Surely, the courts would not extend the concept of coercion to cover more conventional types of therapy, even though the inducement to submit to such therapies may be identical to the inducement to submit to psychosurgery. What this indicates, I think, is that this area of the law, like many others, uses the concept of coercion not simply to invalidate choices made under impermissible pressure, but rather invokes the concept as camouflage when condemning choices the consequences of which are unacceptable." Wexler, D. B. Mental health law and the movement toward voluntary treatment. 62 *California Law Review* 671, 679 (1974). It would be incongruous if an individual who lacks capacity to make a treatment decision could frustrate the very justification for the state's action [of commitment] by refusing such treatments." *Harvard Law Review, supra* note 54, at p. 1344. The frequently cited case of Kaimowitz v. Michigan Dept. of Mental Health, No. 73-19434-AW (Mich. Cir. Ct., Wayne County, 1973) (unreported) raised the issue of voluntary consent in a coercive setting. Although experimental psychosurgical intervention was not permitted, the Court stated: "Second, we specifically hold that an involuntarily detained mental patient today can give adequate consent to accepted neurosurgical procedures." (Court transcript, p. 31) A critical distinction is made in this opinion between "accepted" and "experimental" procedures.

68. Friedman, *supra* note 62, at pp. 73–74.

69. Price v. Sheppard, 239 N.W.2d 905 (minn. 1976).

70. *Id*. at 913. Stone has proposed a balancing test: "Would a reasonable man, given the patient's serious illness and suffering, be willing to give up a certain amount of freedom in that particular institution in exchange for a treatment that in similar cases produces a specific range of results?" Stone, *supra* note 66 at p. 69. Stone has also suggested the possibility of an "incompetent refusal" of treatment in which the patient, in part, gives an irrational reason for his refusal which is based on, or related to, the diagnosed illness,

e.g., "I am radioactive and no one should come near me." A reason that was not a product of the patient's illness, such as, "I do not believe in medicine or physicians," would be considered acceptable for a competent refusal of treatment. *Id.* at 68–69.

71. Wyatt, 344 F. Supp. 373 at section 3.
72. Arizona Rev. Stat. Ann., sec. 36-506 (1974). For a summary of voting statutes in all states, *see* 1 *Mental Disability Law Reporter* 237 (1976).
73. A practical, illustrative booklet informing patients in Pennsylvania of their rights is *Patients' rights—You mean we have some?* prepared by the Mental Patients Civil Liberties Project, Philadelphia.
74. See, New York Association for Retarded Children v. Carey, 393 F. Supp. 715 (E.D. N.Y. 1975) (Memorandum and Order of March 10, 1976, No. 72-C-356) and *infra* note 77.
75. Wyatt, *supra* note 1 at p. 1343.
76. *E.g.,* Wisconsin Stat., sec. 51.61(e) (1977). *See also,* New Mexico H.B. 472 as amended, sec. 8(c)(2)(1977); North Carolina Gen. Stat., sec. 122–51.1 (1976).
77. *See,* Covington v. Harris, 419 F.2d 617 (D.C. Cir. 1969); Dixon v. Weinberger, 405 F. Supp. 974 (D. D.C. 1975).
78. These steps, slightly modified in the text, are adopted from Martin, R. Reader's Forum. 2 *Law and Human Behavior: Quarterly Analysis of Legal Developments Affecting Professionals in Human Sciences* 7 (Spring 1977).
79. Ayllon, T. and Skuban, W. Accountability in psychotherapy: A test case. 4 *Journal of Behavior Therapy and Experimental Psychiatry* 19 (1973). *See* Nicholson v. Han, 162 N.W.2d 313 (Mich Ct. App. 1968) (Therapeutic contracts permissible; in this instance no breach of contract found).
80. Adams, S. and Orgel, M. *Through the mental health maze: A consumer's guide to finding a psychotherapist, including a sample consumer/therapist contract.* Public Citizen's Health Research Group, 2000 P Street N.W., Washington, D.C. 20036 (1975).
81. Alexander, G. and Szasz, T. From contract to status via psychiatry. 13 *Santa Clara Lawyer* 537 (1973); Schwitzgebel, R. K. A contractual model for the protection of the rights of institutionalized mental patients. 30 *American Psychologist* 815 (1975); *and* Treatment contracts and ethical self-determination, 29 *The Clinical Psychologist* 5 (Spring 1976).

CHAPTER 3

Prisoners' Rights

"Any person who attempts to commit suicide is a disorderly person—according to a New Jersey criminal statute.[1] Although a suicide attempt, in itself, would seldom prompt authorities to file a criminal complaint (unless it was so publicly dramatic as to induce others to do the same), certain aberrant behavior can be punished as a "criminal offense" under criminal statutes, as well as treated as a "mental illness" under civil statutes. Persons most likely to come under this dual regulation include sexual psychopaths, mentally defective delinquents, and accused offenders found "not guilty by reason of insanity."[2] Mental health practitioners may be engaged at three different points in the process of criminal litigation. (1) They may help to determine whether the accused person is competent to stand trial. (2) They may present evidence regarding the person's criminal responsibility for his acts. (3) They may make recommendations regarding the person's post-trial treatment and transfer.

COMPETENCY TO STAND TRIAL

The important distinction between "criminal responsibility" and "competency to stand trial" is often overlooked. Criminal responsibility and competency refer to the defendant's mental capabilities at two different points in time. Criminal responsibility (i.e., the insanity defense) concerns the state of mind of the defendant *at the time the alleged offense was committed.* Competency concerns the state of mind of the defendant *at the time of trial.* Thus, a person who might have been "insane" at the time of his offense so as not to be legally responsible might nonetheless later be competent to stand trial because of his improved mental capacity. For example, if a defendant committed a criminal act while under the influence of LSD which was involuntarily digested, he probably would not be criminally responsible because of his confused state of mind at the time of the offense. Later, when the effects of the drug were no longer present, the defendant would be competent to stand trial. (Incidently, the ingestion of LSD or other drugs, including alcohol, must be involuntary to excuse liability. A person who voluntarily ingests a drug that causes mental confusion is liable for his acts.)

It is possible for a defendant to be of sound mind and ciminally responsible at the time of the offense, and then later because of mental illness, become incompetent to stand trial.[3] The trial process itself might be enough to produce insanity in some defendants or at least substantially change their self-perception and patterns of social interaction. This is particularly likely if the mental status of the defendant is one of the issues of litigation.[4]

In terms of the number of persons affected, incompetency to stand trial is much more frequently raised than criminal responsibility.[5] This is due, in part, to the fact that competency is raised procedurally before the issue of insanity. Surveys have indicated that 52 to 78 percent of patients in security mental hospitals are incompetent to stand trial, while less than one percent of such patients are eventually found not guilty by reason of insanity.[6]

In the past, it was customary to confine a mentally ill accused person in a security hospital for a period of 30 to 90 days for evaluation. At the end of this period, there would be a court hearing on the person's competency to stand trial. If, at the hearing, the person was found incompetent, he would be committed to a security hospital for an indefinite period until competent to stand trial.[7] In 1972, the Supreme Court held that a person may be confined only for a reasonable period of time necessary to determine whether there is a substantial chance of his becoming competent to stand trial.[8] If he is not likely to gain such capacity in the foreseeable future, then standard civil commitment proceedings must be instituted (see Chapter 1).

There are three major legal issues involved in determining a person's competency to stand trial: (1) the accused's ability to cooperate with an attorney in the preparation of his defense, (2) his awareness and understanding of the nature and object of the proceeding, and (3) his understanding of the consequences of the proceedings.[9] The particular fact situation of a given case will bear upon the accused person's legally determined competency. For example, a defendant may be "competent" when working with one lawyer but not with another due to the different quality of interaction. Routine assessment procedures have been developed for mental health professionals asked to assist the court in competency hearings.[10]

CRIMINAL RESPONSIBILITY (THE "INSANITY DEFENSE")

The sanity or mental condition of a defendant at the time of the alleged offense is determinative of (1) his criminal responsibility and (2) the court's disciplinary measures. The same person, if convicted, will be punished (*e.g.*, by imprisonment, fines, or probation) and held responsible for his actions. The person adjudged insane will be "treated" and held "not responsible" or not guilty for his action. In an increasing number of jurisdictions, the hospitalization of a person acquitted by insanity may not be automatic. A new hearing must be held. The reasoning is that the insanity defense focuses on the person's past state of mind at the time of the offense. The need for commitment to a hospital focuses on the person's present state of mind.[11]

The standards or tests used to determine criminal responsibility vary considerably among the states, but they usually center around one of three general formulations.[12] The oldest formulation is that of M'Naghten which suggests that the defendant is not responsible if he committed the unlawful act while "labouring under such a defect of reason. from disease of the mind, as not to know the nature and quality of the act he was doing; or, if he did know it, that he did not know he was doing what was wrong."

The second common test of criminal responsibility is a formulation that includes an "irresistible impulse" provision not found in the original M'Naghten rules. Under this test, a defendant might have known the moral or legal wrongfulness of his act but because he was overwhelmed by an impulse there was diminished responsibility. The third common formulation is the one proposed in the Model Penal Code (the so-called ALI test of the American Law Institute). The defendant is not responsible for criminal conduct if, as a result of mental disease or defect, he lacked "substantial capacity either to appreciate the criminality of his conduct or to conform his conduct to the requirements of law."[14] This test, or a variation of it, is commonly used in federal courts.

A defendant is usually presumed to be responsible.[15] He therefore has the initial duty, if he pleads insanity, to present evidence that would raise the question of his criminal responsibility. If he produces such evidence, the burden of persuasion in the federal courts and in about one-half of the states then shifts to the prosecution to prove that the defendant was in fact responsible at the time of the alleged offense.[16] If the prosecution does not succeed in meeting this burden of proof, a jury may, after finding that the defendant committed the act, also find him "not guilty by reason of insanity."

The term "insanity" as used by the jury to characterize the defendant's mental state, is a legal one—not necessarily consistent with a technical/medical definition. In some states, the defendant's attorney may seek a bifurcated trial in which the jury first hears only evidence on the defendant's guilt and then, if found guilty, the same jury or a new one hears evidence on the issue of criminal responsibility. This may avoid some jury confusion because it is difficult to persuade a jury that the defendant did not commit the offense, but if he did, it was because he was insane.[17]

With respect to psychiatric examination, it is quite clear that if the defendant himself first raises the issue of insanity or incompetency, then the defendant waives any objection to examination by court-appointed psychiatrists.[18] If, however, the examination is initiated by the prosecution, the defendant may be able to refuse to answer the psychiatrist's questions concerning facts of the alleged offense on the grounds that answers to these questions would involve self-incrimination.[19] The matter is unsettled as to whether a defendant may have his attorney present at the time of a compulsory psychiatric examination or during the hospital conferences on competency to stand trial. The current trend seems to be toward allowing the attorney to be present.[20] Of course, the defendant or his attorney may automatically waive the right to counsel by not asking that counsel be present.[21]

STANDARDS FOR INSTITUTIONAL CARE AND TRANSFER

The four traditional justifications for using prisons to deal with society's offenders are: (1) isolation, (2) rehabilitation, (3) deterrence, and (4) retribution. "Isolation" refers to the state's authority to separate offenders from society, thus preventing commission of more crimes. "Rehabilitation" refers to the modification of behavior or attitudes to conform more closely to prescribed social standards. ("Habilitation" is sometimes used where initial socialization is required—e.g., with severely retarded individuals.) "Deterrence" refers to the suppressive effect of imprisonment on the commission of future crime; "retribution" to deserved punishment of, or revenge against, the individual who has violated social standards.

Isolation is a seemingly justifiable rationale in view of the need for community protection. Likewise, rehabilitation has been generally accepted as a humanitarian rationale. However, the Federal Bureau of Prisons has officially begun to shift the emphasis on its correctional policies from rehabilitation to deterrence and retribution. Its current goal is not to simply "warehouse" offenders, but neither is it to treat or cure offenders.[22] This reflects an increasing acceptance of the idea of giving offenders sentences they "deserve" as a result of their crime against society—a "just deserts" concept.

A traditional judicial stance with respect to complaints by prisoners has been a "hands off" policy, that is, a refusal to exercise jurisdiction, based upon the notion that "lawful incarceration brings about the necessary withdrawal ... of many privileges and rights.[23] The rationale for such a policy is related to judicial respect for state laws, deference to the alleged expertise of prison officials, and noninterference with prison administration (which is an executive rather than a judicial function of government).[24] Because a prisoner may lose, due to administrative necessity, many rights and privileges, this should not prevent the courts from protecting prisoners from "unlawful and onerous treatment of a nature that, of itself, adds punitive measures to those legally meted out by the court."[25]

An alternative judicial attitude concerning a prisoner's civil rights is that "a prisoner retains all rights of an ordinary citizen except those expressly, or by necessary implication, taken from him by law."[26] The assumption underlying this attitude may be "that the rule of law and legal process are part of the free community's way of life, and every consideration should be given to the inculcation of community values while in prison."[27]

In summary, three principles have appeared to guide the courts in dealing with prisoners' rights issues—lawful incarceration necessarily deprives a convict of certain rights and privileges, certain fundamental rights remain with the convict and are to be protected by the courts, and courts should not interfere with prison administration unless constitutional or other fundamental rights are involved.[28]

Constitutional Standards of Care

Cruel and Unusual Punishment. The Eighth Amendment specifically prohibits the cruel and unusual punishment of prisoners. Typically, a punishment violates the proscriptions of the amendment if it falls into one or more of three categories: (1) that which is contrary to contemporary standards of human decency, (2) that which is unnecessarily cruel, or (3) that which goes beyond legitimate penal aims.[29]

Because there is wide latitude in determining whether a punishment falls into any of these categories, standards of punishment are difficult to summarize succinctly. Some guidelines may be useful, however. Physical force or medication may be temporarily used to prevent a prisoner (or mental patient) from physically injuring himself or others, but these procedures are probably unacceptable as a general practice for long-term management, discipline, or treatment.[30] Prisoners may not be tortured, disfigured, or physically injured.[31] Prisoners may not be deprived of the fundamental physical necessities of food, warmth, light, and personal hygiene for discipline or treatment purposes.[32]

Solitary confinement *per se* has not been found to constitute cruel and unusual punishment, nor has the absence of a rehabilitative program.[33] However, various conditions of solitary confinement and incarceration may make such confinement unconstitutional (e.g., being forced to sleep nude on the floor, to eat dirty food, or to stand for an entire day).[34] Corporal punishment is forbidden by statute in most states and in at least one federal appellate district.[35] Corporal punishment in one case was liberally interpreted to include even a deficient diet of bread and water.[36]

Privacy. The constitutional right of privacy is often ineffective as a protection for prisoners because the Fourth Amendment, which disallows searches and seizures without a warrant and/or "probable cause," is often not legally applicable to the prison environment. Prison administrators customarily conduct searches to discover contraband or stolen property and to prevent escapes. Correspondence is routinely read and censored. Searches should not be more personally intrusive than necessary, and there should be a reasonable basis for suspecting illegal conduct before a search.[37] In a case dealing with mentally ill offenders in a security mental hospital, the court found that the patient has a right to be present during the search of his living area, items must be returned without damage, and the patient must be given a written list of the items confiscated from him.[38]

There is no doubt that a certain degree of privacy is automatically lost through engagement of criminal activities—the facts of indictment, arrest, trial, and conviction are matters of public record. However, to what degree prisoners or ex-convicts may review and challenge their records and to what extent information in criminal records may be disseminated for noncriminal purposes has yet to be determined (see Chapter 12).

The right to privacy might also suggest possible limitations on the intrusiveness of treatment.[39] For example, a treatment that substantially diminishes mental capacity could conceivably be prohibited by the First Amendment provisions of free speech.

Equal Protection. Prison treatment programs should be designed to avoid violations of the "equal protection" clause of the Fourteenth Amendment. Violations occur when prisoners are unfairly treated by discriminations that have no rational relationship to a legitimate objective.[40] One possible violation of the equal protection clause would be the discriminatory regulation of visitation privileges on a racial basis or the capricious and arbitrary assignment of prisoners to treatment programs.[41]

Freedom of Religion. The present trend of cases requires prison administrators to show compelling and substantial justification for restrictions they place on the practice of religion.[42] One aspect of the prisoner's right to religious freedom is the right not to have religious beliefs forced upon him. Although some courts have required church attendance as a condition of probation,[43] other courts have found the requirement unconstitutional.[44] Most recent cases support the view that a civil authority may not require a person to accept any religious belief or practice.[45] A Utah statute expressly forbids the use of mental health services to change religious beliefs.[46] There is a frequently made distinction between the freedom to believe what one wishes and the freedom to exercise that belief. When other persons are seriously disturbed or placed at risk by a religious practice, that practice (not the related belief) may be legally limited.[47]

Due Process. The results of prison disciplinary hearings can have profound effects on the prisoner's future. Although precise determination of those elements of "due process" which the Fourteenth Amendment requires in prison disciplinary hearings have been infrequent, two key holdings have surfaced: (1) Before a prisoner may be deprived of a liberty (even a state-created liberty such as good-time credits), some type of hearing must be held. (2) During a hearing or other disciplinary proceeding, the prisoner is entitled to the minimal procedures required by the due process clause of the Fourteenth Amendment. The most authoritative prison due process case to date has been *Wolff* v. *McDonnell*.[48] In this case, the Supreme Court concluded that prison disciplinary proceedings resulting in loss of good-time credits or the imposition of solitary confinement required (1) written notice of the violation at least 24 hours in advance of an appearance before an adjustment committee, (2) a written statement of facts and reasons for any disciplinary action taken, and (3) an opportunity to call witnesses and present documentary evidence in defense. However, there was no constitutional right to confront or cross-examine adverse witnesses, nor to retain or have appointed counsel. In contrast, some federal and state decisions have held that in disciplinary proceedings, the prisoner has the right to retain counsel,[49] cross-examine witnesses, and call witnesses in his defense.[50] The major procedural requirements suggested in *Wolff* may be required in some jurisdictions not only for decisions involving the loss of liberty but also prior to the deprivation of important privileges such as association with other prisoners, visitation, and attendance at religious services.

Legislative and Judicial Standards of Care

Correspondence. The prisoner will find greater degrees of privacy accorded to his correspondence if it is legal correspondence (i.e., to a court, attorney, or government official) rather than nonlegal correspondence. This is because several federal courts and the Supreme Court have limited the power of prison officials to open, read, or censor legal mail.[51] The prevailing view, supported by the Supreme Court decision in *Procunier* v. *Martinez*,[52] is that the censorship of mail is justified only when it furthers a substantial government interest in security, order, or rehabilitation, and is no more restrictive than necessary. Most prison mail is still subject to at least minimal inspection. Incoming mail may be also inspected with regard to matters such as explosives, escape devices, drugs, obscenity, and inflammatory writing that advocates violence.[53]

Many prisons maintain lists of nonlegal persons who are approved for correspondence. (Usually, approved persons bear a significant relationship, such as family member, to the prisoner.) The courts have generally allowed this practice.[54] The censorship of outgoing or incoming mail to a prisoner in segregation or isolation should not differ from that of other prisoners.[55]

Treatment Programs. A substantial number of correctional institutions have used behavior modification techniques.[56] Although these techniques have sometimes been successful with maladaptive behaviors, unconstitutional practices have at time occurred in prisons under the pretense of behavior control.[57] For guidelines relevant to specific treatment procedures, see Index.

A legally defined right to rehabilitation or psychological treatment for prisoners in general has not yet emerged. Nonetheless, it is rather clear that prisoners have a right to adequate *medical* treatment.[58] Also, there is considerable judicial recognition that youths committed to juvenile correctional facilities have a right to both medical and psychological treatment.[59] This is because juveniles are often considered to be committed under a "parens patriae" obligation that requires the state to provide for the welfare and best interests of the child in place of the parents. Parents ought not deprive their children of useful rehabilitative treatment, assuming that the means of financing it has been provided. On the other hand, the development of a right to treatment for mentally competent adult offenders does not have the support of the parens patriae doctrine because they are confined under a police power doctrine. The primary purpose of this doctrine is the protection of society.

To the extent that a right to treatment exists for prisoners, it is most clearly emerging for severely mentally disabled offenders. In *Bowring* v. *Godwing*[60] the Court held that prisoners were entitled to psychological or psychiatric treatment if: (1) the symptoms indicated a serious disease or injury, (2) the disease or injury was curable or could be substantially alleviated, and (3) the potential for harm to the prisoner by reason of delay or denial of care would be substantial. The essential test, as the Court noted, was one of "medical necessity" and not simply that the treatment would be "desirable." If appropriate treatment cannot be provided in the prison, some courts have required that these severely disturbed offenders be transferred to facilities that can provide the necessary treatment. This is consistent with standards for treatment programs recommended by the National Advisory Commission on Criminal Justice Standards and Goals.[61]

Some reluctance in promoting a right to treatment for other prisoners may stem from at least two sources. One is a concern that punishment and deprivation might be increased by being administered under the guise of treatment (e.g., "time-out" or "reality therapy"). The other source of reluctance is grounded in the re-emerging view, as previously mentioned, that the correctional system should be operated on the basis of the "just deserts" model rather than the rehabilitation model. The Task Force on the Role of Psychology in the Criminal Justice System of the American Psychological Association has attempted to define or redefine the appropriate function of psychology assuming a "just deserts" model.[62]

When psychological services are provided in correctional settings, psychologists should consider following the *Standards for Providers of Psychological Services* also promulgated by the American Psychological Association[63] (see Appendix KK). These *Standards,* although not enforceable as ethical standards,[64] represent considerable agreement on certain acceptable practices that may be given administrative and judicial recognition. The *Standards* expressly mention "correctional/judicial" settings to which they are applicable. Among the many relevant standards, a few are particularly appropriate to prisons. "In delivering psychological services to a recipient, the provider shall not diminish or violate the legal and civil rights of the recipient."[65] "There shall be a written service delivery plan for every consumer for whom psychological services are provided."[66] "Accurate, current, and complete documentation shall be made of psychological services provided."[67]

As previously noted in Chapter 2, the right to treatment does not imply an obligation to accept treatment. Like other rights, the right does not impose a duty to exercise it. (Citizens are not obligated to assemble peaceably, although they have the right to do so.)

The right of prisoners to *refuse* treatment has probably resulted from a need to clarify this understanding that a right to treatment does not impose a duty to accept treatment, particularly when some physically intrusive forms of treatment can be motivated by a desire to punish the offender. The law is unsettled in this area. Judicial decisions seem to depend upon several factors such as the prisoner's mental state (e.g., mental competency), the intrusiveness or aversiveness of the treatment, and the purpose of the treatment. It should be noted that in many right-to-refuse-treatment cases (as interpreted by civil rights advocates) the court does not state *explicitly* that treatment may be refused. It is implied, however, when the court rules that treatment may not be imposed without consent of the patient or inmate. Thus, the inmate's refusal to give necessary consent automatically blocks the treatment.

As a starting point, it may be assumed that an inmate has the right to refuse treatment unless the state has a compelling interest to the contrary. The more intrusive the treatment, the more substantial and certain must be the state's purpose or interest. Obviously, this involves the balancing of competing personal and public interests.

Highly aversive forms of treatment should not be used to enforce prison rules without inmate consent—and such consent is not very likely. In *Knecht* v. *Gillman*,[68] a drug was used to induce vomiting to prevent rule violations such as swearing, lying, talking, and not getting up. The "treatment" in this situation was not directed so much toward rehabilitation as toward institutional management. The Court did not absolutely prohibit this "treatment," but found that it may not be administered without written consent which could be revoked at any time. Otherwise, this "treatment" would be prohibited as cruel and unusual punishment. As current case law is developing, prisoners could also probably refuse this type of aversive treatment even if its purpose was one of rehabilitation to reduce subsequent crime. One reason is that the state would have to justify its intrusion by proving that the treatment was effective in reducing crime—a very difficult problem in light of most research results. Less intrusive forms of treatment might, however, be permissible even without inmates' consent if there was a sufficient rehabilitative purpose.[69]

Treatment, even when there is consent, should be conducted within the context of at least minimal standards of living. Adequate food, light, clothing, space, bed, etc. may not be used as "privileges" to be earned. They must be provided unconditionally.[70] Items beyond these necessities such as cigarettes, home visits, special food or clothing, may be earned conditionally upon participation in treatment.

If, as a part of a treatment program, an inmate is involuntarily transferred to living conditions that are much more depriving than his usual institutional living conditions, the inmate should probably have the opportunity to appear before an impartial hearing panel, treatment committee, or court. In *Clonce* v. *Richardson*,[71] inmates who were disciplinary problems were transferred into a so-called behavior modification program in which the initial level had extremely few privileges. Claims were made that some prisoners were shackled to bare beds and were not allowed to attend religious services. The Court did not decide many constitutional issues because the program was discontinued. The Court did, however, determine that the inmates should be given notice and a hearing before transfer because of the major adverse change in the conditions of their confinement. The hearing procedures should follow those for disciplinary hearings as outlined in *Wolff* v. *McDonnell*[72] mentioned previously. Lesser deprivations, such as brief periods of isolation, would not require a formal hearing.[73]

As with mental patients, a prisoner who refuses reasonable treatment cannot later claim that he should be released because treatment is inadequate.[74] A consequence of refusing treatment may be longer confinement. This is not due to the refusal per se, but because he has not participated in treatment that could increase the probability of his safe release into the community. Treatment decisions affecting mentally ill and legally incompetent inmates should probably be reviewed by a court if substantial deprivation, aversiveness, or intrusiveness is involved. Because legal incompetency requires a finding by a court, the court may establish guidelines for the person's treatment at this hearing.

Many institutions have established a human rights committee to oversee treatment procedures and to make decisions in individual cases. This committee can be used to provide the independent hearings required prior to treatment that is intrusive, hazardous, or experimental in nature.[75] Human rights committees are usually composed of persons who represent the patient or inmate population, law, mental health, and the community. The majority of members are independent of the institution.

Waiver of Rights. In the interest of enhancing self-determination or autonomy, a mentally competent prisoner may in some circumstances be permitted to waive certain constitutional rights in exchange for receiving a form of treatment which could facilitate his/her early release from prison. A waiver of rights frequently occurs when prisoners select release into the community with specific parole conditions rather than continued confinement in prison.[76] The conditions of parole, including the type of treatment required, if any, should be reasonably related to the successful adjustment of the parolee in the community. Valid waivers—those made voluntarily and intelligently—should be knowingly made in writing and perhaps scrutinized by an independent review group. In situations involving mentally incompetent prisoners or patients, the individual's legal counsel or guardian *ad litem* may exercise the power of waiver. As much as possible, the individual and his/her lawyer or guardian should agree upon the nature and effect of the waiver.[77]

Considerable confusion exists as to which constitutional rights are waivable under noncoercive circumstances. Basic necessities and protection against cruel and unusual punishment are not waivable.[78] On the other hand, a prisoner could probably waive rights or privileges such as visitation or certain aspects of privacy (e.g., permitting urine tests of narcotic use). Although some constitutional rights may be waived, state or federal legislation may guarantee them even beyond that which is constitutionally required.[79] Prisoners and program personnel should therefore check state and federal laws to determine the extent of permissible waivers.

Transfer Procedures

The need for therapeutic services for some, perhaps many, prisoners seems apparent even though they were not found incompetent or insane. The transfer of prisoners to mental institutions may be desirable and permissible—given certain procedural safeguards. For example, a prison inmate may not be moved to a mental institution without having the benefit of a customary civil commitment proceeding.[80] A mere administrative decision is not apparently sufficient for a transfer from a prison to a mental institution, but it is for a transfer from one prison to another.[81]

One of the most publicized cases of mentally disabled offenders is *Baxtrom* v. *Herold*[82] in which Baxtrom, after serving his maximum prison sentence of three years for assault, was transferred to a department of correction's mental hospital for another five years until released by a decision of the Supreme Court. The Court held that he had been denied equal protection of the law because there was no proper hearing as to whether he was dangerously mentally ill at the end of his prison term. Baxtrom was transferred to a civil hospital to await a hearing. After a jury trial in which he was found mentally competent and not in need of hospitalization, he was released. It could be argued in this particular case that he was "killed with legal kindness" for less than one month after he gained his freedom, he died at home of bronchial pneumonia and epileptic seizures.[83]

Sexually deviant behaviors are, by far, the most frequent subject of special legislation that permits the confinement of a person for an indeterminate amount of time in a prison or security hospital.[84] An "indeterminate sentence" is a confinement for the maximum period of time allowed by law, with the condition that the sentence may be terminated by a parole board or other agency any time after the established *minimal* time is served. The maximum period of time allowed by law is often the natural life of the offender.

The avowed goal of much of this original legislation in the 1930s was to impose longer sentences for sexually motivated crimes and to provide effective and humane treatment. Unfortunately, even the most casual survey of such legislation will show many procedural ambiguities and questionable results. The release of an offender is often left entirely to the discretion of an institution's staff. The offender must be found "fully recovered" or no longer "dangerous" or meet similarly vague criteria, and after the first year, mandatory review of the offender's eligibility for release may occur only once every three years.[85]

The trend of court decisions is to require that procedural safeguards be included in any quasi-criminal confinement such as the "civil" treatment of sex offenders.[86] These safeguards include a separate hearing in which the accused person has a right to counsel, presentation of evidence, a confrontation of witnesses, and the preparation of a record of the hearing sufficient to permit an appeal.

NOTES

1. New Jersey Stat. Ann., sec. 2A:170-25.6 (1960).
2. Wexler, D. B. *Criminal commitments and dangerous mental patients: Legal issues of confinement, treatment, and release.* Rockville, Md.: NIMH, Center for Studies of Crime and Delinquency, 1976.
3. U.S. *ex rel* Schuster v. Herald, 410 F.2d 1071 (2nd Cir. 1969). It should be noted that if medication such as chlorpromazine is able to bring about a temporary "synthetic sanity," the defendant may be deemed competent to stand trial: ". . . a defendant whose mental capability is maintained only through the use of prescribed medication [is] competent to stand trial. The likelihood that defendant will relapse if the use of the medication is interrupted does not bar her from proceeding to trial." State of Louisiana v. Hampton, 216 So. 2d 311 (1969); State of Tenn. v. Stacy, No. 446 (Crim. App., Knoxville, Tenn., Aug. 4, 1977).
4. Defense psychiatrist M. S. Guttmacher testified that Lee Oswald's assassin, Jack Ruby, ". . . seethes with hostility. Much of the time he is able to keep it under control, but his controls are brittle and when they break, the hostility erupts with volcanic force. Obsequiousness and over solicitude are often reaction formations against hostility. This is often seen in Negroes and in members of other minority groups." Guttmacher, M. S. *The role of psychiatry in law.* Springfield, Ill.: Charles C Thomas, 1968, p. 67. One writer commented on the insanity issue raised in the Ruby trial as follows: "Whatever reasons for killing Oswald, [it was not] to hear himself called 'a mental defective' or a 'goof' or 'came from bad stock.' His own lawyer reports 'this poor miserable specimen.' . . . The trial itself degraded and debased him, a specimen to lawyers and experts. There was not a man in the courtroom who did not feel superior to him. . . . Jack Ruby had his day in court, all right. Unlike Lee Oswald, he was given the full protection of due process of law. It would have been kinder to have stoned him to death." Linn, E. Untold story of Jack Ruby. *Saturday Evening Post* (July 25, 1964), pp. 25, 49.
5. It has been estimated that in 1967 as many as 15,000 persons were committed in various institutions in the United States for incompetency to stand trial. At the same time about 1450 persons were committed in institutions after findings of "not guilty by reason of insanity." Kanno, C. K. and Scheidemandel, P. L. *The mentally ill offender: A survey of treatment programs.* Washington, D.C.: Joint Information Service, 1969, p. 20.

6. Committee on Psychiatry and Law, *Misuse of psychiatry in the criminal courts: Competency to stand trial*. New York: Group for Advancement of Psychiatry, Report No. 89, Feb. 1974, pp. 861–862.

7. Wexler, *supra* note 2 at 131.

8. Jackson v. Indiana, 406 U.S. 715 (1972). It may be noted that the Court dealt with a patient who had not been formally found to be dangerous. Later, in McNeil v. Director, Patuxent Institution, 407 U.S.245 (1972), the Supreme Court observed that a presumably dangerous person could not be held indefinitely "for observation" without a hearing on his commitment. The patient had been confined for six years and during this time refused to cooperate in his mental examination. The GAP committee, *supra* note 6 at p. 907, believes "that new techniques and drugs currently available can bring most persons initially found to be incompetent to a competent state well within 6 months of initiation of treatment."

9. McGarry, A. L., Curran, W. J., Lipsitt, P. D., Lelos, D., Schwitzgebel, R. K., and Rosenberg, A. H. *Competency to stand trial and mental illness*. Rockville, Md.: NIMH, Center for Studies of Crime and Delinquency, 1973, p. 20. *See also* Dusky v. U.S., 271 F.2d 385 (8th Cir. 1959), *rev'd. & remanded* 80 S.Ct. 788 (1960), 295 F.2d 743 (8th Cir. 1961).

10. See Appendix NN for excerpts reprinted from McGarry, et al., *supra* note 9.

11. *See, e.g.,* Bolton v. Harris, 395 F.2d 642 (D.C. Cir. 1968); Allen v. Radack, 426 F. Supp. 1052 (D.S.D. 1977).

12. Prior to 1972, there was a much discussed, but not generally adopted, formulation known as the Durham rule, which stated that the defendant was not responsible if his unlawful act was "the product of mental disease or mental defect." Durham v. United States, 214 F.2d 862 (D.C. Cir. 1954). *But see* United States v. Brawner, 471 F.2d 969 (D.C. Cir. 1972).

13. This language was used by Lord Tindal in the M'Naghton case, 10 Cl. & F. 200, 8 Eng. Reprint 718 (H.L. 1843). *See* Perkins, R. M., *Criminal law and procedure*. Brooklyn: Foundation Press, 1966, p. 463.

14. American Law Institute, Model Penal Code, Tentative Draft No. 4, 1956.

15. ". . . Even if individual responsibility is an illusion, it may be dysfunctional socially for us to 'cease to regard people as agents of dignity and responsibility who are capable of being blameworthy for what they do." Wexler, *supra* note 2 at 51, quoting Wexler, D. B. Therapeutic justice, 57 *Minnesota Law Review* 289, 309 (1972). *Similarly,* Monahan, J. Abolish the insanity defense?—not yet. 26 *Rutgers Law Review* 719 (1973).

16. The leading case is Leland v. Oregon, 343 U.S. 790 (1952) in which the Court held that a criminal defendant pleading insanity could be required to carry the burden of proof. *Supporting* Suzynski v. Oliver, 538 F.2d 6 (1st Cir. 1976). However, Supreme Court cases after *Leland* indicate the prosecution may have the burden of overcoming the defense argument once it is presented. *In re* Winship, 397 U.S. 358 (1970); Mullaney v. Wilbur, 421 U.S. 684 (1975).

17. Shadoan, G. Raising the insanity defense; The practical side. 10 *American Criminal Law Review* 533 (1972).

18. People v. Laudati, 304 N.Y.S.2d 815 (N.Y. 1969); *concurring,* Lee v. County Court, 267 N.E.2d 452 (N.Y. 1971); Parkin v. State, 238 So. 2d 817 (Fla. 1970).

19. Shepard v. Bowe, 442 P.2d 238 (Ore. 1968).

20. U.S. v. Baird, 414 F.2d 700 (C.C.A. 2, 1969) (negative); People v. Abdul Karim Al-Kanani, 260 N.E.2d 496 (N.Y. 1970) (affirmative); Thornton v. Corcoran, 407 F.2d 695 (D.C. C.A. 1969) (affirmative).
21. State v. Canaday, 467 P.2d 666 (Ore. 1970); People v. Ranes, 163 N.W.2d 807 (Mich. 1968).
22. Normal A Carlson, Federal Director of Prisons, quoted in Meyer, L. Crime and punishment: Prisons in flux. *Los Angeles Times,* Part 1-A, p. 8, April 30, 1975. "Rehabilitation—whatever it means, whatever it embraces—must cease to be the claimed purpose of a prison sanction. It is silly to lock people up to do them good. . . . The rejection of the model of coercive curing of criminals does not flow from our lack of power or competence to influence human behavior. Rather, it flows from certain centrally important views about the relationship between individual freedom and state authority. We do not force cures on criminals as a matter of social policy. We know the corruptibility of power, the abuses that attend its exercise. At the moment we cannot coercively change people while also preserving proper respect for their human rights and individual autonomy." Morris, N. Who should go to prison. In B. D. Sales (Ed.), *The criminal justice system.* New York: Plenum Press, 1977, 151-159, at pp. 156-157. Whether a deterrence or retribution approach will be any more effective in reducing subsequent offenses than the rehabilitation approach is a matter for empirical study. *See,* Singer, B. F. Psychological studies of punishment. 58 *California Law Review* 405 (March 1970) (summary of relevant psychological studies).
23. Price v. Johnston, 344 U.S. 266, 285 (1948), quoted in Student Note, The voting booth with steel bars: Prisoner's voting rights and O'Brien v. Skinner. 3 *Capital Law Review* 245, 255 (1974).
24. Millemann, M. A. and Millemann, S. J. The prisoner's rights to stay where he is: State and federal transfer compacts run afoul of constitutional due process. 3 *Capital Law Review* 223 (1974).
25. Jackson v. Godwin, 400 F.2d 529, 532 (5th Cir. 1968).
26. Coffin v. Reichard, 143 F.2d 443, 445 (6th Cir. 1944).
27. Cohen, F. *The legal challenge to corrections.* Washington, D.C.: Joint commission on Correctional Manpower and Training, 1969, p. 78.
28. Rudovsky, D., Bronstein, A.J. and Koren, E. I. *The rights of prisoners: The basic ACLA guide to a prisoner's rights.* New York: Avon Books, 1977, p. 13. (This source is a useful and informative survey of the area.)
29. *Id.* at 30.
30. Peek v. Ciccone, 288 F. Supp. 329 (W.D. Mo. 1968); Nelson v. Heyne, 491 F.2d 352 (7th Cir. 1974), *cert. denied. See also* Ford v. Board of Managers of New Jersey State Prison, 407 F.2d 937 (3rd Cir. 1969); Landman v. Peyton, 370 F.2d 135 (4th Cir. 1966). A state prisoner successfully argued that his constitutional right to be free from cruel and unusual punishment had been violated when he was given succinycholine, a respiratory inhibitor, without his consent. Mackey v. Procunier, 447 F.2d 877 (9th Cir. 1973).
31. *In re* Birdsong, 39 Fed. 599 (S.D. Ga. 1889) (prisoner chained to cell by neck). Hosing of mentally ill prisoners with fire extinguishers would almost certainly be considered cruel and unusual punishment. After allegedly hosing down the prisoners, prison guards in the Wayne County (Mich.) jail opened cell windows in 40-degree F weather. Fox, T.

C. Jail mistreating mentally ill, *Detroit Free Press,* Part 1, p. 1, Jan. 5, 1975. A law in Libya provides for amputation of the right hand for stealing, and the left foot for armed robbery—but permits it to be done by a surgeon, using anesthetics. Note, Marcus Welby, executioner, 3 *Hastings Center Report* 16 (1973).

32. Jordan v. Fitzharris, 257 F. Supp. 674 (N.D. Calif. 1966); Wright v. McMann, 387 F.2d 519 (2d Cir. 1967).

33. Jordan, *supra* note 32 (solitary confinement permissible under some conditions); Neuman v. Alabama, No. 76-2269 (5th Cir., Sept. 16, 1977) as reported in 2 *Mental Disability Law Reporter* 172 (Sept.–Dec. 1977).

34. Hancock v. Avery, 301 F. Supp. 786 (M.D. Tenn. 1969); Holt v. Sarver, 309 F. Supp. 362 (E.D. Ark. 1970); *aff'd* 442 F.2d 304 (8th Cir. 1971); Wright v. McMann, 387 F.2d 519 (2d Cir. 1967); LaReau v. MacDougall, 473 F.2d 974 (2d Cir. 1972), *cert. denied* 414 U.S. 878 (1973). *Contra,* severely restrictive conditions (e.g., complete darkness, steel bunk without mattress) have been upheld in federal court as constitutionally allowable. Novak V. Beto, 453 F.2d 661 (5th Cir. 1971).

35. Jackson v. Bishop, 404 F.2d 571 (8th Cir. 1968).

36. Landman v. Royster, 333 F. Supp. 621 (E.D. Va. 1971).

37. Moore v. People, 171 Colo. 338, 467 P.2d 50 (1970) (not permitting harassing or humiliating the prisoner), *but see* Daugherty v. Harris, 476 F.2d 292 (10th Cir. 1973) (allowing routine rectal searches prior to court appearance); Black v. Amico, 387 F. Supp. 88 (W.D. N.Y. 1974) (suspicion necessary).

38. McGray v. Maryland, 267 Md. 111, 297 A.2d 265 (1972).

39. *See* Shapiro, M. Legislating the control of behavior control: Autonomy and the coercive use of organic therapies. 47 *Southern California Law Review* 237 (1974).

40. Schwartz, B. *Constitutional law, a textbook.* New York: Macmillan Co., 1972, p. 307. If a discrimination abridges a fundamental right or is itself constitutionally suspect, the discrimination must be shown to effectuate a compelling state interest.

41. Henry v. Van Cleve, 469 F.2d 687 (5th Cir. 1972)(racial discrimination); Skinner v. Oklahoma, 316 U.S. 535 (1972)(sterilization of habitual offenders). Although prisoners often invoke the equal protection clause to challenge treatment, they are seldom successful. Courts usually allow programs much leeway in selection of participants, e.g., Sas v. State of Maryland, 334 F.2d 506 (4th Cir. 1964). *See generally,* Schwitzgebel, R. K. *Development and legal regulation of coercive behavior modification techniques.* Crime and Delinquency Monograph Series, DHEW, Public Health Service Publ. No. 2067, Washington, D.C.: 1971 (reprint 1972), pp. 50–54.

42. Rudovsky, *supra* note 28, at p. 57. Cruz v. Beto, 405 U.S. 319 (1972) (practice by Buddhist).

43. Murderer sentenced to Sundays in church, *New York Times,* p. 12, May 27, 1972.

44. Jones v. Commonwealth, 185 Va. 335, 38 S.E.2d 444 (1946).

45. *See* Winters v. Miller, 446 F.2d 65 (2d Cir.), *cert. denied* 404 U.S. 985 (1971).

46. Utah Code Ann., sec. 26-17-7 (1974).

47. In Peek v. Ciccone, 288 F.Supp. 329 (W.D. Mo. 1968), a prisoner convicted of robbery underwent a religious experience in which he came to believe that in his body, "the body of a thief," Christ had reappeared on earth. The Rabbi of the institution refused to allow him to attend services which the prisoner disrupted. The Court upheld this restriction but

did order the prison authorities to mail a "respectful letter" from this prisoner to the Pope.

48. Wolff v. McDonnell, 94 S. Ct. 2963 (1974). An earlier case, Morrissey v. Brewer, 408 U.S. 471 (1972), established some precedential due process standards for parole hearings.

49. Relevant case law suggests that the Sixth Amendment, which guarantees the right to have assistance of counsel in the preparation of a defense, also allows psychologists, hypnotists, or similar practitioners to accompany counsel in consultation with prisoner-clients. Cornell v. Superior Court of San Diego County, 52 Cal. 2d 99, 338 P.2d 447 (1959); *Ex parte* Ochse, 38 Cal. 2d 230, 238 P.2d 561 (1941). *See* Davis, R. P. Annotation: Accused's counsel—consultation, 72 A.L.R.2d 1120.

50. Landman v. Royster, 333 F. Supp. 621 (E.D. Va. 1971); Sostre v. McGinnis, 442 F.2d 178 (2d Cir. 1971); Clutchette v. Procunier, 328 F. Supp. 767 (N.D. Calif. 1971), *mod.* 497 F.2d 809 (9th Cir. 1974).

51. *Ex parte* Hull, 312 U.S. 546 (1946)(prohibited prison officials from determining whether legal documents were properly drawn before forwarding them to the courts); Johnson v. Avery, 393 U.S. 483 (1969)(no obstruction of access to courts permitted); Palmigiano v. Travisono, 317 F. Supp. 776 (D.R.I. 1970)(prohibited prison officials from opening or inspecting incoming or outgoing legal mail).

52. 416 U.S. 396 (1974). (The Court also considered the First Amendment rights of the addressees as well as those of the prisoners.)

53. Gray v. Greamer, 376 F. Supp. 675 (W.D. Pa. 1974).

54. Toal, R. Correspondence and visitation. *Recent developments in correctional case law.* Columbia, S.C.: South Carolina Dept. of Corrections, 1975, pp. 19–23.

55. Collins v. Schoanfield, 344 F. Supp. 257 (D. Md. 1972). A temporary restriction of nonlegal correspondence as a disciplinary measure might be permissible. The Supreme Court in Procunier v. Martinez reserved the question on this matter. The decision to use such a measure would have to conform at least to due process requirements.

56. According to a survey of 47 Commissioners of Corrections, 13 states were using operant conditioning techniques in 1974, 14 states were operating token economy systems, and seven states were using aversion therapy (consent required). Twenty-eight Commissioners reported a favorable attitude toward extending behavior modification programs in prisons. Blatte, H. State prisons and the use of behavior control. 4 *Hastings Center Report* 15 (Sept. 1974).

57. For example, McCray v. Maryland (Misc. Pet. 4363, Montgomery County, Md., Cir. Ct., Nov. 21, 1971), *rev'd on juris grounds* 297 A.2d 265 (1972).

58. Estelle v. Gamble, 97 S.Ct. 287 (1976). The ABA Joint Committee on the Legal Status of Prisoners has recommended establishing a right to dental, physical, psychological, and psychiatric services. *American Criminal Law Review* (special issue, vol. 14, No. 3, Winter 1977).

59. *E.g.* Martarella v. Kelly, 359 F. Supp. 478 (S.D.N.Y. 1973); Morales v. Turman, 383 F. Supp. 53 (E.D. Tex. 1974), *remanded* 562 F.2d 933 (5th Cir., 1977); Krantz, S. *The law of corrections and prisoners' rights in a nutshell.* St. Paul, Minn.: West Publ. Co., 1976, pp. 178–180. *But see* Collins v. Bensinger, 374 F. Supp. 273 (E.D.N.D. Ill. 1974).

60. 551 F.2d 44 (4th Cir. 1977). *See also* White v. Morris, No. 789666 (Super Ct., King County, Wash., Aug. 1, 1975); Newman v. Alabama, 349 F. Supp. 278 (M.D. Ala. 1972), *aff'd*. 503 F.2d 1320 (5th Cir. 1974) *cert denied* 421 U.S. 948 (1975); Laaman v. Helgemo, 437 F. Supp. 269 (D.N.H. 1977); Pugh v. Locke, 406 F. Supp. 318 (M.D. Ala. 1976); *but see* Lunsford v. Reynolds, 376 F. Supp. 526 (W.D. Va. 1974); Bermanger v. State, 307 N.E.2d 891 (Ct. App. Ind. 1974).

61. National Advisory Commission on Criminal Justice Standards and Goals. *Corrections.* Washington, D.C.: U.S. Govt. Printing Office, 1973.

62. Task Force on the Role of Psychology in the Criminal Justice System, *Report.* Washington, D.C.: American Psychological Association, 1978, p. 28.

63. Task Force on Standards for Service Facilities (American Psychological Association), Standards for providers of psychological services. 30 *American Psychologist* 685 (1975).

64. These standards have not been incorporated into the current published ethical standards of the American Psychological Association. The ethical standards are now under revision and may, or may not, be incorporated by reference (i.e., by citation). If so, a violation of the "Standards for Providers of Psychological Services" might become grounds for an ethical violation.

65. Principle 3.2.2, *supra* note 63.

66. Principle 3.3.2, *supra* note 63.

67. Principle 3.3.3, *supra* note 63.

68. 488 F.2d 1136 (8th Cir. 1973).

69. *E.g.,* People ex rel. Stutz v. Conboy, 300 N.Y.S.2d 453 (Sup. Ct. 1969)(confinement and group therapy for drug addiction); Haynes v. Harris, 344 F.2d 463 (8th Cir. 1965).

70. *See e.g.,* Inmates of Boy's Training School v. Affleck, 346 F. Supp. 1354 (D.R.I. 1972).

71. 379 F. Supp. 338 (W.D. Mo. 1974).

72. 94 S. Ct. 2963 (1974).

73. *See* Morales v. Turman, 383 F. Supp. 53 (E.D. Tex. 1974), 535 F.2d 864 (8th 1976), 430 U.S. 322 (1977).

74. Clatterbuck v. Harris, 295 F. Supp. 84 (D.D.C. 1968); Buchanan v. State, 164 N.W.[d. 253 (Wis. 1969); DeBolt v. Cupp, 522 P.2d 1395 C.A. Ore. 1974).

75. Procedures to be used by a human rights committee to review treatment can be found in the Suggested Statute on Civil Commitment prepared by the ABA Commission on the Mentally Disabled. 2 *Mental Disability Law Reporter* 127–159, pp. 153–154.

76. *See e.g.,* an extreme case in North Carolina involving a person who saw three high school students steal 24 soft drink bottles, a case of charcoal lighter fluid, and 60 cents from a gas station. Rather than serve a one-year jail term, the youths agreed to waive their Fourth Amendment protections against illegal search and seizure for five years. Jones, R. A. Rights—can they be lost in a bargain. *Los Angeles Times,* Part 1, p. 1, Jan. 10, 1975.

77. Courts generally scrutinize waivers more carefully in criminal than in civil cases and when the right involved is central to the trial process. Less protected are rights such as freedom from unreasonable searches and seizures which are extraneous to the trial process. *See* Developments in the law: Civil commitment of the mentally ill. 87 *Harvard Law Review* 1190, 1315–16 and n. 289 (1974).

78. Friedman, P. R. Legal regulation of applied behavior analysis in mental institutions and prisons. 17 *Arizona Law Review* 39 (1975), pp. 69–71. The doctrine of "unconstitutional conditions" has been used to limit waivers. Though this doctrine has been variously formulated, it suggests that the right of the government to withhold a benefit does not imply that the government has the privilege to grant it only on the condition that the recipient first surrender a constitutional right. *See* note, Unconstitutional conditions. 73 *Harvard Law Review* 1595 (1960).

79. Wexler, D. B. Reflections on the legal regulation of behavior modification in institutional settings. 17 *Arizona Law Review* 132 (1975) p. 140.

80. Chesney v. Adams, 377 F. Supp. 887 (Conn 1974) (noting possible indignities, stigma, psychic harm and difficulty of parole involved in hospitalization); U.S. ex rel Schuster v. Herold, 410 F.2d 1071 (2d Cir. 1969).

81. Montayne v. Haymes, 427 U.S. 236 (1976); *but see* on remand Haymes v. Montayne, 547 F.2d 188 (2d Cir. 1977).

82. 383 U.S. 107 (1966).

83. As a result of the Baxtrom decision, 967 patients in two New York State correctional hospitals were transferred to civil facilities. A four-year follow-up study showed that "in very few cases were these transfers detrimental to the prisoners or the community." Steadman, H. J. Implications from the Baxtrom experience. 1 *Bulletin of the American Academy of Psychiatry and the Law* 189 (July 1973).

84. A survey and listing of sex offender statutes can be found in Schwitzgebel, R. K. *Development and legal regulation of coercive behavior modification with offenders.* Rockville, Md.: NIMH Center for Studies of Crime and Delinquency, 1971.

85. Stone, A. A. *Mental health and law: A system in transition.* Rockville, Md.: NIMH Center for Studies of Crime and Delinquency, 1975, p. 187.

86. Golten, R. J. Role of defense counsel in the criminal commitment process 10 *The American Criminal Law Review* 385 (1975).

4

Punishment

In one widely discussed behavior therapy program, a Marine Corp psychiatrist told inactive and resistant patients in an overseas military hospital, "If you don't work, you don't eat."[1] This order was enforced up to a length of three days. On the second day, 120 "unmodified electroconvulsive treatments" were also given to motivate the patients. Punishment routines (of even much less drastic nature) are, however, usually low priority strategies in professional behavior-change programs.[2]

DEFINITION AND USE OF PUNISHMENT

"Punishment" is procedurally defined as: (1) the presentation of an aversive consequence or (2) the withdrawal of a positive consequence. Both of these procedures are intended to reduce the strength of the preceding behavior. Punishment may be employed simply to suppress unwanted behavior over an extended period of time, or it may be used to control the unwanted behavior for a brief period during which a competing and more desirable behavior can be specifically strengthened by positive reinforcement. Generally, punishment or aversive conditioning is contraindicated where the unwanted behavior is fear-motivated, as in phobias, because adding a noxious stimulus to a high-anxiety state may lead to pathological disorganization.

The widespread use of punishment procedures in almost all societies is due possibly to the immediate, suppressing effects that the procedure usually has on unwanted behavior. Alternative positive means of controlling behavior may have less immediate effects and are therefore more difficult and less reinforcing for persons in authority to use. Another factor is that physical aggression often occurs as the immediate response to the frustration experienced when a person "misbehaves," or a car will not start, and so forth. The physical expression of anger on the part of a therapist is rarely, if ever, professionally endorsed, although the verbal expression of anger may be encouraged in some therapies.[3]

One way to remove positive consequences is to place a person in social isolation. This procedure, known as "time-out" or "time out from reinforcement," uses brief, swift isolation from a rewarding situation for the purpose of reducing the preceding unwanted behavior. For example, a hospitalized paranoid schizophrenic patient was taken to, and remained in, her room for five minutes whenever she made a delusional statement during therapy interviews.[4] The effectiveness of the time-out procedure is dependent upon the prior, normal occurrence of *positive* consequences at a level *generally* maintaining desirable behavior. Seclusion from an *unrewarding* environment is not punishing. Time-out procedures have been applied to a variety of disruptive social behaviors of normal and mentally handicapped children.[5]

Customarily, short time intervals of five or ten minutes are adequate in terms of cost-effectiveness, and sometimes merely interrupting the ongoing activity is effective. A procedure known as "contingent observation" requires only that the client sit nearby and watch on-going activity.[6] If seclusion is necessary to reduce unwanted behavior, the time-out area should be relatively barren in terms of available reinforcers, free from potentially harmful objects, and have a means (when necessary) of keeping the person in the area (e.g., a latched door).[7] A few classroom teachers have constructed isolation cubicles or booths, but this arrangement may be ineffective, abused, or simply politically unwise due to adverse publicity.[8] The Associated Press reported that in Hamilton, Georgia, a nine-year-old spent several hours in a box approximately the size of a refrigerator carton. She was also given her noon meal while in her box! The teacher explained: "I've paddled her and I've fussed with her. I hate to beat the child."[9]

Nonconvulsive electric shock and chemical conditioning have also been used in aversive therapies. Among disorders treated with electroshock have been alcoholism, sexual variation, obesity, and self-injury.[10] For example, the successful use has been reported of "electric shock rods to decrease self-destructive behavior in an 11-year-old girl who spent three years tied hand-and-foot to prevent her from violently banging her head and severely mutilating her face by digging at skin grafts with her fingernails."[11] Worthy of note is the fact that the previous physical restraint in this case was not part of the operant conditioning program but was allegedly "the only means the frustrated nursing staff had to prevent her from seriously injuring herself."[12]

A chemical conditioning procedure that has been used for decades involves the mixing of an emetic with alcohol to induce vomiting. More recently, a procedure was used with alcoholics that involved injections of succinylcholine chloride to induce terrifying muscular paralysis. However a follow-up study revealed a low success rate.[13] The craving for morphine was temporarily reduced by administering nausea-inducing apomorphine following each "fix" by drug addicts.[14] A variety of less technically precise and more traditional techniques (such as restriction of movement, long-term isolation, degrading tasks, use of crowd-control chemicals or military weapons) are used in society at large to control behavior.

The short-term effectiveness of punishment is well documented.[15] The long-term effectiveness of punishment is primarily a function of the post-treatment environment, and hence rather unpredictable. Among variables found to influence the outcome are: the types of behaviors to be modified (e.g., consummatory, sexual, intellectual), intensity and type of aversive stimulus, pain threshold of the patient, and so on.[16]

CONSTITUTIONAL AND ADMINISTRATIVE GUIDELINES

Broadly interpreted, most aversive conditioning procedures can be legally constrained by use of one of three constitutional amendments or interpretations: cruel and unusual punishment, due process, or least restrictive alternative. A few administrative regulations now exist that relate specifically to the rehabilitative use of time-out and electric shock.

Cruel and unusual punishment

The Eighth Amendment reads: "Excessive bail shall not be required, nor excessive fines imposed, nor cruel and unusual punishments inflicted." The "cruel and unusual punishment" clause has often been used to challenge the treatment of mental patients and offenders—but with mixed results. One crucial issue regarding the amendment's protection concerns whom the amendment was intended to protect. The original legislative intent of the amendment was surely to protect criminal offenders, but has been somewhat broadened. A second issue involves the type or purpose of the penalties imposed. There appears to be a tendency to place fewer or less severe constitutional restrictions on "treatment" than on traditional "punishment" because treatment presumably promises certain benefits to a patient or an offender, and is not limited to the retributive or deterrent functions of traditional punishment. Nonetheless, the mere characterization of a procedure as "treatment" or the classification of a statute by a legislature as "nonpenal," cannot avoid the application of constitutional provisions.[17]

The Supreme Court has ruled that spanking, as usually done to maintain discipline, does not violate the Eighth Amendment.[18] The majority opinion upheld the teacher's option to impose reasonable but not excessive force to discipline a child, and noted that local civil and criminal laws can adequately regulate disciplinary measures used by teachers.[19]

A procedure may constitute cruel and unusual punishment if it violates minimal standards of decency, is wholly disproportionate to the alleged offense, or goes beyond what is necessary.[20] For example, forcing an inmate in a "psychiatric observation cell" for disciplinary purposes, to sleep nude on a concrete floor in cold temperatures without soap, towels, or toilet paper has been held a violation of the Eighth Amendment.[21] With respect to the degree of punishment permissible, a federal district court held: "A prisoner may not be unreasonably punished for the infraction of a rule. A punishment out of proportion to the violation may bring it within the bar against unreasonable punishments."[22] A successful action was maintained by a prisoner who consented to shock treatment but who did not consent to administration of succinycholine.[23] Similarly, the administration of apomorphine (to induce vomiting) to nonconsenting mental patients[24] or forceful intramuscular injection of a tranquilizer to a juvenile inmate[25] for infraction of rules has been held as cruel and unusual punishment. Another court held the institutionalized delinquents cannot be required, as a means of punishment, to perform degrading and unnecessary tasks such as pulling grass without bending their knees on a large tract of ground not used for cultivation or any other purpose.[26]

In general, however, some form of aversive remedial effort is permissible. The courts will examine the necessity for the punishment, evaluate its severity, and determine whether it goes far beyond that which was necessary to achieve its purpose. Compulsory treatment for narcotics addicts has been upheld against constitutional attack,[27] and a claim that confinement in a correctional institution for the treatment of addiction constituted cruel and unusual punishment was overruled.[28] HEW-supported programs "involving use of restraints or aversive stimuli" are permitted with mentally handicapped persons, but only with informed consent of parent or guardian.[29]

Two federal courts have set guidelines for disciplinary measures with delinquents in a training school and with mentally ill inmates.[30]

- No use of physical force by personnel except to the extent reasonably necessary (1) in self-defense, (2) in defense of third persons, (3) in effecting restraint on inmates in the act of escaping, or (4) in preventing substantial destruction of property.
- Inmates in restraints are to be released every two hours to see if threats of serious injury are made to self or others. Placement in seclusion or restraints for longer than two or three consecutive days requires an authorizing statement by the inmate's caseworker or psychiatrist, and a review by an independent psychiatrist.
- No use of Mace or tear gas.
- Repetitive, nonfunctional, degrading, and unnecessary tasks are prohibited.
- Silence during periods of the day other than those that reasonably require some order (e.g., academic or vocational classes) should not be enforced.

The type and purpose of punishment circumscribed by the Eighth Amendment appears to be subject to a variety of interpretations depending upon complex case-by-case fact situation. A county circuit court in Illinois reportedly reversed a school board's dismissal of a teacher for using a cattle prod on several sixth-grade boys who were severe discipline problems.[31]

Due process

Punishment is commonly applied to inmates or residents for violation of institutional rules of conduct. If the rules are too broad or vague to provide adequate guidelines, and if the consequences are severe, then a fair and orderly procedure of enforcement may be violated.[32] In *Morris* v. *Travisono*[33] prisoners successfully contended that placing certain inmates in a "behavioral conditioning unit" (maximum security) without written notice or opportunity for a hearing was unconstitutional. A federal circuit court has similarly held that summary transfer to a behavior modification unit resulted in a substantial reduction of privileges, and therefore procedures compatible with due process requirements must be followed.[34] Again, the relevance of this doctrine is ill-defined with respect to aversion therapy.

"Due process" may also be used in a substantive, rather than strictly procedural, sense to refer to fundamental social values of decency or fairness. In this view, the treatment should be reasonably related to the rehabilitation of the person, should not be unduly restrictive of his liberty, and should not be incompatible with his freedom of conscience. Inmates, for example, should be given an opportunity to protest inclusion in a behavior modification program that employs severe deprivation such as being shackled to a bare bed.[35]

Least restrictive alternative

A constitutional doctrine of "the least restrictive alternative" has developed in the last several decades and has been applied with increasing frequency to educational and treatment programs.[36] Originally applied to the treatment of mental patients within psychiatric facilities,[37] the same principle was expanded in 1972 to mandate that retarded children first be educated in a regular classroom, second in a special classroom, and only after other methods have failed in an institution.[38] *Welsch* v. *Likins*[39] held that civilly committed persons should be placed in appropriate settings least restrictive of their liberties. Other cases[40] have held that the same doctrine applies to the *type* of treatment (e.g., electric shock may be used only after verbal reprimand has failed). This doctrine seems particularly salient in aversive chemical routines where there is a relatively high or undefined risk of harm and, at best, a moderate possibility of benefit.

An Ohio statute[41] requires that "aversive stimulae" (sic) be used for only seriously self-destructive behavior after other forms of therapy have been attempted.

This statute appears overly restrictive inasmuch as it limits aversive conditioning to "self-destructive" behavior (presumably preventing use in cases of alcoholism, sexual violence, drug abuse, and so forth). Furthermore, "aversive stimulae" are not defined, leaving in doubt the application of relatively nonintrusive stimuli such as stale cigarette smoke, loud noise, offensive odors, or undesirable music that have been used in some programs.

Administrative safeguards

Controversial programs would be well advised to use an institutional review board or a human rights committee during the planning and implementation phases.[42] The majority of the committee should be composed of persons unaffiliated with the institution and should include representatives of the patient population such as patients, ex-patients, relatives of patients, a behavioral scientist, and a lawyer.[43] The guiding principle in the use of aversive procedures is that the procedure should entail a relatively small amount of pain and discomfort relative to a large amount of pain and discomfort if left untreated.[44]

The experience of several aversive conditioning programs, which have been legally challenged and still survive, indicates that the following precautions are appropriate using extreme measures such as electric shock:[45] (a) have specific goals and guidelines (including plans for generalization of treatment[46]) written in advance and approved by a review panel, (b) use electric shock only for self-destructive behavior after less aversive means have been tried and documented as ineffective, (c) obtain written consent from proper individuals who have first experienced the shock, (d) obtain written outside consultation, (e) have the therapist administer shock first to him/herself, (f) use graduated intensities—starting with simply the sight of the shock device and then rapidly increasing the intensity using only a few steps (to avoid possible adaptation to a greater number of milder shocks), (g) discontinue the procedure if no substantial improvement occurs within the first hour or the first ten shocks, (h) keep a written record of each administration and of the staff review sessions, and (i) institute a concurrent program to teach positive behaviors that will permit shock to be discontinued. The equipment used should meet safety specifications and be periodically inspected.

Time-out, particularly if it does not involve seclusion in a separate area, is less intrusive and therefore requires fewer safeguards. In contrast to "isolation" which would require due process procedures (e.g., notice and hearing) if longer than three days, time-out should not extend over one hour. Intermediate degrees of punishment, such as one-day of seclusion, may be subject to state administrative regulations[47] as well as guidelines by professional organizations. Recommendations by the Joint Commission on Accreditation of Hospitals relative to "time-out" and "aversive stimuli" are as follows:

Behavior modification programs involving the use of time-out devices or the use of noxious or aversive stimuli shall be:

Reviewed and approved by the facility's research review and human rights committees;

Conducted only with the consent of the affected resident's parents or surrogates;

Described in written plans that are kept on file in the facility;

Restraints employed as time-out devices shall be applied for *only* very brief periods, *only* during conditioning sessions, and *only* in the presence of the trainer.

Removal from a situation for time-out purposes shall not be for more than one hour, and this procedure shall be used *only* during the conditioning program, and *only* under the supervision of the trainer.[48]

Guidelines published by the National Association for Retarded Citizens similarly recommend that time-out, when using a locked room, should be employed only when physical harm is threatened; the room itself is safe and has a window for visual monitoring; a staff member can continuously monitor the client; and records are kept of the time spent in the room.[49] These guidelines fall well within the requirement of several court rulings that required a visit by a staff person every hour or half-hour.[50] There appears to be no legal restraint on the legitimate use of the time-out technique.

DISCUSSION

Many aversive procedures alleged to be "treatment" have never been researched or promoted as prescriptive programs in psychological, medical, or educational literature. This "treatment" smokescreen is of little aid to courts which in the past have found no violation of due process for very vague and unrealistic behavioral goals such as a probation requirement of "stay out of all trouble."[51] Knowledgeable therapists as well as civil rights groups are likely to bring pressure on administrators to more clearly define the conditions under which punishment can be applied.

In one 900-bed state institution for retarded persons, an "achievement" cottage used punishment procedures with young residents that included isolation in a locked room for four hours, forced public masturbation, requiring a boy to wear female underpants (for some reason, the reverse dressing was not observed), and holding feces-stained underwear under a resident's nose approximately ten minutes as punishment for incontinence.[52] An investigating committee found that these abuses were the result of well-meaning but poorly trained personnel working within an inappropriately structured program and without external monitoring. "The person who appeared to be most sadistic and cruel in the log turned out to be a college student who was as sincere, dedicated and conscientious as one could possibly expect of an attendant. He reported to the committee in tears, as to how differently his words appeared in newsprint than they did in the log as he wrote them."[53] The designer and administrator of the program, who held a Ph.D. in education and who was judged by the committee to be inadequately trained and experienced for the task, also appeared to always have the welfare of the patients in mind.

One structural flaw in the institution's program was a policy instructing attendants to (a) emphasize natural consequences, (b) devise their own immediate response if specified instructions should not be provided, (c) follow through on every promise or threat, and (d) escalate the intensity of the consequence if, after a trial period, it is not effective. A second structural flaw was an "up-side-down" token economy system wherein the first phase (for new residents and those most "out of control") did not permit any items or privileges to be purchased with tokens. Thus, at the time when the resident needed the strongest and most immediate reinforcers to control his behavior, he was expected to work for long-term gratification in a later phase of the program when tokens could be spent.[54]

Practitioners who themselves use punishment can hardly object to some form of aversive legal contingencies (or at least periodic monitoring) to prevent treatment abuses. For example, regional panels of professionals and citizens might be empowered to make announced and unannounced visits to certain instititions, to have free access to records, and to interview residents and staff.[55] All routine procedures involving aversive conditioning might have to be documented in advance with references from professional literature, and guidelines for the use of these procedures might be submitted to external peer review. If these procedures are experimental, established rules for human experimentation should be followed (see Chapter 11). Procedures should not violate acceptable cultural standards in the particular situation, and the procedures should be discontinued if they do not provide significant therapeutic benefit. Exit interviews with residents could be randomly conducted by responsible administrators. Finally, a regional panel should also have discretionary funds to use as awards for support of particularly meritorious programs and personnel.

NOTES

1. Cotter, L. H. Operant conditioning in a Vietnamese mental hospital. 124 *American Journal of Psychiatry* 23, 25 (1967). For statements defending the procedure, *see* "Gross but appropriate," 92 *Science News* 81 (July 22, 1967).
2. B. F. Skinner's consistent position on punishment has been to the effect that "our task is . . . to make life *less* punishing and in doing so to release for more reinforcing activities the time and energy consumed in the avoidance of punishment." Skinner, B. F. *Beyond freedom and dignity*. New York: Knopf, 1971, p. 81 [italics added]. For a discussion of the legal definition of punishment, *see* Friedman, P. R. Legal regulation of applied behavior analysis in mental institutions and prisons. 17 *Arizona Law Review* 39 (1975), p. 63, n. 117. In behavioral terms, an aversive situation (such as the deprivation of food) that can be avoided is a "negative reinforcer." Such threats or negative reinforcers are used to *increase* a behavior; punishments are used to *decrease* a behavior.

3. Pearls, F. S. *Gestalt therapy verbatim.* LaFayette, Ca.: Real People Press, 1969; Ellis, A. Rational psychotherapy, 59 *Journal of General Psychology* 35 (1958).

4. Liberman, R. P., Davis, J., Moon, W., and Moore, J. Research design for analyzing drug-environment-behavior interactions. 156 *Journal of Nervous and Mental Disorders* 432 (1973) (statements eliminated after 24 days).

5. *See generally,* H. Leitenberg (Ed.), *Handbook of behavior modification and behavior therapy.* Englewood Cliffs, N.J.: Prentice-Hall, 1976.

6. "A client who is doing something inappropriate is asked to step away from the activity for a few moments, sit in a chair nearby, and watch the appropriate behavior of other clients. The staff member deliberately attends to other clients who are appropriately behaving in ways the client should observe. The client rejoins the activity after a few moments of observation and after indicating that he intends to behave appropriately." Research Advisory Committee, *Guidelines for the use of behavioral procedures in state programs for retarded persons.* Arlington, Texas: National Assoc. for Retarded Citizens, 1976, p. 21.

7. Wahler, R. G. Deviant child behavior with the family: Developmental speculations and behavior change strategies. In Leitenberg, *supra* note 5 at p. 533.

8. "Its use was viewed so negatively in Eugene, Oregon, several years ago that it resulted in cries of torture chamber treatment and clamors in several newspapers. . . . One major reason for teachers' dislike of time out is that it may be difficult to get the child or adolescent into the isolation area." O'Leary, S. G. and O'Leary, K. D. Behavior modification in the school. In Leitenberg, *supra* note 5, at 490.

9. Principal puts problem pupils in boxes. *Los Angeles Times,* Part I, p. 6, May 5, 1977. *Similarly,* Allison, H. Retarded schoolboy is imprisoned in dark airless box in classroom. 50 *National Inquirer* 14 (March 2, 1976). (A 4-½ft. × 4-½ft. × 2ft. box was removed from a school in Butte, Montana.)

10. Vogler, R. E., Lunde, S. E., Johnson, G. R., and Martin, P. L. Electrical aversion conditioning with chronic alcoholics. 34 *Journal of Consulting and Clinical Psychology* 302 (1970). Blakemore, C. F., Thorpe, J. G., Barker, J. C., Conway, C. J., and Lavin, N. I. The application of faradic aversive conditioning in a case of transvestism. 1 *Behaviour Research and Therapy* 29 (1963). Meyer, V. and Crisp, A. H. Aversion therapy in two cases of obesity. 2 *Behaviour Research and Therapy* 143 (1964). Corte, H. E., Wolf, M. M., and Locke, B. J. A comparison of procedures for eliminating self-injurious behavior of retarded adolescents. 4 *Journal of Applied Behavior Analysis* 201 (1971). Electric shock typically used is relatively high voltage (85–150v) at low amperage (3–6ma). Between 50 and 150 Hz are delivered through small electrodes on the skin surface. The intensity must be adjusted for each individual, preferably with the person him/herself slowly increasing the current. Numerous other aversive procedures have been used professionally: olfaction, loud noise, imagined scenes, tickling, and delayed auditory feedback.

11. Myron, N. B. The primary ethical consideration. 19 *Hospital and Community Psychiatry* 226, 227 (1968).

12. *Id.* at 226.

13. Sanderson, R. E., Campbell, D., and Laverty, S. G. An investigation of a new aversion conditioning treatment for alcoholism. 24 *Quarterly Journal of Studies of Alcoholism*

261 (1963). Madill, M. F., Campbell, D., Laverty, S. G., Sanderson, R. E., and Vanderwater, S. L. Aversion treatment of alcoholics by succinycholine-induced apneic paralysis. 27 *Quarterly Journal of Studies of Alcoholism* 483 (1966).

14. Liberman, R. Aversive conditioning of drug addicts: A pilot study. 6 *Behaviour Research and Therapy* 229 (1968).

15. A classic review in this area is Azrin, N. H., and Holz, W. C. Punishment. In W. K. Honig (Ed.), *Operant behavior: Areas of research and application.* New York: Appleton-Century-Crofts, 1966, pp. 380–447.

16. Kohlenberg, R. J. The punishment of persistent vomiting: A case study. 3 *Journal of Applied Behavior Analysis* 241 (1970) (rumination in retarded patient suppressed five months following treatment, then recurred); Rooth, F. G., and Marks, I. M. Persistent exhibitionism: Short-term response to self-regulation and relaxation treatment. 3 *Archives of Sexual Behavior* 227 (1974) (50 percent reduction in exhibitionism at 12 to 14 month follow-up of aversion treatment; relaxation treatment ineffective); Dericco, D. A., Brigham, T. A., and Garlington, W. K. Development and evaluation of treatment paradigms for the suppression of smoking behavior. 10 *Journal of Applied Behavior Analysis* 173 (1977) (elimination of smoking by electric shock in 65 percent of subjects at six-month follow-up).

17. Knecht v. Gillman, 488 F.2d 1136 (8th Cir. 1973). *Cf. also,* Trop v. Dulles, 356 U.S. 86, 78 S. Ct. 590, 2 L. Ed. 2d 630 (1958). For psychological perspectives, *see* Opton, E. M. Psychiatric violence against prisoners: When therapy is punishment. 45 *Mississippi Law Journal* 605 (1974).

18. Ingraham v. Wright, 525 F.2d 909 (5th Cir. 1976), *aff'd* 97 S. Ct. 1401 (1977).

19. *Id.* at 1411, 1415. Massachusetts and New Jersey are the only two states prohibiting such punishment; 21 states authorize moderate use of corporal punishment. *Id.* at 1408. *See generally,* Prosser, W. L. *Handbook of the law of torts.* St. Paul, Minn.: West Publishing Co. (1971), pp. 136–138 ("discipline").

20. *See* Note, The cruel and unusual punishment clause and the substantive criminal law. 79 *Harvard Law Review* 635 (1966). *See also,* Turner, W. B. Establishing the rule of law in prisons: A manual for prisoners' rights litigation. 23 *Stanford Law Review* 473 (1971) (useful review of case law prior to 1971 on disciplinary punishment).

21. Wright v. McMann, 460 F.2d 126 (2d Cir., 1972).

22. Fulwood v. Clemmer, 206 F. Supp. 370, 379 (D.D.C. 1962).

23. Mackey v. Procunier, 477 F.2d 877 (9th Cir. 1973).

24. Knecht v. Gillman, 488 F.2d 1136 (8th Cir. 1973).

25. Nelson v. Heyne, 491 F.2d 352 (1974). One court permitted the forceful, intramuscular administration of a tranquilizer to a schizophrenic inmate. Peck v. Ciccone, 288 F. Supp. 329 (W.D. Mo. 1968). The extent to which this was necessary for temporary management and safety instead of long-term treatment is not clear.

26. Morales v. Turman, 364 F. Supp. 166 (E.D. Tex. 1973), *vac.* 535 F.2d 864 (5th Cir. 1976), *rev'd* 430 U.S. 322, 97 S.Ct. 1189 (1977); *remanded for evidentiary hearing* 562 F.2d 933 (5th Cir., 1977).

27. *In re* Spadafora, 54 Misc. 2d 123, 281 N.Y.S.2d 923 (Sup. Ct. 1967); *see also In re* De La O, 28 Cal Rptr. 489, 378 P.2d 793 (1963), *cert. denied* 83 Sup. Ct. 1927 (1963).

28. People *ex rel.* Stutz v. Conboy, 300 N.Y.S.2d 453 (Sup. Ct. 1969).

29. Standards for intermediate care facilities, HEW Rules and regulations. 41 *Federal Register* 12884 (March 29, 1976).

30. This list is a rough condensation of Morales *et al.* v. Turman, 383 F. Supp. *supra* note 26, and the considerably stricter guidelines set in Negron v. Ward, 74 Civ. 1480 (S.D. N.Y., July 13, 1976) *as reported in* Guidelines on use of "restraint and seclusion" on mentally ill inmates ordered by federal court. 1 *Mental Disability Law Reporter* 191 (Nov.–Dec. 1976).

31. Ruling of Judge Leonard Hoffman supporting complaint of Frank Rolando, teacher at Lincoln School in Oglesby, Illinois, as reported by Lofton, J. D. Jr. Court approves cattle prods. *United Features Syndicate,* June, 1975.

32. *See generally,* doctrine as applied to prisoners, Turner, *supra* note 20.

33. Morris v. Travisono, 310 F. Supp. 857 (D.R.J. 1970).

34. Clonce v. Richardson, 379 F. Supp. 388 (W.D. Mo. 1974). This was the Federal Bureau of Prison's START (Special Training and Rehabilitative Treatment) program which the court stopped, on the basis of violating the due process clause of the Fourteenth Amendment.

35. *Id.; see also,* Rochin v. California, 342 U.S. 169 (1952) (forceful pumping of a suspect's stomach not permitted).

36. This subsection follows a brief, cogent outline by Stepleton, J. V. Legal issues confronting behavior modification. 2 *Behavioral Engineering* 35 (1975).

37. Lake v. Cameron, 364 F.2d 657 (D.C. 1966).

38. Pennsylvania Association for Retarded Children v. Commonwealth of Pennsylvania, 343 F. Supp. 279 (E.D. Pa. 1972).

39. Welsch v. Likins, 373 F. Supp. 487 (D. Minn. 1974).

40. Covington v. Harris, 419 F.2d 617 (D.C. 1969); Wyatt v. Stickney, 344 F. Supp. 373 (1972); Barnett v. Rodgers, 410 F.2d 995 (D.C. Cir. 1969).

41. Ohio Rev. Code. Ann. sec. 5122.271(E) (1977).

42. The original and now notorious START program, *supra* note 34, was designed by only one psychologist. For a cogent legal analysis of the program, *see* Project on Law and Behavior, Program analysis: Prisons. 1 *Law and Behavior* 5 (Winter 1976).

43. Research Advisory Committee, *supra* note 6 at p. 36.

44. *Id.* at p. 29.

45. These are adapted from Project on Law and Behavior, *supra* note 42 at p. 41; Research Advisory Committee, *supra* note 6 at pp. 29–34; and "Aversion and deprivation guidelines," Program and Health Services Div., Dept. of Public Welfare, State of Minnesota, Aug. 8, 1977.

46. A well-known research project with autistic children at UCLA in the 1960s attempted to generalize the effects of punishment by camouflaging a shock prod, with only electrode tips protruding, in an innocuous-appearing lunch box carried by a staff member when accompanying children outside the clinic. This was an attempt to meet the problem that chidren can readily discriminate the source of punishment and may not suppress unwanted behavior in other environments.

47. *E.g.,* Bureau for Health Services, Dept. for Human Resources, State of Kentucky, 3 *Administrative Register* 734 (May 1, 1977).

48. J.C.A.H., Accreditation Council for Mentally Retarded. *Standards for residential facilities for the mentally retarded.* May 5, 1971, p. 22.

49. Research Advisory Committee, *supra* note 6 at pp. 28–29.

50. Morales v. Turman, *supra* note 26; Welsch v. Likins, 373 F. Supp. 487 (D. Minn. 1974).

51. The confusion is compounded by anti-treatment advocates proposing a ''right to punishment.'' *E.g.*, Fox, S. J. The reform of juvenile justice: The child's right to punishment. 4 *Juvenile Justice* 2 (Aug. 1974).

52. Report of Resident Abuse Investigating Committee, dated April 18, 1972 to Division of Retardation, Florida State Department of Health and Rehabilitative Services, pp. 11–12; for summary of report, *see* May, J. G. Ethical and legal contingencies in and upon behavior modification programs, Psychology Dept., Florida State University, May 1974 (mimeo.).

53. Report, *id.* at 18.

54. May, *supra* note 52 at 11. This is probably one of the most common and traditional errors of institutional training programs that contributes to treatment failure and recidivism. Residents about to be released should be ''overtrained'' during the final phase by working hard for minimal reward (i.e., on large-ratio intermittent reinforcement schedules) so that they will be more likely to survive in a relatively unrewarding society.

55. The authors are indebted to Todd Risley and Jack May for making some of these recommendations. *See also* Research Advisory Committee, *supra* note 6 at p. 37.

CHAPTER 5

Organic Therapies

Few procedures of behavior-change have generated more public controversy than psychosurgery and electroconvulsive therapy (also known as electroshock therapy). The popularity of the book and film, *One Flew over the Cuckoo's Nest,* accentuated the public concern about possible violations of patients' civil liberties by such physical interventions. According to one psychiatrist, no somatic treatment in psychiatry, when properly used, has been as consistently or dramatically effective as electroconvulsive therapy (ECT).[1] He cited three factors contributing to the current negative attitude toward ECT: (1) individuals and groups who have over the years misused or abused ECT, (2) dominance of psychoanalytic teaching in medical school, and (3) the scores of articles, horror stories in Sunday supplements, sensational books that portray ECT as a form of punitive therapy controlled by sadistic doctors and nurses. "Anyone familiar with the workings of a modern psychiatric hospital, with its insistence on clear criteria and informed consent, can dismiss this as sensational hogwash, which can only create needless anxieties in the minds of the suggestible lay public."[2]

The concern about ECT and psychosurgery is somewhat puzzling, inasmuch as the use of psychoactive drugs such as tranquilizers and antidepressants is far more common. On the other hand, ECT and psychosurgery may be more painful, less reversible, and more visually dramatic.

DESCRIPTION OF PROCEDURES

Psychoactive Drugs

A psychoactive drug can be defined as any chemical agent that affects living processes used for the purpose of altering mental states and behavior.[3] The most common of these drugs fall into five categories of use:

- *"Major tranquilizers"* such as prochlorperazine (Compazine), trifluroperazine (Stelazine), and thioridazine (Mellaril) for treatment of schizophrenia and psychosis, or *"minor tranquilizers"* such as diazepam (Valium) and meprobamate (Equanil) for treatment of anxiety reactions.
- *Antidepressants* such as isocarboxazid (Marlan), imipramine (Tofranil), and amitriptyline (Elavil) for depression.
- *Amphetamines* such as dextroamphetamine (Dexadrine) and methylphemidate (Ritalin) for mild depression and hyperactivity.
- *Barbiturates* such as barbital (Medinal) and pentobarbital (Nembutal) for sleep disturbances.
- So-called *"psychedelics"* such as heroin, LSD, psilocybin, cocaine, marijuana, mescaline, and methadone for control of pain, and on rare occasions as an experimental adjunct to intensive psychotherapy.[4]

Psychoactive drugs have been used with many thousands of mental patients, and antipsychotic medication has been credited with substantially reducing the number of patients in mental hospitals since 1956.[5] In the United States, only antibiotics are more frequently prescribed than tranquilizing agents.[6] One study found that nine percent of all admissions of a general medical and surgical hospital received a psychoactive drug prescribed by internists, surgeons, and gynecologists, but "the drugs of different groups were often used interchangeably in an unsystematic fashion and there was little evidence as to how effective a drug had been."[7] The efficacy, dosage limits, and reversability of side effects are matters of some ambiguity and debate.[8]

Electroconvulsive Therapy (ECT)

Electroconvulsive therapy involves the application of regulated electrical current of a brief duration (from 0.1 to 1 sec.) through electrodes positioned on the patient's temples.[9] "The optimal dosage is the lowest current for the shortest time that will produce a grand mal or generalized tonic and clonic convulsion."[10] Normally, three treatments are prescribed per week. A minimum of six treatments and a maximum of twenty-five treatments spaced over two to ten weeks are considered normal limits; nine treatments is average.[11]

Paralytic agents such as succinylcholine are commonly used in conjunction with ECT in order to achieve muscular relaxation during the induced seizures.[12] This procedure guards the patient against the violent bodily reactions which can accompany ECT. General anesthesia with very short-acting intravenous barbiturates is also employed in a majority of cases. At one time, complications included broken bones (e.g., vertebral and hip fractures), damaged muscles and brain tissue, disorientation in time and space, relaxation of inhibitions, and loss of memory.[13] Except for reversible memory loss, however, these complications are not very common with the use of muscle relaxants and general anesthesia.[14]

In the nearly four decades since ECT was first introduced by Cerletti and Bini, indications for successful application have become fairly well defined. There is general psychiatric consensus that ECT is 75 to 90 percent effective in alleviating *depressive symptomology* of involutional melancholia and persisting endogenous depressions of middle and older age individuals who have not responded to at least several months of treatment with antidepressant drugs and psychotherapy.[15] One psychopharmacologist reported that due to a suicidal tendency, "data from 15 studies involving over 4,500 depressed persons indicate that the overall death rate is significantly lower with ECT than with psychotherapy."[16] In severe suicidal depressions, initial treatment with antidepressant drugs may similarly prolong the time period of suicidal risk.[17] The appropriateness of ECT for various *schizophrenic psychoses* is a matter of wider controversy.[18] In overall perspective, the use of ECT constitutes only a small percentage of general psychiatric practice, possibly averaging about four percent of psychiatric inpatients.[19]

Psychosurgery

Psychosurgery has been described as "a surgical operation on the intact brain for the relief of mental symptoms"[20] or as "surgical removal or destruction of brain tissue or the cutting of brain tissue to disconnect one part of the brain from another with the *intent of altering behavior.*"[21] Such surgery is usually performed in patients with very serious mental illness and therefore should be distinguished from surgery to correct physical trauma, Parkinson's disease, tumors, clots, and so on. It should also be distinguished from brain surgery for aggressive or violent behavior patterns prompted by temporal lobe epilepsy.

Originally, the most common operation was prefrontal lobotomy, mainly used for schizophrenic psychosis. In recent years, however, this type of operation has become quite rare. Its use is now typically restricted to patients who have not responded to psychotherapy, drugs, or repeated ECT, and who show predominantly depressive symptoms.[22] Some practitioners have claimed that over 75 percent of patients receiving lobotomy were found "virtually free of symptoms."[23] Postoperative seizure activity is estimated at ten to 30 percent, and postoperative death rate at one to three percent.[24] On the basis of two independently commissioned follow-up studies by neuropsychologists, the National Commission for the Protection of

Human Subjects concluded that psychosurgery has potential merit and that risks are not excessive.[25]

Psychosurgery is not the treatment of choice for any psychiatric illness, and it requires highly skilled personnel to carry out very meticulous procedures. The result is that surgery has become infrequently performed in this country, and is so uncommon that most practicing psychiatrists never see a patient who has undergone modern psychosurgery.[26]

COMPETENT INFORMED CONSENT

At common law, administering a somatic treatment without consent of the individual or his/her legal representative constitutes the tort of battery. An exception to this general rule is often allowed in emergency situations. The nature of the consent to be obtained (e.g., informed vs. pro forma, explicit vs. implied) and the manner in which it is obtained (e.g., voluntary vs. coerced) are legally very significant. At present, "competent, informed consent" is the primary legal doctrine relied upon to restrain (or permit) the use of organic therapies. In the absence of more specific statutory or administrative regulations, a treating physician may be properly expected to make reasonable effort to obtain such consent. A general summary of this doctrine will be presented here, followed by more specific recommendations regarding therapies using psychoactive drugs, ECT, and psychosurgery.

Competence

There is general agreement that a person who voluntarily enters a mental facility, despite an existing mental disability (and possibly some coercion by relatives), is capable of giving (or withholding) truly informed consent.[27] Nor does *involuntary* commitment necessarily imply a lack of capacity. "Commitment" and "competency/incompetency" are different legal determinations. For instance, a commitment might be based on potential dangerousness to self or others, not on any lack of decision-making capacity of the person to manage or decide about business affairs or about treatment.

In a few states, a hospitalization order is also an adjudication of incompetency, but the trend is to completely separate the issues of hospitalization and incompetency.[28] Because a person's status regarding competency is usually a separate legal determination made by a court or by established administrative procedure, a practitioner should not normally assume that the committed patient is incompetent. Nonetheless, it should be noted that in practice both voluntary and involuntary patients may be cared for as if they were not entirely competent to choose the specifics of their own treatment. For example, both groups of patients, upon admission, might be housed on a locked unit until some improvement has been seen. Competence, a pragmatic sense, is not a static quality because even the patient who is committed and declared legally incompetent would presumably regain competence during successful treatment.[29] Conversely, a competent patient might become temporarily incompetent.[30] An attempt to obtain full consent, in a literal legal sense, may be very time-consuming or even impossible. A minimal, practical approach is to provide all patients with an on-going series of treatment options.[31] (See Appendix E.)

One of the leading cases involving organic therapies is *Winters* v. *Miller*[32] in which an involuntarily committed Christian Scientist was given heavy doses of a major tranquilizer over her objection. The court held that, in the absence of a judicial determination of incompetence, a diagnosis of mental illness was not sufficient reason to impose medication over her religious objections.

The consent problem, particularly with involuntary patients, is a real one—"How does one obtain consent from a severely ill catatonic schizophrenic who could not even give the time of day much less consent to treatment?" or "How does one obtain consent from a paranoid inmate whose refusal of treatment is a product of his illness?"[33] One approach is to assume that the involuntary patient, though mentally capable, is under such duress that s/he cannot freely give consent to intrusive forms of treatment. But then a paradox develops for certain types of patients: those who lack the legal status to consent may have to forego a treatment of choice (e.g., ECT) for a less effective and less intrusive intervention for which informed consent may not be as critical. One strategy is to place the responsibility of consent with a guardian. But this person may be a relative who wants the patient "treated" or even punished as a matter of retribution. Another approach is to borrow certain criminal law precedents to develop a legal status of "diminished capacity" or "selective incompetency."[34] Still another approach would be to require a court hearing on the merits and dangers of the proposed treatment,[35] but this is administratively very burdensome and expensive, and furthermore the proceeding itself might be damaging to the patient.[36]

The trend appears to be toward allowing the staff to treat a patient who lacks capacity to make an informed decision about treatment if certain procedural requirements are followed. For example, treatment must be planned with the patient as much as possible.[37] The patient's legal counsel must have access to the plans and records. The patient may at any time raise an objection to the treatment and such an objection will be considered by a Human Rights Committee. This committee also generally reviews all treatment within the institution. Approval of the committee would be required prior to initiating the treatment. Hazardous treatment or treatment involving unusual discomfort requires additional procedures such as the sending of a notice of the proposed treatment simultaneously to the patient, attorney, and his/her guardian or conservator, if any.

Many of the newer civil commitment statutes contain express provisions for obtaining consent for specific forms of treatment. New Mexico, for example, requires the judicial appointment of a "treatment guardian" to make a decision on behalf of the incompetent individual if the proposed treatment involves psychosurgery, convulsive therapy, experimental treatment, or behavior modification.[38]

Voluntariness

The second major issue to be considered in obtaining legally adequate consent is the degree to which an involuntarily confined person can freely give consent while in a more-or-less coercive institutional environment. In one well-known psychosurgery case, a county circuit court opinioned that "It is impossible for an involuntarily detained mental patient to be free of ulterior forms of restraint or coercion when his very release from the institution may depend upon his cooperating with the institutional authorities in giving consent to experimental surgery."[39] It can be argued that similarly strong pressures may exist in other "social institutions" such as school or home, yet these pressures do not inevitably destroy a person's decision-making capacity.

A federal district court held that consent of a prisoner to recognized drug therapy was not necessary if such treatment both benefited the prisoner and met a compelling state interest.[40] In another case, however, a state appellate court ruled that due to the unfavorable attitude toward ECT, an outpatient with a psychotic depression could properly refuse ECT and still collect money damages even though ECT might be the treatment of choice. That is, social as well as medical factors may legitimately be considered in refusing a recommended treatment. The legal status of the person, the degree to which a procedure may be experimental, the urgent or nonurgent need for intervention, etc. all affect the nature of the consent that should be sought by a practitioner. Even where some urgency and a compelling state interest exists, a prudent practitioner should have evidence that prior consideration was given to the possibility of using "less drastic means" or "less restrictive alternatives" (including social as well as medical procedures) to accomplish the state's purpose.[41] The weight of legal opinion at present is supportive of the view that institutional conditions do not per se preclude the voluntariness necessary for legally valid consent.[42]

The frequent statement that the patient may withdraw consent at any time is usually true. However, it is sometimes difficult to keep this option available to patients because the treatment itself may induce a temporary loss of rationality and/or the discontinuance of treatment may cause injury.[43] In *Nims* v. *Boland*[44] the Court used a two-step test for determining the liability of the defendant practitioner. First, was there a revocation of consent from a clear and rational mind, leaving no room for doubt in the minds of reasonable men? Second, was it "medically feasible for the doctor to desist in the treatment or examination at that point with the cessation being detrimental to the patient's health or life from a medical viewpoint"?[45] The Legislative and Social Issues Committee of the American Association on Mental Deficiency observes that capacity, information, and voluntariness must be present for the withdrawal of consent to be effective and that "the consenting person always has the right to withdraw consent, usually at any time."[46]

Knowledge

Potential risks to patients are physical, psychological, and sociological in nature. Informed consent requires that consent be based on sufficient knowledge and understanding of the comparative risks and benefits involved. But how much knowledge and understanding is "sufficient"? Many technical details will likely be beyond the patient's comprehension, and a listing of all possible risks may cause excessive concern and anxiety. One writer has claimed that if every patient given a drug by a physician was asked to read the package insert supplied by the pharmaceutical manufacturer and then sign a consent, "it is very doubtful if any patient would ever take any drug, including aspirin."[47] A recitation of risks and benefits of *no* treatment, as well as various treatment alternatives, may be an affirmative duty of the physician to the extent that such a recital aids the patient's decision-making.[48] The description of options should include also the duration and purpose of the treatment, the manner in which the treatment is administered, and the degree to which the treatment is experimental in nature.

Some courts have measured the physician's duty to disclose risks in terms of the patient's perception of the situation—". . . the test for determining whether a potential peril must be divulged is its materiality to the patient's decision."[49] Even a one percent risk of serious disability may in some situations require disclosure.[50] Conversely, no disclosure to the patient himself may be required at all in a situation where great risks to the patient are involved by making such a disclosure.[51]

As the law is developing, a fair summary might be that "the physician is required to disclose all information about a proposed treatment which a reasonable person in the patient's circumstances would find material to his decision either to undergo or to forego treatment."[52]

GUIDELINES FOR SPECIFIC TREATMENTS

Psychoactive Drug Therapy

Frequently asked questions about drug prescription include the following:[53] How strictly must a physician follow a drug manufacturer's directions? How thorough must a physical examination be prior to drug prescription? What are the legal risks in dispensing potent medications to suicidal patients?

The drug manufacturer's package insert is a legally important document that may be used to establish a professional standard of practice. If recommended dosages are exceeded, or even vague warnings (e.g., "use with care in pregnant women'') are not followed, the physician's liability undoubtedly increases. On the other hand, the physician, as a licensed practitioner, "is not precluded from using a commercially available drug in a manner which his knowledge and experience indicate to him is in the best interest of his patient."[54] Nonapproved use of a drug would be investigational, but if it "is available locally on the commercial market, the physician may purchase and use it without filing an IND (Notice of Claimed Investigational Exemption)."[55] Thus, a prescription of diphenylhydantoin as a tranquilizer rather than an anticonvulsant would not require an IND, but there is increased liability and hence the need for informed consent is greater. Package inserts are conservatively written to protect the drug company from liability, but this may unfairly shift responsibility to the prescribing physician. Alternately, these inserts might be reduced in legal status to an "advisory" document but be frequently revised.[56]

More novel treatments require additional safeguards for the patient's welfare. For example, chemical aversive conditioning of an involuntary patient would require special clearance procedures, and would be absolutely prohibited if merely used as a punishment for minor violations of hospital rules.[57] Procedural safeguards for novel applications such as aversive conditioning should include: the recommendation of two mental health professionals and approval of an institutional "human rights" committee, the written informed consent of the patient (which may be withdrawn orally or in writing at any time and has immediate effect), and the administration of each drug given in the physical presence of a qualified mental health professional with training and experience in the use of the particular novel technique.[58]

Regarding physical examination prior to treatment, national standards of acceptable medical practice seem to apply. For example, a physician who prescribes a drug without at least taking a blood pressure measurement or other minimal precautions is probably taking an unnecessary risk. If examination by the psychiatrist is inappropriate or the necessary equipment is not available, referral to an internist is a reasonable expectation.

Standards of practice may have also been promulgated by state administrative agencies, and the prudent practitioner will be aware of these. For example, Michigan standards on the use of psychotropic drugs require a comprehensive drug history, weekly recordation of medication effects on target symptoms, and possibly a "drug holiday" one day a week for all patients.

A physician might not meet an acceptable standard of care if s/he prescribed potentially dangerous pills to a known suicidal patient,[60] or did not review an inpatient's medication at least monthly.[61] But a conscientious practitioner who merely fails to predict a reasonably unforeseeable suicide would not be liable.[62] Furthermore, it is generally recognized that calculated risk must be taken for therapeutic purposes (e.g., prescribing antidepressants). As long as the physician is informed about, and alert to, the patient's condition, lack of professional due care is difficult to prove. For example, hoarding of pills at home and attempted suicide after a patient had been placed on a semi-open hospital ward did not create liability.[63]

Electroconvulsive Therapy

Case law indicates that a moderately controversial treatment such as ECT requires more than simply getting a patient to read and sign a brief, standardized consent form.[64] The following conditions have been recommended as minimally adequate to assure adequate consent for ECT:[65]

1. The person must be specifically informed by the treating physician about the right to refuse shock therapy. If an individual agrees to shock therapy:
   a. S/he must sign an informed consent; such a consent form should include:
      (1) description of procedure (i.e., how it will be done, duration or number of treatments, what physical and emotional phenomena the individual may experience).
      (2) an explanation of the risks and an indication of the anticipated benefits (previously explained orally in more detail).
      (3) statement of rationale for the use of this treatment as opposed to other modalities or no treatment at all (previously explained orally).
      (4) statement that the individual, guardian, or conservator has read the consent and has had an opportunity to discuss its meaning with the physician.
      (5) patient's and/or relative's dated and witnessed signature.
   b. S/he has the right to refuse further treatment at any time.
2. If the person agrees to shock therapy but is not competent to give consent, the consent is not valid.
3. If the person refuses shock treatment, treatment may be given only if the following conditions are met:
   a. The individual's condition is life-threatening and the intervention is the last-resource treatment of choice. Treatments are limited in number or duration and are adequately documented in writing in the individual's chart, by urgent circumstances.
   b. The parent, responsible family member, guardian, or conservator has signed an informed consent form on behalf of the individual in those cases where the person is a minor or legal ward.
   c. At least two physicians also sign the consent form agreeing with the prescribed treatment.
4. Consent should be obtained at the time treatment is indicated, not at admission.

Considerably more stringent procedures for administration of ECT were specified in *Wyatt* v. *Hardin*[66] stating, in part, that: The patient must be over 18 years of age; written consent must be knowing, intelligent, and voluntary with the option of immediate termination of such consent; approval must be obtained from another mental health professional, the medical director of the institution, and a five member review committee; appointed legal counsel shall represent the patient at all proceedings; a complete physical examination, including neurological, shall be given 10 days prior to each series of treatments; and regressive, multiple, or depatterning techniques are not to be used nor are more than 12 treatments in any one series in any 12-month period to be given without special committee approval.

Psychosurgery

The legal status of psychosurgery is ambigious at present. *Wyatt* v. *Hardin* prohibited the procedure without exception.[67] Similarly, *Kaimowitz* v. *Department of Mental Health*[68] removed the opportunity for experimental psychosurgery from involuntary patients, even with the consent of a legally appointed guardian. The Court held, however, that when such psychosurgical intervention "becomes an accepted neurosurgical procedure and is no longer experimental, it is possible, with appropriate review mechanism, that involuntarily detained mental patients could consent to such an operation."[69] This case is also noteworthy as an apparent anomaly in arranging for a legal custodian.[70]

Many states have established administrative guidelines for psychosurgery through their departments of health or similar agencies.[71] A few states have amended statutes to include this technique. An Oregon statute regulates all psychosurgery practice by setting specific standards of consent and by requiring prior approval of a nine member Psychosurgery Review Board.[72] Federal administrative guidelines are more ambiguous but follow a general pattern requiring advanced review by at least an institutional consent committee.[73] Some provisions of a state statute to limit psychosurgery were struck down because the statute prohibited mentally competent patients from obtaining the treatment and because relatives had to be notified prior to surgery.[74] The court considered these provisions to be an excessive invasion of privacy. Given the present degree of controversy and ambiguity, the most prudent course would be to obtain a court hearing and approval on a case-by-case basis.

CONSTITUTIONAL ISSUES

Constitutional issues that have been raised with respect to organic therapies usually follow a pattern similar to those raised with other behavioral interventions. For example, in *Kaimowitz* v. *Department of Mental Health,* psychosurgery was prohibited, in part, on the grounds that "a person's mental processes, the communication of ideas, and the generation of ideas, come within the ambit of the First Amendment.''[75] Medication which might also interfere in the communication of ideas would probably be subject to similar criticism and restriction. A federal district court in Pennsylvania held that a former patient could bring a class action suit under the Federal Civil Rights Act alleging that he was forcibly treated with psychotropic drugs in a manner that might have violated the First and Eighth Amendments.[76]

Conversely, in a situation where a drug has been proven behaviorally effective, a patient may sue in tort for lack of proper treatment if withholding that drug was contrary to generally accepted medical practice.[77]

Efforts to overthrow statutory restrictions against the use of psychoactive substances such as marijuana or LSD without prescription on the basis of First Amendment protection of freedom of religion have been notably unsuccessful.[78]

"Due process" arguments asserting that some organic therapies violate the right to make a contract, to liberty, to equal education, and so forth have been made, but case law is not well developed in these matters.[79] Another argument against organic therapies has been grounded in the eighth amendment's mandate against cruel and unusual punishment.[80] The most frequently cited case is an aversive conditioning treatment, now discontinued, with prisoners involving intravenous administration of succinylcholine (anectine) to induce conscious cessation of respiration for approximately two minutes.[81] There is ambiguity as to whether or not officials at the three prisons involved in this treatment regime considered the use of anectine for psychological purposes to be "investigational." Nonetheless the case should be distinguished from chemical treatments without such intense aversive effect and those used in a more routine therapeutic manner. Due to the interactive complexity of an individual's presenting problem, the range of optimal treatments, the particular practitioner's skill, various economic considerations, and other factors, a categorical claim that ECT or drug therapy is more violative of a patient's constitutional protections (e.g., of privacy or against cruel and unusual punishment) than is psychoanalysis or behavior therapy does not seem justified.

Fifth Amendment prohibitions against compulsory self-incrimination in criminal trials and investigations have been raised in relation to drug-use offenses. New York, for example, requires a medical examination of any arrested person who appears to be a narcotic addict.[82] Although the state has a clear and justifiable interest in obtaining information for the prosecution of criminal suspects, incriminating statements made to a psychiatrist doing a compulsory interview may not be used by the prosecution during the trial in some states.[83] This immunity has been extended by federal statute to persons involved in addict-diversion programs.[84] Federal legislation provides that "records of the identity, diagnosis, prognosis, or treatment of any patient which are maintained in connection with the performance of any drug abuse prevention function conducted, regulated, or directly or indirectly assisted by any department or agency of the United States shall, except as provided in subsection (e) of this section, be confidential and be disclosed only for the purposes and under the circumstances expressly authorized. . . . ''[85] The exception involves disclosures compelled by ''a court of competent jurisdiction'' after ''application showing good cause therefor.''[86] The regulation apparently makes the scope of confidentiality similar to that traditionally protected by the physician-patient privilege, but extends this to all program personnel whether or not they are medically trained.[87]

Researchers using experimental drugs (including apparently methadone) or doing treatment follow-up with addicts may, after making application to the Departments of HEW or Justice, assert an absolute privilege against disclosure concerning certain information.[88]

A more controversial aspect of prevention programs involves compulsory urinalysis. Urine samples ''voluntarily'' given by a parolee are constitutionally acceptable.[89] Moderate physical force may be used once the person is reasonably suspected of a crime.[90] Previously identified users in the military services may be compelled to submit to unannounced urinalysis as part of a rehabilitation program.[91] However, a general order directing all military personnel to give urine samples as part of a drug-use prevention program was held illegal.[92]

Psychiatrists who usually have general responsibility for the treatment of severely disabled persons are in a difficult situation with respect to the use of organic therapies—they're ''damned if they do and damned if they don't.'' Attorneys and psychologists without medical training are seldom required to take legal responsibility for severely disabled persons. These interested parties (who are not obliged to find realistic compromise in difficult situations or to cope with the day-to-day behavioral management of such persons) have the option of being radically supportive or radically opposed to any particular treatment, as their attitudes and beliefs may dictate. This makes for interesting debates. But the degree to which the welfare of patients has been or can be improved by legal intervention is an empirical question for which criteria and data are notoriously lacking.

NOTES

1. Lebensohn, Z. M. The place of electroshock therapy in present-day psychiatry. In R. C. Allen, E. Z. Ferster, and J. G. Rubin (Eds.), *Readings in law and psychiatry.* Baltimore: Johns Hopkins Univ. Press, 1975, p. 92.
2. *Id.*
3. Goodman, L. S. and Gilman, A. *The pharmacological basis of therapeutics,* 4th ed. New York: Macmillan, 1970. *See generally,* Van Praag, H. M. *Psychotropic drugs: Guide for the practitioner.* New York: Brunner/Mazel, 1977; Werry, J. S. *Pediatric psychopharmacology: The use of behavior modifying drugs in children.* New York: Brunner/Mazel, 1977; Honigfeld, G. and Howard, A. *Psychiatric drugs: A desk reference,* 2nd ed. New York: Academic Press, 1978.
4. Introduction of the term ''psychedelic'' is usually attributed to an article by Osmond, H.

A review of the clinical effects of psychotomimetic agents. 66 *Annals of the New York Academy of Science* 418 (1957). Regarding clinical use, *see* Chandler, A. L., and Hartman, M. A. LSD-25 as a facilitating agent in psychotherapy. 2 *AMA Archives of General Psychiatry* 286 (1960); recent issues of *Journal of Altered States of Consciousness* (Baywood Publishing Co.); and Note, LSD, clinical use and research: A proposal for legislated change. 7 *University of California (Davis) Law Review* 113 (1974). For detailed description of standard prescribed medications, see *Physician's desk reference* issued yearly by Medical Economics, Inc.

5. Davis, J. M. and Cole, J. O. Antipsychotic drugs, In A. Freedman, H. Kaplan, and B. Sadock (Eds.), *Comprehensive textbook of psychiatry,* 2d ed. Baltimore: Williams & Wilkins, 1975, vol. 2, at p. 1921.

6. Greenblatt, D. J. and Shader, R. I. *Benzodiazepines in clinical practice.* New York: Raven Press, 1974.

7. Davidson, J. R. T., Raft, D., Lewis, B. F., and Gebhardt, M. Psychotropic drugs on general medical and surgical wards of a teaching hospital. 32 *Archives of General Psychiatry* 507 (April 1975).

8. "Drugs have largely supplanted convulsive therapy and surgery . . . because they are more effective, . . . treatment complications are fewer, . . . and their effects are generally reversible." Goodman and Gilman, *supra* note 3, p. 152. "Convulsive shock therapy has doubled the number of recoveries [of involutional melancholia]. Eighty to 90 percent of patients are benefited. About 60 percent will respond to antidepressants (imipramine, amitriptyline)." D. N. Holvey (Ed.), *Merck Manual of Diagnosis and therapy.* Rahway, N.J.: Merck Sharp & Dohme, 1972 (12th ed.), p. 1404. *See also* special issue, Vol. 5, of *Psychiatric Annals* (1975) on side effects of various prescription psychoactive drugs.

9. Solomon, P. and Patch, V. D. *Handbook of psychiatry.* Los Altos, Calif.: Lange Medical Publications, 1971, p. 394. A useful source of apparatus description can be found in U.S. Patent Office classification 128-419s.

10. Solomon, *id.* at 391.

11. *Id.*

12. Asnis, G. M., Fink, M., and Saferstein, S. ECT in Metropolitan New York hospitals: A survey of practice, 1975–1976. 135 *American Journal of Psychiatry* 479 (Apr. 1978).

13. Ilaria, R. and Prange, A. J., Jr. Convulsive therapy and other biological treatments. In E. F. Iliach and S. C. Draghi (Eds.), *The nature and treatment of depression.* New York: Wiley & Sons, 1975, p. 298.

14. *Id.* at 280.

15. *Id.* at 273; Kalinowsky, L. B. The convulsive therapies. In A. Freedman, H. Kaplan, and B. Sadock (Eds.), *Comprehensive textbook of psychiatry,* 2d ed. Baltimore: Williams & Wilkins, 1975, vol. 2, p. 1969; Abrams, R. and Taylor, M. A. Unipolar and bipolar depressive illness. 30 *Archives of General Psychiatry* 320 (March 1974); Cole, J. and Davis, J. Antidepressant drugs. In Kalinowsky, *id.,* at 1950.

16. Avery, D. The case for "shock" therapy. 11 *Psychology Today* 104 (Aug. 1977).

17. Ilaria, *supra* note 13, at p. 274. Generally *contra* Friedberg, J. *Shock treatment is not good for your brain. Call me. . . .* San Francisco: Glide Publications, 1975.

18. Ilaria, *supra* note 13, at p. 272; Peck, R. E. *The miracle of shock treatment.* Jericho, N.Y.: Exposition Press, 1974 (recommending ECT for schizophrenia as well as "psychosomatic disorders such as ulcers, spastic and ulcerative colitis, asthma,

psoriasis, trigonitis.''—p. 23). Special section: Electroconvulsive therapy—current perspective. 134 *American Journal of Psychiatry* 991 (Sept. 1977).

19. Asnis, *supra* note 12. Estimate based on 45,063 new admissions to 69 hospitals, ranging from one percent in public hospitals to 21 percent in private for-profit hospitals.

20. Freeman, W. Psychosurgery. In S. Arieti (Ed.), *American handbook of psychiatry*. Vol. 2. New York: Basic Books, 1959, p. 1521. *See generally* Mark, V. and Ervin, F. *Violence and the brain*. New York: Harper & Row, 1970; Balenstein, E. S. *Brain control*. New York: Wiley & Sons, 1973; Note, Symposium on psychosurgery. 54 *Boston University Law Review* 215 (1974); Note, Physical manipulation of the brain. *The Hastings Center Report* (Special Supplement) (May 1973).

21. National Institute of Mental Health, *Psychosurgery: Perspectives on a current problem*. Washington, D.C.: HEW, 1973, p. 1, as cited in Shapiro, M. H. Legislating the control of behavior control: Autonomy and the coercive use of organic therapies. 47 *Southern California Law Review* 273 (1974) (a valuable general survey of this topic).

22. Ilaria, *supra* note 13, at pp. 271–307.

23. Bernstein, I. C., Callahan, W. H., and Jaronson, J. M. Lobotomy in private practice. 32 *Archives of General Psychiatry* 1041 (Aug. 1975).

24. Solomon, P. and Patch, V. D., *supra* note 9, at p. 394.

25. Trotter, S. Federal commission OKs psychosurgery. 6 *Monitor* (American Psychological Assn.) 4 (Nov. 1976).

26. Redlich, F. and Mollica, R. F. Overview: Ethical issues in contemporary psychiatry. 133 *American Journal of Psychiatry* 125, 131 (February 1976); Shevitz, S. A. Psychosurgery: Some current observations. 133 *American Journal of Psychiatry* 266–267 (March 1976).

27. Lebensohn, *supra* note 1, at 391.

28. New York law (N.Y. Estates, Probates and Trust Law, sec. 1–2.9) requires a judicial declaration. *See also* Negron v. Preiser, 382 F. Supp. 535 (S.D. N.Y. 1974)(criminally ill not automatically incompetent).

29. Hoffman, B. D. and Dunn, R. C. Guaranteeing the right to treatment. 6 *Psychiatric Annals* 258 (June 1976).

30. ''ECT treatment has complicated consent problems because it is a continuing treatment, over a period of time, and during the therapy there is progressive memory loss, loss of rationality, and an increase in regressive behavior. . . .'' Robitscher, J. Informed consent: When can it be withdrawn? 2 *Hastings Center Report* 10, 11 (June 1972).

31. Slovenko, R. Commentary on psychosurgery. 5 *Hastings Center Report* 19, 22 (Oct. 1975).

32. Winter v. Miller, 446 F.2d 65 (2d Cir.), *cert. den.* 404 U.S. 985 (1971). Among the ambiguities in this case is the degree to which the Court relied upon the absence of judicially determined incompetence versus a violation of the First Amendment as the basis for its decision.

33. Note, Conditioning and other technologies used to ''treat?'' ''rehabilitate?'' ''demolish?'' prisoners and mental patients. 45 *Southern California Law Review* 161 (1972), at 673.

34. Shapiro, *supra* note 21, at 309–310 supports this alternative.

35. ''. . . The fact of involuntary certification demonstrates that the patient has not consented to treatment and that such lack of consent is tantamount to a request for release, thereby

triggering the patient's right to counsel and to seek habeas corpus, . . .'' Thorn v. Superior Ct., 1 Cal. 3d 666, 464 P.2d 563, 604 (1970). *See generally, Southern California Law Review, supra* note 33, at 673–678; Note, Legislative control of shock treatment, 9 *University of San Francisco Law Review* 738 (Spring 1975).

36. Lester v. Aetna Casualty and Surety Co., 240 F.2d 676 (5th Cir. 1957) (informed consent of wife, but not of patient, adequate where great risk existed of worsening patient's psychological state). A survey of legal criteria for determing the competency of a patient to consent (e.g., the patient's ability to understand) can be found in Roth, L. H., Meisel, A., and Lidz, C. W. Tests of competency to consent to treatment. 134 *American Journal of Psychiatry* 279 (1977).

37. American Bar Association, Commission on the Mentally Disabled, Suggested statute on civil commitment, *Legal issues in state mental health care: Proposals for change* (as reprinted in 2 *Mental Disability Law Reporter* 127 (1977)).

38. New Mexico H.B. 472 as amend. sec. 14 (1st session 1977).

39. Kaimowitz v. Department of Mental Health (Civil Action No. 73-19434-AW; Wayne County, Michigan, Cir. Ct. July 10, 1973), at p. 27.

40. Ramsey v. Ciccone, 310 F. Supp. 600 (W.D. Mo. 1970). *See generally,* Sitnick, S. A. Major tranquilizers in prison: Drug therapy and the unconsenting inmate. 2 *Williamette Law Journal* 378 (Summer 1975).

41. Jackson, J. E. The coerced use of Ritalin for behavior control in public schools: Legal challenges. 10 *Clearinghouse Review* 181 (July 1976).

42. Wexler, D. B. Reflections on the legal regulation of behavior modification in institutional settings. 17 *Arizona Law Review* 39, 80–87 (1975). Friedman comments in his discussion that ''Sound public policy requires that courts and legislators formulate standards of consent which balance the threat of coercion against the equally serious threat of paternalism.'' *Id.* at 83.

43. Knecht v. Gilman 488 F.2d 1136 (8th Cir. 1973)(the right to withdraw consent may not be absolute when, for example, treatment has begun and its discontinuance would seriously harm the patient). *See also,* Robitscher, *supra* note 30.

44. 138 S.E.2d 902 (Ga. App. 1964).

45. *Id.* at 907.

46. *Consent handbook.* Washington, D.C.: AAMD, 1977, p. 8.

47. Lebensohn, *supra* note 1, at 390.

48. Slovenko, R. Commentary on psychosurgery. 5 *Hastings Center Report* 19, 22 (Oct. 1975).

49. Cobbs v. Grant, 8 Cal. 3d 229, 245, 502 P.2d 1, 11 (1972).

50. Canterbury v. Spence, 464 F.2d 772 (D.C. Cir.), *cert. den.,* 409 U.S. 1064 (1972); Trogun v. Fruchtman, 58 Wis. 2d 569, 207 N.W.2d 297 (1973). *Contra* Tatro v. Lukin, 512 P.2d 529 (Kan. 1973). Lebensohn, *supra* note 1.

51. Lester v. Aetna Casualty & Surety Co., 240 F.2d 676 (5th Cir. 1957).

52. Meisel, A. The expansion of liability for medical accidents: From negligence to strict liability by way of informed consent. 56 *Nebraska Law Review* 51, 56 (1977).

53. Appleton, W. S. Legal problems in psychiatric drug prescription. 124 *American Journal of Psychiatry* 877 (Jan. 1968). The paraphrased questions and responses in the text are based on findings of a conference on psychiatric drugs and the law summarized in Dr. Appleton's paper.

54. Excerpt from letter, April 1967, from James L. Goddard, Commissioner of FDA, published in Appleton, *id.* at 879.

55. *Id.*

56. Appleton, *supra* note 53 at p. 381.

57. Knecht v. Gilman, 488 F.2d 1136 (8th Cir. 1973) (apomorphine used to induce vomiting for minor breach of hospital rules); Nelson v. Heyne, 491 F.2d 352 (7th Cir. 1974) (thorazine to control outbursts of juvenile residents).

58. Adapted from guidelines for aversive drug conditioning specified by 8th Circuit Court, Knecht v. Gilman, 488 F.2d 1136, and the more stringent requirements set by the federal district court in Wyatt v. Hardin [No. 3195-N (M.D. Ala., Feb. 28, 1975, modified July 1, 1975) formerly known as Wyatt v. Stickney, 344 F. Supp. 387 (M.D. Ala. 1972), *aff'd.* in part *sub nom* Wyatt v. Aderholt, 503 F.2d 1305 (5th Cir. 1974)]. Wyatt v. Hardin requires additional approval of a five-member Extraordinary Treatment Committee appointed by the court and the representation of the patient by legal counsel appointed by the Committee [cf., sec. 2d–e, as reprinted in 1 *Mental Disability Law Reporter* 55, 56 (July–August 1976)].

59. Michigan Dept. of Mental Health Administrative Manual, Ch. 04, sec. 005-0002, as amended Oct. 1976.

60. *Id. See generally,* Schwartz, V. E. Civil liability for causing suicide. 24 *Vanderbilt Law Review* 217 (1971).

61. Terri Lee Halderman, et al. v. Pennhurst State School and Hospital, et al., C.A. No. 74-1345 (E.D. Pa. March 17, 1978) as reported in 2 *Mental Disability Law Reporter* 213, 215 (Sept.–Dec. 1977).

62. Frederic v. U.S., 246 F. Supp. 368 (D.C. Ala. 1965); Hernandez v. Baruch, 224 A.2d 109 (N.J. 1968).

63. Katz v. State, 46 Misc. 2d 61, 258 N.Y.S.2d 912 (Ct. Cl. 1965).

64. In *Aiken v. Clary* (396 S.W.2d 668, Sup. Ct. Mo. 1965) the patient's signing of a brief 125-word standard form (AMA form No. 31 "Consent to Shock Therapy," 1961) was held inadequate.

65. These recommendations are adapted from *Report of the Department of Mental Hygiene [California] Task Force on Patients' Rights* (Nov. 4, 1972), in Shapiro, M. H. Legislating the control of behavior control: Autonomy and the coercive use of organic therapies. 47 *Southern California Law Review* 237 (1974), 350–351. Slightly different guidelines have been specified by the Minnesota Supreme Court in Price v. Sheppard, 239 N.W.2d 905 (Minn. 1976), and by statute in Tennessee, Public Ch. 489, S.B. 997 (March 1976).

66. No. 3195-N (M.D. Ala., Feb. 28, 1975, modified July 1, 1975).

67. "No lobotomy, psychosurgery or other unusual, hazardous or intrusive surgical procedure designed to alter or affect a patient's mental condition shall be performed on any patient confined at any institution maintained by or under the control of the defendants." Wyatt v. Hardin, *supra* note 58, as reprinted in 1 *Mental Disability Law Reporter* 55–56 (July–August 1976).

68. Kaimowitz, *supra* note 39.

69. *Id.* at 40.

70. According to one commentary on the Detroit psychosurgery case, attorney Gabe Kaimowitz, representing himself and other individual taxpayers, filed suit on behalf of the patient "John Doe," without first consulting the patient. The suit asked that "John

Doe's'' custody be removed from the Lafayette Clinic physicians (against their wishes) and be given to law professor Ralph Slovenko, despite the fact that Professor Slovenko had not previously agreed to this arrangement. Detail reported in Slovenko, R. Commentary on psychosurgery. 5 *Hastings Center Report* 19, 22 (Oct. 1975). The *Kaimowitz* decision has been soundly criticized for its confused reasoning by several legal commentators. *See, e.g.,* Friedman, *supra* note 42 at p. 82; Singer, R. Consent of the unfree: Medical experimentation and behavior modification in the closed institution, Parts I and II. 1 *Law and Human Behavior* 1, 101 (1977).

71. E.g., Mass. Mental Health Regulations 181 (May 1, 1973) (psychosurgery); DHEW, 39 *Federal Regulations* 18914 (1974). *See generally,* Note, Beyond the "cuckoo's nest'': A proposal for federal regulation of psychosurgery. 12 *Harvard Journal of Legislation* 610 (June 1975).

72. Oregon Revised Statutes, sec. 426.700-.755 (1974).

73. E.g., 39 *Fed. Reg.* 18914 (1974); 39 *Fed. Reg.* 30655-56.

74. Aden v. Younger, 129 Cal. Rptr. 535 (App. Ct. 1976).

75. Civil Act. No. 73-19434-AW (Wayne Co., Mich., Cir. Ct. July 10, 1973) quoted in 2 *Prison Law Reporter* 433, 477 (1973).

76. Memorandum opinion in Souder v. McGuire, No. 74-590 (M.D. Pa., Dec. 9, 1976) as reported in 1 *Mental Disability Law Reporter* 264 (Jan.–Feb. 1977).

77. Whitree v. State, 65 Misc. 2d 691, 290 N.Y.S.2d 486 (1968).

78. Foster, C. T. Free exercise of religion as a defense to prosecution for a narcotic or psychedelic drug offense. 35 A.L.R.3rd 940; [Finer, J. J. Psychedelics and religious freedom. 19 Hastings Law Journal 667 (1968).] Leary v. U.S., 383 F.2d 851 (C.A. 5 Tex. 1967), 392 F.2d 220, *rev'd in part* 395 U.S. 6, 23 L. Ed. 2d 57 (1969); U.S. v. Kuch, 288 F. Supp. 439, 35 A.L.R.3rd 922 (D.C. Dist. Ct. 1968).

79. Lester v. Aetna, *supra* note 36 (patient's "full freedom to contract'' argument not sustained). *See generally,* Bomstein, M. S. The forcible administration of drugs to prisoners and mental patients. 9 *Clearinghouse Review* 379, 386–387 (Oct. 1975); Jackson, *supra* note 41.

80. Note, Conditioning and other technologies used to "treat?'' "rehabilitate?'' "demolish?'' prisoners and mental patients. 45 *Southern California Law Review* 616, 665–666; Bomstein, *supra* note 79. However, the Minnesota Supreme Court held the ECT was not per se a violation of the 8th amendment. Price v. Sheppard, 239 N.W. 2d 905 (Minn. 1976).

81. Mackey v. Procunier, 477 F.2d 352 (9th Cir. 1973). *See also,* Reimringer, M. J., Morgan, S. W., & Bramwell, P. F. Succinylcholine as a modifier of acting-out behavior. 77 *Clinical Medicine* 28 (July 1970); Sanderson, R. E., Campbell, D., and Laverty, S. G. An investigation of a new aversive conditioning treatment for alcoholism. 24 *Quarterly Journal of Studies on Alcohol* 261 (June 1963).

82. N.Y. Mental Hygiene Law, sec. 81.19(a) (Supp. 1974): "Every person charged with a crime who, while in custody or when he appears before the court, shall state, indicate, or show symptoms or it otherwise appears, that he is a narcotic addict, shall undergo a medical examination to determine whether he is a narcotic addict.''

83. Shepard v. Bowe, 250 Ore. 288, 442 P.2d 238 (1968); Kastigar v. U.S., 406 U.S. 441 (1972).

84. Sec. 408 of the Federal Drug Abuse Office and Treatment Act of 1972 (cf., 21 U.S.C.

sec. 1175, Supp. 1974); Comprehensive Drug Prevention and Control Act of 1970 (*cf.,* 42 U.S.C. sec. 242a, 1970; and 21 U.S.C. sec. 872c, 1970).

85. 21 U.S.C. sec. 1175(a) (as amended 1974).

86. 21 U.S.C. sec. 1175(b) (2) (C), as amended 1974.

87. Perlman, H. and Jaszi, P. *Legal issues in addict diversion.* Lexington, Mass.: Lexington Books, 1976, pp. 100–101. This volume is an excellent and comprehensive source of case and statute law relative to addict identification, right to counsel, confidentiality, and termination from diversion programs.

88. 21 U.S.C. sec. 872(c) (1970); 37 Fed. Reg. 6943 (April 6, 1972).

89. People v. Saldivar, 249 Cal. App. 2d 670, 57 Cal. Rptr. 731 (1967). Probably some coercive pressure exists to "volunteer," but whether *Miranda*-type warnings are appropriate is debatable (*cf.,* Miranda v. Arizona, 384 U.S. 218 [1973]).

90. Schmerber v. California, 384 U.S. 757 (1966) (blood sample from unconsenting driver okay); Blackford v. U.S., 247 F.2d 745 (9th Cir. 1957) (rectal search okay); Huguez v. U.S., 406 F.2d 366 (9th Cir. 1968) (forceful rectal search prohibited); Blefare v. U.S., 362 F.2d 870 (9th Cir. 1966) (use of emetic okay).

91. Committee for GI Rights v. Callaway, 307 F. Supp. 934 (D.D.C. 1974), *rev'd* 518 F.2d 466 (D.C. Cir. 1975) (appealed on basis of 4th Amendment search and seizure protection, not 5th Amendment). The circuit court noted, at p. 474, that the need for discipline may render procedures constitutionally permissible in the military that would not be so outside of it.

92. U.S. v. Ruiz, 23 U.S.C.M.A. 181, 48 C.M.R. 797 (1974) (based on Article 31 of Code of Military Justice banning forced self-incrimination).

CHAPTER 6

Token Economies

A *token economy* is an environmental arrangement, normally found in institutional settings, whereby tokens or similar evidence of earned credits are used to purchase items, services, and privileges. The tokens or credits are issued by one person to another to reinforce certain desired behaviors.[1] In an institution, a token economy can act as a motivating environment to prevent behavioral deterioration and the weakening of social behaviors because, presumably, tangible feedback motivates the individual to participate in socially useful activities during the period of treatment.

EXPERIMENTAL AND THERAPEUTIC APPLICATIONS

Tokens may be used to reinforce behaviors that will later generalize to social situations outside the institution, or tokens may be used directly in normal social situations. Researchers have established token economies in various social settings and among diverse populations—for example, in a halfway house with delinquents, in a psychology clinic with stutterers, on a college campus with automobile drivers or bus riders, in classrooms with retarded children, in a community agency with low-income parents, and in a campground with a general population.[2] Tokens or credits control behavior only to the extent that they can be eventually exchanged for goods, services, and privileges which a particular individual desires. Money is the most common generalized token reinforcer.

The selection of effective reinforcers is sometimes made difficult by the idiosyncratic nature of individual preferences or by an apparent lack of convenient reinforcers. In some human and animal research, a "deprivation operation" is used.[3] This involves the withholding of food, water, sexual contact, and so on for the purpose of potentiating the reinforcing aspect of a particular item or activity. Another approach involves the use of the "Premack Principle," which states that the opportunity to engage in those behaviors that occur naturally with the *higher* frequency (or probability) can be used to strengthen a *lower* frequency (or probability) behavior.[4] Thus, a school child who works 15 minutes on math problems (a less probable activity) can be "rewarded" by five minutes of reading (a more probable activity).

In institutions, effective reinforcers have typically included ground and visitor privileges, supervised walks, more attractive meal arrangements, the opportunity to wear one's own clothes, improved sleeping arrangements, special room decorations, and the like. Questions have been raised in the courts, however, as to whether some contingent reinforcers are not, in fact, rights that are guaranteed in the Constitution.

CONSTITUTIONAL PROTECTIONS

The use of token economies should be viewed, as any other specialized behavior modification procedure, in the general context of civil rights and duties.[5] Hence, case and statutory law relative to prisoners and to civilly committed mental patients serve as relevant guidelines. (See Chapters 2 and 3.) The use of deprivation procedures to increase motivation should be employed, if at all, with considerable caution. Generally, "privileges" may be withheld but basic "rights" may not—unless there is a valid consent or waiver. Furthermore, almost any withdrawal procedure, even those involving only privileges, may be interpreted as "punishment." (See Chapter 4.)

A treatment procedure that withdraws or withholds substantial privileges from patients should probably involve due process procedures such as notifying the patients, giving them an opportunity to present questions and an opposing view, and allowing them to appeal to an impartial group such as a human rights committee.

There has been considerable discussion in the literature about which items and activities in institutions can be considered basic, constitutionally guaranted rights, and those which may be considered privileges (or "contingent rights"). Because opinions differ, it has sometimes been difficult for treatment personnel to design token economies. *Wyatt* v. *Stickney*[6] has provided perhaps the most detailed and extensive specification of rights as "minimum constitutional standards." The following list is a summary of rights enumerated in *Wyatt*. Patients must be permitted to:

Visit and make telephone calls (similar to the right of patients at other
     public hospitals)
Send sealed mail
Wear own clothes
Attend religious services
Interact with the opposite sex (with supervision)
Avoid forced labor
Take a shower and use the toilet in privacy
Use a day room area with reading lamps, television, and other recreational
     facilities
Have a comfortable bed, a closet or locker, a chair, and a bedside table
Have frequent changes of bedding and other linen
Have meals in dining rooms (that provide at minimimum the Recom-
     mended Daily Dietary Allowances as developed by the National
     Academy of Sciences
Have an individualized treatment plan
Have appropriate treatment for mental disorders and physical illnesses
Have transitional treatment and care when released from the hospital
Have a humane psychological and physical environment that is comforta-
     ble and safe.

Four years later the same Court established similar but less extensive standards
for inmates in the Alabama penal system.[7] The following list summarizes some of
the rights that inmates must be permitted:

Send or receive an unlimited number of letters (with postage and paper
     supplied by the institution for five letters per week)
Receive visitors on at least a weekly basis (with reasonable time and space
     for each visit)
Participate in a meaningful job based on abilities and interests and accord-
     ing to institutional needs
Have toothbrushes, toothpaste, shaving cream, razors, razor blades, soap,
     shampoo, and combs without charge
Have adequate clean clothing
Have a storage locker with a lock
Have clean bed linen and towels weekly
Have access to household cleaning supplies
Have a bed, clean mattress, and blankets
Have a minimum of 60 sq. ft. of living space.
Have three wholesome and nutritious meals per day (served with proper
     eating and drinking utensils)
Have a special diet if required for reasons of health or religion

Have the opportunity to participate in educational, vocational, and recre-
    ational programs
Have the opportunity to participate in a transitional program designed to
    aid in re-entry into society
Be released from voluntary segregation immediately upon request
Be transferred if mental health care is required at another institution (with
    some care provided within the prison)
Be protected from violence.[8]

This list is not intended to be a complete summary of all rights. Nor is it likely
that the Court listed all of the protected rights. For example, adequate medical care
is mentioned only for inmates in isolation, but it must also be provided for the
general inmate population. In addition, access to religious services should be
allowed, but it is not mentioned by the Court.

A sample of an impermissible program was the short-lived involuntary problem at a federal prison psychiatric facility for troublesome convicts.[9] In this program, there were three levels of privileges, and prisoners could work their way up to
a more privileged level after meeting well-defined behavioral goals of the previous
level. The plaintiffs alleged that the lowest level consisted of an environment
stripped of amenities in which inmates were sometimes shackled to bare beds,
forced to eat out of large bowls with their hands, and not released for toileting. Two
of the three court-appointed investigators prepared less than favorable reports for the
Court.[10] The plaintiffs' argument—that the beginning level was cruel and unusual
punishment and a violation of privacy—was not adjudicated because of the prison's
termination of the program. The court did, nonetheless, establish that a behavior
modification procedure that begins by substantial deprivation represents a sufficient
change in status that prospective participants must be accorded the *due process* of
notice, hearing, and an opportunity to protest.

Apparently the use of aversive stimuli is rather rare in published reports. In
one out of 10 surveyed studies, patients were served a blended diet or had to sleep
on a cot. Over a period of one year, no patient was served the blended diet longer
than one day or had to sleep on a cot for more than a total of three nights.[11]

Another possible precedent involved several high school students, suspected of
inciting a lunchroom disturbance, who were summarily suspended from school.[12]
The majority of the Supreme Court justices held that this action sufficiently influenced the students' freedom of association and the way other people viewed them
that due process required at least a notice and a hearing. By analogy, establishing a
token economy within an institution that would isolate and socially stigmatize
participants without giving them or their legal guardians notice and an opportunity
to protest might be unconstitutional.

Because token economies involve overt compensation for therapeutic tasks,
they fall more obviously under the Thirteenth Amendment protections (prohibiting

slavery and involuntary servitude) than under other therapeutic requirements placed upon patients by mental health professionals (e.g., "Keep a diary," "Do not drink alcohol at work," "Do not get into arguments with the boss, or "Attend group sessions") where no tangible compensation is given for patient compliance. If the therapeutic task involves labor for which a person would normally receive compensation, then the Thirteenth Amendment is applicable. The general thrust of case law suggests that if: (1) hospital operation and maintenance is not involved, (2) the task is professionally approved and integrated into an individualized treatment program, and (3) the task is supervised by a staff member to assure therapeutic worth, then Thirteenth Amendment requirements have been met.[13] These particular guidelines do not appear to handicap any patient-oriented, legitimate token economy.

Where hospital operation and maintenance is involved, all *involuntary* labor may be prohibited whether therapeutic or not, and *voluntary* labor will have to be compensated (perhaps at the level of the prevailing federal minimum wage) as well as have a therapeutic purpose. Persons who voluntarily engage in therapeutic labor may be unable to perform as efficiently as a person not physically or mentally labeled. On that theory, the person might be compensated at a rate that bears the same approximate relation to the statutory minimum wage as his ability to perform that particular job bears to the ability of a person not so afflicted. Residents may also be required to perform tasks of a *personal* housekeeping nature such as the making of one's own bed. A summary record of all therapeutic tasks and compensated labor should be noted in the patient's record. Most token economies have a "banking system" that provides a convenient and participant-monitored accounting routine.

If necessary, the institution might remove some rights, only temporarily, to protect the health or safety of the patient or other persons in the institution. Neither patients nor other citizens have the right to physically attack other persons, to frighten others by falsely shouting "fire," or to swallow razor blades as an act of worship. Furthermore, some basic rights, such as freedom of assembly, are frequently removed from committed mental patients for purposes of safety and public order. These rights should not be unilaterally removed for the purposes of treatment. It is important to distinguish between the purpose of safety and the purpose of treatment.

RIGHT TO TREATMENT

Token economies appear to be particularly well adapted to meeting some of the "right to treatment" requirements for involuntary patients. As detailed in *Wyatt*, individual treatment plans should contain, among other elements, a statement of the particular problem, description of treatment goals, description of staff involvement, and criteria for discharge. Because token economies must specify target behavior, the contingencies for reinforcement, a method of token delivery, and a range of back-up reinforcers (e.g., special entertainment or greater access to telephones), the efforts of the staff are more accountable.

Some authors and institutional personnel have found it convenient to misuse the phrase "token economy" or other treatment terms to describe or disguise improper discipline and control practices. In *Morgan* versus *Sproat*,[14] the court carefully examined the Progressive Phase Program (a tier privilege system) at the Oakley Training School in Mississippi which was labeled as a behavior modification program. The court observed, "The Progressive Phase Program is supposed to be based upon behavior modification techniques. However, the behavior modification specialists who evaluated the phase program found that it violated all of the basic principles of behavior modification."[15] The court thus appropriately declined to decide, in the abstract, constitutional aspects of behavior modification programs.

Another federal district court similarly noted the lack of adequate professional treatment design by holding that "It is not sufficient for defendants to contend that merely removing a child from his environment and placing him in a 'structured' situation constitutes constitutionally adequate treatment.... Nor do the Texas Youth Centers' sporadic attempts at...' behavior modification' through the use of point systems rise to the dignity of professional programs geared to individual juveniles."[16] Clearly, the use of a point system in an irratic or traditionally "common sense" manner is not a token economy in the sense that it was originally intended by the psychologists who developed such systems. Such inadvertent misleading of clients, or deliberate deception, has resulted in both public misunderstanding and technically ill-conceived legislative proposals.[17]

In enumerating and protecting inmate or patient rights, courts frequently rely on philosophical concepts such as "freedom" or "liberty." It is these concepts, operationally translated into conditions of privacy and comfort, that can be arranged to make an individual's behavior more appropriate and self-fulfilling. It has been argued that only the most primitive consequences (e.g., food, beds) can motivate the development of socially adaptive behavior in certain chronic patients.[18] If these effective contingent reinforcers were legally restricted, then chronic patients might be not only destined to spend their lives functioning poorly in an institutional setting, but also be deprived of their right to the best treatment available. "In the psychologist's view it would surely be an ironic tragedy if, in the name of an illusory ideal such as freedom, the law were to deny the therapist's only effective tools he has to restore the chronic psychotic to his health—and his place in the community."[19]

Legal restraints may, however, force treatment personnel to be more creative with certain chronically disabled persons; or perhaps the continued disability of such individuals will be the social price paid to prevent more general abuse of administrative power (as in *Clonce* v. *Richardson*). The effectiveness of a treatment regime may be weighed in the judicial determination of the legal adequacy of a program.[20] Several studies indicate that token economies, especially those involving patient decision-making groups, are frequently more effective than traditional and often vaguely defined treatment regimes in achieving community adjustments after release.[21] There is no legal requirement that any given treatment be successful with any given patient. But institutions should adopt treatment programs that demonstrate good-faith efforts and provide some system of accountability to those purchasing their service.

DISCUSSION

By this time, the reader should be sensitive to the discrimination the law makes between a "right" or a "privilege" versus an "obligation." The right to worship does not impose an obligation upon a citizen to go to church. Rights may sometimes be waived in a variety of matters (e.g., formal hearing on a traffic ticket, confidentiality of hospital records). Mental patients may also waive rights, but courts will examine more closely than in normal circumstances the voluntariness of the waiver and the patient's understanding.[22] Most patient and state interests can be served by permitting waivers to participate in effective treatment programs. For example, in the area of behavioral programming, the state may have an interest in promoting the rehabilitation, independence, and productiveness of its citizens. "To the extent certain hazardous or intrusive procedures are useful for behavior modification, permitting waiver of due process rights or rights of privacy and autonomy may further those state interests."[23] Because treatment is, according to *Wyatt* and other cases, the primary goal of confinement, courts may feel justified in authorizing restrictions of patients' rights in order to further such goals. Several courts have ordered the establishment of a permanent human rights committee. An advocacy committee of this nature could well be the appropriate body to approve any non-routine contingency management system involving basic patient ammenities.[24]

Although a waiver may be made by an incompetent patient's legal counsel or guardian *ad litem*, a thorough review procedure should be followed, especially when the patient does not wish to waive his right.[25] Even procedurally suitable waivers could be challenged under two theories: (1) A person is not permitted to waive a right that produces a result contrary to social policy—for example, allowing mutilation by another person or giving up the right to have children as a condition of probation for robbery.[26] (2) The doctrine of "unconstitutional conditions" suggests that the right of the government to withhold a benefit does not imply that the government may grant the benefit only on the condition that the recipient surrender a constitutional rights (particularly in an unrelated area). That is, a government which offers many benefits should not be permitted, through bargaining procedures, to erode fundamental liberties.[27] In situations where the goals of the treatment program are legally permissible and the reinforcers to be used do not jeopardize fundamental rights (i.e. involve only "nonbasic" consequences), special consent or waiver from patient might not be required.[28]

If a patient waives a right, as a condition to participate in a treatment program, s/he may also revoke that waiver. However, a program using only mild deprivation would probably lack motivational force if a patient revoked whenever s/he felt the deprivation. One approach might be to permit a patient to revoke his/her waiver with immediate effectiveness one or two times. Subsequently, however, when s/he wanted back into the program, it might be with the agreement that revocation would be subject to a brief, reasonable delay.[29]

With respect to waivers and revocation of waivers which are permissible by prisoners and involuntary mental patients, the situation is unclear and ambiguous. "The law" is not a static list of rules, but rather a constantly changing code of permissible conduct molded from complex conflicts of value and interest. Token economies represent only one small subset of behavioral interventions inducing social conflict which might be partially resolved by the application of legal thought and procedure.

NOTES

1. Allyon, T. and Azrin, N. *The token economy: A motivational system for therapy and rehabilitation.* N. Y.: Appleton-Century-Crofts, 1968, p. 216. For a brief historical and somewhat critical commentary on token economies, *see* Gagnon, J. H. and Davison, G. C. Asylums, the token economy, and the metrics of mental life. 7 *Behavior Therapy* 528 (1976).

2. Phillips, E., Wolfe, M., and Fixsen, D. Achievement place: Modification of the behaviors of predelinquent boys within a token economy. 4 *Journal of Applied Behavior Analysis* 45 (1971); Ingham, R. J. and Andrews, G. An analysis of a token economy in stuttering therapy. 6 *Journal of Applied Behavior Analysis* 219 (1973); Foxx, R. M. and Hake, D. F. Gasoline conservation: A procedure for measuring and reducing the driving of college students. 10 *Journal of Applied Behavior Analysis* 61 (1977); Everett, P. B., Hayward, S. C., and Meyers, A. W. The effects of a token reinforcement procedure on bus ridership. 7 *Journal of Applied Behavior Analysis* 1 (1974); Zimmerman, E. H., Zimmerman, I., and Russell, C. D. Differential effects of token reinforcement on instruction-following behavior in retarded students instructed as a group. 2 *Journal of Applied Behavior Analysis* 101 (1969); Miller, L. K. Freedom money: A token economy approach to organizing self-help activities among low-income families. In Annual Report No.1 (University of Kansas, Family and Community Research Project), Dec. 1969 (mimeo.); Allyon, *supra* note 1 at 48 (campground). For an authoritative summary of token economies, *see* Kazdin, A. E. and Bootzin, R. R. The token economy: An evaluative review. 5 *Journal of Applied Behavior Analysis* 1 (1972).

3. Laboratory animals are often systematically underfed to bring them to 80 percent of normal body weight. For less severe human laboratory studies, *see* McClelland, D. C. and Atkinson, J. W. the projective expressions of needs: The effect of different intensities of hungr drive on perception. 25 *Journal of Psychology* 205 (1948); Dinsmoore, J. A. the effect of hunger on discriminated responding. 47 *Journal of Abnormal and Social Psychology* 66 (1952).

4. Premack, D. Toward empirical behavior laws, 1: Positive reinforcement. 66 *Psychological Review* 219 (1959).
5. Wexler, D. B. Token and taboo: Behavior modification, token economies, and the law. 61 *California Law Review* 81, 93 (1973).
6. Wyatt v. Stickney, 325 F. Supp. 781 (M.D. Ala. 1971), *enforced in* 344 F. Supp. 373 (M.D. Ala. 1972), *aff'd.sub non*. Wyatt v. Aderholt, 503 F.2d 1305 (5th Cir. 1974). *Critized in* Burnham v. Dept. Public Health of State of Georgia, 349 F. Supp. 1335 (1972) (no federal statute requiring right to treatment).
7. Pugh v. Locke, 406 F. Supp. 318 (M.D. Ala. 1976).
8. *Id*. at 332–335.
9. Clonce v. Richardson, 379 F. Supp. 338 (W.D. Mo. 1974). O'Brien, K. E. Tokens and tiers in corrections: An analysis of legal issues in behavior modification. 3 *Northeast Journal on Prison Law* 15 (Fall 1976).
10. Reports cited in Singer, R. Consent of the unfree: Medical experimentation and behavior modification in the closed institution, Part I. 1 *Law and Human Behavior* 1, 36, n. 142 (1977).
11. Greenberg, D. J. and Meagher, R. B., Jr. The courts and the token economy: An empirical approach to the problem. 8 *Behavior Therapy* 377, 381 (1977).
12. Gross v. Lopez, 95 S. Ct. 729 (1975).
13. Wyatt, 325 F. Supp. 781 at sec. 18A&B. Jobsen v. Henne, 355 F.2d 129 (2d Cir. 1966). *See generally*, Wexler, *supra* note 5 at 90, 93, 132.
14. 432 F. Supp. 1130 (S.D. Miss. 1977).
15. *Id*. at 1147.
16. Morales v. Turman, 364 F. Supp. 166 (E.D. Tex. 1973), *vac*. 535 F.2d 864 (8th Cir. 1976), *rev'd on other grounds* 430 U.S. 322, 97 S. Ct. 1189 (1977).
17. *See,e.g.*, "Patients have a right not to be subjected to treatment procedures such as lobotomy, adversive [sic] reinforcement conditioning, or other unusual or hazardous treatment procedures without their express and informed consent after consultation with legal counsel. . . ." State of Montana, An Act to Provide for Determination and Treatment of the Seriously Mentally Ill and those Suffering from Mental Disorders, Senate Bill No. 377 (May 1975), at sec. 22. The phrase "adversive reinforcement conditioning" is at best a technically inaccurate phrase, probably referring to punishment procedures and/or negative reinforcement. Under this law, withholding T.V. privileges from residents could apparently be restricted along with "other [?] unusual or hazardous treatment procedures". Furthermore, who is to pay for legal counsel?
18. Allyon, *supra* note 1, at 269; *also*, Bandura, A. *Principles of behavior modification*. New York: Holt, Rinehart & Winston, 1969, p. 227.
19. Wexler, *supra* note 5 at 101.
20. *See,e.g.*, Faucette v. Cunbar, 61 Cal. Rptr. 97 (App. 1967) (suggesting that a parole authority waive its usual requirement of Nalline test for a drug addict to permit his participation in a new, potentially effective treatment program); Sas v. State of Maryland, 334 F.2d 506 (4th Cir. 1964); People ex rel. Blunt v. Narcotic Addiction Control Commission, 295 N.Y.S.2d 276 (Sup. Ct. 1968).
21. Greenberg and Meagher, *supra* note 11 (summary of ten studies; data on post-treatment effectiveness are minimal but somewhat positive). For contrary opinion without data, *see* Gagnon and Davison, *supra* note 1: "The success of token economies in mental hospitals

rests on the fact that patients are not suffering from economic irrationality, and that they will learn to adapt pre-existing economic modes of behavior to deal with token environments. . . . The token economy teaches the wrong things—the first is that the world is just and the second that good behavior is generally rewarded.'' (p. 534). (Couldn't a token economy be run with variable schedules and contingencies, thus making it "less just" and more realistic?)

22. *See, e.g.*, Pate v. Robinson, 383 U.S. 375 (1966) (the Supreme court did not permit the state to claim both that the alleged offender was mentally incompetent to stand trial *and* that he had waived his right to a hearing on his incompetency); *In re* Walker, 77 Cal. Rptr. 16 (1969) (lack of understanding of consequences).

23. Friedman, P. R. Legal regulation of applied behavior analysis in mental institutions and prisons. 17 *Arizona Law Review* 39, 70 (1975).

24. Baer, D. M. Behavior modification and the law: Implications of recent judicial decisions. 4 *Journal of Psychiatry and Law* 171, 205 (1976).

25. *See* guardian consent procedures in Chapter 5. *Also*, Quesnell v. State, 517 P.2d 568 (1973) (guardian waiver not valid over patient's objection).

26. *Cf.* People v. Domingues, 64 Cal. Rptr. 290 (App. 1967).

27. *See*, Note, Unconstitutional conditions. 73 *Harvard Law Review* 1595 (1960).

28. Wexler, D. B. Behavior modification and legal development. 18 *American Behavioral Scientist* 679 (1975); *see generally*, Wexler, D. B. Of rights and reinforcers. 11 *San Diego Law Review* 957 (1974).

29. Noted by Wexler in Reflections on the legal regulation of behavior modification in institutional settings. 17 *Arizona Law Review* 133, 139 (1975). In *Mims v. Boland*, 110 Ga. App. 477, 138 S.E.2d 902 (1964), a patient was not permitted to withdraw her consent to a medical procedure until it was "medically feasible" to terminate the procedure without detriment to the patient's health or life. Similarly, the repeated revocation of a waiver might be briefly delayed in the absence of harm to the patient until it was "therapeutically feasible" to terminate her from the program.

CHAPTER 7

Psychological Testing

If the "I.Q. test" were a new drug, it would probably never reach the marketplace. Manufacturers of new drugs are required by federal regulations to demonstrate that the material is both effective and safe. Intelligence tests:

- are probably not effective in measuring what the general public assumes intelligence to be (i.e., an inherited ability to succeed in high-prestige tasks)[1]
- have serious defects in some of the standard forms[2]
- can result in harm (e.g., placement in inappropriate educational programs)[3]

In everyday practice, there is the understandable tendency to conceive of test scores as cognitive potential even though the predictive validity of many tests for certain populations is unknown, particularly for those populations apparently in need of special treatment or remediation.[4] Projective personality tests such as the TAT and Rorschach have also come under social and legal attack.[5] In some instances, testing has been curtailed[6] and in its place other forms of evaluation such as, interviews and questionnaires for educational or job placement have been used in the decision process. Some types of interviews and questionnaires, however, also have low reliability and validity.[7] Of course unfair discriminations were made long before psychological testing became popular. If all testing (regardless of validity) were to stop, the impact, if any, is uncertain.[8]

Perhaps one of the most useful goals of legal inquiry into assessment procedures is to clarify the differences between using tests to make skilled placement decisions versus using tests to isolate individuals from education and employment opportunities due to some presumed biological deficit. Standardized assessment procedures might systematically describe what behavior is being measured, the task to which that behavior is demonstrably related, the conditions of the technique's proper use, and known distortions and potential risks. From a consumer perspective, the most common potential risks of testing involve unfair discrimination, self-incrimination, and invasion of privacy.

UNFAIR DISCRIMINATION

Two Supreme Court cases on testing[9] have outlined the procedures by which one can determine whether or not an assessment technique meets the nondiscrimination requirement of the 1964 Civil Rights Act.[10] Although both cases dealt with employment practices, a similar pattern of enforcement based on the Civil Rights Act can be expected in educational matters. According to the Education of the Handicapped Act[11], states are required to select and administer tests or other evaluation materials to handicapped children that are not unfairly discriminatory. The sequence of legal maneuvers is usually as follows:

1. A complaining party must make out at least a prima facie case of discrimination—that is , show that "the tests in question select applicants for hire or promotion in a racial pattern significantly different from that of the pool of applicants."[12]
2. After this *appearance* of discrimination is established, the burden shifts to the employer (or school, hospital, etc.) to prove that the tests are "job-related" (or educationally relevant). If the employer cannot meet this burden by having an adequate validation of the test procedure, then the court may award damages such as back pay and attorneys' fees to the plaintiff.
3. If the employer meets the burden of validation, then the plaintiff must show that "other tests or selection devices, without a similarly undesirable racial effect, would also serve the employer's legitimate interest in efficient and trustworthy workmanship.[13]

Good intention or the absence of any unfair discriminatory intent does not redeem testing procedures unrelated to job capabilities.[14] Even uniformly applied standards as measured by tests may be illegally discriminatory if they have an unfairly disproportionate impact upon minority persons, unless the employer can prove that the standards measure qualities essential to job performance.[15] A test may discriminate *between* individuals or groups but may not discriminate *against* them.

Several published guidelines exist for determining whether or not a test is job-related and professionally constructed.[16] In the case of *Albemarle Paper Com-*

pany v. *Moody,* the Supreme Court did not prohibit testing but found that the company's validation study was defective.[17] Abuse and incomplete analysis of validity is typically found where unsubstantiated inferences are made that some particular verbal and/or quantitative ability (such as a certain I.Q. score) is required to perform a job.[18] The general reputation of a test or its author is not sufficient evidence of validity. To the extent that construct or apparent validity is relied upon, it should be backed up by evidence of predictive validity.[19] There seems to be increasing emphasis upon the need to measure on-the-job performance rather than some ability indirectly related to job performance. Local or in-house validity studies may be helpful or necessary, although the extent to which employment test validities are situation-specific is a matter of discussion. Some investigators have suggested the possibility of validity generalization to new settings without additional studies.[20] Tests need substantial, not necessarily perfect, validity. Furthermore, other methods of assessment such as interviews, observation, and ratings by knowledgeable persons should supplement tests, if appropriate.

Both *Ethical Standards of Psychologists* and *Standards for Educational and Psychological Tests*, prepared by the American Psychological Association, make the test user responsible for supporting claims of validity and reliability.[21] Psychologists who are not members of the American Psychological Association may also be affected by these standards because these standards are incorporated into the licensing laws of at least 31 states.

Carefully developed testing programs may provide the best defense for selection procedures that *appear* to be discriminatory because of an adverse impact on a particular ethnic, age, or sex group.[22] But there is a potential risk of social stigma when selection criteria become explicit. For example, in some jurisdictions certain students must be tested in their primary language, using appropriate norms, and so on.[23] Such procedures may encourage the development of separate norms that appear on the surface to be discriminatory—for example, the acceptable score for male clerical applicants on the Short Employment Test is 93, while for a female, a score of only 79 is required.[24] In the interpretation of scores, it may be useful to discuss with the client the concept that a test score usually does not represent a specific point on a scale but rather a range of probable scores determined by the standard error of measurement. If the range of probable scores considerably overlap between two persons, there may not be the "marked difference in ability" required for selecting one person over the other on the basis of the test scores.[25]

In situations involving the use of tests for placement or research that require the classification of applicants by race, the examiner might consider obtaining permission from the state employment commission or similar agency before proceeding with the tests.[26] Although such permission might not be necessary, it could avoid misunderstanding and fears of unfair discrimination. Unnecessary testing of religious beliefs and practices, which are often strongly protected by the courts, should be avoided. As previously noted, unfair discrimination need not be intentional or deliberate for the examiner and/or employer to be legally liable.

Many of the problems involved in testing for employment can also be found in testing for educational admission, professional careers, and placement in special education or treatment programs. Examiners should be able to show that the tests are necessary and accurately assess the characteristics required for success in the program.[27] The use of I.Q. tests for placement in mental health treatment programs, special education classes, or decision-making in child custody cases requires special care.[28] This is because of the potentially coercive nature of these settings and the possibility of long-term, negative labeling effects.

The leading court cases have *not* held intelligence testing or ability grouping per se to be illegal.[29] But misuse of tests or grouping is. The factors to be considered, as a total system, include test validity, the avowed purpose of the testing, and the actual results of the testing. If, for example, testing is designed to assign students to a temporary compensatory educational program, but afterward almost no students ever leave the program, then assignments based on that testing can be prohibited.[30]

Unfair discrimination should be avoided against *all* persons. In a few instances, bias has been found in *favor* of minority group applicants or applicants from working-class backgrounds, but apparently some "benign discrimination" is acceptable.[31] The well-known and delicately balanced *Bakke* decision[32] decreed that race may be an element in university admissions policy but not serve as a basis for numerical quotas, unless a previous history of discrimination is involved. Shortly thereafter, the Supreme Court let stand—without comment—a federal appellate court ruling that approved numerical goals for one of the country's largest employers who had apparently previously discriminated against minorities and women.[33]

SELF-INCRIMINATION

Psychological testing in the employer-employee relationship has been analogized to the extraction of involuntary confessions and to the demand for self-incrimination.[34] Knowing that one's employment is possibly contingent upon submission to a test, an applicant may be economically persuaded into submitting. Conversely, psychological testing can be viewed as a voluntary procedure because the applicant or employee has implicitly consented to testing by completing the test or by accepting employment. An issue relevant to all situations where consent is required is whether such consent is truly voluntary and informed. In the school situation, the examiner should be sure that the parent clearly understands the purpose and uses of the tests given to the child prior to signing a consent form.

Two particular complications may arise with the use of personality tests: "Certain answers might be an admission of factual data which constitute a felony"[35] and people "could be falsely labeled neurotic, schizophrenic, or emotionally disturbed, even though they have committed no antisocial behavior. . . ."[36]

In situations of involuntary commitment to a mental institution, one commentator has suggested that the privilege against self-incrimination should apply to psychiatric examinations if the defendant has not raised an insanity defense or if post-conviction treatment is not provided.[37] The patient may remain silent at mental examinations or testing that could lead to involuntary commitment. The Supreme Court held that a state's attempt to force a prisoner into a psychiatric exam by an indefinite sentence after he had served maximum time was a violation of the Fifth Amendment.[38] Similar logic may be applied to tests, but there is very little case law on this matter. It may be necessary in some jurisdictions to inform (or warn) the person about the potential use of test information in order for it to be admissible later in a judicial hearing.[39] For example, a criminal defendant might have the right to have legal counsel present during his mental examination if the information from the examination is to be used to determine his quilt or innocence.[40] Generally, however, the courts have not found that a right exists to have legal counsel present during mental examinations that are to be used in determining whether a person should be committed to a mental health facility.[41]

The use of data from psychological tests in trials or formal hearings may be compared to the use of other types of information upon which expert opinion is based (e.g., breathalizers, electroencephalographs, X rays, as well as the traditional structured or unstructured interview). The admissibility of test data often seems to be based upon some judicial assessment of the scientific accuracy of the test weighted against costs in time, financial expense, and distraction of the jury.[42] The usefulness of psychological tests in legal proceedings is a matter of sharply divergent opinion. If tests are presented, the purpose for which the data are being used should be clearly defined, the rationale explained, reliability and validity standards presented (including appropriate norms for the individual tested), and some measures of probable error.

The likelihood of self-incrimination on the part of the test-taker may be reduced if the examiner is careful to avoid the erroneous assumption that the data answer the ultimate legal question being litigated. A defendant's guilt or mental competence is not finally determined by test data (or by any other kind of data). That matter is ultimately decided by the jury or judge using data and expert opinion as they see fit.[43]

INVASION OF PRIVACY

Privacy is a complex, subtle right concerned with maintaining individuality. Its scope and nature are still being defined by case law. In 1890, Samuel Warren and Louis Brandeis wrote a frequently quoted article, "The Right to Privacy," in which they stated that "the right to life has come to mean the right to enjoy life—the right to be let alone."[44] Later, Brandeis, dissenting in *Olmstead* v. *United States*, again wrote: "The makers of our Constitution ... sought to protect Americans in their beliefs, their thoughts, their emotions, and their sensations. They conferred, as against the Government, the right to be let alone—the most comprehensive of rights and the right most valued by civilized man.''[45] The forms of invasion may include public disclosure of private facts, publicly placing a person in a false light, commercial exploitation, and intrusion into the person's physical or mental solitude.[46] For conduct to constitute such an invasion, it must be such as would be offensive or objectionable to the reasonable man of ordinary sensibilities.[47] Mental health professionals *might* be held to a higher standard of conduct than the typical citizen in avoiding harm to a client's privacy.

To what extent psychological testing might constitute a wrongful invasion of privacy has not been significantly determined by the courts.[48] Commentators have suggested that the constitutional doctrine of privacy established by the Supreme Court in *Griswold* extends to governmental efforts to compel individuals to disclose information through lie detectors and psychological tests.[49] However, the court was reluctant in *Merriken* v. *Cressman*[50] to expand the interpretation of *Griswold* and *Roe's* precendental values beyond the family relationship context in which they were decided. The questionnaires used in *Merriken* contained intimate questions about family relationships and asked students to identify other students who made unusual or odd remarks. Although the results were to be confidential, information about potential drug abusers was to be distributed to school personnel including athletic coaches, PTA officers, and school board members of the senior high school. The Court noted that although the students were juveniles, they still maintained a right to privacy.

The following letter was sent to the parents to obtain consent on behalf of their children:

> Dear Parent:
>
> This letter is to inform you that this fall we are initiating a Drug Program the aim of which is to identify children who may be susceptible to drug abuse and to intervene with concrete measures to help these children. Diagnostic testing will be a part of this program and will provide data enabling the prevention program to be specific and positive.
>
> This program will be started in Grade 8. We ask your support and cooperation in this program and assure you of the confidentiality of these studies. If you wish to examine or receive further information regarding the program, please feel free to contact the principal in your school. If you do not wish your child to participate in the program, notify your principal of this decision.[51]

The Court did *not* consider this letter an adequate request for consent for several reasons: The parents were not given information about the use of the results as a criterion for initiating treatment, nor were they told about what persons might see or use the information. The parents were required to notify the principal if they did *not* want their children to participate, rather than signing a form granting permission. The Court called the letter a 'book-of-the-month club' approach in which a parent's silence would be construed as acquiescence."[52] The Court also characterized the letter as a promotional inducement to buy that lacked "the necessary substance to give a parent the opportunity to give knowing, intelligent, and aware consent."[53]

The *Merriken* court further noted that there was a need to balance individual privacy against the right of the government to invade that privacy for the sake of public interest. But the Court concluded that the test and the resulting program did not have sufficient authenticity and credibility [validity?] in fighting the drug problem to justify the invasion of privacy. "There is too much of a chance that the wrong people for the wrong reasons will be singled out and counselled in the wrong manner."[54]

An invasion of privacy of the tested persons might occur if their test scores or interpretations are distributed to unauthorized individuals without consent of the person who was tested. In *Detroit Edison* v. *NLRB*,[55] a labor union wanted actual test scores for use in a grievance proceeding. Several employees who took tests were not recommended for advancement by the company on the basis of their test scores. The company psychologist refused to supply the test scores to the union until the employees tested signed a waiver releasing the psychologist from his pledge that the test scores would be kept confidential.[56] The union refused to obtain these releases. The case eventually came before the Supreme Court which upheld the confidentiality of the test scores. The Court noted, "There is nothing in this record to suggest that the Company promised the examinees that their scores would remain confidential in order to further parochial concerns or to frustrate subsequent union attempts to process employee grievances. . . . Under these circumstances, any possible impairment of the function of the Union in processing the grievances of employees is more than justified by the interests served in conditioning the disclosure of the test scores upon the consent of the very employees whose grievance is being processed.[57] Anonymously coded data would perhaps meet the needs of the union while at the same time preserving the privacy rights of the tested individuals.

As illustrated here, the enforcement of the right to privacy usually involves the balancing of competing and legitimate interests. The Supreme Court in *Poe* v. *Ullman*[58] observed that "the right to privacy . . . is not an absolute." A balance between *Griswold* and *Poe* might be struck by strictly limiting investigative incursions via testing procedures to (1) those observed or reliably inferred behaviors that have a demonstrated relevance to the matter at hand, and (2) those methods that are scientifically valid and are the least intrusive necessary to achieve a legally permissible objective.[59]

NOTES

1. Cronbach, L. J. Five decades of public controversy over mental testing. 30 *American Psychologist* 1 (1975) (subtle shift of purpose of tests from prediction to potentiality);

Kagan, J. The magic aura of the I.Q. 57 *Saturday Review* 92 (Dec. 4, 1971) (popular notions critiqued).

2. "The Stanford-Binet Intelligence Scale is an old, old vehicle. It has led a distinguished life as a pioneer in the bootstrap operation that is the assessment enterprise. Its time is just about over. Requiescat in pace." Review by Freides, D., in Buros, O. K. (Ed.), *The seventh mental measurements yearbook* (Vol. 1). Highland Park, N.J.: Gryphon Press, 427, 428 (1972). *See also* McClelland, D. C. Testing for competence rather than for "intelligence." 28 *American Psychologist* 1 (1973). Tests should conform, unless there are reasonable grounds for exception, with essential requirements as set forth in the American Psychological Association's *Standards for educational and psychological tests*. Washington, D.C.: APA, 1974.

3. Diana v. State Bd. of Education, Civil No. C-70 RFR (N.O. Cal. Jan. 1970) (court-ordered retesting of 30,000 children using a Spanish language test resulted in reclassification of 45 percent of the children and a 15-point increase in I.Q. scores. The suit, settled when the defendant agreed to change classification procedures, alleged that the school district previously refused to reclassify because it stood to lose a subsidy of $550 per child in state aid for special education classes). Hobson v. Hansen, 269 F. Supp. 401 (D.D.C. 1967), *aff'd sub nom* Smuck v. Hobson, 408 f.2d 175 (D.C. Cir. 1969) (two-thirds of students misclassified into 1 of 4 tracks on basis of I.Q. scores alone). PARC v. Pennsylvania, 343 F. Supp. 279 (E.D. Pa. 1972) (25 percent of retarded children misclassified).

4. If a person's score is low and the test is interpreted as an index of *aptitude*, then educational resources may be withdrawn and the validity of the test therefore challenged by an interest group. If the same test is interpreted as an index of *achievement*, then resources may be increased and the validity of the test may be at least covertly accepted by the same group. Flaugher, R.L. The many definitions of test bias. 33 *American Psychologist,* 671, 672 (1978). *See also* Lewardoski, D. G. and Saccuzzo, D. P. The decline of psychological testing. 7 *Professional Psychology* 177 (1976) (overall predictive validity acceptable for groups but not for individuals. This has been a long-standing criticism by operant psychologists of nearly all normative research).

5. Note, Legal implications of standardized ability tests in employment and education. 68 *Columbia Law Review* 708 (1968); Lykken, D. T. Psychology and the lie detector industry. 29 *American Psychologist* 725 (1974); Mercer, J. R. I.Q.: The lethal lable. 6 *Psychology Today* 44 (1972); Williams, R. L. Scientific racism and I.Q.: The silent mugging of the black community. 8 *Psychology Today* 32 (1974).

6. Smuck, *supra* note 3; Larry P. v. Riles, 343 F. Supp. 1306 (N.D. Cal. 1972) (restrained state and county school boards from use of standardized individual ability or intelligence tests with black school children that do not properly account for background and experiences); Lancaster, H. Job tests are dropped by many companies due to anti-bias drive. 92 *Wall Street Journal* 1 (September 3, 1975).

7. "It is difficult to come up with so much as one single well-designed research study in which the clinician's predictions are better than the statistical table or formula; in most studies the clinician is significantly worse." Meehl, P. E. Psychology and the criminal law. 5 *University of Richmond Law Review* 1 (1970); Meehl, P. E. *Clinical versus statistical prediction*. Minneapolis: University of Minnesota Press, 1954; New York State

statute requires disclosure of test forms and answers to persons taking test. Truth in testing movement, 10 *APA Monitor* 3 (Sept. 1979).

8. The revaluation ordered in *Diana*, *supra* note 3, had no significant impact on the disproportionate number of minorities, state-wide, in EMR programs. For example, black children who constituted nine percent of the school population in California were reduced from 27 to 25 percent in EMR programs from 1969 to 1972. As reported in, Lambert, N. and Meyers, C. E. . . . Children are being deprived of their rights to services. . . . 8 *Monitor* (American Psychological Assn.) 20 (May 1977). Similarly, no impact from court-ordered moritorium on I.Q. testing in *Larry P. v. Riles* case. Holden, C. California court is forum for latest round in I.Q. debate, 201 S*cience* 1106, 1109 (Sept. 22, 1978).

9. Griggs v. Duke Power Company, 401 U.S. 424; 91 S. Ct. 849 (1971); Albemarle Paper Company v. Moody, 474 F.2d 134, *vac*. 95 S. Ct. 2362, 45 L. Ed. 2d 298 (1975) Court specifically noted Amer. Psychological Assn. guidelines at 422 U.S. 405, 431 (1975).

10. Employers may use "any professionally developed ability test provided that such test, its administration, or action upon the results is not designed, intended, or used to discriminate because of race, color, religion, sex, or national origin." Title VII of the Civil Rights Act of 1964, Sec. 703(h), 42 U.S.C. 2000c-2(h). *See also* Uniform guidelines on employee selection procedures, 43 *Federal Register* 38290 (Aug. 25, 1978) (criterion and content validity).

11. Sec. 613(a)(13)(c).

12. Griggs, 401 U.S. 432.

13. Griggs, 401 U.S. 436.

14. Fincher, C. personnel testing and public policy, 28 *American Psychologist* 489 (1973).

15. Sherman, M.J. Anti-intellectualism and civil rights. 8 *Change* 34 (1976).

16. American Psychological Association, Office of Scientific Affairs, *Standards for educational and psychological tests*. Washington, D.C., 1974.; American Psychological Association, Division of Industrial-Organizational Psychology. *Principles for the validation and use of personnel selection procedures*. Washington, D.C., 1975; Equal Employment Opportunity Commission, Guidelines on employee selection procedures, 29 C.F.R. PP 1607. *See also*, Cleary, T. A., Humphreys, L. G., Kendrick, S. A, and Wesman, A. Educational uses of tests with disadvantaged students. 30 *American Psychologist* 15 (January 1975).

17. Albemarle, *supra* note 9.

18. Sharf, J. C. What you can and cannot do in the employment process: The current status of testing. Talk given at the Third Annual Personnel Compliance Conference, Washington, D.C., November 1975, p. 15 (a succinct and knowledgeable summary by a staff psychologist of the EEOC). This issue has been raised in relation to professional qualifications and tests, such as state bar exams, by Robert B. McKay, of the New York University School of law, in a program sponsored by The Committee on Minority Groups, New Orleans, April 24, 1971. Reported in S. J. Rosen and S. E. Lee (Eds.) *Committee on Minority Groups Newsletter* (Association of American Law Schools). Washington, D.C.: Foundation Press, May 1972 (No. 72–2). *Similarly*, ". . . I find no reason to assume the bar examination is job related. . . . I find strong reason to presume any test invalid until empirically demonstrated to be valid." in a brief filed by Opton, E. Jr., Henry Espinoze

v. the Committee of Bar Examiners of the State Bar of California, No. SF22928 S. Ct. (1972), as quoted in Sachs, B. Challenging testing in the courts. 1 *Social Action and the Law* 5, 6 (1974).

19. Fincher, *supra* note 14.

20. *See*, *e.g.*, Schmidt, F.L. and Hunter, J.E. Development of a general solution to the problem of validity generalization. 62 *Journal of Applied Psychology* 529 (1977).

21. APA, *Ethical Standards of psychologists* (1977 revision). Washington, D.C.: APA, 1977, at p. 6; APA *Standards for Educational and Psychological Tests*. Washington, D.C.: APA, 1974 at p. 32.

22. Sharf, *supra* note 18, at 24.

23. Ringelheim, D. *What a difference a day in court makes*. New Jersey State Department of Education, August 1973, pp. 3–4 (mimeo.). According to California Education Code, no group intelligence test may be administered, for the purpose of planning special education programs, to any pupil from a non-English-speaking country who has not resided in the U.S. for two years. Legislative Counsel's Digest, Assembly Bill No. 283 amending Educ. Code sec. 21821.5 (Dec. 1974), p. 1.

24. Ash, P. The implications of the Civil Rights Act of 1964 for psychological assessment industry. 21 *American Psychologist* 797, 801 (1966).

25. *See* Metzler, J.H. and Kohrs, E. Tests and "a marked difference in ability." 19 *The Arbitration Journal* 229 (1964).

26. See Columbia Law Review, *supra* note 5, ftns. 64, 65.

27. *See* Plotkin, L. Coal handling, steamfitting, psychology, and law. 27 *American Psychologist* 202 (1972).

28. Sussman, A. Psychological testing and juvenile justice: An invalid judicial function, 10 *Criminal Law Bulletin* 117 (1974) (a sharply negative article on the use of I.Q. tests, particularly practices in New York State courts). Galliher, K. E., Jr. Termination of the parent-child relationship: Should parental I.Q. be an important factor? 1973 *Law and Social Order* 855 (1973); and Thomas, H. W. Low intelligence of the parent: A new ground for state interference with the parent-child relationship? 13 *Journal of Family Law* 379 (1973–74). *See* Larry P. v. Riles, 502 F.2d 963 (9th Cir. 1974) (use of I.Q. test with black children).

29. Moses v. Washington Parish School Bd., 330 F. Supp. 1340 (E.D. La. 1971), *aff'd* 456 F.2d 1285 (5th Cir. 1972), *cert. den.* 409 U.S. 1013 (1972) (particular use of test was denial of equal protection, but no ruling on validity); Smuck, *supra* note 3 at 189 (unnecessary to rule on verbal tests as adequate predictors of performance). *See* summary critique in Shea, T. E. An educational perspective of the legality of intelligence testing and ability grouping. 6 *Journal of Law and Education* 137 (Apr. 1977).

30. The *Hobson* court said that a shift of only 3.1 or 6.3 percent of students from their assigned track in a two-year period was an "unkept promise." Hobson, 269 F. Supp. at 459.

31. Rock, D. A. Motivation, moderators, and test bias, 1970 *Toledo Law Review* 527 (1970). Cleary, T. A. Test bias: Prediction of grades of Negro and white students in integrated colleges. 5 *Journal of Educational Measurements* 115 (1968) (overprediction in favor of black applicants on the Scholastic Aptitude Test) *but see* Clark, K. and Plotkin, L. Aptitude test bias. 174 *Science* 1278 (24 December 1971). The New York State Court of Appeals ruled that reverse discrimination is constitutional "in proper circumstances" (e.g., when temporary and necessary to promote equality). The court cautioned, how-

ever, that this recognition of "benign discrimination" was not to be taken as blanket approval of preferential policies. The plaintiff, Martin C. Alevy, was denied admission to the Downstate Medical Center of SUNY even though his Medical College Application Test Score "was higher than every one of the accepted minority students." *Cf.,* Reverse discrimination ruled legal in some cases. 12 *The Chronicle of Higher Education* 9 (April 19, 1976).

32. Regents of the University of California v. Bakke, 98 S. Ct. 2733 (1978). (Bakke's attorney has requested public payment of $437,000 in legal fees because of "significant social issue.")

33. Equal Employment Opportunity Commission v. American Telephone and Telegraph, 556 f.2d 167 (3rd Cir. 1977). (Although AT&T did not admit to an allegation of discrimination by the Labor Department's Contract Compliance Office, the company had previously agreed to pay $15 million compensation to 15,000 employees.)

34. Kirkwood, J. H. Selection techniques and the law. To test or not to test? 44 *Personnel* 18 (November 1967). During Congressional hearings investigating the use of psychological tests by government agencies, it was alleged the "search and seizure of the contents of men's minds by a forced submission to psychological testing should be denounced as offensive to those canons of decency and fairness which express the notions of justice of English-speaking people." Kirkwood, *id.* at 27.

35. Sherrer, C. W. and Roston, R. A. Some legal and psychological concerns about personality testing in the public schools. 30 *Federal Bar Journal* 111, 115 (1971); Note, Constitutional requirements for standardized ability tests used in education. 26 *Vanderbilt Law Review* 789 (1973).

36. ". . . their test scores merely vary from a group norm. In this tyranny of group statistical guilt, there are no safeguards, no psychological habeas corpus, no impartial judge or jury to review or rebuke or to even find the tests are in scientific contempt." Kirkwood, *supra* note 34, at 21, quoting Martin Gross. *See generally,* Aronson, R. H. Should the privilege against self-incrimination apply to compelled psychiatric exams? 26 *Stanford Law Review* 55 (1973); People v. Clark, 77 Cal. Rptr. 50 (1959) (counsel not necessary to protect against self-incrimination during expert examination at a "non-critical" stage of commitment proceeding), reported in Robitscher, J. Psychiatric testimony: Why the conflict? *Medical World News* (Special Psychiatry Supplement) (1969) at 95.

37. Aronson, R. H. Should the privilege against self-incrimination apply to compelled psychiatric examinations? 26 *Stanford Law Review* 55, 93 (1973). *See also* Lessard v. Schmidt, 349 F. Supp. 1078 (ED. Wisc. 1974), *vac.* 414 U.S. 473 (1974), *on remand,* 379 F. Supp. 1376 (E.D. Wisc. 1974), vac. 421 U.S. 957 (1975), *on remand* 413 F. Supp. 1318 (E.D. Wisc. 1976) (evidence from a mental exam may not be used to commit a person unless the person voluntarily agrees).

38. McNeil v. Director, Patuxent Institution, 407 U.S. 245 (1972) (this decision did not, however, deal directly with psychological testing or situations of involuntary confinement).

39. Lessard v. Schmidt, *supra* note 37.

40. *See* Lee v. County Court of Erie County, 318 N.Y.2d 705, *cert. den.* 404 U.S. 823 (1971).

41. Lessard v. Schmidt, *supra* note 37; Lynch v. Baxley, 386 F. Supp. 378 (M.D. Ala. 1974).

42. *See* McCormick, C. T. *Handbook of the law of evidence*, 2d ed. St. Paul, Minn.: West Publishing Co., 1972.

43. For a broader discussion of the use of psychological and social science data in legal proceedings, as in Brown v. Board of Education, 347 U.S. 483 (1954), *see* Rosen, P. L. *The Supreme Court and social science*. Urbana, Ill.: University of Chicago Press, 1972.

44. Warren, S. and Brandeis, L. The right to privacy. 4 *Harvard Law Review* 193 (1890–1891).

45. Olmstead v. United States, 277 U.S. 438, 478 (1928) (Brandeis, J., dissenting). *Accord* Roe v. Wade, 410 U.S. 113 (1973). For comment, *see* Greenawalt, K. Privacy and its legal protections. 2 *Hastings Center Studies* 45 (September 1974); *also* Westin, A. F. *Privacy and Freedom*. New York: Atheneum, 1967.

46. L. R. Frumer and M. I. Friedman (Eds.), *Personal injury: Actions, defenses, damages*, Vol. 5. Albany: Matthew Bender, 1965, p. 764.106.

47. *Id.*, at 764.23.

48. *See* Sherrer & Roston, *supra* note 35.

49. *See* Emerson, C. D. Nine justices in search of a doctrine. 64 *Michigan Law Review* 219, 231–234 (1965); McKay, The right of privacy: Emanations and intimations. 64 *Michigan Law Review* 259, 272–282 (1965); Emerson, C. D. Personality tests for prospective jurors. 56 *Kentucky Law Journal* 832 (1968); Griswold v. Connecticut, 381 U.S. 479 (1965).

50. Merriken v. Cressman, 364 F. Supp. 913 (E.D. Pa. 1973). For a summary of opinions and reasoning in *Merriken*, *see* Recent cases (Constitutional law—Right of privacy), 27 *Vanderbilt Law Review* 372 (1974).

51. This letter is quoted in a discussion of the case by Bersoff, D.N. Professional ethics and legal responsibilities: On the horns of a dilemma. 13 *Journal of School Psychology* 359, 361–366 (1975).

52. Merriken v. Cressman, *supra* note 50, at 914.

53. *Id.* at 920.

54. *Id.* at 921.

55. 97 S. Ct. 2669 (1977); *infra* note 57.

56. *See* APA *Ethical Standards* at p. 6 and APA *Standards for Educational and Psychological Tests* at p. 68, *supra* note 21.

57. Detroit Edison Co. v. NLRB, U.S. Supreme Court, No. 77–968 (March 5, 1979) advance sheet, p. 17. *See also* Note, Psychological aptitude tests and the duty to supply information, 91 *Harvard Law Review* 869 (Feb. 1978).

58. Poe v. Ullman, 367 U.S. 497 (1961).

59. *See* Anonymous v. Henry A. Kissinger, 499 F.2d 1997 (D.C. Cir. 1974) (least intrusive methods for psychiatric examination for employment screening).

CHAPTER 8

Hypnosis, "Lie Detectors", and Instrumentation

At the turn of this century, when the X ray was just beginning to become known to the general public, a state legislature passed a bill forbidding the use of X-ray machines in movie theaters—on the grounds that such apparatus might be used by unscrupulous men to peer through women's clothes.[1] As it turns out, the sight of bones is just not that exciting to most people, and therefore this potential application of X-ray technology has not required specific legal regulation and enforcement.[2] Nonetheless, judges and legislators are constantly pressed to deal with innovative technologies of questionable safety and efficacy (e.g., "subliminal advertising") as these become used and abused by experimenters, practitioners, entrepreneurs, and entertainers.

Among the peripheral but more enduring forms of psychological interventions presently subject to statutory or administrative regulation are hypnosis, "lie detection" (using polygraphs or voice analyzers), and various types of behavioral instrumentation used for biofeedback training, treatment of enuresis, and so on. Each of these intervention strategies suffers from a lack of substantial and rigorous experimentation as well as a science-fiction type of popularity. Their legal status is for the most part, understandably and appropriately, rather ambiguous. This chapter briefly reviews the technical definitions, most frequent applications, and some general legal issues related to these three interventions.

133

HYPNOSIS

Hypnosis is generally thought of as an altered state of consciousness wherein there is an increased susceptibility to suggestion.[3] "Hypnotism" is a multidimensional term that refers not only to the altered state itself but also to the variables antecedent to the state such as repeated suggestions to relax, imagine, or sleep, and the behaviors during the state.[4] These behaviors include analgesia (inability to feel pain), age-regression (verbal and nonverbal behaviors reminiscent of an earlier chronological age), and hallucination (perception of stimuli that do not exist). Hypnosis and hypnotism are phenomena that presumably occur in everyday life.[5]

A classical legal definition of hypnotism has included any act or process which induces in another person a trance in which the susceptibility to suggestion or direction is increased. Hypnotism, in a legal sense, normally does not include acts or processes that are self-induced.[6]

The psychological and medical literature has not solved fundamental questions regarding the nature of hypnosis (viz., Is hypnosis the result of the hypnotist's externally applied force, the subject's willingness to be hypnotized, or a combination of both?).[7] Nonetheless, certain clinical uses of hypnosis are widely acknowledged.[8] Hypnotic techniques are typically used in psychotherapy, not as the treatment per se, but as an element of the overall therapeutic approach.[9] Hypnosis has reportedly been helpful in controlling pain,[10] breaking smoking habits,[11] treating migraine headaches,[12] suppressing hiccups,[13] and reducing phobias.[14] As a general principle, hypnosis appears more effective in attentuating sensation than in enhancing it.[15] The use of hypnosis in legal proceedings has been suggested in the literature,[16] but such application is infrequent. Hypnotism is also practiced by entertainers, but generally stage hypnotists select only highly suggestible individuals and demonstrate only limited novel behaviors.[17]

Unauthorized Practice of Medicine or Psychology

Because of alleged dangers of hypnotism,[18] some jurisdictions have limited it by construing certain hypnotic situations as the practice of medicine. Where a particular statute, for instance, deems diagnosis, prescription, and treatment to be constituents of the practice of medicine, a hypnotist will be found guilty of practicing without a license if s/he tries to cure a patient of nervousness, headaches, and weight problems.[19] However, where a statute (e.g., in Delaware) designates physicians only as persons who, for a fee, prescribe remedies and perform surgical operations for the cure of any bodily disease or ailing,[20] personal treatment through hypnotism, *unaccompanied* by directions as to the use of drugs, medicines, or other remedies, may not be considered an illegal practice of medicine.[21]

As a general rule, hypnotism is not prohibited unless a statute specifies that such practice constitutes the unauthorized practice of medicine or psychology. And the same rationale would permit hypnosis for purposes of entertainment or learning.[22] Whether or not a particular event amounts to unauthorized practice depends upon the facts of the particular situation.

Diminished Responsibility for Antisocial Behavior

May a defendant claim "diminished responsibility" for a criminal act committed while under hypnosis? Hypnotized persons will sometimes commit apparent crimes when they know such acts are part of an experiment and they can trust the hypnotist. However, most responsible opinion considers that the hypnotized subject could not commit a really serious crime unless the person would be inclined to do so in the ordinary state.[23] To the authors' knowledge, no significant court case has accepted diminished responsibility as an adequate defense of an alleged hypnotized defendant.[24]

Use in the Judicial Process

An important state supreme court case[25] held that the Sixth Amendment (right to counsel) guarantees access to a hypnotist if counsel thinks that a hypnotic examination will help in compiling the facts of the case. The decision did not imply that information obtained during the examination would be admissible as evidence. But the possibility that such an examination could produce leads to admissible evidence, or even an admissible alibi, served as the court's rationale.[26] *In re Ketchel*[27] similarly held that there was no reason to disallow private hypnotic examinations because such examinations do not harm prison safety or orderly administration. An earlier case,[28] however, held against the right to certain private hypnotic examinations.

Until the 1960s, the courts consistently rejected the admission of testimony involving hypnosis. The leading case had been *People* v. *Ebanks*.[29] In *Ebanks*, the testimony by the defendant's hypnotist was not admitted because "the law of the United States does not recognize hypnotism."[30] Similarly, another court rejected the expert testimony of a physician-hypnotist insofar as his opinions were based on the use of hypnosis.[31]

A 1963 state supreme court case[32] held, however, that the admission of tape recordings of examinations under hypnosis *to substantiate* testimony of experts was within the discretion of the trial court. One court subsequently permitted the admission of a 47-minute film of the defendant under hypnosis for the purpose of evaluating the testimony of a defense psychiatrist.[33] Decisions on this matter are far from unanimous. At least two courts have denied admission of recordings made under hypnosis, evidently deciding that the danger of prejudicing the jury was too great.[34] In a 1968 Maryland case, a prosecution witness was hypnotized to refresh her waking memory.[35] The court admitted the witness's post-hypnotic testimony. In another appellate case, the court held that a defendant could be hypnotized to help him prepare a defense, but it did not rule on the admissibility of evidence thus obtained.[36]

The courts have rarely allowed hypnosis to take place in the courtroom itself. In *State* v. *Nebb*[37] the defendant was hypnotized in court but out of the presence of the jury. As a result of the hypnotic recall of events, the prosecuting attorney moved to amend the charge against the defendant from first-degree murder to manslaughter and assault. A Canadian case permitted the hypnotism of an amnesiac defendant with the stipulation that there would be no questioning during the hypnotic trance.[38] The hypnotist was allowed only to suggest to the defendant that she remember the missing information after the trance. Sirhan Sirhan, the convicted murderer of Senator Robert Kennedy, was hypnotized in his cell, and his attorney subsequently asked that Sirhan be hypnotized in court. This request was denied.[39]

Ethical Aspects

The *Ethical Standards of Psychologists* of the American Psychological Association requires that psychological services for the purpose of diagnosis, treatment, or personal advice be provided only within the context of a professional relationship.[40] These services are not to be provided by means of public demonstration, by newspaper or magazine articles, or by radio, television, or related media. (The National Association of Broadcasters code has a similar prohibition.) Interpretation of this standard by the Committee on Scientific Affairs, Ethics and Conduct of the APA has prohibited the demonstration of hypnotic techniques on stage or by television to the general public without control over the effects on the audience.[41] Hypnotic techniques are not to be provided to persons otherwise inadequately trained for their use. Hypnotic techniques may be demonstrated to mental health professionals or trainees.

The Society for Clinical and Experimental Hypnosis has adopted an ethical code that includes, among others, the following requirements:

> I. (a) A person who uses hypnosis shall continue in good (ethical) standing in his own professional organization. (e.g. APA, ADA, etc.) If the individual is not a member of his own professional organization, he may be requested to obtain such membership or show cause as to why he should not meet such a requirement.
>
> (b) A person who uses hypnosis shall neither claim directly nor imply professional qualifications that exceed those that he has actually attained.
>
> (c) A person who uses hypnosis must refer his patient to an appropriate specialist when there is evidence of a difficulty with which he is not competent to deal.
>
> (d) A person who uses hypnosis shall not employ any procedure, which in the informed opinion of competent persons, is likely to mislead a patient or subject. A cardinal obligation is to protect the welfare and respect the integrity of the individual with whom one is working.

(e) Guarantees of easy solutions or favorable outcomes must not be made nor may one claim to have secret techniques.

(f) A person who uses hypnosis shall not offer his services for the purpose of public entertaiment or advisement via newspapers, magazine articles, radio, television or similar media. Such a person, if he makes public announcement of his services, is obligated to describe such services with accuracy and dignity, adhering to professional rather than commercial standards. Direct solicitation is unethical.

(g) Demonstrations should only be conducted for serious purposes, such as the training of professional workers. It is unethical to display subjects or patients to satisfy casual curiosity.[42]

LIE DETECTION

In the late 1800s, the well-known Italian criminologist Cesare Lombroso measured changes in the blood pressure and pulse rate of suspected criminals during interrogation. In 1938, William Marston, a criminal lawyer and psychologist, published the early and classic study of empirical research on physiology and deception.[43] The standard commercial polygraph today consists of a compact machine that records, on a paper chart, blood pressure fluctuations, depth and rate of breathing, pulse rate, and skin resistance.[44] Inasmuch as the device records physiological changes, not "lies" or "truths" as such, the accuracy of results depends greatly upon the method of conducting the examination (e.g., what questions are asked in what order) and on the interpretation of the results.

The polygraph technique has, at least in the past, been used extensively by private industry and the federal government for initial screening of job applicants and for periodic evaluations such as regular and routine examination for possible stealing.[45] Numerous law enforcement agencies have used and perhaps misused it as an aid in criminal investigations.[46] In one early case, the defendant's confession was not admitted in court because, reportedly, the defendant remained attached to the apparatus for 12 hours and was told that it would not be removed until he gave the desired information.[47] Some psychiatric uses have also been reported.[48]

The reliability and accuracy of polygraph examinations in ascertaining truthful or deceptive statements is still subject to considerable controversy.[49] About a dozen states now license polygraph operators, and the American Polygraph Association favors such legislation.[50]

Employee Screening Using the Polygraph

Among constitutional issues raised by the useof the polygraph technique with employees or potential employees are "invasion of privacy," "privilege against self-incrimination," and the "right to cross examination."[51] It has been argued that the technique penetrates into individual beliefs and inclinations (rather than dealing with overt behavior) and therefore violates his/her sense of personal autonomy.[52] The degree of "voluntariness' in most situations when taking the test has also been questioned.[53] But this issue is not necessarily more relevant to lie detection than to pencil-and-papaer tests, treatment, or experimentation. Self-incrimination may occur when damaging personal information which one would ot normally reveal is exposed. Furthermore, the nature of the information to be obtained is usually unknown to the examinee.

The Washington State Supreme Court ruled that a police officer could be compelled to submit to a polygraph examination by a superior.[54] But such a holding may be limited to public safety employees, because an increasing number of states (15 in 1975) enacted statutes prohibiting private employers from requiring polygraph tests.[55] The statutes typically state: "No employer shall cause (require, demand, request) an employee or prospective employee to take a polygraph examination as a condition of employment or continued employment."[56] Most states exclude from this prohibition government employees, particularly law endorcement and drug treatment personnel.

Polygraph Evidence in Court

The courts have traditionally rejected the results of lie detector tests submitted, whether by the defense or the prosecution, as evidence of guilt or innocence.[57] Recently there has been some loosening of this prohibition. Some jurisdictions admit expert witness opinions based on lie detector results if the examinee has given full cooperation and if an established test procedure is used.[58] The usual rationale is that agreement between the parties as well as interpretative screening of the results by a qualified expert will compensate for the fact that polygraph methods have not yet obtained general scientific acceptance for being reliable and accurate.[59] The New Mexico Supreme Court set five criteria for the admissibility of evidence:

> Both parties would stipulate to the test and its admission as evidence,
> No objection to its admission would be offered at trial,
> The court would hear evidence of the qualifications of the examiner to establish his expertise,
> Testimony to establish the reliability of the testing procedure would be heard to determine whether it is approved by authorities in the field,
> Validity of the tests would be established.[60]

Some courts, however, still prohibit use of polygraph information even as a data source for expert opinion in any phase of a criminal proceeding.[61] The resistance lies, in part, in the fact that experts are traditionally permitted to testify about matters relevant to the case but not directly on the issue of guilt or innocence, which is a matter for the jury to decide. The more reliable polygraph examinations become, the more probable their impact upon the jury prerogative.

Can a person who presumably wants to prove his/her innocence in a criminal trial insist that the police or other qualified operators administer a lie detector test?—apparently not. A police agency may deny the request on the grounds that both parties should agree to its use in opinion (expert) testimony.[62] If, however, the police or prosecution do agree to a defendant's request, the defendant cannot then later prevent the admission of unfavorable results by claiming that s/he was unaware of the fallibility of the technique.[63]

Narcoanalysis, Breathalyzer, Voiceprints

Other widely publicized techniques to ascertain legally relevant facts involve "truth serums" (narcoanalysis), breathalyzers, and "voiceprints" (voice spectrography). Narcoanalysis employs the intravenous injection of sodium pentothal or sodium amytal to relieve anxiety and produce temporary euphoria and emotional fluidity.[64] With larger dosage levels, the patient tends to engage in complex interweaving of fact and fantasy. Medical consensus is that "without knowledge of the suspect's emotional substructure, the results can probably not be evaluated with any degree of reliability."[65] Rarely, if ever, are the results (e.g., interview transcript) of narcoanalysis directly admitted as evidence, even if a psychiatrist is willing to testify as to the validity of the information.[66] On the other hand, if the patient has consented, use of the drug does not preclude the psychiatrist from stating a professional opinion in court based on information obtained during narcoanalysis.[67] As with polygraph tests, a defendant's request to be given a "truth serum" can be properly denied.[68]

Breathalyzer tests that measure blood-alcohol concentration have fared better in the courts than polygraph tests or narcoanalysis. If the accuracy of the instrument has been recently verified,[69] and the test is given by a qualified person, most courts accept the results as collaborative evidence of other testimony.[70] All states have statutes authorizing the use of breathalyzers. Presumably the breathalyzer procedures are more like fingerprinting than lie detection because they rely more directly upon physical evidence and less upon interpretation by the operator.[71] In some states, an automobile driver who refuses a breathalyzer test may be presumed guilty and have the burden of proving innocence of a drunk driving charge.[72]

"Voiceprints" are oscillographic representations of spoken sounds used for the purpose of identifying the speaker.[73] Most recent appellate court cases have upheld the use of spectrograms as evidence in criminal cases.[74] The favorable rulings on the technique are typically hedged with qualifications and limitations—e.g., to be used only as collaborative evidence, to justify an arrest warrant but not necessarily sustain a conviction, or to be admitted without contradictory expert testimony or literature.[75]

In summary, courts tend to give limited approval of experimental techniques if (1) there is some evidence of acceptance within the scientific community, (2) a qualified operator has used a standard procedure, and (3) there is no substantial objection by the litigants.

PSYCHOLOGICAL INSTRUMENTATION

One of the notable effects of contemporary technology is the proliferation of electromechanical devices and instruments designed to influence our behavior or emotions in some manner (e.g., motion pictures, traffic lights, burglar alarms). A "psychological device" can be defined as an instrument used principally for the observation, assessment, or modification of behavior, emotions, learning, perception, and other mental processes of individual persons.[76]

Some devices have multiple uses, and their classification as psychological, medical, or scientific, and so on, depends on their primary intended use. For example, an X ray machine can diagnose a bone fracture of a patient or can determine structural weakness in an aircraft frame. Biofeedback[77] devices are multiple-use items that have received wide publicity. If such a device is used, for example, to treat a migraine headache, then it may be classified as a medical device. If the instrument, however, is used to enhance thought processes or teach techniques of control of emotional responses (without being used to treat a disease or to substantially affect a health-related physiological function), then it may be classified as a psychological device.[78] Other similar apparatus of multiple classification include alarm systems to prevent bed-wetting and automated desensitization recordings to treat phobias.

Psychological practitioners occasionally use one of at least a dozen different types of behavioral devices such as aversive condition apparatus, timers, token dispensers, anti-stuttering or snoring devices, breathalyzers, etc.[79] The range of application is so broad and the results are so varied that any overall conclusion as to the safety or efficacy is impossible. As a generalization, it is probably fair to assert that most devices are not as effective as claimed[80] and not as dangerous as feared.[81]

Sources of Regulation

An important first step is to determine whether a device is "medical", and thus potentially subject to regulation by the Food and Drug Administration. Considerable confusion exists with regard to the delineation of "medical devices" and "psychological devices" by the FDA and other regulatory agencies.[82] The FDA may require medical devices to meet various labeling requirements, performance standards, and other conditions to insure safety and effectiveness.[83] A practitioner should usually select a device meeting FDA requirements unless there are good reasons for not doing so, such as the need for a custom device. The practitioner should also follow label warnings and instructions carefully. The device label might state that the device is to be used only under the supervision of or in consultation with a physician. Regulations by other agencies such as the Federal Trade Commission (fraudulent claims in interstate commerce) or the Consumer Product Safety Commission (physical safety of items not covered by the FDA) should also be examined.[84] Additionally, many states have statutes covering medical devices.[85]

Guidelines for use in Practice

The following tentative guidelines are applicable only to standard practice situations and not for experimental use.

1. The device should be safe when used as directed for its intended purpose. It should also present little risk even when it is misused in a foreseeable manner. Written informed consent for use of the equipment should be obtained from the patient or client prior to treatment.
2. The therapists or practitioners using a psychological device with patients or clients should be specially qualified by training and experience to do so. They should be capable of reasonably assessing risks and preventing them to the extent possible. Devices that present substantial physical risk to patients or clients should be used only when necessary and with adequate safeguards and under the supervision of or in collaboration with a licensed physician or other qualified practitioner licensed by law to use the device. If such physical risk derives from the properties of the device itself, then its use should be subjected to periodic inspection and approval at reasonable intervals by a qualified engineer or technician.
3. The device should be effective in performing its intended function when used as directed. Directions for use should be clear and specific.[86] The device itself should be clearly and accurately labeled, with hazards and contraindications for use plainly visible to users.[87]
4. The device should function reliably and have a reasonably long life.
5. The therapists or practitioners using a psychological device should collect information on any adverse effects and unexpected risks. In the event of serious harm, this should be promptly reported to the manufacturer, distributor, and to appropriate authorities, professional groups, and regulatory agencies to help prevent subsequent harm to others.
6. The therapeutic use of psychological devices should be conducted within the broader context of a treatment program that is sensitive to the general rights, welfare, and benefits of patients and clients.

These guidelines are, of course, subject to reasonable modification depending upon the particular circumstances of use. Some devices, when properly labeled, may be safely and effectively used by patients or clients with minimal or no direct supervision by therapists.

Guidelines for Experimental Use

If the safety and efficacy of a psychological device has not been established, the use of the device should be considered experimental. In addition to the general procedural standards for experimentation (see Ch. 11), certain more specific guidelines can be suggested for instruments:[88]

- Clinical utilization of the device should have the reasonable potential of improving the quality of life of the individual patient on whom it is applied.[89]
- The expected reliability of the device in investigative clinical use must be stated; this reliability must be exceeded by a reasonable margin of safety in preclinical testing.
- The functioning and the effects of the device must be characterized in detail in bench testing and in experimental animals where an animal test is feasible.
- The device must be fully described as to construction, materials, and methods of use.
- There must be evidence of reasonable safety against such potential ordinary hazards of devices as electrical shocks.
- The investigative team must have specific and extensive familiarity and actual experience with the device.

If the device also has medical applications so as to be classified as a medical device by the Food and Drug Administration, there may be additional requirements for investigational use. The FDA should be contacted for an investigational device exemption. To obtain such an exemption, the investigator must obtain approval from a local institutional review committee that is charged with reviewing, approving, and monitoring the research study. An independent professional individual may also have to be designated as a "monitor" to oversee the progress of the study. The "monitor" would make periodic visits at the site of the study and prepare reports of findings.[90]

Certain diagnostic devices may be exempt from these requirements if they are not invasive, do not introduce energy into the subject, and are used in the diagnosis simultaneously with a similar, approved diagnostic device.[91] Custom devices that are individually designed to meet the health needs of particular patients or health professionals, may also be exempt from these investigational requirements. Custom devices are not generally available in finished form for dispensing, prescription, or commercial distribution. Also, they must not be generally available to other health professionals.

NOTES

1. Goldiamond, I. Statement on subliminal advertising. In Ulrich, R., Stachnik, T. and Mabry, J. (Eds.) *Control of human behavior*. Glenview, Ill.: Scott, Foresman & Co., 1966, p. 279.
2. Other uses of X ray in medicine and in industry are highly regulated under the Federal Food, Drug, and Cosmetic Act, Title 21 of the Code of Federal Regulations.
3. Hilgard, E. Hypnosis. In P. R. Farnsworth (Ed.) *Annual review of psychology*, vol. 16. Palo Alto, Calif.: Annual Reviews, Inc., 1965, p. 160.
4. Barber, T. X. *LSD, marihuana, yoga, and hypnosis*. Chicago: Aldine Publishing Company, 1970, p. 281.
5. Barber, T. X. and Silver, M. J. Fact, fiction, and experimenter bias effect. 70 *Psychological Bulletin* 1 (1968).
6. Hypnotism Act, 1952 (Great Britain), 15 and 16 George 6, Ch. 46, sec. 6: "Hypnotism includes hypnotism, mesmerism and any similar act or process which produces or is intended to produce in any person any form of induced sleep or trance in which the susceptibility of the mind of that person to suggestion or direction is increased or intended to be increased but does not include hypnotism, mesmerism or any such similar act or process which is self-induced." Quoted in Bryan, W. J., Jr. *Legal aspects of hypnosis*. Springfield, Ill.: Charles C Thomas, 1962, p. 25.
7. A summary review of the controversies and theories of hypnosis may be found in Hilgard, E. Hypnosis. In M. R. Rosenzweig and L. W. Porter (Eds.), *Annual review of psychology*, vol. 26. Palo Alto, Calif: Annual Reviews, Inc., 1975.
8. *See generally*, Hilgard, *id*.; Cheek, D. B. and LeCron, L. M. *Clinical hypnotherapy*. New York: Grune & Stratton, 1968; and Platonov, K. I. *The word as a physiological and therapeutic factor*. Moscow: Foreign Languages Publishing House, 1959; Volgyesi, F. A. *Hypnosis of man and animals*. Hollywood, Calif.: Wilshire Book Co., 1968 reprint of 1963 2nd ed. trans. of *Menschen und Tierhypnose* by Tindall & Cassell, Ltd. (London, 1966) (includes a collection of approximately 150 photographs).
9. *See* Wolberg, L. R. Hypnotherapy. In S. Arieti (Ed.), *American handbook of psychiatry*, vol. 2. New York: Basic Books, Inc., 1959; M. V. Kline (Ed.), *Hypnodynamic psychology*. New York: Julian Press, 1955; Dengrove, E. Uses of hypnosis in behavior therapy, 21 *International Journal of Clinical and Experimental Hypnosis* 13 (1973); Erickson, M.H., Rossi, E.L., and Rossi, S.I. *Hypnotic realities: The induction of clinical hypnosis and forms of indirect suggestion*. N.Y.: Irvington, 1976.
10. Crasilneck, H. B. and Hall, J. A. Clinical hypnosis in problems of pain. 15 *American Journal of Clinical Hypnosis* 153 (1973); Orne, M. T. and Hammer, A. G. Hypnosis. In *Encyclopedia Brittanica*, 15th ed. Helen Hemingway Benton, 1974, p. 139; Scott, D. L. Hypnoanalgesia for major surgery: A psychodynamic Process. 16 *American Journal of Clinical Hypnosis* 84 (1973); Marmer, M. J. Unusual applications of hypnosis in anesthesiology. 17 *International Journal of Clinical and Experimental Hypnosis* 199 (1969).
11. Johnston, E. and Donoghue, J. R. Hypnosis and smoking: A review of the literature. 13 *American Journal of Clinical Hypnosis* 265 (1971); Spiegel, H. A single-treatment method to stop smoking using ancillary self-hypnosis. 18 *International Journal of Clinical and Experimental Hypnosis* 235 (1970).
12. Harding, H. C. Hypnosis in the treatment of migraine. In J. Lessner (Ed.), *Hypnosis and psychosomatic medicine*. New York: Springer-Verlag, 1967.

13 Rubin, R. B. The hypnotherapeutic management of intractible hiccups. 2 *British Journal of Clinical Hypnosis* 82 (1972).

14. Cautela, J. R. Desensitization factors in the hypnotic treatment of phobias. 64 *Journal of Psychology* 277 (1966).

15. Weitzenhofer, A. M. *Hypnotism: An objective study in suggestibility*. New York: Wiley, 1953.

16. *See* Bryan, *supra* note 6, and same author, Hypnosis and the unreliability of eye witness testimony. 10 *California Trial Lawyers Association Journal* 50 (1971). *See also*, Hanley, F. W. Hypnosis in the courtroom. 14 *Canadian Psychiatric Association Journal* 351 (August 1969); Note, Hypnosis as a defense tactic. 1969 *Toledo Law Review* 691 (1969); Arons, H. *Hypnosis in criminal investigation*. Springfield, Ill.: Charles C Thomas, 1967; Note, Hypnosis as an evidentiary tool. 8 *Utah Law Review* 78 (1962).

17. Barber, T. X. Experimental analysis of "hypnotic" behavior: A review of recent empirical findings. 70 *Journal of Abnormal Psychology* 132 (1965).

18. Numerous case histories of persons presumably harmed through stage hypnotism are presented in Bryan, *supra* note 6, at pp. 20–22.

19. Masters v. State, 341 S.W. 2d 938 (Tex. Crim. 1960) (defendant, as the director of an "Institute of Hypnosis," gave paid treatments for headaches, nausea, and dizziness—found guilty of practice of medicine). *Similarly* People v. Cantor, 198 Cal. App. 2d Supp. 843, 18 Cal. Rptr 363 (1961). *See* Annot., Hypnotism as illegal practice of medicine, 85 A.L.R.2d 1129.

20. Annotation, *supra* note 19.

21. State v. Lawson, 65 A. 593 (Del. 1907), reported in Annot. *supra* note 19.

22. 54 *Opinions of the California Attorney General* 63 (1971); *see also*: Harris, M. Tort liability of the psychotherapist. 8 *University of San Francisco Law Review* 405, 407 (1970); Brennan, J. Statutory regulation of hypnosis. 14 *Cleveland-Marshall Law Review* 112 (1965).

23. "After 30 years of experience in the field of hypnosis and hypnotherapy, it is my opinion that, under ordinary circumstances, it would be impossible to cause another person to commit a crime, or even to have a crime committed against them under hypnosis, if that person did not have the corresponding inclimation to do so. . . ." Hartland, J. An alleged case of criminal assault upon a married woman under hypnosis. 16 *American Journal of Clinical Hypnosis* 188, 191 (1974) (sexual relations during vaginal exam). *Concurring*, Bryan, *supra* note 6 at p. 165; Hilgard, *supra* note 3 at 164. Under experimental conditions of trust, apparent crimes can be committed: Conn, J. H. Is hypnosis really dangerous? 20 *International Journal of Clinical and Experimental Hypnosis* 61 (1972); Weitzenhoffer, A. M. The production of antisocial acts under hypnosis. 44 *Journal of Abnormal and Social Psychology* 420 (1949).

24. In the trial of Dr. Coppolino [Coppolino v. State, 223 So.2d 68 (Fla. 1968)], in which he was acquitted for the death of William Farber, Mrs. Farber turned state's witness and asserted that she was in a hypnotic state for more than one year, during which time she tried to kill her husband. . . . "Two physicians see no strangulation," . . . *New York Times* (Dec. 14, 1966), p. 1. Psychiatrist Bernard Diamond in the Sirhan Sirhan trial argued unsuccessfully that Sirhan was in a "disassociated state" induced by self-hypnosis at the time of the Kennedy killing.

25. Cornell v. Superior Court of San Diego County, 52 Cal 2d 397, 338 P2d 447 (1959).

26. *See* Note, Hypno-induced statements: Safeguards for admissibility. 1970 *Law and the Social Order* 97 (1970); Davis, R. P. Annotation: Accused's counsel—consultation. 72 A.L.R.2d 1120.

27. *In re* Ketchel, 68 Cal. 2d 397, 438 P.2d 625, 66 Cal. Rptr. 881 (1968). Reported in Note, *supra* note 26. *See also*, Arons, *supra* note 16 (examples of admitted evidence).

28. State ex rel. Sheppard v. Koblentz, 174 Ohio St. 120, 187 N.E.2d 40 (1962).

29. 117 Cal. 652, 49 P. 1049 (1897).

30. *Id.* at 665, 49 P. at 1053, cited in Bryan, *supra* note 6, at p. 33.

31. "Opinions based on hypnotic analysis have never been received in the courts of this state, or in any other jurisdiction to which the defendant refers." People v. Bush, 56 Cal. 2d 868, 877; 366 P.2d 314, 319 (1961).

32. People v. Modesto, 59 Cal. 2d 722, 382 P.2d 33 (1963).

33. People v. Thomas, (Cal. Ct. App., 1969). Reported in Note on defense tactics, *supra* note 16, at 695; photographs in *Time Magazine*, 57 (April 12, 1968).

34. State v. Harris, 241 Ore. 224, 405 P.2d 492 (1965); People v. Hiser, 267 Cal. App. 2d 47, 72 Cal. Rptr. 906 (1968).

35. Harding v. State, 5 Md. App. 230, 246 A.2d 302 (1968), *cert. denied*, 395 U.S. 949 (1969). *See generally*, Physiological and psychological deception tests. 23 ALR2d 1310 (Later case service 731).

36. Cornell v. Superior Court of San Diego, 52 Cal.2d 99(1958). A discussion in favor of courtroom hypnosis can be found in Hanley, F.W. Hypnosis in the court room. 14 *Canadian Psychiatric Association Journal* 351 (1969).

37. No. 39, 540 (Ohio C. P., Franklin Co., June 8, 1962).

38. Regina v. Pitt, 68 D.L.R.2d 513 (1967), reported in Hanley, *supra* note 16.

39. Kaiser, R. B. *RFK must die*. New York: Dutton, 1970.

40. American Psychological Association, *Ethical standards of psychologists* (1977 revision). Washington, D.C.: APA, 1977, p. 4.

41. American Psychological Association, *Casebook on ethical standards of psychologists*. Washington, D.C.: APA, 1967, pp. 27–28. *See also* Kline, M. V. Dangerous aspects of the practice of hypnotism and the need for legislative regulation. 29 *Clinical Psychologist* 3 (Winter 1976).

42. Society for Clinical and Experimental Hypnosis, *Code of ethics*, New York: author, 1977.

43. Marston, W. M. *The lie detector test*. New York: Smith, 1938.

44. For general description with sample records, *see* Smith, B. M. The polygraph. 216 *Scientific American* 3 (January 1967).

45. An estimated 500,000 tests were given by 3000 polygraph operators in 1968 at a cost of $15 to $65 per test. Ferguson, R. S., Jr. *The scientific informer*. Springfield, Ill.: Charles C Thomas, 1971, p. 130. In the first three-quarters of 1974, the Department of Defense reported having 416 polygraphs and 49 examiners who conducted a total of 5351 exams. Hearings before Subcommittee of the Committee on Government Operations, House of Representatives, *The use of polygraphs and similar devices by federal agencies*. Washington, D.C.: U.S. Government Printing Office, 1974, pp. 430–432 (a useful, 790-page source of opinion and data).

46. In 1974, the FBI reported conducting approximately 200 examinations. Hearings, *supra* note 45, at 418; Reid, J. and Inbau, F. The lie detector technique: A reliable and valuable investigative aid. 50 *Journal of the American Bar Association* 470 (May 1964).

47. Bruner v. People, 113 Colo. 194, 156 P.2d 111 (1945).

48. For a useful summary, *see* Abrams, S. *A polygraph handbook for attorneys*. Lexington, MA: D.C. Heath, 1977.

49. One of the most favorable reports is Berch P.J. A validation study of polygraph examiner judgments. 53 *Journal of Applied Psychology* 399 (1969); *similarly* Barland, G. and Raskin, D. An evaluation of field techniques in detection of deception, 12 *Psychophysiology* 224 (1975) (abstract of an LEAA study).. For a thoughtful and critical analysis, *see* Lykken, D.T. Psychology and the lie detector industry. 29 *American Psychologist* 725 (1974).

50. Listing on p. 36 of J. K. Barefoot, (Ed.), *The polygraph story*, 3rd ed. Linthicum Heights, Md.: American Polygraphic Association, 1974.

51. See comprehensive report of Shattuck, J., Brown, P. and Carlson, S. *The lie detector as a surveillance device*. Report of ACLU of New York, 1973, and reprinted in Hearings, *supra* note 45, at 7–48. The issue of cross-examination seems rather spurious—who would want to cross-examine a machine anyway, especially when the operator who makes the critical interpretations is available?

52. Westin, A. *Privacy and freedom*. New York: Atheneum, 1967, p. 238, as cited in Shattuck, *supra* note 51, at 34.

53. *Id.* at 36.

54. Seattle Police Officers Guild v. City of Seattle, 80 Wisc. 2d 307, 474 P.2d 485 (1972).

55. States with limiting statutes include: Alaska, California, Connecticut, Delaware, Hawaii, Idaho, Maryland, Massachusetts, Minnesota, Montana, New Jersey, Oregon, Pennsylvania, Rhode Island, and Washington. *Listed in* Romig, C.H. State laws and the polygraph. 4. *Polygraph* 95 (1975).

56. Abrams, *supra* note 48 at p. 133.

57. Annot. "Lie detectors" 25 A.L.R.2d 1310; United States v. Frogge, 476 F.2d 969 (5th Cir.), *cert. den.* 414 U.S. 849 (1973); United States v. Wilson, 361 F. Supp. 510 (D. Md. 1973).

58. State v. South, 346 A.2d 437 (N.J. Super. 1975) (stipulation and approved procedure required); United States v. Oliver, 525 F.2d 731 (C.A. Mo. 1975) (full cooperation); United States v. Zeiger, 350 F. Supp. 685 (D.D.C.), *rev'd per curiam* 475 F.2d 1280 (D.C. Cir. 1972) (technique found effective); United States v. Ridling, 350 F. Supp. 90 (E.D. Mich. 1972) (technique improving and acceptable).

59. State v. Green, 531 P.2d 245 (Ore. 1975); People v. Leone, 307 N.Y.S. 2d 430 (N.Y.1969). For a comprehensive review favoring admissibility, *see* Tarlow, B. Admissibility of polygraph evidence in 1975: An aid in determining credibility in a perjury-plagued system. 26 *Hastings Law Journal* 917 (1975); *similarly* Note, The emergence of the polygraph at trial. 73 *Columbia Law Review* 1120 (1973).

60. State v. Lecaro, 86 N.M. 686, 926 P.2d 1091 (1974). The first two criteria were dropped later in an unreported case, New Mexico v. Dorsey (N.M. Sup. Ct., Feb. 12, 1975), for being excessively restrictive. *Cited in* Beatty, T. Admissibility rules eased in *New Mexico v. Dorsey*. 4 *Polygraph* 339 (1975), and *reported in* Abrams, *supra* note 48 at p. 131.

61. People v. Liddell, 234 N.W.2d 669 (Mich. App. 1975) (prohibiting opinion testimony in trial, sentencing, or any administrative procedure); *similarly* People v. Reves, 234 N.W.2d 673 (Mich. App. 1975); Crawford v. State, 321 So.2d 559 (Fla. App. 1975).

62. State *ex rel* De Concini v. Sup. Ct., 541 P.2d 964 (Ariz. App. 1975); State v. Perlin, 268 Wisc. 529, 68 N.W.2d 32 (Wisc. App. 1960).

63. State v. Lassley, 545 P.2d 383 (Kan. 1976).

64. McGraw, R. B. and Oliven, J. F. Miscellaneous therapies, in S. Arieti (Ed.), *American handbook of psychiatry*, vol. II. New York: Basic Books, 1959, p. 1573.

65. *Id.* at 1575. *Similarly*, Sadoff, R. L. *Forensic psychiatry: A practical guide*. Springfield, Ill.: Thomas, 1975, pp. 64–69. The classical experimental study showing extremely diverse reactions among subjects is Redlich, F. C., Ravitz, L. J., and Dession, G. H. Narcoanalysis and truth. 107 *American Journal of Psychiatry* 586 (1950).

66. State v. Hemminger, 502 P.2d 791 (Kan. 1972). *See generally*, Polen, E. The admissibility of truth serum tests in the courts. 35 *Temple Law Quarterly* 401 (1962).

67. People v. Esposito, 287 N.Y. 389, 9. N.E.2d 925, 142 A.L.R. 946 (1942); People v. Cartier, 51 Cal.2d 590, 335 P.2d 114 (1959). *See generally*, Annot., Admissibility of physiological or psychological truth and deception test or its results to support physician's testimony, 41 A.L.R.3d 1369.

68. People v. McCraken, 39 Cal.2d 336, 246 P.2d 913 (1952).

69. For sample field-testing of breathalyzer reliability, *see* Ettling, B. V. and Adams, M. F. In vitro studies on a breathalyzer. 17 *Journal of Forensic Sciences* 79 (1972).

70. Davis v. State, 541 p.2d 1352 (Okla. Cr. 1975); Commonwealth v. Bernier, 322 N.E.2d 414 (Mass. 1975); City of Cincinnati v. Duhart, 322 N.E.2d 897 (Ohio App. 1974); People v. Meikrantz, 351 N.Y.S.2d 549 (N.Y.Co. Ct. 1974).

71. Clearly, no data system is immune from accidental or purposeful error. For a report of a purposeful laboratory forgery of a fingerprint resulting in a false bank robbery conviction, *see* Morantz, P. The fingerprint that lied: Justice v. De Palma. 2 *Coast Magazine* 61 (Dec. 1974).

72. The state's increased efficiency and legitimate interest in prosecuting drunk drivers versus the individual's constitutional protection against self-incrimination produced the convenient and perhaps necessary legal fiction that a driver who uses state roads gives implied consent (which cannot be withdrawn) to the test and the use of the results in court. The informality and irrevocability of this consent procedure is not permitted for even the most routine psychological testing or psychiatric treatment. In Massachusetts a driver can refuse, but it results in an automatic 90-day suspension of the driver's license (Mass. Gen. Laws Ann., ch. 90, sec. 24 e,f). *See* Randolph, C. C. and Randolph, D. G. Breathalyzer—statutory and constitutional deficiencies. 9 *Wake Forest Law Review* 331 (June 1973).

73. For an informative and critical review, *see* Siegel, D. M. Cross-examination of a "voiceprint" expert: A blueprint for lawyers. 12 *Criminal Law Bulletin* 509 (Sept-Oct. 1976).

74. *Supporting*: U.S. v. Franks, 511 F.2d 25 (6th Cir. 1975); U.S. v. Baller, 519 F.2d 463 (4th Cir.); Commonwealth v. Lykus, 327 N.E.2d 671 (Mass. Supreme Jud. Ct. 1975); State v. Andretta, 269 A.2d 644 (N.J. 1972). *Denying admissibility*: U.S. v. Addison, 498 F.2d 747 (D.C. Cir. 1974); People v. Law, 40 Cal. App.3d 69 (1974).

75. Alea v. State, 265 So.2d 96 (Fla. App. 1972) (collaborative evidence); State *ex rel*

Trimble v. Hedman, 192 N.W.2d 432 (Minn. 1972) (warrant only); U.S. v. Franks and U.S. v. Baller, *supra* note 74 (no challenge).

76. Schwitzgebel, R. K., Butterfield, W. H., Obrist, P. A., and Sidowski, J. B. *Draft statement on the medical device bill H.R. 5545.* Washington, D.C.: American Psychological Association, 1975, p. 6 (mimeo.). In contrast, the current definition used by the Food and Drug Administration defines a "medical device" more vaguely, in part, as one which is "intended for use in the diagnosis of disease or other conditions, or in the cure, mitigation, treatment, or prevention of disease, in man or other animals" or "intended to affect the structure or any function of the body of man or other animals." Medical Device Amendments of 1976, *Congressional Record-House* 1746 (March 9, 1976).

77. "Biofeedback in its current state refers to techniques whereby the bioelectric analog of physiological responses is connected to a visual, auditory or tactile display which is seen, heard, or felt by the user." Mulholland, T. B. Ethical issues in biofeedback. Paper read at the Biofeedback Research Society Meeting, Colorado Springs, Colorado, February 1974, p. 1 (mimeo.).

78. Schwitzgebel, et al., *supra* note 76, at 7.

79. For general overview, see R. L. and R. K. Schwitzgebel (Eds.), *Psychotechnology: Electronic control of mind and behavior.* New York: Wiley, 1973; J. B. Sidowski and S. Ross (Eds.), Instrumentation in psychology. 30 *American Psychologist* 191 (1975, Special issue); *Behavior Research Methods and Instrumentation* (serial publication).

80. Note the following claim with respect to EEG devices: "We can now state as fact that in approximately 48 hours we can train a group of subjects to function at lower, more stable, more energetic and very valuable brain frequencies for specific applications. . . . The human brain, mind and intelligence functioning at these levels have tremendous problem-solving potential. This indicates that human intelligence is not only capable of sensing information impressed on its own brain, but is also capable of sensing information on other brains at a distance." Silva Mind Control International, Inc. History of the Silva method, in J. and N. Regush (Eds.), *PSI catalogue.* New York: Putnam, 1974, p. 146.

81. With respect to lie detectors, "every American should be concerned and shocked that machines are being used to compel citizens to reveal their innermost thoughts about personal matters in order to obtain employment." Senator S. J. Ervin, Jr. Statement for the record, in Hearings, supra note 45, p. 789.

82. Schwitzgebel, R. K. Federal regulation of medical devices. 27 *Harvard Law School Bulletin* 34 (1976).

83. Medical Device Amendments of 1976, *supra* note 76, at 1746–1748.

84. Consumer product: "Any article or component part produced or distributed for personal use, consumption, or enjoyment of a consumer in or around permanent or temporary household, residence, school, in recreation or otherwise." Michael Lemov, Counsel, Subcommittee on Commerce and Finance, House Interstate and Foreign Commerce Committee, Nov. 27, 1972, as quoted in I. Scher (Ed.), *Consumer Product Safety Act.* New York: Practicing Law Institute, 1973, p. 12. For relevant code sections of the act (P.L. 92–573), *see* 15 U.S.C. section 2051 *et seq.* For alleged misuse of FDA-banned "Relaxacisor" exercise device for punishment, *see* Shocking tales of therapy, 92 *Newsweek* 106 (Nov. 20, 1978).

85. *E.g.*, California's Health and Safety Code, sections 28740–28792 (hazardous substances) and Business and Professional Code, section 17500 (misleading statements to induce person to buy goods or services).

86. " 'Programs-of-use' should be supplied with the hardware. They should permit a reasonably intelligent user to progress to a realization of the full capabilities of the hardware." Mulholland, *supra* note 77, at 4. A survey of 44 advertising brochures and 38 instruction manuals for biofeedback devices showed that 21 of the 44 brochures did not provide specifications on the device's input impedance and other critical user variables; 28 of the 38 manuals did not provide technical specifications. Reported in Rugh, J. D. and Schwitzgebel, R. L. Instrumentation for behavioral assessment. In A. Ciminero, W. Calhoun, and H. Adams (Eds.), *Instrumentation for behavioral assessment*. New York: Wiley-Interscience, 1976.

87. The FDA brought action against two biofeedback distributors allegedly for inaccurate labeling. Alpha Dynamics, civil action No. A-73-CA-78, May 14, 1973, U.S. W.D. Court, Austin, Tx.; Toomim Biofeedback Laboratories, court order to submit to inspection. File No. 5–649, Jan. 24, 1973, Federal Central District Court, Los Angeles, Ca.

88. Following items excerpted from "Criteria for clinical investigative use for therapeutic devices under contract to the National Heart and Lung Institute." 3 *NIH Guide for Grants and Contracts* 1, 2 (Aug. 7, 1974). These selected criteria appear applicable to some but not all psychological devices.

89. The demonstration of reliability and efficacy, rather than prevention of physical harm, is probably the more costly aspect of testing psychological devices. One estimate of cost in order to comply with proposed FDA regulations for a wireless shocker was $300,000. Farrall, W. R. Publisher's page, 2 *Behavioral Engineering* 57 (1975).

90. Regulations regarding clinical investigations are tentative. Initial proposed regulations by the Food and Drug Administration resulted in such a significant number of comments and concerns that substantial revisions may be made. *See* FDA, Clinical investigations: Proposed establishment of regulations on obligations of sponsors and monitors. *Federal Register* 49612 (Sept. 27, 1977).

91. FDA, Medical devices; Proposed investigational device exemptions. *Federal Register* 35282 (Aug. 20, 1976).

9

School Law

Schools are often a focal point of social conflict and change. Although controversial matters such as budget and unionization may not directly involve human service professionals, other practices of the school certainly do. Relevant practices that have come under the greatest legal scrutiny include disciplinary action, class or program assignments, and the educational rights of handicapped children.

"DISCIPLINE"

The rules for behavioral conduct that a school may legally adopt, and the methods for enforcing such rules, are directly related to three legal theories that may be chosen to characterize the student-teacher relationship: "in loco parentis," "contract," or "fiduciary."[1] The in loco parentis ("in place of parents") doctrine relies on the implied delegation of parental power to the school to supervise and punish. Students under the age of 18 have long been viewed as a special class that needs more "protection" or "control" than adults need. The Supreme Court used this rationale in upholding a New York State statute that prohibited the sale of nude pictures to children even though the pictures were not obscene by adult standards.[2] Justice Potter Stewart, concurring in the opinion, wrote: "a child—like one in a captive audience—is not possessed of that full capacity for individual choice which is the presumption of the First Amendment guarantees. It is only upon such a premise, I should suppose, that a state may deprive children of other rights—the right to marry, for example, or the right to vote.''[3] The in loco parentis theory, however, has gradually given way to a greater emphasis on the constitutional and contract rights of students.

In recent years, the strain has been most dramatically demonstrated in cases involving the search of students or their property by school officials suspecting the use of drugs. In *Moore v. Student Affairs Committee of Troy State University*[4] the plaintiff's name was on a list of students suspected of possessing marijuana. The list was presented by federal agents to the dean of the university requesting permission to search rooms. The search turned up a quantity of marijuana, and the plaintiff was suspended indefinitely. He sought reinstatement primarily on the basis of the Fourth Amendment freedom from unreasonable search and seizure. The court sustained the suspension and declared that a reasonable inspection was necessary to allow the institution to perform the duty of protecting campus order and to promote a learning environment even though such inspection might infringe on the outer limits of Fourth Amendment rights. In contrast, where there has been merely a suspicion, rather than a probable cause, to believe that a student possesses illegal drugs, the student may prevail.[5] A search must come within the scope of the school official's duties and must be reasonable under the facts and circumstances of the case.[6]

The existence of a contract, expressed or implied, between a student and a private institution such as a college or a university has been recognized by some courts. These courts generally follow the rationale of a well-known case at the turn of the century which stated that, ''he [the student], upon making that contract, agrees to submit himself to the reasonable discipline of the school.''[7] Some of the conditions of these early contracts now seem a bit strange: professors were not to drawl; and they were subject to fines for lecturing beyond quitting time. Students were fined if they groaned or threw stones in class. More recently, a student attempted to avoid paying tuition because, he asserted, the university had promised in its publications to teach him virtues such as wisdom, which had obviously not been accomplished, inasmuch as the university refused to graduate him due to low scholastic standing. The university trustees took the student to court and won the tuition money but not without some embarrassment, for the court held that ''wisdom is not a subject which can be taught, and . . . no rational person would accept such a claim made by any man or institution.''[8]

Presumably a student and an institution (by signing admission forms, etc.) enter into a contract which binds them to the rules of the institution. The preponderance of cases seems to support this arrangement, but a few courts have questioned the validity of this doctrine because of the student's lack of negotiating power. The contractual capability and negotiating power of students increase as the students get older. Generally, the in loco parentis theory would be more appropriate for elementary school students than for college students, whereas the contract theory would be more appropriate for college students.

A more recent theory applied to the student-teacher relationship has been that of a fiduciary.[9] The institution's trustees are under an obligation to preserve a fair balance between the competing interests of faculty and students. This theory seems to place the greatest restraint upon the disciplinary actions by teachers or administrators while giving the students the most privileges. In contrast to the contract theory, the duties of students, if any, under the fiduciary theory are not clear.

Corporal Punishment

Because corporal punishment of military personnel, domestic servants, and prisoners has generally been prohibited[10], such punishment remains a live issue only in elementary and secondary schools. "Maintaining order" in the classroom has become almost synonymous with "discipline" and "punishment."

Corporal punishment of school children is permitted unless such punishment is excessive or indiscriminate.[11] Some legal restraints have developed in both constitutional law (relying primarily on the Eight Amendment's prohibition against cruel and unusual punishment) and in tort law (alleging an intentional act of battery). Criminal sanctions may also be applied for child abuse if the individual is below the age of a person legally recognized as an "adult" or perhaps as an "emancipated minor." All punishment—whether conventional (spanking, suspension) or unconventional (loud noises, odors[12])—should be reasonable and necessary.[13] Practitioners should work within guidelines established by professional organizations and state administrative agencies.[14] Although there might be general agreement that a teacher who suddenly pulls a chair from under a high school student during study hall is administering a cruel and unusual punishment,[15] most determinations of legality rest upon an analysis of the particular fact situation. For example, the use of a large club when threatened with a gun seems reasonable in terms of necessary force.[16] On the other hand, a two-hundred-pound teacher sitting on a ninety-pound, ten-year-old student to subdue a temper tantrum is probably excessive force.[17]

An important Supreme Court decision has established procedural "due process" requirements for administering corporal punishment.[18] The Court held that corporal punishment per se did not violate the Eighth Amendment's prohibition of cruel and unusual punishment, but procedural safeguards were outlined by which, presumably, the likelihood of such punishment becoming excessive and harsh could be minimized. "Except for those acts of misconduct which are so anti-social or disruptive in nature as to shock the conscience, corporal punishment may never be used" unless, according to the Court, the following conditions are met: (a) inform the student beforehand that specific behavior could result in punishment; (b) try to modify unwanted behavior by some other means prior to corporal punishment; (c) administer the punishment in the presence of a second school official (teacher or principal) who has been informed in advance of the reason for the punishment; and (d) provide a written explanation to the parent, upon request, for the punishment and the name of the witness.[19] Each school district should establish some schoolwide policy stating the means of punishment that can be used, its duration, and so forth. The witness and the person administering the punishment, as paid public officials, may be held liable for violations if they knew or reasonably should have known that a basic constitutional violation of the student's rights was occurring.[20] They cannot plead ignorance. They have a professional duty to know the law regulating essential aspects of their craft.

Academic Discipline

A school may not impose academic punishment for nonacademic conduct.[21] Academic credits may be withheld for inappropriate content in a Ph.D. dissertation,[22] but not for violation of school social rules,[23] illness,[24] or fooling naive professors into authorizing fewer course requirements.[25] At least one court has gone so far as to suggest that academic credit could not be withheld from a high school student for cheating on a test.[26] Another court ordered a 10th-grade pupil, who had been suspended for striking teachers, readmitted because the school board disregarded the advice of a school psychologist and a school psychiatrist that the youngster be allowed to return.[27]

Courts generally will not review the issue as to whether a student deserves a particular grade. Determining the quality of student's work is a matter for teacher judgment. On the other hand, the teacher should not act arbitrarily or maliciously by giving a low mark for reasons unrelated to the quality of the work. Thus, a court was willing to review the failure of a medical school student in a course when he claimed that the instructor told him that he could not pass the course regardless of the quality of his work.[28] At the same time, the Supreme Court upheld the dismissal of another medical student where it was shown that the school, without being arbitrary or capricious, made a judgment that her general academic performance (despite satisfactory course grades) was inadequate.[29] The majority of the Court held that there was a significant difference between dismissing a student for academic reasons versus dismissal for violating valid rules of conduct. "This difference calls for far less stringent procedural requirements in the case of an academic dismissal.[30]

Discipline for Violation of Rules

The essential purpose of due process procedures is to give the person who may be adversely affected an opportunity to respond to the allegations by showing that the presumed facts are inaccurate or that additional facts can logically lead to a different conclusion. The more serious the disciplinary action, the more procedural the safeguards required. Thus, if a high school student is forced to sit in the back of the classroom because he is noisy, no hearing with a disciplinary officer or other school official is required. Conversely, if the student is suspended from school, the opportunity for a hearing should be provided.[31] If a student is to be suspended for 10 days or less, s/he should be given oral or written notice of the charges against him/her, an explanation of the evidence against him/her if requested, and an informal opportunity to present his/her side of the story.[32] Suspensions longer than 10 days may require more formal procedures such as advance written notice, a fair hearing, the right to confront the witness, and perhaps the right to legal counsel.[33]

Advance Notice. Immediately interested parties, parents as well as students in the case of minors, should usually be given suffcent notice to allow time to gather relevant details.[34] The Supreme Court has noted, however, that there does not always need to be a delay between the time the "notice" is given and the time of the hearing. The disciplinarian may discuss the alleged misconduct with the student minutes after it has occurred.[35] The amount of prior notice required will depend on what is "fair" to the student. A formal hearing on a complex matter may require an advance of at least several days. In the case of continuing danger to person or property or the "academic process," removal from school may be immediate with the notice and hearing held later as soon as practicable.[36]

One obvious source of information for students and parents will be school records to which the so-called Buckley Amendment[37] provides access. Although test protocols and professional interview notes may be specifically excluded from school records,[38] some evidence as to how the decision in question came about should be available. In one case, a dean of students at a state university was compelled to provide records on the basis that, as a public officer, whenever a written record is an "appropriate mode of discharging the duties of his office, it is not only his right, but his duty, to keep that memorial whether expressly required to do so or not; and when kept it becomes a public document which belongs to the office rather than to the officer.[39] A good general rule may be that anything in writing to be seen by another person is legally part of the record. Personal notes to one's self would not be available as part of the record.

Fair Hearing. One aspect of a fair hearing is to have an impartial hearing officer.[40] This might be only the dean[41] or might include faculty members and the college president.[42] In cases where assignment of an elementary or secondary school student into special education classes may be in question, an outside school psychologist might be the most knowledgeable person.[43] Nonetheless, such persons may be biased toward the school's position. Absolute objectivity is clearly impossible for any hearing officer, but a sincere effort should be made to select a chairperson who will facilitate both the conditions of "fairness" and its appearance (psychologically important in conflict-resolution).

Confrontation and Cross-examination. Students should have an opportunity to make a personal presentation.[44] In more severe cases, the student may have the right to cross-examine witnesses, although cases can be found denying this opportunity.[45]

In quasi-judicial proceedings, the right to counsel is probably justified only in extreme circumstances where the student's honor and reputation are at stake or where there is the possibility of criminal action following expulsion.[46] "Guidance conferences" that may be contingent upon misbehavior but which do not jeopardize academic standing are not "disciplinary actions," and therefore are not subject to the restraint of procedural due process.[47] Similarly, probation (considered a minor sanction) may not require a notice and a hearing.[48]

STUDENT CLASSIFICATION AND PROGRAM ASSIGNMENT

Assigning children to special education classes on the basis of standardized tests that are assertedly prejudicial has been challenged in numerous cases (see Chapter 7). An early and well-known case prohibited the Washington, D.C. school district from placing all children into one of four tracks based on test scores standardized primarily on white middle-class students.[49] In addition to case law that has restricted or abolished racially biased tests, federal administrative regulations have also been issued to this effect.[50] The use of procedures other than tests, such as structured interviews, for placement purposes has not come under legal attack, although similar or even greater bias might exist. Conversely, initial class assignment by a procedure such as a lottery[51], while removing bias, might also remove the opportunity for educational remediation, and therefore is not a viable alternative. Some regular but unbiased procedure with reasonable criteria should be followed. Labeling and assigning a 15-year-old student as "emotionally disturbed" for verbally abusing a teacher and for failing to follow instructions has been held, for example, to be a violation of procedural due process.[52]

Two precedent-setting cases[53] regarding classification substantially agree in placing the burden of proof for the need of a nonregular assignment on the school. When an unordinary status is recommended, the following safeguards are mandated: notice to parents including alternative assignments, right to a hearing, right to legal counsel, right to examine records, right to have own expert witnesses and a state-provided independent psychological examination, and right to cross-examine school witnesses. Furthermore, the hearing officer is not to be an employee of the school.

Certain classification procedures have been successfully challenged as a violation of the right of privacy. A federal district court held that a school's use of a personality test that asks intimate questions about family relationships (e.g., requesting true or false answers as to whether parents "hugged and kissed me good night when I was small') in order to identify potential drug abusers, without first obtaining informed parental consent, violates the student's and the parents' privacy.[54] The court also condemned the program, in part, because assertedly the program was conducted by "untrained" personnel (i.e., school psychologists with only master's degrees from an education department, rather than Ph.D.'s with clinical experience, as parents might reasonably expect the label of "psychologist" to represent). To insure adequately informed consent, the earned degrees and subject area of personnel administering classification and remedial procedures should be listed.

RIGHT TO EDUCATION

Although education is not mentioned as a right in the United States Constitution, a doctrine (similar to the one of "privacy") is gradually being articulated through case law. In the famous integration case of *Brown* v. *Board of Education,* the Supreme Court asserted that "education is perhaps the most important function of state and local governments."[55] In 1971 the Pennsylvania Association for Retarded Children (PARC) initiated a civil action against the Commonwealth of Pennsylvania[56] in which convincing testimony was presented to the effect that no child is ineducable, that behavior modification techniques are useful with this population, that some retarded children regress rapidly when out of school, and that many children were misclassified into classes for emotionally or mentally retarded. The three-judge district court approved a consent agreement under which the Commonwealth of Pennsylvania could no longer, in violation of the Fourteenth Amendment's "equal protection clause," deny any mentally handicapped child access to free public education.

A second landmark case held that a jurisdiction which requires parents to send their children to school under threat of criminal penalties presupposes that an educational opportunity will be made available.[57] Thus, a failure to provide necessary facilities and programs for all children (including educationally handicapped) violated the due process clause of the Fifth Amendment. Nearly all states have now established administrative or statutory mandates for the education of handicapped children.[58]

The U.S. Office of Education has developed regulations implementing the "Education for All Handicapped Children Act of 1975" which applies to programs or activities receiving federal financial assistance.[59] Basically, school districts are required to identify and evaluate all handicapped children and to provide them with appropriate classification and educational services. Handicapping conditions include mental retardation, deafness, hearing loss, speech and visual impairment, deformities, heart conditions, leukemia, serious emotional disturbances, as well as specific learning disabilities.

Educational services should be designed to meet handicapped children's individual educational needs to the same extent that those of the nonhandicapped are met.[60] Emphasis is placed upon the education of handicapped children in regular classroom settings with the use of supplementary services (ie. "mainstreaming").

An Individualized Education Program (IEP) is required for each youngster. This IEP is to be developed in a meeting with a representative of the educational agency, the teacher, the parents, the child (when appropriate), and other persons requested by the parents or agency. The parents must be given advance notice of the IEP meeting and a written copy of the IEP must be given to them upon request. The parents may also inspect the child's cumulative record file, although there may be a waiting period not to exceed 45 days.[61]

The IEP is to include, among other matters, a statement of the child's present educational performance, a statement of annual goals and short-term objectives, and a statement of the services to be provided.[62] The school is not to be held accountable should a child not achieve the goals or level of growth set forth in the IEP. The school should, however, have made a "good faith effort" to help the student achieve the goals and objectives.[63]

As with many rights, *Brown* v. *Board of Education* as an example, the translation of legal ideals into practice is difficult to accomplish. The public's reaction to the financial cost of the asserted "right" of handicapped children to special education, in private schools if necessary, at public expense, will probably cause a substantial delay.[64] Other legitimate but competing claims (e.g., assistance for the elderly) also impinge on public policy and budgets.[65] Nonetheless, greater opportunities for handicapped persons are being sought and created.

NOTES

1. See Appendix B for definitions of these three terms. The purpose of this chapter is to summarize briefly certain issues especially relevant to the mental health practitioner. Readers may consult annual editions of the *Yearbook of School Law*, published by the National Organization on Legal Problems of Education (Topeka, Kansas) for authoritative and current summaries of broader issues.
2. Ginsberg v. New York, 390 U.S. 629 (1968).
3. *Id.*, Justice Stewart at p. 635.
4. Moore v. Student Affairs Committee of Troy State University, 284 F. Supp. 725 (N.Y.S. 1968). *See also* State v. Stein, 456 P.2d 1 (Kan. 1969), *cert. denied* 397 U.S. 947 (1970).
5. People v. Bowers, 72 Misc. 2d 800, 339 N.Y.S.2d 783 (Crim. Ct. 1973).
6. *In re* W., Cal. App. 3d 777, 105 Cal. Rptr. 775 (1973)
7. Koblitz v. Western Reserve University, 21 Ohio Cir. Ct. R. 144 (1901) as cited in Mills, J. L. *The legal rights of college students and administrators*. Washington, D.C.: Lerner Law Book Publishing Co., 1971, at 44.
8. Columbia Univ. v. Jacobsen, 148 A.2d 63, 67 (N.Y.S. 1959). *See also* Jones v. Vassar, 299 N.Y.S. 283 (1969) (no breach of contract).
9. People *ex rel* Tinkhoff v. Northwestern University, 33 Ill. App. 224, 77 N.E.2d 345, *cert. denied* 335 U.S. 829 (1947) (supporting the theory of fiduciary relationship).
10. *E.g.*, Jackson v. Bishop, 404 F. Supp. 571 (8th Cir. 1968) (prohibition of punishment of prisoners); Nelson v. Heyne, 491 F. Supp. 352 (7th Cir. 1974) (prohibition of punish-

ment of mental patients); Glaser v. Marietta, 351 F. Supp. 555 (W.D. Penn 1972) (permitted in school with parent's approval).

11. Sims v. Bd. of Education, 329 F. Supp. 678 (N.M. 1971); Ingraham v. Wright, 498 F.2d 248 (5th Cir. 1974), 525 F.2d 909 (1976) (*en banc*), 97 S.Ct. 1401 (1977) (limiting application of the Eighth Amendment but allowing criminal charges or civil actions of battery against the person inflicting).

12. Foreyt, J. P. and Kennedy, W. A. Treatment of overweight by aversion therapy. 9 *Behaviour Research and Therapy* 29 (1971); Greene, R. J., Hoats, D. L., and Hornick, A. J. Music distortion: A new technique for behavior modification. 20 *The Psychological Record* 107 (1970).

13. *Restatement of Torts*, section 153 (1965).

14. Resolution on use of corporal punishment, Council of Representatives, American Psychological Assoc., as reported in *Behavior Today*, April 14, 1975, p. 449.

15. Patton v. Bennet, 304 F. Supp. 297 (E.D. Tenn. 1969). *See also* Ingraham v. Wright, 492 F.2d 248 (5th Cir. 1974); Frank v. School Board, 195 So. 2d 451 (1967) (liability for unnecessarily rough disciplining).

16. Metcalf v. State, 17 S.W. 142 (Tex. App. 1886).

17. Calway v. Williamson, 130 Conn. 575, 36 A.2d 377 (Conn. 1944).

18. Baker v. Owen, 395 F. Supp. 294 (M.D.N.C. 1975), *aff'd.* 96 S. Ct. 210, 423 U.S. 907 (1975).

19. *Id.* at 302.

20. Wood v. Strickland, 348 F. Supp. 244 (W.D. Ark. 1973), *rev.* 485 F.2d 186 (8th Cir. 1974), *vac. & remand.* 420 U.S. 308, 95 S.Ct. 992, 1001 (1975) (school board member not immune from liability for damages due to discipline).

21. Traditional academic punishments such as extra homework for classroom misbehavior have not been tested, but logically might be ruled illegal. What about the logic of after-school detention which combines the aversiveness of punishment with studying? According to classical conditioning theory, the frequent pairing of aversive stimuli with academic behavior might reduce positive responses of the student toward studying.

22. Edde v. Columbia University, 168 N.Y.S.2d 643, 154 N.E.2d 558, 359 U.S. 956 (1958) ("The court will not substitute its own opinion as to the merits of a doctoral dissertation for that of the faculty members whom the university has selected to make a determination as to the quality of the dissertation."); *accord, In re* Johnston, 365 Mich. 509, 114 N.W.2d 255 (1962) (high school may change course requirements at any time).

23. Strank v. Mercy Hospital, 383 Pa. 54, 117 A.2d 697 (1955) (school could not withhold previously earned credits of expelled student). *Contra*, Carr v. St. John's University, 17 App. Div. 2d 632, 231 N.Y.S.2d 410, *aff'd mem*, 187 N.E.2d 18, 235 N.Y.S.2d 834 (1962) (upheld refusal of university to confer degree on student who served as a witness in a civil wedding ceremony contrary to tenets of the Catholic Church).

24. Connelly v. University of Vermont, 244 F. Supp. 156 (Vt. 1965).

25. Woody v. Burns, 188 So. 2d 56 (1st Dist. Fla. 1966) (professor signed card on which student crossed off a required course); Blank v. Board of Higher Education, 273 N.Y.S.2d 796 (1966) (college could not refuse to give the student a degree because the chairperson of the psychology department was not aware of an academic rule. The chairperson permitted the student to pass two courses by examination which was contrary to college policy. The Court considered the chairperson an agent of the dean and thus the

decision had binding effect upon the college.): Coats v. Cloverdale Unified School District (Sonoma County) (Cal. Sup. Ct. 1975) (a high school could not deny diploma to student who refused to run a lap as punishment for losing a volleyball game), as reported in *Los Angeles Times,* Part 3, p.3, Jan. 24, 1975.

26. *In re* Carter, 262 N.C. 360, 137 S.E. 150 (1964).

27. R. K. v. Board of Education of Twp. of Lakewood. M.J., January 17, 1974, as cited in Delon, F.G. *Yearbook of school law.* Topeka, Kan.: National Organization on Legal Problems in Education, 1974, p. 159.

28. Connelly v. University of Vermont and State Agricultural College, 244 F. Supp. 156 (D. Vt. 1965) as cited in Levine, A.H. and Cary, E. *The rights of students: The basic ACLU guide to a student's rights* (revised ed.). New York: Avon, 1977.

29. Board of Curators of the University of Missouri v. Charlotte Horowitz, 98 S. Ct. 948 (1978).

30. *Id.* at 953.

31. Goss v. Lopez, 372 F. Supp. 1279 (S.D. Ohio 1974), *aff'd.* 419 U.S. 565, 95 S. Ct. 729 (1975); *see also* Koenings, S.L. and Ober, S.L. Legal precedents in student rights cases, in V.H. Haubrich and M.W. Apple (Eds.) *Schooling and the rights of children.* Berkeley, CA: McCutchan Publ. Co., 1975, pp. 132–158.

32. Koenings and Ober, *Id.* For a more extended discussion of due process requirements in colleges and universities, *see* Chambers, M.M. *The colleges and the courts: The developing law of the student and the college.* Danville, Il: Interstate Printers, 1972, 213–246.

33. Just as due process procedures can be used in a serious manner to limit administrative actions, they can also be used frivolously: "Even if you are as quilty as hell and haven't got a thing to defend yourself with, you should still demand your due process rights. A full-dress hearing, to start with, takes time.... The last thing [school administrators] want to do is kill a few evenings listening to a parade of witnesses testifying whether or not they actually saw you substitute that stag movie for Miss Nerdlinger's geography film.... You might rerun the movie as part of your defense, or cross-exame Miss Nerdlinger on her sexual hang-ups, or present evidence as to the 'redeeming social merit' of the flick. The local press—which you would be free to invite to your public hearing—would lap it up. All in all, your school would much prefer to let you off with a warning rather than submit to the three-ring circus you might plan. Such is the power of procedural due process." Sandman, P.M. *Students and the law.* New York: Collier Books, 1971, p. 126.

34. Sturm v. Trustees of Boston University, Equity No. 89433 (Suffolk County Super. Ct., April 18, 1969); Knight v. State Board of Education, 200 F. Supp. 174 (M.D. Tenn. 1961); Scoggin v. Lincoln University, 291 F. Supp. 161 (W.D. Mo. 1968); in part *contra,* Wright v. Texas Southern University, 277 F. Supp. 110 (S.D. Tex. 1967).

35. Goss, *supra* note 31.

36. *Id.*

37. Section 438 of the General Education Provisions Act, Title 4 of Public Law 90–247, as amended by section 513, Public Law 93–380 (August 21, 1974).

38. Explicitly excluded from educational records, by at least one version of the Buckley Amendment are: "Records of institutional, supervisory, and administrative personnel and educational personnel ancillary thereto which are in the sole possession of the maker

thereof and which are not accessible or revealed to any other person except a substitute.''
40 *Federal Register* 1210 (Jan. 6, 1975). Several states (e.g., New York, Ohio, Maryland, Colorado) have legislation pending or passed requiring disclosure of actual test forms and individual answers at the request of those taking exams. Foltz, D. ''Snowball effect'' seen in truth in testing movement. 10 *APA Monitor* 3 (Sept./Oct. 1979).

39. Morris v. Smiley, 378 S.W.2d 149, 152(Tex. Civ. App. 1964) quoting 45 *Am. Jur.* 420.

40. Morrissey v. Brewer, 408 U.S. 471 (1972).

41. Tanton v. McKenney, 226 Mich. 245, 197 N.W. 510 (1924); Wright v. Texas Southern University, 277 F. Supp. 110 (S.D. Tex. 1967).

42. Barker v. Harway, 283 F. Supp. 228 (S.D. W.Va. 1968), *aff'd per curiam* 399 F.2d 638 (4th Cir. 1968).

43. Buss, W. What procedural due process means to a school psychologist: A dialogue. 13 *Journal of School Psychology* 298, 308 (1975).

44. Goss v. Lopez, *supra* note 31.

45. Pro: *see*, *e.g.* Parker v. Lester, 227 F.2d 708 (9th Cir. 1955); Esteban v. Central Missouri State College, 407 F.2d 1077 (8th Cir. 1969). Con: *see*, *e.g.* Dixon v. Alabama Board of Education, 294 F. 2d 150 (5th Cir. 1961), *cert. denied*, 368 U.S. 930 (1961); Mitchell v. Long Island University, 309 N.Y.S.2d 538 (Sup. Ct. Nassau County, 1970).

46. Esteban, 407 F.2d; *contra*, Dixon, 294 F.2d.

47. Cosme v. Board of Education, 270 N.Y.S.2d 231 (1966); Madera v. Board of Education, 267 F. Supp. 356, 386 F.2d 778 (1967).

48. Sill et al. v. Pennsylvania State University, 318 F. Supp. 608 (M.D. Pa. 1970).

49. Hobson v. Hansen, 320 F. Supp. 720 (D.D.C. 1971). Boys outnumber girls about 5-to-1 in EMR classes, but no class action suit, to the authors' knowledge, has been filed on behalf of young males.

50. Education of the Handicapped Amendments of 1974, 20 U.S.C.A., section 1413(a) (13).

51. Used for admission of the first class in 1968 by Federal City College, Washington, D.C.

52. Walton v. City School District of Glen Cove, Index No. 18209–71 (N.Y. Sup. Ct. 1972) as cited in Gorlow, L. The school psychologist as expert witness in due process hearings. 13 *Journal of School Psychology* 311, 333 (1975).

53. Pennsylvania Association for Retarded Children v. Commonwealth of Pennsylvania, 334 F. Supp. 1257 (E.D. Pa. 1971); Mills v. Board of Education of the District of Columbia, Civ. Action No. 1939–71 (D.D.C. 1972).

54. Merriken v. Cressman, 364 F. Supp. 913 (E.D. Pa. 1973).

55. 347 U.S. 483, 493 (1954).

56. 334 F. Supp. 1257 (E.D. Pa. 1971).

57. Mills, *supra*, note 53, as cited in Mental Health Law Project, *Basic rights of the mentally handicapped*. Washington, D.C., 1973, at p. 47.

58. E.g., Tennessee Public Law chapter 839, 1972; Massachusetts chapter 81, sec. 46a. *See also*, summary in *Basic rights of the mentally handicapped*, *supra* note 57, pp. 38–58.

59. Public Law 94–142, sec. 504 of Rehabilitation act of 1973 (1975 ammend.).

60. Dept. of Health, Education, and Welfare, Office of the Secretary, Nondiscrimination on the basis of handicap. 42 *Federal Register* 22676 (May 4, 1977) and 42474 (Aug. 23, 1977).

61. ''Family Educational Rights and Privacy Act of 1974,'' Public Law 93–380. Complaints regarding noncompliance may be filed with the Family Educational Rights and Privacy Complaint Office, U.S. Dept. of Health, Edcuation, and Welfare, 330 Independence Ave., S.W., Washington, D.C. 20201.

62. *See* Weintraub, F.J. Understanding the individualized Education Program (IEP). 2 *Amicus* 26 (1977); Paine, S.C. The individual educational plan: Concept, guidelines, issues. 2 *Forum for Behavioral Technology* 1 (1977) (a behavioral approach toward implementing IEPs).

63. Clarification of final regulations to Public Law 94–142. 3 *Amicus* 8 (1978).

64. A New York State court required that a child certified as handicapped by the board of education be provided approximately $6500, in addition to a $2000 state grant, for the purpose of attending a special school in Florida. *In re* Downey, 72 Misc. 2d 772, 340 N.Y.S.2d 687 (Fam. Ct. 1973). Similar case requiring a public school to pay for private school: Howard S. v. Friendswood Independent School District, 454 F. Supp. 634 (S.D. Tex. 1978).

65. *See, e.g.*, Rehabilitation Act of 1973 (Public Law 93–112) section 504; Dept. of HEW, Office of the Secretary, Implemention of Executive Order 11914: Nondiscrimination on the basis of Handicap in federally assisted programs. 43 *Federal Register* 2132 (Jan. 13, 1978).

CHAPTER 10

Family Law

The family is the primary social environment in which most of us are raised, for better or for worse. It is also the primary institution that structures the legal rights and obligations of husband, wife, and child. Family law deals inevitably, and perhaps more directly than any other branch of law, with intense human emotions.[1]

As developed in American case law in the 1800s, marriage was viewed as a lifelong community of equals—one partner working in the home and one working outside the home, reinforced by the doctrine of community property.[2] Economic and social changes such as the increased divorce rate, cohabitation of unmarried couples, and employment of both partners outside the home have forced a revision of traditional legal doctrine. Recent reforms in family law can be characterized by two trends: (1) general withdrawal of the State from regulation of private adult relationships, and (2) a focus by the State on the economic and psychological consequences of cohabitation, whether inside or outside a formal marriage, on any children involved.[3]

A plethora of social alternatives (e.g., serial marriage, open marriage, group marriage, homosexual marriage) have had advocates seeking social legitimization. The government may have retreated from the bedroom, but it certainly has not left

The authors wish to acknowledge the assistance of Donald W. Pike, Commissioner in the Los Angeles County Superior Court, for his comments on an early draft of this chapter. Unfortunately, the authors cannot hold him responsible for what errors of commission and omission may be herein contained.

the home. The loosening of traditional family structure has seemingly required that the State more actively support and promulgate rules for birth control, abortion, child care, special education, nutrition, old-age pension, and so forth. It may be useful to begin with a brief summary of what remains of the State's interest in formal legal marriage.

MARRIAGE

Marriage is not only a religious or civil act, it is also a contractual agreement in which the State has a definite and legitimate interest.[4] The regulation of marriage and divorce has generally been left to state prerogative.[5] Individual states have therefore set the various conditions necessary for marriage (e.g., minimal age, physical examination, purchase of license, solemnization by a ceremony) and also some of the rights and duties expected of the married couple. Case law,[6] as well as the Uniform Marriage and Divorce Act,[7] has now firmly established marriage as a fundamental civil freedom. This legal development may be the logical consequence of greater diversity of life styles and the popular acceptance of the doctrine of privacy.[8]

Except perhaps for bigamy and marriage of close relatives or persons of the same sex, any prohibition of marriage is constitutionally suspect.[9] Furthermore the ease of traveling to a state which has fewer marriage restrictions makes enforcement of more stringent requirements in another state quite difficult. Marriage is now, both in fact and in law, little more than a matter of registration by the prospective couple.[10] Similarly, no-fault divorce statutes bring the legal routine into conformity with the de facto situation wherein termination of marriage is unilaterally terminable at will.[11] The enactment of the Uniform Parenting Act[12] and the enforcement of fair and reasonable distribution of property accumulations reduces the importance of sanctioned marriage and divorce. Few State interests are now served by civil or religious ceremonies.

The "withering away" of marriage and divorce regulation does not, as noted earlier, mean that the relationship is of no concern to the State. The freedom to enter into a contractual relationship does not mean that valid contracts are left unenforced. Where property or child custody disputes have arisen, the courts have occasionally recognized as a "legal family" a social unit consisting of an unmarried man and woman (and children, if any) who live together as an ostensible married family.[13] The traditional proof of sexual intercourse as an element of common law marriage is probably unnecessary.[14] Two adults of opposite sex simply living at the same address becomes "an association of two independent individuals" and can create the presumption of a de facto marriage.[15] However, mere temporary sexual relationships, as for example between swinging couples, are not sufficient to constitute a family. More than two adults cohabiting (e.g., "group marriages") do not meet this presumption and indeed may be discouraged by the application of statutes forbidding adultery, bigamy, fornication, and prostitution. More subtle but effective means of discouraging collectives of unrelated persons rely upon the enforcement of "single family residential" zoning ordinances or classifying such persons as ineligible for certain federal and state programs such as food stamps and aid to dependent children.[16]

Marriage laws are presumably designed to encourage an enduring relationship between a man and a woman, although the sex of partners may not be specified by statute. In Minnesota where the statute does not specify the sex or the number of parties who can be married,[17] two men were denied a marriage license by the clerk of court on the ground that the applicants were of the same sex. The denial was upheld by the courts.[18] The equal protection provision of the Fourteenth Amendment restraining the government from classifying persons in a discriminatory manner without a pressing public necessity has been the basic, though thus far unseccessful, rationale of advocates of homosexual and other nontraditional marriages.[19] The factors to be balanced include how important being married is to the nontraditional partners, and the legitimate interest of the state in maintaining the classification that makes certain persons ineligible. Where same-sexed persons have been married "accidentally," the court has voided the wedding.[20] An English court held that the "true" legal sex of a person was not altered by a sex-change operation, and annulled a 14-day marriage between a male transsexual and her transvestite husband.[21]

Because the act of marriage presumes a rational state of mind (although "being in love" may not), a marriage will be held invalid if a person consents because of a delusional belief. Concealment of severe mental disability will usually justify annulment. Mental disability without intentional concealment will not, however, in itself be cause for annulment unless the disability has resulted in a number of years of institutionalization.

Formal contracts between prospective spouses are called "ante-nuptial" or "pre-nuptial" agreements. In common law, the wife's legal identity merged with that of her husband—she adopted the husband's family name. Thus, agreements made prior to marriage as well as any made during the marriage were held to be invalid. Numerous restrictions still exist as to what may be negotiated in an antenuptial agreement, but such agreements (whether written, oral, or implied) are now generally recognized as valid and binding if they are equitable and reasonable,[22] untainted by fraud or undue influence, entered into by competent parties with full knowledge of their rights and the material consequences, and not promotive of divorce.[23] If facilitation of sex is the consideration,[24] the contract is universally void.

Other typical marriage contract restrictions do not permit the husband to relinquish his duty to at least partly support the family,[25] either party to refrain from cohabitation,[26] prior agreement for a fixed amount or waiver of alimony in event of divorce,[27] or an agreement as to the custody of the children.[28] The rationale is that private agreements should not make a spouse or children wards of the state by encouraging the wage-earner to avoid his/her duty of support. On the other hand, in situations of out-of-wedlock pregnancies, contracts specifying support and living arrangements might actually encourage marriage rather than adoption, foster care, or abortion.[29]

Contracts usually focus on financial arrangements (e.g., property settlement if divorced or at time of death, separate bank accounts), household responsibilities (e.g., baby-sitting, washing dishes), and sexual or social behavior (e.g., extramarital affairs). (See Appendixes V and W for sample contracts.) Jacqueline and Aristotle Onassis reportedly drew up a 170-point marriage contract covering many details of their living arrangements.[30] The parties are usually considered to be in a confidential relationship, and are thus required to give a full and frank disclosure of relevant matters. It may be helpful—but is not necessary[31]—for each party to have an independent legal counsel to avoid any future claim of fraud or over-reaching because one of the parties has, for example, much more knowledge of financial matters.[32] Agreements should be in writing and properly witnessed.[33]

Some contracts contain provisions for the reexamination and revision of the terms of the contract and for arbitration by a mutually agreed-upon third party. The arbitration process is universally acknowledged as a privilege of contracting parties in general, although the privilege is probably more limited in marriage or separation contracts.[34] Some agreements have stated that either partner can terminate the marriage after six weeks, six months, or at any time for any reason.[35] The courts have usually taken a dim view of these ''self-destruct'' arrangements, and voided them all. Courts may also void those contracts that compel the performance of personal services such as having two children or those that require marital or nonmarital sex.[36]

The only uniform enforcement of ante-nuptial agreements by the courts has been in financial matters of a limited and personal nature. Because the preservation of marriage is generally held to be socially desirable, courts and legislatures have traditionally refused to enforce arrangements that appear to defeat the relationship. A New Jersey court refused to enforce an ante-nuptial agreement where the wife promised to allow her mother-in-law to live in the household indefinitely.[37] The fact that invalid portions are included in an otherwise valid agreement does not necessarily invalidate the entire document. It should be noted, in summary, that much of the confusion and publicity surrounding *Marvin* v. *Marvin*[38] is because the couple did not have a written contract of any kind.

CHILD ABUSE AND NEGLECT

''Child abuse''—the intentional use of force resulting in physical injury serious enough to endanger the health or life of the child—is a criminal offense in all states.[39] ''Neglect'' is a less certain concept but generally refers to persistently inadequate child care of a physical nature, and sometimes to the failure to insure conditions for positive social-psychological development.[40]

Statutes typically prohibit cruel corporal punishment, physical neglect, and sexual exploitation. Some states include emotional abuse.[41] Idaho has one of the broadest and most psychologically-oriented negligence statutes. It gives the court jurisdiction over any child whose behavior indicates social or emotional maladjustment.[42] Criminal negligence has been found even where there are no physical signs of abuse.[43] The Federal Child Abuse Prevention and Treatment Act refers generally to situations of "physical or mental injury, sexual abuse, negligent treatment or maltreatment of a child."[44]

Very rarely are positive standards of care specified because of the difficulty of obtaining consensus. The United Nations General Assembly in a "Declaration of the Rights of the Child," asserted that all children are entitled to:

Have a name and nationality

Enjoy the benefits of security, including adequate nutrition, housing, recreation, and medical services

Receive special treatment, education, and care if handicapped

Grow up in an atmosphere of affection and security and, wherever possible, in the care and under the responsibility of his parents and in any case in an atmosphere of affection and moral and material security

Receive free education and opportunity for play and recreation

Be among the first to receive protection and relief in times of disaster

Be protected against all forms of neglect, cruelty, and exploitation

Be protected from practices that may foster racial, religious, or any form of discrimination.[45]

Children may be removed from homes for many diverse reasons such as parental chronic alcoholism,[46] sexual promiscuity,[47] and mental incompetency.[48] The wording of neglect statutes permits wide judicial discretion in terminating parental custody, but the predominate concern is the welfare of the child rather than the punishment of the deviant parents (or securing the right of the parents to privacy and freedom from State intrusion). For example, a 16-year-old mother convicted of thefts to support her heroin addiction lost custody of her 18-month-old child due to a previous lack of contact with the child (only one month out of 18), previous prison record, poor prognosis for curing drug addiction, and the child's psychological need for a stable home.[49] By focusing on the welfare of the child, even severe mental disability of the parent is, in itself, not sufficient to terminate parental custody if the parents have arranged for alternate care.[50]

After termination of custody, some appropriate remedy (e.g., return to home under welfare agency supervision, placement in a foster home, adoption) must be arranged. The options have customarily been assessed on the basis of the "best interests of the child" or the more modest principle of "least detrimental among available alternatives.''[51] Psychological considerations may be factored into the judicial determination. Mental health practitioners might gather factual data regarding behavioral deficits and strengths of the child, age-appropriateness of the child's behavior, motivation of potential caretakers, ratios of reward/punishment in alternative environments, exposure to peer and adult role models, probable duration of relationships, and coping strategies used by the child under stress.[52]

All states require physicians to report suspected cases of child abuse, and the majority of states have expanded this requirement to nurses, school teachers, social workers, and mental health professionals.[53] An American Medical Association resolution has recommended the inclusion of lawyers.[54] Some states require that ''any'' person who has knowledge or a reason to suspect abuse should report it. Most states instruct the reporting individual to make a report by telephone, followed by a written report, to departments of welfare, juvenile courts, or law-enforcement officials.[55]

Every state provides some form of immunity for the reporter against possible defamation of character, invasions of privacy and breach of confidence, although, even without such statutes, a person acting in good faith and without malice would probably have a successful defense.[56] The majority of states also provide penalties for *failure* to report. Violation of the reporting statute may, in itself, constitute negligence and therefore support a civil suit against the professional. The parents of an abused youngster (who is frequently a behavior problem) may also be subject to civil suit for the misbehavior of their child when, for example, they have negligently entrusted the family car to a mentally incompetent son[57] or giving a mentally ill child a semi-automatic rifle.[58]

Although the concept of *emotional* abuse or neglect is gaining acceptance, this wider recognition is not without cost or danger. It permits the state to set and enforce standards of child-rearing in private homes where physical injury has not occurred and where the primary evidence might be the more-or-less informed opinion of mental health professionals.[59] Furthermore, relatively few middle-class homes, compared to poor and minority class homes, are subject to inspections by social case workers. Therefore the constitutional issue of due process could be raised.

CHILD CUSTODY

In custody disputes, the court is required to determine which of the competing parties is to be the legal guardian of the child. The dispute usually arises out of a divorce proceeding in which the emotional trauma is felt by the child as well as by the parents.[60] In early English common law, the father, as head of the household, automatically had custody of the children unless it could be proven he was an unfit parent. In Blackstone's words: ''A mother, as such, is entitled to no power but only to reverence and respect.''[61] A general preference for maternal custody developed gradually after the women's suffrage movement and with the doctrine of "tender-years" (i.e., children of tender years need their mothers more than their fathers). The tender-years doctrine has now been replaced by the concept of the "best interests of the child." In principle, both parents have equal custody rights. However, mothers gain custody in a large majority of the cases[62] because they are usually the more psychologically important parent. Nonetheless, fathers are increasingly being given custody of even preschool children, particularly if the best interests of the child can be supported by findings of an unfit mother or abandonment by the mother.[63]

The phrase "best interests of the child" is quite vague. In an effort to make it less so, the Michigan legislature established standards upon which a trial court's decision should be based:

1. The love, affection, and other emotional ties existing between the competing parties and the child.
2. The capacity and disposition of competing parties to give the child love, affection and guidance and continuation of educating and raising of the child in its religion or creed, if any.
3. The capacity and disposition of competing parties to provide the child with food, clothing, medical care or other remedial care recognized and permitted under the laws of this state in lieu of medical care and other material needs.
4. The length of time the child has lived in a stable, satisfactory environment and the desirability of maintaining continuity.
5. The permanence, as a family unit, of the existing or proposed custodial home.
6. The moral fitness of the competing parties.
7. The mental and physical health of the competing parties.
8. The home, school, and community records of the child.
9. The reasonable preference of the child, if the court deems the child to be of sufficient age to express preference.
10. Any other factor considered by the court to be relevant to a particular child custody dispute.[64]

The Uniform Marriage and Divorce Act is similar in its "best interest" test, although it specifically forbids the trial court to consider "conduct of a proposed custodian that does not affect his relationship to the child."[65] In such matters the court must exercise its discretion and cannot automatically deny custody, for example, to a homosexual mother.[66] The court may, however, specify living relationships.[67] In limiting the scope of relevant behavior of prospective custodians, the drafters of the Uniform Act wrote, "There is no reason to encourage parties to spy on each other in order to discover marital (most commonly, sexual) misconduct for use in a custody contest.''[68]

Similarly, because one of the competing parties is financially more secure does not necessarily justify placement in the more affluent home.[69] Nor does the mere existence of a mental disorder, past or present, disqualify a parent.[70] ''Case after case which have been decided in various jurisdictions have uniformly held that a mother who has suffered and recovered from mental illness and otherwise shown to be a fit and proper person *retains* preference for custody of her minor children. This is so notwithstanding that she may later suffer a relapse. The cases make it clear that when the issue of unfitness for custody is raised on the grounds of mental illness, the court's function is limited to ascertaining what the mental condition and health of the mother is *at the time of application* for custody is made.''[71] When, however, the mental disablement is severe and potentially damaging to the child, custody can be removed.[72] A parent adjudged incompetent or committed to a mental hospital is assumed to be unfit.[73]

The Federal Rules of Civil Procedure (Rule 35), followed in many states,[74] permits a court, upon a motion (usually *habeas corpus*) and a showing of good cuase, to order a party to submit to a mental examination by a qualified physician.[75] In at least one case, refusal to be examined resulted in awarding custody to the competing party.[76] The following steps have been recommended in preparing a custody evaluation:[77]

1. Receive permission from the parent-client to use confidential information. If you believe that revealing certain information such as test scores would be detrimental to the client, the client and his/her lawyer should be told.

2. If the youngster is in a treatment center or there is reason to believe that his/her best interests are likely to be overlooked, raise the matter with the client or both attorneys about appointing a guardian *ad litem* or counsel for the child.[78]

3. Inform the parties as to how information in the diagnostic or therapeutic process might be used so that they can be selective in their revelations if they so choose. The individual may have to choose between protecting privacy and appearing evasive to the court.

4. Carefully conduct the examination. As a general guideline, an adequate clinical examination of the parent may last between one to three hours, supplemented by psychological tests.[79] Examination of a child may last between two to five hours and one or two hours may be spent going over background information such as school records, home observations, and so forth.

5. Organize observations and conclusions in a manner to withstand the validating procedure of cross-examination. Cross-examination is the means

used by an opposing attorney to bring relevant information to the attention of the court.[80]

Whether the cost of mental health consultants to the judicial system can be justified in terms of observable benefit to the children is open to debate. Fiscal prudence suggests that controlled, longitudinal outcome studies of the accuracy of professional predictions and recommendations should be undertaken.[81]

In contrast to adoption decisions, custody orders are often modified when there has been a significant change in circumstances that would bear on the welfare of the child (e.g., remarriage of parents, illness of parent or child).

ADOPTION

Adoption is a procedure by which the legal responsibility for an individual, minor or adult, is transferred with court approval from the natural parents to another party. At common law, adoption was not permitted, even with parental consent. Voluntary adoption was first authorized in the United States by statute around 1850.[82] Adoption *without* parental consent is a later development and authorized only in special circumstances where there is clear and convincing proof of parental unfitness.

A widely accepted statement of objectives of adoption programs reads as follows:

> To protect the child—from unnecessary separation from parents who might give him a good home and loving care if sufficient help and guidance were available to them; from adoption by persons unfit to have the responsibility for rearing a child; and from interference after he has been happily established in his adoptive home, by his natural parents, who may have legal claim because of defects in the adoption procedure. To protect the natural parents—from hurried decisions to give up a child, made under strain and anxiety.
>
> To protect the adopting parents—from taking responsibility for children about whose heredity or capacity for physical or mental development they know nothing; from later disturbance of their relationship to the child by natural parents whose legal rights had not been given full consideration.[83]

A considerable body of statutory and case law has developed around procedures for adoption. The Uniform Adoption Act[84] outlines a three-step procedure: (1) termination of the parental rights of the natural parents, (2) interlocutory decree giving adoptive parents custody and allowing time (e.g., six months) for a placement evaluation, and (3) final decree of adoption based on the best interests of the child.

Parental consent is usually required unless the parents are incapable of giving consent, or they have relinquished their rights by abandoning the child, or their rights have been terminated by court order. The Uniform Adoption Act also permits dispensation of consent if a court finds such consent unreasonably withheld contrary to the child's best interests.[85] Again, the courts have wide discretion in determining what constitutes "abandonment," "best interests," and so forth, depending upon a particular fact situation and the court's philosophy.[86] The common-law doctrine of "intrafamilial tort immunity" generally prevents civil action against other family members for alleged harm.

Consistent with the trend, previously mentioned, to presume cohabitation as a "marriage," the parents of illegitimate children require notice of a proposed adoption as a matter of due process.[87] Because the leading case, *Stanly* v. *Illinois,*[88] involved a father who successfully claimed his illegitimate child from an adoption agency to which the mother surrendered the child at birth, adoption agencies and adopting parents have understandably pressed for definable limits to such rights. The present situation can be described as "fluid," and has resulted in some "awkward" situations.[89] Supreme Court cases as well as the Uniform Parentage Act[90] reflect the shift toward establishing rights of children as co-equal with those of the parents. In general, except for some limitation on inheritance, children born in or out of wedlock or by means of artificial insemination are all granted similar rights to insurance proceeds, custody, visitation, adoption, and so forth.[91]

Most jurisdictions permit children of severely mentally disabled parents to be adopted without parental consent.[92] Otherwise, a child of mentally disabled parents could not be adopted because persons presumed or judged to be incompetent cannot give legally valid consent. Low I.Q. scores of the natural parents as well as mental fitness may be sufficient grounds for ordering adoption.[93] A statute, upheld by the Illinois Supreme Court,[94] stated that a parent's consent was unnecessary if the parent had been mentally ill for three years or more and if two qualified physicians selected by the court testified that the parent was not likely to recover in the foreseeable future. Obviously, these statutes mandate not only a history of mental incapacity but also some professional estimate of the future course of the natural parents' disability—a prediction of varying validity and reliability. The Illinois statute recognized a need for a court-appointed guardian or counsel to act on behalf of the disabled parents to assure more adequate representation of their interests.

After it is established that the parental rights of the natural parents may be severed, a determination must be made that the proposed adoptive family can meet at least the minimal physical and emotional needs of the child. Factors usually considered are the ethnic background, age and health of both adoptee and prospective parents, religious preferences, marital status, economic stability, and the "emotional climate." In most states, an agency investigation of the prospective home and an examination of the child is mandated by statute.[95] The investigation is to help assure that the prospective home is suitable, not necessarily ideal, and that the child is not severely handicapped physically or intellectually. One study found that 80 percent of agency rejections of prospective adoptive parents were because the parents were too restrictive about the type of child they wanted, were emotionally unstable, had undesirable motives, or had unrealistic expectations for the child.[96]

Once an adoption has been court-approved, it is usually permanent and irrevocable. Exceptions include instances where the adoptive parents fraudulently misrepresented the stability of their marriage,[97] or where they were unaware that the child was disabled.[98] Upon finalization of adoption, almost all states place the court record and birth certificate under seal, and an adoptee cannot have access without court authorization for "good reason."[99]

INCOMPETENCY OF A FAMILY MEMBER

State statutes traditionally required conditions of "insanity," "lunacy," "idiocy," or "unsoundness of mind" as a justification for guardianship. More recent statutes do not use these terms, but designate as incompetent a person who for *any* reason is mentally incapable of caring for himself or his property.[100] A New York statute allows surrogate management of an individual's property "if he is incompetent to manage himself or his affairs by reason of age, drunkenness, mental illness or other cause, or is a patient... who is unable adequately to conduct his personal or business affairs."[101] Note, however, that parents and guardians must be sensitive to the Constitutional rights applicable to children, especially as the minors approach physical and legal maturity. For example, parents or guardians cannot "voluntarily" commit children, on their behalf, to a mental hospital without some "due process' review.[102]

Contracts

Probably the most important aspect of business affairs is making contractual agreements. As a general rule, a person is bound by his agreements as long as he knows what he is doing. Only if the person is so mentally disabled that he believes he is entering into a completely different type of agreement will he be allowed to void the contract on the grounds of incapacity. Even if the person is so "senile and feeble-minded"[103] that he badly misjudges the consequences of his acts, the transaction is still probably valid. Thus, a person with manic-depressive psychosis was not allowed to void a contract to purchase a $3,000,000 golf range,[104] and a husband was not granted a marriage annulment on the grounds that his wife was mentally incompetent at the time of marriage.[105] The involuntary commitment of a patient to a hospital does not necessarily mean that the person is incompetent to contract, for example, to conduct business or to marry.[106] Such hospitalization may, however, alert others to the possibility of incompetency and suggest an evaluation of the person's personal and business transactions (except those involving petty cash). It may also be noted that a person may be incompetent with regard to some matters and not others. To have legal significance, the mental disability must be causally related to the contract. If the mental disability does not affect or motivate the contract, it has no effect upon contract validity. The law generally recognizes that there are different mental capacities required for different types of conduct such as making a will, consenting to treatment, or committing a violent crime. Thus a delusion that the local librarian is transmitting evil ideas into one's mind does not preclude that person from entering into contracts related to real estate, unless the real estate happens to involve the librarian. The present trend has been toward expanding the contractual rights of patients.[107] and toward examining how the mental characteristics of an individual affects his/her contractual ability rather than concluding that an entire class of persons is incompetent.[108] A contract may be voided, of course, if the other party has used undue influence or fraud.[109]

In order to avoid possible controversy where an individual's competence to make contracts is marginal or might be legitimately questioned, interested parties should strive to meet as many of the following conditions as possible:[110]

1. Have the mentally disabled person actively participate in the determination of the terms and conditions of the contract.
2. Execute the contract in an attorney's office.
3. Explain the meaning of the contract in nonlegal terms to the mentally disabled person.
4. Have a disinterested third person experienced in handling similar dealings explain the meaning and consequences to the party.
5. Have the mentally disabled person note on the contract itself or on an attached paper that he recognizes the legal consequences of his actions (e.g., that he will move when his house is sold).
6. Have the witnesses at the execution of the contract ask the mentally disabled person if he is satisfied with the results of the contract.
7. Be certain the contract is fair and just.

In addition to the ability to make valid contracts, modern statutes focus upon the person's ability to care for himself and his property. Very difficult situations sometimes arise when an elderly person begins to "squander" his estate. Relatives and prospective inheritors may wish, for obvious reasons, to conserve the estate—or at least to help spend it. In one relatively typical case, an 85-year-old man made arrangements with a rest home to care for him until his death, including prepayment of his burial expenses. He had approximately $20,000 of assets remaining, and in the course of a few years he spent about $9,000. He gave $2,000 to a widow whom he felt needed it, and entrusted the remainder of approximately $12,000 in stocks to his sister-in-law. Later when he asked for return of the stock, she initiated incompetency proceedings against him. There was no psychiatric examination. The evidence of incompetency consisted only of a physician's testimony (based upon a 15-minute examination of the man in the jury room) and the court's own observations. Although the court conceded that the man had lucidly conducted a number of recent transactions, it overruled his wishes and appointed a guardian to "conserve" his estate, for reasons not stated.[111]

An even more bizarre turn of affairs occurred in 1958 when the wife of a middle-aged man precipitated his commitment by claiming that her husband was delusional because, among other things, he had charged her with infidelity. The same charges led to a judicial declaration of incompetency. In 1962, while her "incompetent" husband was still committed at the state hospital, the woman gave birth. A divorce was subsequently granted to the husband on the grounds of adultery.[112] The misuse of institutionalization is sometimes an honest error. Most courts would probably concur that "[M]ental deterioration due to old age should not serve as an excuse for bundling off to a mental institution an aged hospital patient suffering from a multitude of physical ailments."[113] The usual remedy for unnecessary guardianship is to petition the probate court where the original proceeding took place for a hearing on "restoration to competency."[114]

Wills

Less capacity is required to execute a will than to conduct business or to enter into contracts because there is less possibility of fraud by other parties. Hence, the burden is even greater in legal actions to invalidate a will than to void a contract or to determine guardianship.[115] A psychiatric patient may well possess the necessary capacity and may in fact make a will as long as there has not been a prior judicial determination of incompetency.[116]

The most important factor to be determined by a psychological or psychiatric examiner is whether or not any essential element of testamentary capacity is impaired. The traditional legal criteria have been the following: (1) Does the testator know the nature and extent of his property? (2) Does he have a plan for its disposition? (3) Is he aware of the natural objects of his bounty?[117] A checklist of items to be investigated could reasonably include:[118]

- Physical appearance, demeanor, communication skill
- Age
- Physical condition
    Recent illness (nature and duration)
    Operations
    Hospitalization
    Physical disabilities
    Invalid (length of time)
    Severe pain
- Mental capacity
    General intelligence
    Education
    Memory (recent and long-term recall)
    Reasoning ability (only at intervals or constant)

- Record of mental illness in family
- Person's own mental health history
  Hospitalization (voluntary or involuntary, control of business affairs)
  Guardianship (original proceedings, restoration)
  Private treatment (reason for initiation, duration)
  Other problems (alcohol, drugs, suicide attempts, eccentricities)
- Opinion of family, acquaintances (personal care, business judgment)

In many circumstances such a survey will be too broad. A typically difficult case is one in which the alleged incapacity is quite specific—for example, a successful businessman who may suddenly disinherit a child on the basis of a delusion of his wife's earlier infidelity.

The aged in their last few years are often eager "to do important things while time is left." These may involve projects beyond the scope of the immediate family whose members may anticipate an inheritance or understandably want to be compensated for caretaking. This normal developmental interest of old people is certainly in itself no justification for depriving them of their legal right to dispose of their possessions.[119] In affirming the validity of a marriage of a 90-year-old man (and the division of his estate 14 months later following his death), a Missouri court stated: "Every person is presumed to be sane until the contrary is shown."[120] And in that there is some solace, for all of us, of any age.

NOTES

1. Many lawyers are reluctant to accept family law cases, particularly divorces, or they routinely reject such cases as a matter of policy. The emotionalism of the clients and the time spent listening to complaints are two commonly reported reasons. Siegel, M. I. New challenges to the family law practitioner. 6 *University of California, Davis Law Review* 371, 374 (1973). The practitioner of family law had the lowest median income of 20 legal specialties surveyed. Economics of Law Practice Committee, ABA, *reported in* Fixing adequate fee and fee arrangements in domestic relations cases. 1 *Family Law Quarterly* 92 (Dec. 1967).
2. Glendon, M. A. The American family in the 200th year of republic. 10 *Family Law Quarterly* 335, 338 (1977); Glendon, M. A. Marriage and the state: The withering away of marriage. 62 *Virginia Law Review* 663 (1976).
3. Glendon, The American family in the 200th year of the republic, *id.* at 339.
4. Williams v. North Carolina, 317 U.S. 287, 325 U.S. 226.
5. Subject to the "full faith and credit" clause of Article 4, Section 1 of the U.S. Constitution. Schiffman v. Askew, 359 F. Supp. 1221 (D.C. Fla. 1973); Beller v. Beller, 124 C.A.2d 679, 682, 268 P.2d 1074 (1954).
6. *E.g.*, Loving v. Virginia, 388 U.S. 1 (1967).
7. National Conference of Commissioners on Uniform State Laws, Uniform Marriage and Divorce Act of 1970 (amended 1971, 1973).

8. *E.g.*, Griswold v. Connecticut, 381 U.S. 479 (1965). Roe v. Wade, 410 U.S. 113 (1974).

9. Foster, R. Marriage: A "basic civil right of man." 37 *Fordham Law Review* 51 (1966).

10. Glendon, The American Family in the 200th year of the republic, *supra* note 2, at 341.

11. *Id.* at 346.

12. National Conference of Commissioners on Uniform State Laws, Uniform Parentage Act (1974); *see* Krause, H. D. The Uniform Parentage Act. 8 *Family Law Quarterly* 1 (1974) for a copy of the Act.

13. Omer v. Omer, 11 Wash. App. 386, 523 P.2d 957 (1974); *contra* Marvin v. Marvin, 134 Cal Rptr 815, 557 P2d 106 (1976). *see generally* King, M. D. *Cohabitation handbook: Living together and the law*. Berkeley, Ca.: Ten Speed Press, 1975.

14. A probable interpretation of Eisenstadt v. Baird, 405 U.S. 438 (1972), wherein the Supreme Court held that the anti-contraceptive law of Massachusetts was unconstitutional when applied to *unmarried* couples.

15. California Civil Code sec. 4801.5.

16. Use of zoning: Palo Alto Tenants' Union v. Morgan, 321 F. Supp. 908 (N.D. Cal. 1970); *contra*, Boraas v. Village of Belle Terre, 476 F.2d 806 (2d Cir. 1973); *see also* Note, Excluding the commune from suburbia: The use of zoning for social control. 23 *Hastings Law Journal* 1459 (1972). For denial of aid: Moreno v. U.S. Department of Agriculture, 345 F. Supp. 310 (D.D.C. 1972), 37 L. Ed. 2d 782, 93 S. Ct. 2821 (1973); *see also* Comments, *All* in the "family": Legal problems of communes. 7 *Harvard Civil Rights—Civil Liberties Law Review* 393 (1972).

17. "Marriage, so far as its validity in law is concerned, is a civil contract, to which the consent of the parties, capable in law of contracting, is essential." Minn. Stat. Ann., Sec. 517.01 (1969).

18. Baker v. Nelson, 291 Minn. 310 (Sup. Ct. Minn. en banc 1971), 191 N.W.2d 185, *appeal dismissed* 409 U.S. 810, 34 L. Ed. 2d 65 (1972).

19. Note, The legality of homosexual marriage. 82 *The Yale Law Journal* 560 (1973).

20. Anonymous v. Anonymous, 325 N.Y.S.2d 499, 67 Misc. 2d 982 (1971).

21. Corbett v. Corbett, 1970 2 W.L.R. 1306, 2 All E.R. (P.D.A.), as cited in Davidson, K. M., Ginsburg, R. B., and Kay, H. H. *Text, cases, and materials on sex-based discrimination*. St. Paul, Minn.: West Publishing co., 1974, pp. 196–213.

22. Marvin v. Marvin, 134 Cal Rptr 815, 557 P2d 106 (1976) (division of property based on oral or implied agreement by unmarried couple).

23. For possible guidelines regarding competency, see Murray, J. B. Marriage contracts for the mentally retarded. 21 *Catholic Law Review* 22 (Summer 1975). Cases supporting ante-nuptial agreements: Spector v. Spector, 23 Ariz. App. 131, 531 P.2d 176 (1975); Eule v. Eule, 24 Ill. App. 3rd 83, 320 N.E.2d 506 (1974); Rocker v. Rocker, 13 Ohio Misc. 199, 232 N.E.2d 445 (1967); In re Harris' Estate, 431 Pa. 293, 245 Atl. 2d 647 (1968); Loftin's Estate, 285 N.C. 717, 208 S.E.2d 670 (1974). *See* sample statutory provision in General Obligations Law, State of New York, Section 3–303, and *also* comprehensive survey of this topic in Lindey, A. *Separation agreements and ante-nuptial contracts*. New York: Matthew Bender, 1976.

24. See Appendix B for glossary of legal terms such as "consideration" in contract law.

25. Eule v. Eule, *supra* note 23.

26. Gregg v. Gregg, 133 Misc. 109, 231 N.Y.S. 221 (1928).

27. Reynolds v. Reynolds, 217 Ga. 234, 123 S.E.2d 115 (1961); Mitchel v. Mitchel, 310
Atl. 2d 837 (C.A. D.C. 1973); Kunde v. Kunde, 52 Wisc. 2d 559, 191 N.W.2d 41
(1971); *contra* Unander v. Unander, 506 P.2d 719 (Ore. 1973).

28. Mengal v. Mengal, 201 Misc. 104, 103 N.Y.S. 292 (Dom. Rel. Ct. 1951). *See
generally*, Clark, H. H., Jr. *The law of domestic relations in the U.S.* St. Paul, Minn.:
West Publishing Company, 1968, at pp. 28–30. This restriction may change. Contracts
might include custody and support agreements that could be subsequently enforced or
voided by a court if litigation occured. Provisions of the contract should be severable
(cf; appendix V).

29. Articles supporting this trend include: Fleischman, K. Marriage by contract: Defining
the terms of relationship. 7 *Family Law Quarterly* 32 (Spring 1974); McWalter, C.
Marriage as contract: Towards a functional redefinition of the marital status. 9 *Columbia Journal of Law and Social Problems* 607 (1973); Weitzman, L. J. Legal regulation
of marriage: Tradition and change. 62 *California Law Review* 1169 (July–Sept. 1974)
(a comprehnsvie review of this topic, including eleven pages of excerpts from sample
contracts).

30. "Ties that bind," 106 *Time* (Sept. 1, 1975), p. 62.

31. Klein, D. M. A "checklist" for the drafting of enforceable ante-nuptial agreements. 19
Miami Law Review 615 (1964); Pniewski v. Przybysz, 89 Ohio L. Abs. 385, 183
N.E.2d 437 (1962).

32. Matter of Sunshine, 82 Misc. 2d 363, 369 N.Y.S.2d 304 (1975): Britven v. Britven,
145 N.W.2d 450 (Iowa 1966); *but see* Matter of Moore, 53 Misc. 2d 786, 41 N.Y.S.2d
697 (1967).

33. Loftin's Estate, *supra* note 23.

34. Robinson v. Robinson, 296 N.Y. 778, 71 N.E.2d 214 (1947) (wife support arbitrated);
Matter of Hill, 199 Misc. 1035, 104 N.Y.S.2d 755 (1951) (arbitration of custody
denied).

35. Schibi v. Schibi, 136 Conn. 196, 69A.2d 831 (1949) (six weeks); Lannamann v.
Lannamann, 171 Pa. Sup. 147, 89 A.2d 397 (1952) (six months); Fincham v. Fincham,
160 Kan. 683, 165 P.2d 209 (1946) (any time); *similarly*, Censor v. Censor, 28 Misc.
2d 702, 208 N.Y.S.2d 95 (1960).

36. Corbin, A. *Contracts*. St. Paul, Minn.: West Publishing Co., 1962 ed., at 621–622.

37. Kock v. Kock, 95 N.J. Sup. 546, 232 A.2d 157 (1967); *but see* Fleischman, *supra* note
29, arguing that marriage contracts are "fundamentally conservative, inasmuch as they
aim at preserving conventional forms of marriage."

38. Marvin, *supra* note 22.

39. See generally, Katz, S., Howe, R. W., and McGrath, M. Child neglect laws in
America. 9 *Family Law Quarterly* 1 (1975) for a comprehensive 375-page survey of
abuse and neglect laws. For an unusual case of brutal punishment of 3-year-old *see*
Adelson, L. Homicide by pepper. 9 *Journal of Forensic Sciences* 391 (July 1974).

40. *Id*. at 4–5.

41. *E.g.*, Arizona, California, Delaware, Idaho, Louisiana, Tennessee, and Texas. Mental
injury is included in the model statue by the Education Commission of the States, *Child
abuse and neglect: Model legislation for the states*. Denver, 1976, report no. 71, p. 14.

42. Idaho Code Ann., sec. 16–1623 (Supp. 1969). "Emotional maladjustment" is defined in the statute as, "the condition of a child who has been denied proper parental love, or adequate affectionate association, and who behaves unnaturally and unrealistically in relation to normal situations, objects and other persons." As quoted in Katz, N. *When parents fail*. Boston: Beacon, 1971 at 61.

43. *In re* Rowe, 196 Misc. 830, 92 N.Y.S.2d 882 (Dom. Rel. Ct. 1949); *in re* Halmeda, 85 C.A. 219, 192 P.2d 781 (1948).

44. P.L. 93–247, 93rd Congress, S.1191, January 1974.

45. Summary of Declaration, UN Office of Public Information, September 1968, as published in *Standards for child protective service*. New York: Child Welfare League of America, 1973, at 4.

46. Sumner v. Superior Court, 19 Wash. 2d 5, 140 P.2d 784 (1943).

47. Shrout v. Shrout, 224 Ore. 521, 357 P.2d 935 (1960) (mother had children bring beer to her while in bedroom with paramour); *see also*, McNatt v. State, 330 P.2d 600 (Okla. 1958).

48. *In re* Dehart, 114 So. 2d 13 (Dist. Ct. Fla. 1959); *In re* McDonald, 201 N.W.2d 447 (Iowa 1972) (mentally retarded parents).

49. *In re* Levi, 131 Ga. App. 348, 206 S.E.2d 82 (1974).

50. *In re* Vilas, 475 P.2d 615 (Oklà. 1970) (alternate care given by grandparents).

51. A principle popularized, though not originated, by Justice Cardozo in Finlay v. Finlay, 240 N.Y. 429 (1929). *See* Goldstein, J., Freud, A. & Solnit, J. *Beyond the best interests of the child*. New York: Free Press, 1973, at 53.

52. Westman, J. C. and Hanson, A. S. Guidelines for determining the psychological best interests of children. In Allen, R.C., Ferster, E. Z. and Rubin, J. G. (Eds.) *Readings in law and psychiatry*, 2d ed. Baltimore: Johns Hopkins, 1975, at 583; Patterson, J. R. and Cobb, J. A. A dyadic analysis of "aggressive" behaviors. In J. P. Hill (Ed.) *Minnesota symposia on child psychology*. Vol. 5. Minneapolis: University of Minnesota Press, 1971, 72–129; Wahler, R. G. Deviant child behavior within the family: Developmental speculations and behavior change strategies. In H. Leitenberg (Ed.) *Handbook of behavior modification and behavior therapy*. Englewood Cliffs, N.J.: Prentice-Hall, 1976, 516–546.

53. Sussman, A. Reporting child abuse: A review of the literature. 8 *Family Law Quarterly* 257, 272 (Fall 1972). For summary of legislation, *see* De Francis, V. and Lucht, C. L. *Child abuse legislation in the 1970's*. Denver: American Human Assn., 1974.

54. Sussman, *id*. at 274.

55. Sussman, *id*. at 280.

56. Paulsen, M. G. Child abuse reporting laws: The shape of the legislation. 67 *Colorado Law Review* 1, 31 (1967); In a survey using a hypothetical case of child abuse under Nebraska law, large percentages of psychologists (87%), psychiatrists (63%), and social workers (50%) said they would not report. Swoboda, J.S., Elwork, A., Sales, B.D. and Levine, D. Knowledge of and compliance with privileged communication and child-abuse-reporting laws. 9 *Professional Psychology* 448 (Aug. 1978).

57. Gossett v. Van Egmond, 176 Or. 134, 155 P.2d 304 (1945).

58. May v. Golding, 356 Mich. 143, 111 N.W.2d 862 (1961).

59. Burt, R. A. Protecting children from their families and themselves: State laws and the constitution. 1 *Journal of Youth and Adolescence* 91 (1972).

60. Approximately 60 percent of all divorces involve children five years old or younger. Of these divorces, approximately one-third are litigated. Broel-Plateris, A. A. Divorce statistics analysis. 21 *Vital Health Statistics* 1 (1965); Wheeler, M. *No-fault divorce*. Boston: Beacon Press, 1974, at 72. The stressful effects on children have been noted in McDermott, J. F. Divorce and its psychiatric sequelae in children. 23 *Archives of General Psychiatry* 421 (1970).

61. Quoted in Slovenko, R. *Psychiatry and the law*. Boston: Little, Brown, 1973, at 361.

62. "Surveys of sample cases indicate that maternal custody is awarded in 85 to 95% of the cases." Slovenko, *id*. at 361.

63. *Ex parte* Hendrix, 186 Okla. 712, 100 P.2d 444 (1940). For a popular account of father custody cases, *see* Molinoff, D. D. Living with father, *New York Times Magazine*, May 22, 1977, 13–17; *also* Dr. Lee Salk's theories on family are challenged in own divorce case. 3 *People* 8 (June 9, 1975).

64. Michigan Comp. Laws Ann., sec. 7222.23, as quoted in Watson, A. S. Contested divorces and children: A challenge for the forensic psychiatrist. In C. Wecht (Ed.) *Legal medicine annual, 1973*. New York: Appleton-Century-Crofts, 1973, at 493.

65. Uniform Marriage and Divorce Act, sec. 402.

66. People v. Brown, 49 Mich. App. 358, 212 N.W.2d 55 (1973) (acknowledged lesbian mothers were permitted to retain custody of their children and live together); Nader v. Superior Court, 255 C.A.2d 523, 63 Cal. Rptr. 352 (Ct. App. 1967).

67. Schuster v. Schuster, No. D-36868 (Wash. Supr. Ct. King Cty. Dec. 22, 1972) summarized in Davidson, K. M., Ginsburg, R. B., and Kay, H. H. *Text, cases, and materials on sex-based discrimination*. St. Paul, Minn.: West Publishing Company, 1974, 276–277. *See generally*, Note, Custody and homosexual parents. 2 *Women's Rights Law Reporter* 19 (1974); Riley, M. The avowed lesbian mother and her right to child custody. 12 *San Diego Law Review* 799 (1975). A.A., 514 P.2d 358 (Ore. Ct. App. 1973) (change of custody from alleged homosexual father denied but conditions set).

68. Uniform Marriage and Divorce Act at 46–47.

69. Marum v. Marum, 265 P.2d 723 (Okla. 1964).

70. Prouty v. Prouty, 16 Cal. 2d 190, 105 P.2d 295 (1940); Repetti v. Repetti, N.Y.L.J. Aug. 26, 1975, p. 10, col. 2 (Sup. Ct. Suffolk County) cited in Saxe, D. B. Some reflections on the interface of law and psychiatry in child custody cases. 3 *The Journal of Psychiatry and Law* 501, 511 (1976).

71. DuCanto, A. Mental illness and child custody. 7 *Journal of Family Law* 636, 637 (1967).

72. Bowler v. Bowler, 355 Mich. 686, 96 N.W.2d 129 (1959); Brown v. Brown, 92 Cal. App. 276, 268 P. 401 (1928).

73. Annot. Mental health of contesting parents as a factor in award of child custody, 74 *ALR 2d* 1068 (1960).

74. E.g., New York Family Court Act, sec. 653; California Civil Procedures, Code sec. 263.

75. Some practitioners have asserted that there is a reluctance on the part of physicians to get involved in custody cases (due to lack of knowledge about the legal process and anxiety about being questioned in court) and that there is a preoccupation with the *practitioner's* own best interest. Benedek, E. K. and Benedek, R. A. New child custody laws: Making them do what they say. 42 *American Journal of Orthopsychiatry* 825 (1972). There's nothing the matter with physicians, or anybody else, protecting their own interests. The solution is to make participation in the legal process by nonlawyers less aversive. Custody and divorce proceedings are not, apparently, very popular among lawyers either. "The legal profession has its caste system, and those who handle divorce are stuck with the stigma of dealing with a slimy area of the law. Divorce is to the practice of law as proctology is to medicine." Wheeler, *supra* note 60 at 120.

76. Withrow v. Withrow, 212 La. 427, 31 So. 2d 849 (1947).
77. Adapted from Watson, A. S. The children of Armageddon: Problems of custody following divorce. 21 *Syracuse Law Review* 55, 75 (1969).
78. The court may "appoint guardian ad litem or counsel for the child and assess the costs and reasonable fees against any or all parties involved, totally or partially." Child Custody Act of 1970, P.A. 1970, No. 91, April 1, 1971, Mich. Comp. Laws Ann. 722.2. Maine, Oregon, and a number of other states have a similar statutory provision. "It may be, however, that there are already too many lawyers involved in custody disputes." Wheeler, *supra* note 60, at 89. It increases litigation costs, and "what child would want to live with his parents after stopping them from getting divorced?" Wheeler, *id*. at 85.
79. In one case, projective tests with children (ages five, seven, and nine years) as well as MMPI scores and the expert testimony of clinical psychologists, were heavily relied on in granting custody of the children to a father who was believed to be able to fulfill more adequately the nurturing functions than the mother. Moezie v. Moezi, Fam. Div. No. D3535–71 (Sup. Ct. D.C. 1973), reprinted in Davidson, K. M., Ginsburg, R. B., and Kay, H. H. *Text, cases, and materials on sex-based discrimination*. St. Paul, Minn.: West Publishing Co., 1974, at 250–255. Despite the notoriously suspect validity of projective tests, they may provide a pseudo-objective reason for a judge to "disperse the blame" for an inevitably difficult decision.
80. "It is not difficult to embroil the legally uninitiated expert into all kinds of logical inconsistencies once he is on the witness stand. These inconsistencies often reflect the expert's lack of legal gamesmanship rather than any intrinsic errors in his material. Therefore, the presentation of expert testimony in these custodial cases must be well-controlled by the courts if accuracy and good judgment are to prevail." Watson, A. S. The children of Armageddon: Problems of custody following divorce. 21 *Syracuse Law Review* 55, 76. See generally, chapter 14, on Expert Witness.
81. Even in more thoroughly studied areas, such as hospitalization on the basis of dangerousness to self or others, there are few if any structured or projective tests which adequately predict, or even postdict, violent behavior. Megargee, M. The prediction of violence with psychological tests. In C. Spielberger (Ed.) *Current topics in clinical and community psychology*. New York: Academic Press, 1970, p. 98.
82. The earliest adoption statutes were in Mississippi in 1846 and in Massachusetts in 1851 as detailed in Huard, R. The law of adoption: Ancient and modern. 9 *Vanderbilt Law Review* 743, 748 (1955).
83. Children's Bureau, Department of Health, Education and Welfare, Legislative guides for the termination of parental rights and responsibilities and the adoption of children. Washington, D.C.: U.S. Printing Office, 1961.

84. Drafted by the National Conference of Commissioners on Uniform State Laws, available in numerous texts including *The family law reporter* (Bureau of National Affairs, Inc.), reference file, section 2 (1977).

85. Sec. 19, 1971 Amendment.

86. Adoption without parental consent approved: Benjamin v. Buch, 208 Ga. 453, 67 S.E.2d 476 (1951) (child left in woods covered with dirt and straw); Schwartz v. Hudgins, 12 Md. App. 419, 278 Atl. 2d 652 (1971) (mother made no contact for two years); Dyer v. Howell, 212 Va. 453, 184 S.E.2d 789 (1971) (child emotionally upset by contact with father who had killed the mother). Adoption without parental consent denied: Meyer v. Georgia, 124 Ga. App. 146, 183 S.E.2d 42 (1971) (newborn baby left in phone booth with $25 followed by call to suicide prevention center); Logan v. Coup, 238 Md. 253, 208 Atl. 2d 794 (1965) (father's failure to support or visit not extreme enough).

87. Stanley v. Illinois, 405 U.S. 645, 92 S. Ct. 1208 (1972); Rothstein v. Lutheran Social Services of Wisconsin and Upper Michigan, 405 U.S. 1051, 92 S. Ct. 1488 (1972). Barron, J. A. Notice to the unwed father and termination of parental rights: Implementing Stanley v. Illinois. 9 *Family Law Quarterly* 527 (1975).

88. 408 U.S. 645, 31 L. Ed. 2d 551 (1972).

89. For example, a Michigan statute requires that an unmarried father must file what might be termed a "notice of fornication" with the probate court prior to the birth of the child in order to avoid automatic termination of his right to consent to adoption of the child. Upon filing the form, he must also acknowledge liability for contributing to the support and education of the child and to pregnancy-medical expenses of the mother. Mich. Comp. Laws Ann. Vol. 37, sec. 710.3a (Supp. 1973–74). A copy of the notice is to go to the prospective mother whether or not she is married (to someone else, of course). So-called scientific determination of paternity also has its limitation. Reportedly one re-check of blood-typing reports found that approximately one-third of the reports were in error! Sussman, L. *Blood grouping tests—Medico-legal uses*. Springfield, Ill.: Charles C Thomas, 1968, p. ix. *See also*, Joint AMA-ABA guidelines: present status of serologic testing in problems of disputed parentage. 10 *Family Law Quarterly* 247 (Fall 1976).

90. Drafted by the National Conference of Commissioners on Uniform State Laws, 1973, ABA approval 1974. *See* H. D. Krause, The Uniform Parentage Act, 8 *Family Law Quarterly* 1 (1974) for copy of the Act.

91. Krause, *id*. at 3–4, 8.

92. Katz, N. *When parents fail: The law's response to family breakdown*. Boston: Beacon Press, 1971, at 117, 135–136 (listing of state statutes and summary of case law).

93. In re McDonald, 201 N.W.2d 447 (Iowa 1972). *See* Galliher, K. E., Jr. Termination of the parent-child relationship: Should parental IQ be an important factor? 1973 *Law and Social Order* 855 (1972); Thomas, H. W. Low intelligence of the parent: A new ground for state interference with the parent-child relationship? 13 *Journal of Family Law* 379 (1973–74).

94. Ill. Ann. Stat., ch. 4; People *ex rel*. Nabstedt v. Barger, 3 Ill. 2d 511, 121 N.E.2d 781 (1954).

95. 10 Okla. Stat. 60.15 (1966); California Civil Code, sec. 226 (1961). A set of standards and procedures to be used by social workers in such an investigation has been issued by the California State Department of Social Welfare titled "Manual of Policies and Procedures, Adoptions in California."

96. Schapiro, I. *A study of adoption practice.* New York: Child Welfare League of America, 1965.

97. Adoption of Emery, 191 C.A.2d 428, 12 C.R. 685 (1961).

98. *In re* Anonymous, 352 N.Y.S.2d 743 (N.Y. 1968) (child returned to adoption agency when adoptive parents learned that they had been wrongfully informed by a physician prior to adoption that an autistic child was in "good health").

99. See Chapter 12, text at note 66.

100. *E.G.*, Ariz. Rev. Stat. Ann., sec. 14–861 (1956); Ore. Rev. Stat., sec. 126.006 (3) Supp. (1968); Utah Code Ann., sec. 75-13-19 (1953).

101. N.Y. Mental Hyg. Law, sec. 100 (McKenney Supp. 1969). *See generally*, Alexander, G.J. and Lewin, T.H.D. *The aged and the need for surrogate management.* Syracuse, N.Y.: Syracuse Univ. Press, 1972 (Contains a summary of statutes of the 50 states and a "Model Estate Advisors and Managers Act").

102. Bartley v. Kremens, 402 F. Supp. 1039 (E.D. Pa. 1975), *calendared for rehearing* 98 S.Ct. 762 (1978); J.L. & J.R. v. Parham, 412 F. Supp. 112 (M.D. Ga.) (1976), *vac. & remanded* due to statutory changes 97 S.Ct. 1709 (1977).

103. Sheffield v. Andrews, 440 S.W.2d 175 (Mo. 1969).

104. Fingerhut v. Kralyn Enterprises, Inc. 337 N.Y.S.2d 394 (Sup. Ct. N.Y. 1971).

105. DeMedio v. DeMedio, 215 Pa. Super. 255, 257 A.2d 290 (Super. Ct. Pa. 1969).

106. Slovenko, R. Contractual Capacity. *Psychiatry and law.* Boston: Little, Brown, 1973, Chapter 17.

107. *E.g.*, Alexander, G.J. and Szasz, T.S. From contract to status via psychiatry. 13 *Santa Clara Lawyer* 537 (1973).

108. Some legal decisions and statutes appear to attempt to exempt entire classes of persons from contracting or consenting (e.g., all patients in mental hospitals may not contract for or consent to psychosurgery). This notion of the differential capacity of an entire class of persons to contract is similar to prohibiting, for example, all women over 80 from disposing of estates valued at over one million dollars. R. Singer in Consent of the unfree: Medical experimentation and behavior modification in the closed institution, Pt. I. 1 *Law and Human Behavior* 1, 147 (1977) argues effectively that there is little support in the law for the differential contractual capacity of an entire class of persons.

109. Hannah v. Central Bank of Biringham. 341 So.2d 669 (Ala. 1977) (undue influence used to obtain deed of land from 86-year-old woman).

110. Slightly modified from a list in Selzer, M. L. Outline checklist of evidence for and against incapacity, in E. D. Shapiro and R. H. Needham (Eds.) *Psychiatry for lawyers handbook* Ann Arbor, Mich.: Institute of Continuing Legal Education, 1967, p. 143.

111. In the Matter of Guardianship of Tyrrell, 174 Ohio St. 552, 190 N.E.2d 687 (1963); similarly, *In re* Conservatorship of Hartshorne, 498 P.2d 406 (Okla. 1972) (conservators appointed for 95-year-old lady who trusted "everyone" except commercial banks); *see generally*, Stone, A. A. *Mental health and law: A system in transition.* Rockville, Md.: NIMH, Center for Studies of Crime and Delinquency, 1975, ch. 10.

112. Based upon a summary of a file examined in a survey of New York state mental institutions as reported in Alexander, G. J. and Lewin, P. H. D. *The aged and the need for surrogate management.* (Privately printed, Santa Clara University School of Law, and Syracuse University College of Law, funded by the Frederick and Amelia Shrimper Fdn. of New York City), 1971, at p. 74.

113. Application for the Certification of Anonymous. No. 1 to No. 12, 206 Misc. 909, 138 N.Y.S.2d 30 (Supr. Ct. 1954); Confirming policy statement: State of New York, Department of Mental Hygiene, Policy Manual, sec. 400 (g), January 15, 1969. *See also* Note, Disguised oppression of involuntary guardianship: Have the elderly freedom to spend? 73 *Yale Law Journal* 676 (1964).

114. "If the petition alleges and if it is determined that the conservatee is able to properly care for himself and for his property, the court shall make such finding and enter such judgment accordingly." Cal. Stat. Ann. Probate Procedure, section 853 (1965).

115. Smith, R. G. and Hager, L. M. The senile testator: Medicolegal aspects of competency. 13 *Cleveland-Marshal Law Review* 97, 99 (1964); Newhall, G. *Settlement of estates and fiduciary law in Massachusetts*, 4th ed. Rochester, N.Y.: Lawyers Co-operative Publishing Co., 1958, p. 399.

116. Waple v. Hall, 238 A.2d 544 (Md. 1968); Willis v. James, 227 So.2d 573 (Ala. 1969).

117. Lord Cockburn test in Banks v. Goodfellow, L.R. 5 Q.B. 549, 565 (1870), quoted and summarized in Smith, *supra* note 115, at 99. *See generally*, Note, Psychiatric assistance in the determination of testamentary capacity. 66 *Harvard Law Review* 1116 (1953).

118. Excerpted, with modifications, from Selzer, *supra* note 110 at 141.

119. "A son obtained a declaration of incompetency for his 81-year-old mother after discovering that she had given away $10,800 to 'Bible groups.' He then protected his 'involutional paranoid' mother from further dissipation of her $17,200 estate." From a case file summarized in Alexander, *supra* note 101, at 72.

120. Sheffield, *supra* note 103, at 176. The Court also provided some poetic dicta: "Certainly there are vast differences between the marriages of youth and the marriages of age. . . . Marriages entered upon during the twilight years are after the season is done. The seed has been sown, the crop has been blended, and the harvest has been reaped. The surviving partner then needs mostly care and companionship. Should he be denied this solace because his faculties have deteriorated as they must with age?''

CHAPTER 11

Research with Human Participants

Every student of psychology has heard of "Little Albert"—the nonconsenting eleven-month-old child behind whose head the behaviorist John Watson pounded on a steel bar to make a frightening noise.[1] Watson initially had the guardian's permission to conduct some tests. Two months later Albert was removed from the institution according to plan but against medical advice by a wet-nurse. When a request was made that Albert be returned for more "study" (the intended nature of which is not clear), the nurse claimed that she had "given Albert away."[2]

This classic study of human conditioning raises a number of complex legal questions—for example: What interventions should be labeled "research" (in contrast to "treatment")? How, if at all, should the practitioner's standard of care or the patient's level of informed consent differ between research and treatment? Who, under what circumstances and by what means, should have authority over minors or mentally disabled persons to consent on their behalf?

Much has been written on such topics as essays on professional ethics, and some administrative regulations have been established, but relatively little statutory or case law exists.[3] One reason for this lack of formal regulation may be that research in the behavioral and social sciences is comparatively recent. Also, research in medicine (though having a long and distinguished history) has not been viewed as part of routine medical practice.[4] A national survey of research activity with adult humans showed that approximately 60 percent of the research was biomedical, 30 percent behavioral, and 20 percent archival or secondary statistical analysis.[5]

Presumably, by most any formulation, our celebrated "Little Albert" would be a member of a class of people that public laws and regulations should be designed to protect. The Department of Health, Education, and Welfare (DHEW) has defined a "subject" as "any individual who may be exposed to the possibility of injury, including physical, psychological, or social injury, as a consequence of participation as a subject in any research, development, or related activity which departs from the application of those established and accepted methods necessary to meet his needs, or which increases the ordinary risks of daily life, including the recognized risks inherent in a chosen occupation or field of service."[6] The DHEW regulations encompass activities other than research. The rationale of this is that research is not the only activity of health professionals that may put a person at risk. For example, even a broad definition of research (e.g., "any manipulation of a human done for purposes of developing new information and which differs in any way from customary medical or other professional practice")[7] may not cover departures from routine practice that are not legitimate research yet are necessary to meet individual needs or advance the state of the art.[8] There is also research that does not require the manipulation of persons, but instead involves only observation, recording, and analysis of data.

PROFESSIONAL STANDARDS

Protection of Human Participants

Article 7 of the U.N. draft *Covenant on Civil and Political Rights* reads:

> No one shall be subjected to torture or to cruel, inhuman or degrading treatment or punishment. In particular, no one shall be subjected without his free consent to medical or scientific experimentation.[9]

More specialized guidelines have been developed by biomedical researchers, psychiatrists, psychologists, and others.[10] Policies specifying the rights of human research subjects have been published by several governmental agencies,[11] and the National Commission for the Protection of Human Subjects of Biomedical and Behavioral Research was charged with investigating problem areas and with recommending regulatory mechanisms.[12]

Children and institutionalized persons may have impaired capacity or be more easily coerced into making decisions; hence, special attention must be given to the conditions under which interventions occur with these individuals. The National Commission for the Protection of Human Subjects of Biomedical and Behavioral Research has promulgated standards for research with children, prisoners, and institutionalized mentally infirm.[13]

Before conducting research with children it is prudent to obtain authorization from parents or guardian, the potential subject if over seven years of age, and an institutional review board of diverse membership. The board should be empowered to monitor the recruitment procedure, assess the reasonableness of the parental consent, and provide an unbiased representative with whom the parent or the child can confidentially consult at any time.[14]

The traditional legal authority by which parents and guardians can consent to medical procedures on behalf of their children extends only to interventions necessary for the child's care. By extension, parental consent is usually accepted for innovative or experimental procedures where there is some possibility of benefit to the minor.[15] For example, researchers involved in a controversial treatment program to reduce extreme stereotypically feminine behavior among male children who "are in a chronic state of lonely misery" asserted that proper legal consent from the child was impossible because "the very process of obtaining consent from the child . . . would be an anxiety-producing encounter, and it might adversely determine the boy's psychological and sexual development."[16] Presumably, only parental consent was obtained.

If parental consent is impossible for legitimate reasons (e.g., child abuse by parents) and waived by the institutional review board, some additional appropriate procedure should be used to protect the child. This might be court approval or consent of the child if the youngster is a "mature minor." A "mature minor" is a minor who has sufficient intelligence to understand and appreciate the nature and consequences of the proposed treatment or research. (Courts have usually recognized mature minors at the age of 15 or older.)[18]

It has been recommended that research having greater than minimal risk and which is not necessarily beneficial to the individual child or to an institutionalized mentally disabled person should be conducted only when certain conditions have been met, such as the possibility of furthering the alleviation of a serious health problem.[19] (See Appendixes BB and CC) Persons holding themselves out as researchers owe a certain standard of care to participants. Assuming the absence of more explicit guidelines, a parallel to the physician-patient relationship can be assumed. Thus, unless otherwise indicated, the subject can rightfully expect that "(a) the proposed study is for legitimate and justifiable ends, (b) the investigator is well qualified, (c) the investigator will supervise the experiments, follow them closely, and discontinue them if serious unanticipated risks develop, (d) where pertinent, preliminary tests have been conducted, and (e) the investigator is aware of possible side effects and is prepared to cope with them."[20] The less familiar the subject is with the experimental procedure or situation (hence putting him/her at a disadvantage relative to the investigator), the greater the reliance of the subject on the competency of the investigator. This reliance and trust may establish a fiduciary responsibility on the part of the investigator.

Potential Benefits and Knowledge

"The values held by an individual or by a society are, and must be, in competition since no single value can be absolute. Even the right to life is supervened by a society seeking to protect itself from criminal behavior."[21] Some risk is expected in any research endeavor. But the degree of risk, the manner of calculating the risk (and balancing benefits), and the extent to which a potential subject may voluntarily assume greater-than-normal risks, are among the immediately apparent complexities in determining a cost/benefit ratio. In some circumstances, the benefit side of the formula is extremely difficult, if not impossible, to determine.

It has been traditionally assumed that where research is designed to gain general knowledge rather than promote the idividual subject's "best interest," less risk or discomfort is permitted. Yet in many situations, the distinction between "research," "treatment," "normal volunteer," and "patient" is blurred.[22] Furthermore, in the very situation in which the subject has the most to gain (e.g., when critically ill or when in prison), the person may overestimate the potential benefits and underestimate the experimental risks.[23] The researcher must therefore share the responsibility to assess risks (physiological, psychological, sociological, and legal) and benefits (to the individual subject and the society). There may also be risks to the investigator such as physical harm or litigation. The predictive validity of such assessments, however, except for probably rather benign and dull instances, is highly suspect.[24] In all these matters, a general guideline is that "greater care must be taken when the proposed procedure is experimental, dangerous, or intrusive than when it is routine."[25] In situations of greater risk or stress, the subject should be provided in advance and in writing the name and telephone number of a third party for direct and confidential appeal; if medical procedures or drugs are involved, that third party should be a licensed physician.

The trend in present regulations is toward the process of "negotiating" approval of the research project or treatment program among various interested parties—potential subjects, institutional subjects-rights committee, funding agency peer review panel, principal investigator.[26] Consent is no longer seen as the rapid signing of a document. State or federal law may require approval of the research by a review committee.[27]

Legally Effective Consent

An individual's voluntary assumption of personal and foreseeable risk for the public good has wide social acceptance (e.g., blood donations). When, however, the (a) individual is not competent or (b) his/her act is not voluntary or (c) the risks are unforeseen by the subject, participation in research—even if requested by the prospective subject—should be routinely denied until special arrangements are made. The necessity of consent lies in the tradition of *tort* law in which the unconsented touching of another person gives rise to a legal action of "technical battery" even though that touching (e.g., physical examination, aversive noise, administration of a drug) actually benefits that person. If the person consents, there is no battery.

To be legally effective, however, the consent must be *informed* consent. Ideally, the patient/subject/participant should understand (a) the diagnosis or purpose of the treatment or research, (b) the nature and duration of the treatment or research, (c) the risks involved, (d) the prospects of success or benefit, (e) possible disadvantages if the treatment or experiment is not undertaken, and (f) alternative methods of treatment or fulfilling a requirement. HEW regulations also require that (g) prospective subjects be allowed to ask questions and (h) if there is risk of physical harm, they should be informed whether they will be financially compensated for injuries.[28] The institution does not have to provide financial compensation, but the subjects must be informed of this if the research is funded by HEW.

Legal questions frequently arise regarding the amount and type of information that must be given to a prospective patient or subject. There is current ambiguity as to whether the standard of information to be disclosed should be based on: (a) the amount and type that would be given by a similar practitioner (by local or national comparison) in like circumstances, or (b) a "client standard" determined by how much and what kind of information such a person would normally require to reach a reasonable decision about participation.[29]

Because, in psychological or psychiatric research, the procedures of any particular investigation may be relatively unique, establishing a standard among practitioners "in the same or similar circumstances" could be difficult. Researchers can, alternatively, assume that they have a duty to disclose all foreseeable serious inherent and potential hazards that a reasonable person would consider significant. The fact that an individual may not reach a reasonable conclusion, in the view of the researcher or outside parties, is not sufficient evidence of itself to conclude that there was an absence of necessary information.

Information essential to making an informed decision about participation should be given, preferably in writing, to the prospective subject. This duty to disclose information is based on the person's "right of self-decision."[30] The information to be presented would certainly include expected substantial risks and benefits. If the potential harm is severe even though quite improbable, or if the potential harm is relatively mild but statistically frequent, a presentation of these facts should be made. Biomedical or behavioral research that may result in physical injury requires, as previously mentioned, "an explanation as to whether compensation and medical treatment is available if physical injury occurs and, if so, what it consists of or where further information may be obtained."[31]

There has been much emphasis upon obtaining *written* informed consent. (See guidelines for constructing consent forms, and samples, in Appendix Z, DD, EE and FF.) Although written consent is desirable, it may not always be required.[32] Legally effective consent may sometimes be obtained verbally, with witnesses.

Tape or video recordings might be made of the consent process in which the subject expresses his understanding of the procedure, including its risks and benefits, and his voluntary desire to participate. Writing primarily serves evidential purposes; it does not guarantee understanding. One study found that 17 percent of those who signed consent forms later reported that they did not know that they were going to be involved in a research project.[33] One experimental advantage of a written rehearsal of risk/benefits and a consent form is that it provides a standardized protocol. The manner in which subjects are informed about the nature of a research project can sometimes drastically alter the results.[34]

It is often said that a subject should be free to withdraw consent at any time. Although this is a good general principle for maximizing a person's freedom of choice and self-determination, it may not in some circumstances be feasible or reasonable after a medical or experimental procedure has begun. In *Mims* v. *Boland,* the Court noted that the effective withdrawal of consent must come from a rational mind, and when it is "medically feasible for the doctor to desist in the treatment or examination . . . without . . . being detrimental to the patient's health or life from a medical viewpoint."[35] A surgical patient may not be permitted to jump off an operating table or a mental patient to withdraw consent for treatment which involves restraint while standing on a ninth-floor balcony. Thus, while consent may be withdrawn at any time, it becomes legally advisable to terminate treatment or research at a time when such termination is safe. It has even been suggested that, in social policy research (as distinct from potentially life-threatening medical research), moderate penalities might be imposed upon subjects who withdraw from such research without adequate reasons.[36] Generally, however, the withdrawal of consent by research subjects should be quickly recognized, and perhaps even encouraged, so that subjects will not later become hostile or harmed in ways unforeseen by the researcher.

Researchers should carefully consider the various categories of persons placed at risk in the research and obtain appropriate consent from these persons or their representatives. High school students identified as potential drug abusers by other high school students for a drug prevention program are subjects from whom consent should be obtained.[37] In the examination of court files of mental illness hearings, committed patients might be at risk. If their consent cannot be obtained because it would be impossible to locate them, a guardian ad litem might be appointed by the court to represent the interests of these patients to help insure adequate procedures for confidentiality.

Consent is not only to be informed, it is also to be "competent" and "voluntary." The doctrine of mental competency (or incompetency) has been extensively developed in areas of wills and contracts. Many of the concepts developed there are applicable in developing a doctrine of competency to consent. Among those who have most extensively studied the issue, there seems to be considerable agreement that the status per se of being an institutionalized mental patient or prisoner should not automatically preclude participation in research—at least that which may be therapeutically beneficial to the individual. With regard to prisoners, one legal scholar has concluded, ''The notion that the confined are 'institutionalized' to such a degree as to invalidate consent, leaving aside the inducement argument, should be rejected, for at least two reasons: (1) There is little factual evidence to sustain it; and (2) its acceptance might lead to unwarranted intrusions upon other rights of prisoners.''[38]

Granting the capacity of at least some institutionalized persons to consent competently and voluntarily to research, the next step would seem to be to establish additional safeguards to insure the rights of this class of persons. Thus DHEW has issued regulations limiting the type of research that can be conducted with prisoners and specifying certain conditions that must be approved by institutional review boards.[39] (See Appendix AA.)

There may be situations where consent of subjects is not necessary because the added risk or stress is minimal or nonexistent, and there are practical reasons for not seeking consent.[40] Rearranging signs and benches in a university park or setting up a bonus token-system for bus riders appear to be sufficiently benign.[41] But asking nonsuspecting bar patrons about ''alcoholism'' while riding in a cab[42] is more ethically ambiguous. Sometimes there is no practical way of getting informed, and certainly not written, consent in advance (e.g., from help-line callers).[43] More ethically suspect experiments involve purposeful deception. Some mild deception may be justified if the potential results are ''important,'' alternative deception-free methods of producing comparable results are not available, and the degree of deception is not harmful or socially repugnant.[44]

In summary, when a subject is at risk, the researcher is expected to have made reasonable efforts to assure that the following elements of consent are present: (a) the subject's consent is voluntary, competent, and informed, (b) provision is made for the subject to withdraw from the experiment, and (c) a method of appeal to a third party is specified. In studies of social issues, some modification of these requirements may be made and found legally acceptable.[45]

RESEARCH CONTRACTS

The relationship between an experimenter and a subject can be viewed legally as a form of contract. Although not commonly done in medical or psychological practice, a practitioner may enter into an express contract, written or oral, to produce a specific result or cure.[46] Similarly, it is possible to enter into contracts with other persons who provide professional services such as dentists, stockbrokers, accountants, and attorneys. One does not ordinarily ''consent'' to the services of a stockbroker or an attorney.

''Consent'' and ''contract'' are different legal concepts. Consent, an aspect of tort law, allows the touching of another person without subsequent legal liability.

There are, however, many issues that ought to be clarified in the conduct of research that are not, strictly speaking, related to consent, such as payment of fees, mutual duties of researcher and participants, and confidentiality of the data. The research contract usually includes informed consent provisions and then specifies other aspects of the agreement. For example, contracts have been written for contingency management in behavior therapy (including the therapist's fees).[47] The traditional notion of consenting to treatment or research seems to reflect an authoritarian orientation toward a patient-subject. While obvious inequality exists in a research situation with respect to technical knowledge, there is no necessity for such inequality to be reflected in civil status.

In the research context, a researcher can be viewed as an offeror, and the subject as the offeree (who can accept or reject the researcher's offer or make a counter-offer). In this way, alternatives can be discussed, the terms of the contract can specify possible benefits and risks to both parties, and the agreement can be mutually modified or rescinded should unforeseen circumstances arise. Because agreement might be reached in experimental situations without complete understanding by the scientifically unsophisticated subject, provision to modify or rescind the agreement should be stipulated in clear terms.[48] (See sample contract, Appendix DD.)

It is important to note that both contract agreements and consent may not be valid (or may be voidable) if they involve duress, coercion, fraud, certain types of mistakes, or certain types of activities. For example, one may not legally consent to, or contract for, being made insane or being killed.[49] Committed mental patients, unless specifically judged incompetent, are not necessarily presumed incapable of disbursing assets, making contracts, and in general managing their own affairs.[50] Prisoners also retain at least some contractual rights.[51] Across-the-board prohibition of research opportunities for such individuals may diminish potential income and social status.[52] The propriety of the prohibition will depend, in part, on whether the environment is believed to be so coercive that even unreasonable inducements cannot be voluntarily refused. If there is gross inequity in the bargaining power of the parties to a contract so that the weaker party has no meaningful choice or no real alternative, the contract may be considered legally unconscionable.[53] The court may also consider whether the weaker party (such as a prisoner, patient, or minor) was reasonably able to protect his/her interests because of physical or mental infirmities, ignorance, or inability to understand the language of the agreement.[54]

DISCUSSION

Common law does not restrain individuals from voluntary participation in private hazardous undertakings that demonstrably serve public purposes. Furthermore, social tradition in this country vigorously champions the right of a person to know anything that may be known or discovered about any part of the universe—

BOX 11.1   RESEARCH METHODS

"Once aloft, at 5,000 feet, subjects completed one irrelevant test and then waited for the plane to reach a higher altitude. In the case of the Experimental group flights, the aircraft lurched while changing altitude. Subjects saw that one propeller had stopped turning and heard about other malfunctions over the intercom; they were then informed directly that there was an emergency. A simulated pilot-to-tower conversation was provided to the subjects over their earphones to support the deception. As the aircraft passed within sight of the airfield, subjects could see fire trucks and ambulances on the airstrip in apparent expectation of a crash landing.

After a specified period of time, the aircraft made a safe landing at the airport. Subjects . . . were thoroughly informed as to the true nature and purpose of the experiment. . . . Urines were collected at 3 hours after landing.''

Source: Berkun, M. M., Bialek, H. M., Kern, R. P. & Yagi, K., Experimental studies of psychological stress in man. 76 *Psychological Monographs* (No. 15), 1962, p. 3.

---

including other human beings. Freedom of the press is one expression of this tradition. However, there are similarly strong traditions supporting the individual's right to self-determination and to privacy.

Numerous studies in psychology, sociology, and medicine have been the target of criticism for their apparent invasions of privacy (e.g. observation of micturition or sex in a public restroom),[55] or excessive coercion (e.g. army recruits on a "stricken" airplane apparently forced to crash land).[56] Psychologists in particular have acquired a dubious reputation for not merely failing to inform participants but actively misinforming (e.g. false feedback regarding homosexual desires)[57] and deception (e.g. presumed traumatic shocking of a subject).[58] Seemingly, the decision of when a researcher may expose some of the members to risk for their own or others' benefit cannot be left to the individual investigator (or any other affected party) because vested interests may be quite strong.[59] Ethical discussions often produce many words with very little observable effect.

Although opinion varies as to the desirability of legal regulation of research and treatment,[60] one conservative prediction can be made: in the midst of "information overload," researchers (like other human beings) will simply ignore even the wisest and most saintly words unless such verbalizations are backed up by tangible consequences. Therefore if experimentation is to be consciously regulated by society, a contingency analysis of professional reinforcers (e.g., economic, social, emotional payoffs) would likely be an effective first step. Renee Fox has suggested the goal: "Some kind of dynamic equilibrium between the promises and perils of research, between individual and societal considerations should ideally be struck— an equilibrium that does not immoderately embolden investigators and their subjects, unduly fetter them; or relegate them to an irresolute state of limbo."[61]

NOTES

1. Watson, J. B. and Rayner, R. Conditioned emotional responses. 3 *Journal of Experimental Psychology* 1 (1920); Watson, J. B. and Watson, R. R. Studies in infant psychology. 13 *Scientific Monthly* 493 (1921).

2. Ellen Reese, personal communication (with R. L. S.), October 18, 1974. Details of this transaction are difficult to verify. The Heckscher Foundation of New York City which might have old records has moved offices, and Mary Cover Jones, who conducted the classic companion study eliminating fears of 3-year-old Peter, reported: "I am saying, among other things, that one of my disappointments is that I don't know what happened to Albert or Peter—that if I were to repeat my experiment, I would want to know much more about the 'patient' and be able to follow-up." Letter to author (R. L. S.) from M. C. Jones, November 11, 1974. *See generally,* Jones, M. C. A laboratory study of fear: The case of Peter. 31 *Pedagogical Seminary* 308 (1924); Jones, M. C. Albert, Peter, and J. B. Watson. 29 *American Psychologist* 581 (1974).

3. *See* Fletcher, J. Human experimentation: Ethics in the consent situation. 32 *Law and Contemporary Problems* 620, 623 (1967); Lowe, C. U., Alexander, D., and Michkin, B. Nontherapeutic research with children: An ethical dilemma. 84 *The Journal of Pediatrics* 468 (Apr. 1974).

4. Ladimer, I. Ethical and legal aspects of medical research on human beings. 3 *Journal of Public Law* 467 (1954): "Medical research on human subjects, except as it is an inherent but not a predominant incident to such [medical] practice, would appear to be outside the scope of medical practice . . ." as quoted in Perlman, J. L. Human experimentation. 2 *The Journal of Legal Medicine* 30, 32 (Jan. 1974). Some differences between medical and socially oriented research include (1) influence of the social context upon outcome measures, (2) use of relationships between individuals or groups as dependent and independent variables, and (3) influence of subject awareness of the experiment on outcome measures. *See* Schwitzgebel, R. K. Ethical problems in experimentation with offenders. 38 *American Journal of Orthopsychiatry* 738 (1968).

5. Cooke, R. A. and Tannenbaum, A. S. Research subjects report they are adequately informed; cite immediate and future benefits of participation. *ISR (Institute for Social Research) Newsletter* 7 (Summer 1977). With children, 50 percent of the research is biomedical; 40 percent behavioral. In prisons practically all research is biomedical.

6. Title 45, *Code of Federal Regulations,* sec. 46.103(b) (revised Jan. 11, 1978). This definition defines the role of "subject" in terms of risk but does not consider the factor of active or passive participation in investigative procedures. Deceased persons are sometimes the "subjects" of investigation, but they are not "at risk" in the usual meaning of the term. In this situation, could the surviving relatives (or even employers) be considered "subjects" by DHEW definition?

7. Guidelines for preparation of protocols for review by the Human Investigation Committee. Yale University School of Medicine, Sept. 1973, as quoted in Levine, R. J. Guidelines for negotiating informed consent with prospective human subjects of experimentation. 22 *Clinical Research* 42 at 42 (Feb. 1974).

8. "The mere fact of a departure from the manufacturer's reccommendation where such departure is customarily followed by physicians of standing in the locality does not make that departure an 'experiment.'" Salgo v. Leland Stanford Jr. University Board of Trustees, 317 P.2d 170 (Cal. App. Ct. 1957) (injury resulting from a drug used in a medical examination).

9. Report of the Third Committee, doc. A/4045, 13 *United Nations General Assembly Official Records,* Annex agenda item no. 32 (1958) as quoted in Katz, J. *Experimentation with human beings.* New York: Russell Sage Foundation, 1972, at p. 837.

10. *E.g.,* Position statement of the American Federation for Clinical Research on the DHEW proposed rule, 23 *Clinical Research* 53 (Feb. 1975); *Ethical principles in the conduct of research with human participants.* Washington, D.C.: American Psychological Assn., 1973; American Psychiatric Assn., Code of ethics on human experimentation. 38 *American Journal of Orthopsychiatry* 589 (1968); Statement of the American Bar Association on the mentally disabled before the national human experimentation group. 1 *Mental Disability Law Reporter* 155 (1976); Bureau of Social Science Research, *BSSR policy on the protection of human subjects.* Washington, D.C.: Author, 1973; May. J. G., Risley, T. R., Twardosz, S., Friedman, P., Bijou, S. W., Wexler, D. et al. Guidelines for the use of behavioral procedures in state programs for retarded persons. 1 *Mental Retardation Research* (National Assn. for Retarded Citizens) 1 (1975).

11. DHEW Regulations, title 45, *Code of Federal Regulations,* subtitle A, part 46 published in 39 *Federal Register* 18914 (May 30, 1974) (benefits should outweigh risks); FDA Regulations, 21 *Code of Federal Regulations,* sec. 130.37 (requiring written consent of subject); Bureau of Census, 13 *U.S.C.,* sec. 8 & 9a (preserving confidentiality of data and prohibiting use for nonstatistical purposes); Office of Education, Bureau of Research, *Support for research and related activities,* 1967, at p. 14 (anonymity and confidentiality of questionaire responses); DHEW, Protection of human subjects: Proposed amendments concerning fetuses, pregnant women, and in vivo fertilization. 45 *Code of Federal Regulations,* part 46 published in 42 *Federal Register* 2792 (Jan. 13, 1977).

12. P.L. 93–348 (the ''National Research Act''); for related Congressional activity, *see* Staff report of Subcommittee on Constitutional Rights of the Committee on Judiciary, *Individual rights and the federal role in behavior modification,* U.S. Government Printing Office (Nov. 1974).

13. DHEW, Protection of human subjects: Proposed regulations on research involving prisoners, 43 *Federal Register* 1050 (Jan. 5, 1978); DHEW, Protection of human subjects: Proposed regulations on research involving children, 43 *Federal Register* 2084 (Jan 13, 1978) and 43 *Federal Register* 31786 (July 2, 1978); DHEW, Report and recommendations: Research involving those institutionalized as mentally infirm, 43 *Federal Register* 11328 (March 17, 1978). (Apr. 1974). *See generally,* Keith-Spiegel, P. Children's rights as participants in research. In G. P. Koocher (Ed.) *Children's rights and the mental health professions.* New York: Wiley, 1976, pp. 53–81.

14. Lowe, et al., *supra* note 3 at p. 469.

15. Fiorentino v. Wenger, 227 N.E.2d 296 (N.Y. 1967) (informed consent necessary from parents of 14-year-old for experimental surgery). Note, Common law and clinical investigation. 203 *Journal of the American Medical Association* 231 (Feb. 5, 1968). ''Sound practice from a legal standpoint requires that the informed consent of the legal guardian be obtained for such an individual's research participation. . . . When a child, a mentally retarded person, or a disturbed patient is incapable of making some reasonable judgment . . . permission should be obtained from the participant as well as the responsible adult or guardian.'' *Ethical principles in the conduct of research with human participants.* Washington, D.C.: American Psychological Association, 1973, pp. 35–36.

16. Rosen, A. C., Rekers, G. A., and Bentler, P. M. 34 *Journal of Social Issues* 122,127; Rekers, G. A. and Lovaas, O. I. Behavioral treatment of deviant sex-role behaviors in a male child. 7 *Journal of Applied Behavior Analysis* 173 (1974), and rejoinder asserting the project to be "the most insidious attempt to stamp out the development of gay identity in young children, Morin, S. F. and Schultz, S. J. The gay movement and the rights of children. 34 *Journal of Social Issues* 137, 142 (1978).

17 DHEW, Protection of human subjects: Proposed rules on research involving children, 43 *Federal Register* 31792 (Jl. 21, 1978).

18. Grisso, T. and Vierling, L. Minors' consent to treatment: A developmental perspective. Unpublished paper, 1978. In this detailed review, the authors conclude that "There is little evidence that minors of age 15 and above as a group are any less competent to provide consent than are adults. In the age range of 11–14, existing research suggests caution regarding any assumptions about these minors' abilities to consider intelligently the complexities of treatment alternatives." *Id.* at 20.

19. DHEW, *supra* note 17. In situations of great risk where no benefit is to be obtained by the minor, parents or guardians alone may not be able to give legally valid consent on behalf of their children or wards. In such situations with only parental authorization, parents and the investigator might be liable for battery or "child abuse." *See* Morse, H. Legal implications of clinical investigation. 20 *Vanderbilt Law Review* 747 (May 1967).

20. Dykstra, D., in "Invited discussion," *Proceedings of Conference on use of human subjects in safety evaluation of food chemicals*, Washington, D.C.: National Academy of Science/National Research Council, 1967, at pp. 229–247; as quoted in Perlman, *supra* note 4 at 37–38. *Similarly,* Kelman, H. C. The rights of the subject in social research. 27 *American Psychologist* 989, 992 (Nov. 1972).

21. Office of Science and Technology, *Privacy and behavioral research*. Washington, D.C.: U.S. Government Printing Office, 1967, at pp. 9–10; as quoted in Katz, *supra* note 9, at p. 730.

22. Fletcher, *supra* note 3, at p. 653; e.g., Schwitzgebel, R. K. *Streetcorner research*. Cambridge, Mass.: Harvard University Press, 1965 (traditionally defined "clients" and "offenders" paid as "research subjects" for purpose of behavior-change).

23. Katz, *supra* note 9, ch. 11 (a comprehensive series of commentaries on balancing the interests of science, society, and individuals).

24. In a controversial study of obedience (Milgram, S. *Obedience to authority*. New York: Harper & Row, 1973) in which 15 subjects showed "full-blown uncontrollable seizures," 84 percent of the subjects on a follow-up questionnaire stated that they were glad to have been in the experiment, and an interview by a third party 12 months later found that none of the 40 "worst cases" showed signs of having been harmed. Errera, P. Statement based on interviews with 40 "worst cases" in the Milgram obedience experiments, unpublished manuscript (1963) reprinted in Katz, *supra* note 9, at p. 400. On the vicissitudes of potential benefits or harms to a subject, *see* Mead, M. The problem of an unpredictable future position of an individual identified in a research project. 98 *Daedalus* 382 (1969).

25. Friedman, P. R. Legal regulation of applied behavior analysis in mental institutions and prisons. 17 *Arizona Law Review* 40, 76 (1975). *See also* Guidelines for psychologists for the use of drugs in research, 27 *American Psychologist* 335 (Apr. 1972).

26. Brown, B. S., Wienckowski, L. A., & Stolz, S. B. *Behavior modification: Perspective* *on a current issue.* Rockville, Md.: National Institute of Mental Health, 1975 (DHEW Publ. No. ADM 75–202), p. 21. *Also,* Cooke & Tannenbaum, *supra* note 5, and Gray, B. H., Cooke, R. A. and Tannenbaum, A. S. Research involving human subjects. 201 *Science* 1094 (Sept., 22 1978) (one-fourth of projects required changes for informed consent, usually addition of content rather than in way consent was to be obtained).

27. Settlement stipulation, *In the matter of alleged violations of Article 24–A of the Public Health Law by State University of New York at Albany, et al.* State of New York, Dept. of Health, Oct. 27, 1977. (SUNYA officials admitted that members of the psychology department violated state law by failing to give subjects a description of the discomforts and risks reasonably expected). 198 *Science* 383 (Oct. 28, 1977); an outrageous description can be found in "Experiments 'peril' pupils," *Times Union* 1 (Sept. 24, 1977).

28. DHEW, Informed consent: Definition amended to include advice on compensation. 43 *Federal Register* 51559 (Nov. 3, 1978).

29. Although many states use the "similar practitioner" standard, the "client" standard appears to be gaining acceptance (e.g., Wilkinson v. Besey, 295 A.2d 676 (RI 1972) (patient has right to decide on basis of all material risks, even if medical community practice does not disclose certain dangers of radiation burns); Canterbury v. Spence, 464 F.2d 772 (D.C. Cir. 1972), *cert. denied* 409 U.S. 1064 (1972) (patient's right of self-determination shapes the boundaries of physician's duty to disclose dangers of laminectomy); Cobbs v. Grant, 502 P.2d 1 (Cal. 1972) (in duodenal ulcer treatment, patient need not be given a "mini-course in medical science," but physician must explain complications in lay terms). For an extensive discussion of the legal doctrines of consent, see Meisel, A. The expansion of liability for medical accidents: From negligence to strict liability by way of informed consent. 56 *Nebraska Law Review* 51 (1977).

30. Canterbury v. Spence, *supra* note 29.

31. DHEW, Protection of Human Subjects: Informed consent. 45 *Code of Federal Regulation* 46.103(c), as published in 43 *Federal Register* 51559 (Nov. 3, 1978).

32. Notice, Prohibited or restricted research, 5 *NIH guide for grants and contracts* (Oct. 8, 1976) prohibits support of "any research program or project, or program or course which is of an experimental nature, without the written informed consent of each participant or subject, or if the participant or subject is under 18 years of age, the written informed consent of his parents or legal guardian." However, in response to the question as to whether written consent is *always* necessary, Dr. D. T. Chalkley, Director, Office for Protection from Research Risks, NIH, DHEW, replied, "Insofar as DHEW regulations are concerned, no. We would agree that the writing serves only evidentiary purposes, and is in effect protection for the researcher rather than the subject. Any number of good research institutions much prefer the oral approach because it improves investigator/subject rapport, and it offers a far better opportunity to judge subject competence and subject comprehension. Personal communication with R. K. S., Jan. 25, 1977.

33. Cooke & Tannenbaum, *supra* note 5.

34. Resnick, J. H. & Schwartz, T. Ethical standards as an independent variable in psychological research. 29 *American Psychologist* 134 (Feb. 1973) (sharply divergent outcome on a trivial but rather traditional verbal-conditioning task).

35. 138 S.E.2d 902 (Ga. Ct. App. 1964) (barium enema continued).

36. "While the subject should not be forced to perform his contract if he wishes to cancel it, it may be appropriate to include a provision for liquidated damages should the subject

withdraw without adequate reasons, spelled out in advance, which reflect the nature of the risks and inconveniences involved in the research." Capron, A. M. Social experimentation and the law. In A. M. Rivlin and P. M. Timpane (Eds.) *Ethical and legal issues of social experimentation*. Washington, D.C.: Brookings Institution, 1975, 127–163, at 139–140.

37. Merriken v. Cressman, 369 F. Supp. 913 (Pa. 1973).
38. Singer, R. Consent of the unfree: Medical experimentation in the closed institution. 1 *Law and Human Behavior* 1, 162 (1977): Shapiro similarly argued: "It is a mistake to assume that because of the inescapably coercive conditions of institutionalization and an overwhelming desire for freedom from confinement, a person involuntarily confined can *in principle* never render a competent, free decision, untainted by loss of capacity or duress, concerning the use of organic therapies upon him. Such a blanket assumption is itself an assault upon the value of personal autonomy." Shapiro, M. H. Legislating the control of behavior control: Autonomy and the coercive use of organic therapies. 47 *Southern California Law Review* 237, 338 (1974).
39. DHEW, Additional protections pertaining to biomedical and behavioral research involving prisoners as subjects. 43 *Federal Register* 53652 (Nov. 16, 1978).
40. "Insofar as the research involves comparisons of reasonable variations in the normal program of institutions or agencies, there would seem to be no compelling case for insisting absolutely on the informed consent of the participants." APA *Ethical principles, supra* note 15, at p. 34.
41. Hayes, S. C. and Cone, J. D. Decelerating environmentally destructive lawn-walking behavior. Paper presented at American Psychological Association meetings, Chicago, Nov. 1974 (mimeo. Psychology Dept., West Virginia University) (manipulation of signs and benches with observation of 1885 persons); Everett, P. B., Hayward, S. C., and Meyers, A. W. The effects of a token reinforcement procedure on on bus ridership. 7 *Journal of Applied Behavior Analysis* 1 (1974) (use of bonus tokens at state university).
42. McMartin, J. A. The taxicab as a mobile laboratory for the study of social influence. Paper presented at the Western Psychological Association meetings, Portland, Sept. 1972 (mimeo. San Fernando Valley State College, Calif.).
43. Editorial comments, "Hotline research: Critique, response, and rejoinder. 7 *Professional Psychology* 236 (May 1976).
44. Adapted from Kelman, *supra* note 20. "With children, the primary objective of the postinvestigation clarification procedure is to assure that the child leaves the research situation with no undesirable after-effects of his participation. This may mean, for example, that certain misconceptions should not be removed or *even that some new misconceptions should be induced*. If a child erroneously believes that he has done well on a research task, there may be more harm in trying to correct this misconception than in permitting it to remain." [italics added] APA *Ethical standards, supra* note 15, at p. 81.
45. *See* Aguayo v. Richardson, 473 F.2d 1090 (2d Cir. 1973) (additional work programs and assignments for families receiving aid for dependent children allowed to continue); California Welfare Rights Organization v. Richardson, 348 F. Supp. 491 (N.D. Cal. 1972) (small charges for medical services that might otherwise have been free found permissible).
46. Guilmet v. Campbell, 385 Mich. 57, 188 N.W.2d 601 (1971).
47. Ayllon, T. & Skuban, W. Accountability in psychotherapy: A test case. 4 *Journal of*

Behavior Therapy and Experimental Psychiatry 19 (1973); *see also,* Knox, D. Behavior contracts in marriage counseling. 1 *Journal of Family Counseling* 22 (1973); Alexander, G. J. and Szasz, T. S. From contract to status via psychiatry. 13 *Santa Clara Lawyer* 537 (1973): "When the right to contract is severed from the individual, so is a large portion of his humanity. Yet in contract, as in other areas of the law, the right is taken away with astonishing regularity in the name of mental health."

48. Panel on Privacy and Behavioral Research (President's Office of Science and Technology), Privacy and behavioral research. 155 *Science* 535 (1967); *see generally,* Simpson, L. P. *Law of contracts,* 2d ed. St. Paul: West Publishing Co., 1965, ch. 22.

49. For illegality of contracts, *see generally,* Simpson, *supra* note 48, at ch. 23; for commentary on informed consent in experimentation, including issues of duress, fraud, and misunderstanding, *see* Katz, *supra* note 9, at pp. 521–724. For consent problems in behavior therapy in institutions, *see* Freedman, *supra* note 25, at pp. 80–88.

50. Wexler, D. B. Forward: Mental health law and the movement toward voluntary treatment. 62 *California Law Review* 671, 678 (1974); Winters v. Miller, 446 F.2d 65, 68 (2d Cir. 1971), *cert. den.* 404 U.S. 985 (1971) (refusal of medication on religious grounds).

51. "A prisoner retains all rights of an ordinary citizen except those expressly, or by necessary implication, taken from him by law." Coffin v. Reichard, 143 F.2d 443, 445 (6th Cir. 1944).

52. "All but a half-dozen inmates interviewed here [Jackson State Prison] by the Federal [National] Commission on the Protection of Human Subjects said they opposed American Civil Liberties Union and other efforts, including some in Congress, to halt medical experiments on prisoners. The men said they wanted the money they earned from drug companies for participating in experiments. In addition they enjoy the change from prison routine, the physical care they receive and, some said, the chance to help others." Cohn, V. Prisoners insist on the right to act as paid guinea pigs. *Los Angeles Times,* Nov. 16, 1975, sec. A-1, p. 1. ". . . Prisoners currently participating in research consider, in nearly all instances, that they do so voluntarily and want the research to continue." National Commission for the Protection of Human Subjects, Research involving prisoners. 42 *Federal Register* 3076, 3079 (Jan. 14, 1977).

53. The American Law Institute, *Restatement of the law, 2d: Contracts.* (Tentative draft no. 5) Philadelphia: The American Law Institute, 1970 ("contracts of adhesion"). Schwitzgebel, R. K. A contractual model for the protection of the rights of institutionalized mental patients. 30 *American Psychologist* 815 (1975). For a theoretical argument against the medical contract model, *see* Sedgwick, P. Medical individualism. *Hastings Center Studies* 69 (Sept. 1974); for similar arguments against consensual model, *see* Oppenheim, M. Informed consent to medical treatment. 11 *Cleveland-Marshall Law Review* 249 (1962)

54. *See generally,* The Committee on Federal Agency Evaluation Research, National Research Council, *Protecting individual privacy in evaluation research.* Washington, D.C.: National Academy of Sciences, 1975 (includes a detailed discussion of the confidentially of research data and a draft statute to guard against the compulsory disclosure of research data).

55. Humphreys, L. *Tearoom trade.* Chicago: Aldine Publishing Co., 1970 (sex); Middlemist, R. D., Knowles, E. S. & Matter, F. C. Personal space invasions in the lavatory: Suggestive evidence for arousal. 33 *Journal of Personality and Social Psychology* 541, 1976 (micturation).

56. Berkun, M. M., Bialek, H. M., Kern, R. P., and Yagi, K. Experimental studies of psychological stress in man. 76 *Psychological Monograph* (Whole No. 534, 1962).

57. Bramel, D. Selection of a target for defensive projection. 66 *Journal of Abnormal and Social Psychology* 318 (1962). The public reputation of psychological research may be illustrated by the following news story: "A New York judge stated that a man may use any nonviolent means, 'even deceit,' to get a woman to say yes. Martin Evans, 36, had bedded a 20-year-old woman after telling her he was a psychologist doing research. But, concluded Justice Edward J. Greenfield, he used no violence or threats. . . . Agreed Evans: 'I seduce. I don't rape.' " The law. 106 *Time* 58 (May 12, 1975).

58. Milgram, S. Behavioral studies of obedience. 69 *Journal of Abnormal and Social Psychology* 371 (1963).

59. "The researcher has to weigh many conflicting considerations of losses and gains, which vary both in likelihood of occurrence and in seriousness. . . . The fact that such decision must be based on such complex factors, subjectively weighed and susceptible to bias, implies that the researcher should check it against the judgments of others." APA *Ethical standards,* supra note 15, at pp. 22–23.

60. Generally favorable: Dorken, H. and Associates (Eds.) *The professional psychologist today*. San Francisco: Jossey-Bass, 1976. Generally negative: Gergen, K. J. The codification of research ethics: Views of a doubting Thomas. 28 *American Psychologist* 907 (Oct. 1973); Goldiamond, I. Singling out behavior modification for legal regulation: Some effects on patient care, psychotherapy, and research in general. 17 *Arizona Law Review* 105 (1975).

61. Fox, R. Introduction to the cases, *Experiments and research with humans: Values in conflict*. Washington, D.C.: National Academy of Sciences, 1975, at p. 59.

CHAPTER 12

Confidential Communications

When a mental health professional receives a request for information about a client, the first thought should be to deny the request and to consult with the client. Among the privileges or rights granted to citizens is one involving private communications (e.g., with a spouse, attorney, or psychotherapist). *Privileged communication* refers to a legal right existing by statute which protects the client from having his or her confidences revealed publicly, without permission, during legal proceedings. Generally, the right *belongs to the client, not to the therapist.*[1]

Confidentiality is a broader concept and protects a client from unauthorized disclosures of information given, in confidence, without the consent of the client.[2] These disclosures may be in the form of film or other recordings[3] as well as information given by the therapist to third parties. Confidentiality is an ethical practice, not a legal right authorized by statue. Various professional organizations have codes of conduct designed to safeguard the client's confidentiality and to provide sanctions for professional misconduct.[4]

RATIONALE

The presentation of evidence is an essential aspect of judicial proceedings and presumably of making fair decisions. In order to facilitate such presentation, courts are empowered to subpoena witnesses and to compel answers to any questions, except those which may result in self-incrimination (Cf., Fifth Amendment). However, in certain circumstances, exclusion of materially relevant evidence is permit-

---

BOX 12.1 CONFIDENTIAL COMMUNICATION

"TITICUT FOLLIES"

Among the notable legal follies in the area of psychology was "Titicut Follies," a well-known documentary film by Frederick Wiseman. The film revealed conditions among patients at the Massachusetts Correctional Institution at Bridgewater. Allegedly, Wiseman represented that his film would be noncommercial and that he would not photograph patients unless he had obtained written releases from those competent to sign such releases (as decided by institutional staff).

In an action brought against Wiseman by the Commonwealth of Massachusetts, the trial judge characterized the film as "crass . . . commercialism." Regarding releases, the court found that some of the 62 inmates identified in the film were incompetent to understand a release and that releases were obtained from only 11 or 12 of the inmates. Said the court: "There is a collective, indecent intrusion into the most private aspects of the lives of these unfortunate persons in the Commonwealth's custody." The court granted an injunction against commercial showings but permitted showings to mental health professionals, students, and organizations.

Cf., Commonwealth v. Wiseman, 356 Mass. 251, 249 N.E.2d 610, *cert. denied,* 398 U.S. 960 (1969).

---

ted (i.e, "privilege" is granted) on the theory that the suppression of evidence will best serve the public interest. Professional therapeutic relationships would presumably be hampered if the privilege were not available. An arsonist would probably be reluctant to divulge intimate details of his activities to a mental health professional, knowing that the information could be revealed by the professional in court.

A classic treatise on the subject has listed four requisites for the establishment of the privilege: (a) the communications must originate in a *confidence* that they will not be disclosed; (b) this element of *confidentiality must be essential* to the full and satisfactory maintenance of the relationship between the parties; (c) the *relation* must be one which in the opinion of the community ought to be sedulously *fostered*; and (d) the *injury* that would inure to the relation by the disclosure of the communication must be *greater than the benefit* thereby gained for the correct disposal of litigation.[5]

DEGREES OF PRIVILEGE

Protected Professional Relationships

The only privileged professional relationship recognized in all jurisdictions as a matter of common or statutory law is the attorney-client relationship. Privileged status for other professional communications is sometimes granted by statute. At least 44 states recognize the privileged aspect of the clergyman-penitent relationship, justified by the First Amendment's religious protections.[6] In 40 states communications between psychiatrists and patients are privileged.[7] Connecticut, Florida, Georgia, and Kentucky do not have a general physician-patient privilege but have a specific psychiatrist-patient statute. The proposed *Rules of Evidence for U. S. District Courts and Magistrates* abolishes the physician-patient privilege, but it contains a psychotherapist-patient privilege.[8] The rationale of this policy was that in actual practice so many exceptions to the physician-patient privilege have been found necessary, in order to prevent fraud or to promote the public interest, that the privilege is meaningless. Psychotherapists are protected because, presumably, the matters dealt with are less understandable or more socially sensitive. Therefore, these matters should not be accessible to the public or to the patient for the patient's own welfare.

Twenty-seven states have a psychologist-client privilege. (Five of these states—Alaska, Alabama, Delaware, New York, and Tennessee—grant the privilege to psychologists but not psychiatrists because psychiatrists are physicians.) A few states have extended the privilege to counselors and psychometrists. School personnel are granted statutory privilege in 19 states,[9] but legislation and case law have not generally extended the privilege to social workers and probation officers.[10] Other professions such as architects, accountants, and private detectives have occasionally obtained special legislative privilege.[11] Privileged communications when authorized by statute may be narrowly interpreted to exclude information the patient did not "communicate" (e.g., therapist's appointment book). This information can be subpoenaed if there is litigation.[12]

Approximately one-fourth of the states that allow a psychotherapist-patient privilege use the prevailing attorney-client statute as a model, or perhaps a slightly weaker version:

> The confidential relations and communications between a certified psychologist and his client are placed on the same bases as provided by law for those between an attorney and his client. Nothing in this act shall be construed to require such privileged communications to be disclosed.[13]

Nonetheless, ethical guidelines established by the American Medical Association and the American Psychological Association, as well as much case law, requires that, although confidentiality is an important duty of the psychotherapist, *disclosure* of information is "necessary in order to protect the welfare of the individual or the community" or required "when there is a clear and imminent danger to an individual or to society".[14]

Standard ethical procedure requires that the express (and, if feasible, written) permission be obtained from the client prior to transmittal of identifying information. (See Appendix O, P, and Q) From 1950 to 1976, the American Psychiatric

BOX 12.2 WHAT TO DO WHEN SERVED WITH A SUBPOENA

(1) Determine the nature of the subpoena and its legality of service. A "plain" subpoena may require attendance (but not records) either at a court session or at a deposition outside court to discover material facts. A subpoena "duces tecum" (which bears that name plainly on its face) requires records. Some duces tecum subpoenas state that a personal appearance is not necessary, but this is no assurance that an appearance may not be later required by subsequent subpoena. Attorneys have an absolute right to obtain "plain" subpoenas from the court clerk. Subpoenas duces tecum are theoretically subject to judicial review, but are also, in practice, routinely issued without review. Some governmental administrative agencies or commissions may have subpoena power; some may only use a subpoena-like form hoping to produce information. A paper issued from a court and titled a subpoena can be assumed valid and should not be ignored if properly delivered. (In Federal law and in many states, the subpoena must be handed to the person— not merely mailed or left on the premise.)

(2) Initially claim the privilege not to reveal by verbal testimony or by records any material pertaining to the person in question. In many jurisdictions, the practitioner *must* claim the privilege on behalf of the client unless or until: (a) the client (or his/her lawyer) especially waives privilege, or (b) despite a lack of waiver by the client, the legal proceedings in court waive the privilege as a matter of law (e.g., the client places his/her own mental condition in evidence in a lawsuit). Failure of the practitioner to initially claim the privilege may result in an unauthorized disclosure and legal liability (e.g., defamation of character) to the client. As a general rule, also make the same claim to anyone requesting personal information by telephone.

(3) Notify the appropriate administrator (if employed by an institution). Do not destroy or alter records to prevent disclosure. Tampering constitutes a misdemeanor or a felony. Good professional practice requires some record-keeping, and the time to consider the appropriate nature and extent of such records is, obviously, prior to subpoena.

(4) Contact the client and/or the client's attorney. Explain the probable impact, if any, on the client of public disclosure. A client's waiver should be informed as well as voluntary. If it is the client's attorney who has requested the information (in some states an individual's own attorney has the right of access without a subpoena), demand a written authorization from the client. If there is reason to believe that the disclosure will have a detrimental effect, advise the attorney in writing and (possibly) send a copy to the client.

(5) Consider the following options if an adequately informed and specific (not blanket or general) waiver cannot be obtained from the client:

(a) Do nothing. Failure to comply with a subpoena does not automatically constitute a contempt of court which subjects the practitioner to fines or imprisonment. Contempt occurs by disobeying a specific order from a judge, and presumably would be found only upon judicial consideration of the validity of the particular subpoena.

(b) Request in writing a conference *in private* with the appropriate judge. Make an effort to limit demands for information to those matters essential to the legal proceedings.

(c) Let the court act to violate your professional confidentiality and the patient's privilege. You are immune from malpractice when acting under court order. Subpoenaed records may be sent to the court under seal with particular reference to the court's obligation, under statutory or case law, to protect the privilege.

Source: Adapted and condensed from a memorandum of the same title issued by the Northern California Psychiatric Society Task Force on Confidentiality; Maurice Grossman, Chairperson, in 1 *Bulletin of the American Academy of Psychiatry and Law* 245 (1973). This is intended merely as a general guide and should not be construed as a legal opinion appropriate to a particular situation.

Association received 28 complaints of alleged unethical conduct by psychiatrists involving confidentiality; about 12 percent of the complaints eventually result in some form of sanction (ranging from expulsion to warning).[15] From 1970 to 1976, the American Psychological Association took similar action against seven psychologists for violation of the principle of confidentiality.

There are emergency situations such as temporary hospitalization for the purpose of observation that may require transmittal of information within professional channels or to public officials. In such situations, the person's consent may either be unobtainable or irrelevant. Personally identifiable information from school records may be disclosed without prior consent for similar reasons.[16]

Possible Mandatory Disclosure by Practitioner

What represents "clear and imminent danger" is usually left to the discretion of the psychotherapist. The mere announcement by a patient of a plan or intention to commit a crime or fraud does *not necessarily* demand disclosure by the therapist to authorities—more evidence is probably needed to warrant such a disclosure. However, it should be noted that a revelation by a client to his attorney of a plan or intention to commit a crime or fraud *does* constitute an exception (known as the "future crime or fraud" exception) to their privileged relationship and *does* demand disclosure by the attorney.

The best-known case on this point is *Tarasoff* v. *Regents of the University of California*.[17] The state supreme court, in a rare rehearing of the case, held that "Once a therapist does in fact determine, or under applicable professional standards reasonably should have determined, that a patient poses a serious danger of violence to others, he bears a duty to exercise reasonable care to protect the foreseeable victims of that danger."[18] An amicus curiae brief filed by several professional organizations,[19] in addition to contending that psychotherapeutic communications would be hampered, argued that such a duty would be impractical because

THE TARASOFF CASE

The facts of the case appear to be the following: In the fall of 1968, Prororsenjit Poddar, a graduate student from India studying naval architecture at the University of California at Berkeley, met Tatiana (Tanya) Tarasoff at a folk dancing class. They saw each other weekly during the fall, and on New Year's Eve she kissed him. Poddar interpreted this act as a sign of formal engagement (as it might have been in India where he was a member of the Harijam or "untouchable" caste). Tanya told him that she was involved with other men, and indicated that she did not wish to have an intimate relationship with him.

Poddar became depressed as a result of the rebuff, but he saw Tanya a few times during the spring (occasionally tape recording their conversations in an effort to understand why she did not love him). Tanya left for Brazil in the summer, and Poddar at the urging of a friend went to the student health facility where a psychiatrist referred him to a psychologist for psychotherapy. When Tanya returned in October, 1969, Poddar discontinued therapy. Based in part on Poddar's stated intention to purchase a gun, the psychologist notified the campus police, both orally and in writing, that Poddar was dangerous and should be taken to a community mental health center for psychiatric commitment.

The campus police interviewed Poddar who seemed rational and promised to stay away from Tanya. They released him, and notified the health service. No further efforts at commitment were made because apparently the supervising psychiatrist decided that such was not needed and, as a matter of confidentiality, requested that the letter to the police as well as certain therapy records be destroyed.

On October 27th, Poddar went to Tanya's home armed with a pellet gun and a kitchen knife. She refused to speak to him. He shot her with the pellet gun. She ran from the house, was pursued, caught, and repeatedly and fatally stabbed. Poddar was found guilty of voluntary manslaughter rather than first or second degree murder. The defense established, with the aid of the expert testimony of three psychiatrists, that Poddar's diminished mental capacity (paranoid schizophrenia) precluded the malice necessary for first or second degree murder. After his prison term, he returned to India where, according to his own report, he is happily married.

psychotherapists typically overpredict violence.[20] The majority of the court rejected this contention. They reasoned that judgments of this nature must be made regularly by psychiatrists and psychologists and that, recognizing the difficulty of such prediction, "within the broad range of reasonable practice and treatment in which professional opinion and judgment may differ, the therapist is free to exercise his or her own best judgment without liability. . . ."[21]

Although the duty in *Tarasoff* is still vaguely defined and will vary from jurisdiction to jurisdiction, it may be briefly summarized as the duty to protect (by warning or other means) the foreseeable potential victim. Such a duty does not extend to relatives of a potentially suicidal patient.[22]

In the wake of the *Tarasoff* rulings has come a plethora of commentary. One article advised that "since actual violence is relatively rare among psychiatric patients, especially those with no history of previous violence, it is prudent to rely on the odds and not warn. . . . The psychiatrist must not be stampeded, even by *Tarasoff*, into providing frequent warnings to third parties."[23] In an article sharply critical of the majority opinion, one reviewer claimed that the new duty will increase, rather than decrease, public risk—"It is highly disruptive of the patient-therapist relationship and a less appropriate way of protecting those threatened by dangerous patients than the traditional alternatives of commitment or simply informing the police. . . . It is a disservice to the citizens of California."[24] Long-term, complex empirical issues of public safety seldom evoke such high levels of professionally organized altruistic expression. Elsewhere, however, the same reviewer suggested that, "The duty they [the decisions] impose is designed as much to protect patients from the power of psychiatrists as to protect the public from dangerous patients."[25] That is probably, for better or worse, an accurate assessment.

The parents of Ms. Tarasoff lost their suit to collect damages.[26] Most professionals feel that they also lost (i.e., have a burdensome and vaguely defined duty imposed upon them). One of the appropriate functions of law is to distribute the unhappiness of tragedy as equitably as possible. How well this was accomplished in *Tarasoff* will be a matter long debated.

"After-the fact" crimes are generally covered by the privilege, and do not require disclosure. However in some jurisdictions, statutes have been enacted presumably requiring mandatory disclosure of specific types of crimes—usually child abuse or drug abuse when it becomes known to a physician, dentist, chiropractor, religious practitioner, or professional school employee.[27] Mandatory disclosure statutes typically provide civil immunity for practitioners from private suits by patients alleging harm.

Under certain conditions, the duty to report information about patients may be reduced. For example, the confidentiality of information collected from research subjects in mental health research funded by HEW can be specially protected by a Confidentiality Certificate that permits the researcher to withhold names and other identifying characteristics from any legal proceeding.[28]

Possible Loss of Privilege by Patient

The patient does not have absolute privilege. Exceptions to privilege are often explicitly identified in state statutes. But even in the event they are not identified statutorily, there is some agreement that loss of privilege is probable in the following situations:

- When the services of the psychotherapist are sought to aid in the commission of a crime or tort;
- When a psychotherapist, in the course of diagnosis or treatment of the patient, determines that the patient is in urgent need of treatment in a hospital for mental illness;
- When the client is being prosecuted for homicide;
- When the client is involved in workmen's compensation litigation;
- When there is a dispute between persons involved in the privileged relationship (e.g., malpractice action);
- When there is a contest regarding the validity of a document, such as a will of the client; and
- When permitted and ordered by judicial discretion "in the interest of justice."[29]

Automatic Loss of Privilege by Patient

It is generally agreed that there are at least three situations in which a patient automatically waives his/her privilege of relevant communications:

(a) In a civil proceeding in which the patient introduces his/her mental condition as an element of his/her claim or defense. When psychotherapeutic records are sought only on a speculation of some connection, and when the patient does *not* introduce his/her mental condition, there may be *no* waiver. This might hold even though a "mental component" is involved (e.g., pain from physical injury in an auto accident), and the patient has signed a consent form.[30]

(b) In child custody cases in which either party raises the mental condition of the other party as part of claim or defense, or in cases where the therapist has knowledge or reasonable suspicion of child abuse.

(c) When a judge finds that the patient, after having been informed the communications would not be privileged, has made communications to a psychiatrist in the course of a psychiatric examination ordered by the court.[31] However, only communications related to the patient's mental condition may be admissible. Recommendations, if any, regarding disposition should *not* be included in the *body* of an expert's pre-trial report because the judge might be prohibited by procedural rules from admitting information not introduced at trial. If information is gathered during examination that might be useful for sentencing, one experienced examiner has suggested that the following statement be placed at the end of the pre-trial report: "As is our practice after examining a defendant thoroughly, we enclose under seal, a complete report on him (or her) which the court may use for the purposes of disposition, should he (or she) be found guilty or not-guilty by reason of insanity."[32]

Procedure for Revealing Confidential Information

As a customary practice, patients should, prior to treatment, be informed of and give consent to circumstances under which confidential information might be disclosed. Consent is usually not difficult to obtain.[33] (For a sample form used to provide information about confidentiality to clients, see Appendix K and L.) Because the consent to disclose information is to be an informed consent, it would be desirable, perhaps essential, to explain to the patient the major possible consequences of the disclosure prior to obtaining consent.

If obtaining consent would, in a few cases, prevent treatment, and the communication did not occur as part of a court-ordered examination, the therapist might conduct therapy until, and if, a reason arose for disclosure. In the rare instance when a patient began to speak convincingly of proposed violence, the therapist could explain various options (that may or may not involve the protection or warning of third parties.)[34]

Three steps are recommended in breaching confidentiality in situations of danger to others:

1. The practitioner should first encourage the patient to turn in weapons (if involved), to allow the practitioner to have the dangerous items (e.g., explosives, poison) removed without revealing the source, involve the endangered party in the therapy, and/or have the patient himself reveal the information to the endangered party.

BOX 12.3

"*Problem:* A 34-year-old methadone addict appeared at the emergency ward crying and agitated the day after his wife's suicide. He was carrying a loaded pistol, which he agreed to hand over to the hospital staff. He told the evaluating psychiatrist that he absolutely did not want hospitalization, that he wanted the gun back, and that if anyone on the street irritated him, he would kill that person. Despite the patient's threats of harm, there was no one to warn.

Resolution: The gun was not returned, the patient was not committed, and the police were not notified. He returned to the clinic for treatment, and five days later the unloaded weapon was returned to him. Two months later he threatened to kill his ex-father-in-law. The patient at this time decided not to carry the weapon since he feared he might hurt someone.''

Source: From Roth, L. H. & Meisel, A. Dangerousness, confidentiality, and the duty to warn. 134 *American Journal of Psychiatry* 508, 510 (1977).

2. Failing this, the practitioner should reveal the information with the patient's consent or in the presence of the patient to a responsible family member or a responsible authority in society.

3. Finally, if the patient does not cooperate in revealing information which the practitioner feels is necessary to divulge, then the practitioner should consult with other professionals. If there is consensus that an emergency situation exists with clear and imminent danger to the patient or others, information may be revealed to a responsible authority or other appropriate persons—even without the patient's consent—if it is likely to prevent violence or save a life.

Group Therapy

It is unclear to what extent multiple-person interactions are protected by the rules of privileged communication. If a "casual third party" is present during communications between patient and therapist, then such communications usually are *not* privileged. There is a presumption that the patient did not intend that the information remain confidential. Thus, persons in group therapy appear to be unprotected from other group members who may, without malice, reveal problems discussed during therapy to outsiders.[35] (However, "the therapist may have aides present without destroying the confidential nature of the communication.")[36]

The development of a privilege for group therapy, family therapy, joint marital counseling, and other multiple-person relationships is in the beginning stages. The most likely case-law extention will be to marriage counseling where only husband and wife are involved.[37] There certainly is no privilege which is typically recognized by state statute for multi-patient relationships. An ammendment to a Colorado statute is trend-setting to the extent that it prohibits the questioning of any persons who have participated in group therapy sessions "concerning any knowledge gained during the course of such therapy without the consent of the person or persons to whom the testimony sought relates."[38] If a privilege statute exists and is written so the patient, rather than the therapist, clearly holds the privilege, then disclosure by anyone who was a party to the communication would apparently be prohibited.[39]

As one means of avoiding misunderstanding, the therapist should spell out as clearly as possible the limits of confidentiality at the beginning of the relationship. This might be most effectively accomplished by having each group participant sign a contract binding him to preserving the anonymity of group members unless otherwise required by law or professional ethics.[40] (See appendix M.) The contract should be made without duress by legally competent individuals and should perhaps give some benefit (or "consideration") to the signers. The contract might also include a mutually agreed-upon dollar amount ("liquidated damages") in the event of a breach. To date, however, there are few precedents supporting an action for violation of confidentiality based on contract theory. In one notable case, a psychiatrist who published an extensive verbatim account of a patient's disclosures during psychoanalysis was found liable for breach of an implied contract to maintain professional confidences.[41] Compensatory damages of $20,000 were awarded, but no punitive damages were assessed because the court held that the "defendant's acts were not willful, malicious, or wanton . . . merely stupid."[42]

Privileged communication in group therapy situations is, at best, tenuous and unclear. It is prudent to assume that privilege does *not* exist inasmuch as a federal court rule specifies that federal courts shall be "governed by the principles of the common law as they may be interpreted . . .in the light of reason and experience."[43] This rule also weakens *individual* psychotherapy as well because neither physician-patient or psychotherapist-client privilege exist at common law, although attorney-client privilege does. Even in states that have passed privilege statutes, a patient cannot be sure that his/her communications will be protected should the matter at issue fall into federal jurisdiction.[44] Generally, courts tend to construe privileged communications narrowly because such privileges serve to exclude evidence from the courts.

FREEDOM OF INFORMATION VS. CONFIDENTIALITY

Disclosure, as well as nondisclosure, may be compelled by statute or case law. A state supreme court, for example, unanimously upheld a contempt charge against a psychiatrist for nondisclosure that resulted in a three-day jail term.[45] The court did not accept arguments based on published statements of ethics by professional organizations, or the claim that the psychotherapist-patient privilege should be equal to that of clergyman-penitent. The court did, however, restrict the content of the communications it forced to be disclosed.

Nontherapeutic communications (e.g., research proposals and data) are also regulated by statute and case law.[46] These state statutes usually deal with the confidentiality of research information collected in the area of public health which, broadly defined, includes mental health. Often the information must be collected by a state agency, under its auspices, or with its express authorization in order for it to be confidential. The statutes typically grant the right to withhold the disclosure of information to both the person giving the information as well as the agency collecting it.[47] Research information collected in association with some federal agencies[48] or in programs funded by the federal government such as for drug abuse may be specially protected.[49]

The Freedom of Information Act (5 U.S.C. 552) provides that anyone has the right of access to and may receive copies of any document, file, or other record in possession of the federal government, subject to certain specific exemptions. Particularly relevant to psychological practice are the public information regulations of the National Institute of Health.[50] Among items generally available from N.I.H. are:

approved grant applications, applications (even disapproved ones) for renewal or continuation of an approved initial application, and progress reports. Documents that may be denied in whole or in part are: pending or disapproved applications for new research or training grants, financial information regarding a person (e.g., project personnel salaries), information subject to provisions of the Privacy Act of 1974 (PL 93–579), information of a personal or medical nature, inter- or intra-agency memoranda (including opinions of advisory boards), information that would adversely affect patent or commercial rights, law enforcement records which would interfere with a fair trial, and certain national defense information.

A request for information from the federal government should: (1) clearly state that the request is being made under the Act (5 U.S.C. 552), (2) describe the information wanted, (3) include a notarized statement affirming the requestor's identity and date and place of birth, and (4) be addressed to the Freedom of Information Office of the particular federal agency where the information is believed to be on file.[51] The requestor need *not* state any reason for the request, and government employees are prohibited from inquiring about its intended use. When documents have been requested from N.I.H., it is N.I.H. policy to notify the grantee institution and affected parties of the request and to whom the documents will be released. Information that is inaccurate or substantially misleading may be removed from the file.

The revised Family Educational Rights and Privacy Act of 1974 (the "Buckley amendment") similarly gives students 18 or older (or those attending an institution of post-secondary education) and their parents the right to inspect relevant school records. Generally, the Freedom of Information Act refers to the ability of third parties to obtain information from Federal files, whereas the Privacy Act refers to the ability of a person (or a relative) to obtain information about himself. One commentator has warned institutional personnel not to "purge files too eagerly" because the record must be adequate to support major, critical decisions.[52]

Some "education records" may not be available to students over 18 or to their parents. Among such records are those "created or maintained by a physician, psychiatrist, psychologist, or other recognized professional or paraprofessional acting in his or her professional or paraprofessional capacity, or assisting in that capacity" and those records "created, maintained, or used only in connection with the provision of treatment to the student."[53] Also, these records are not to be "disclosed to anyone other than individuals providing the treatment."[54] Although interpretations of these regulations vary, it appears that if a mental health professional transfers the treatment record to persons other than the treatment personnel, the student or his/her parent may then have access to the record. However, if the student requests that a physician or other appropriate treatment professional of the student's choice be allowed to see the treatment record, that record must be disclosed. Finally, it may be noted that these regulations apply to students 18 or over. Thus, the records of those students under 18 in secondary or elementary schools may need to be made available to the parents of the students. The Privacy Act generally requires written consent from the student or parent before disclosing the record to a third party. There are a few notable exceptions to this consent requirement such as in an emergency when it is necessary to protect the health or safety of the student or others.[55]

Outside of the educational context, requests by insurance companies constitute the most frequent type of request for treatment information. As mental health professionals lobby for insurance coverage for their services, insurance companies may be reasonably expected to escalate demands for information relevant to estimating the cost of such coverage. Most psychiatric facilities routinely have a patient sign a release of information form upon admission, and will subsequently forward admission and discharge diagnoses to insurance companies without a physician's approval. A more protective procedure would permit the treating physician merely to certify that the patient required treatment of a given frequency for ''an emotional disorder characterized by. . .''[56] (rather than citing a standard diagnosis from the APA *Diagnostic and Statistical Manual for Mental Disorders).* If treatment is long-term or extensive, a review and verification by an insurance review committee could be required.[57]

States and private organizations may not be required by the Freedom of Information Act or the Privacy Act to disclose information. In such a situation, case and statutory law is sparse and ambiguous. Hospital records are normally the property of the hospital, but reasonable inspection must be allowed by parties with a legitimate interest when such is not likely to cause danger or harm to the patient.[58] Several states give statutory permission to medical and surgical patients or to mental patients to examine and copy (but not to remove) their medical records.[59] Most states with access statutes (e.g., Illinois, Kansas and New York) explicitly prohibit disclosure of records of patients in mental hospitals to third parties except: (a) on the consent of the patient, (b) by consent of the hospital director if necessary for the treatment of the patient,(c) as a court may direct upon determination that disclosure is necessary for the conduct of proceedings before it, and if failure to disclose would be contrary to the public interest, *and* (d) in hospitalization proceedings upon request of the patient's attorney.[60] Access may be further limited to a professional intermediary, such as an independent psychiatrist or psychologist retained by the patient to examine the record and report relevant conclusion.[61]

In states without statutes granting mental patients access to their medical records, a review of the record by the patient is likely to be difficult unless the institution or practitioner voluntarily agrees. In case law, patient access is the exception rather than the rule. In *Gotkin* v.*Miller*,[62] for example, the plaintiff and her husband brought suit to obtain access to her records at two private New York mental hospitals. She wanted the records to be made available for inspection and coping for the purpose of writing a book about her experiences. The court concluded: "We can find no basis for the proposition that mental patients have a constitutionally protected property interest in the direct and unrestricted access to their records. . . ."[63] The court further noted that because the plaintiff wanted the records to write a book, not to evaluate her medical condition, no serious interest in privacy or the control over one's body was at issue.

Finally, some distinction may be made between records such as transcripts or test protocols, in which the patient has a proprietary interest, and the more informal professional products such as technical notes, comments, or uninterpreted data, which are meaningful only to the practitioner.[64] These informal products are usually in the sole possession of the practitioner or assistants and are not accessible to or transmitted to other persons.

A claim of informality of administrative procedure (e.g., a parole board's decision about an individual's release) cannot hide "agency process" leading to "final disposition" where privacy could be protected by simply deleting certain identifying details.[65] In very difficult situations, some critical incidents might be recorded but kept out of a patient's folder and view by sending the information directly to the institution's attorney where it is protected by attorney-client privilege.

A matter of confidentiality involving considerable controversy is the family history of adopted children. Many adoptees want an explanation of why their natural parents gave them away.[66] Possibly relevant information can be found in adoption agency records, court records, and office of the registrar of vital statistics. Most states seal the original birth certificate, as well as court records. An amended birth certificate is issued substituting the names of the adopting parents. Partial exceptions occur in Alabama, Connecticut, Florida, Kansas, and Louisiana, where adult adoptees have access to the original birth certificate, although court proceedings may be sealed. Only Virginia permits access to court records.[67] Ironically, most state statutes do not specifically restrict access to agency records where the most (although typically scanty) information exists.

Some social agencies will release nonidentifying information about nationality, inheritable diseases, and so forth, but general policy discourages release of identifying data.[68] Such restriction is believed to solidify the adoptive family as a social unit, protect the privacy of the natural parents, and prevent possible emotional stress caused by a reunion. After a person has reached adulthood, the state's interest in protecting the adoptive family unit may be diminished.

Constitutional arguments of freedom of speech ("free flow of information"), equal protection ("suspect classification" without a compelling state interest), and right to privacy (broadly construed as control over information that will permit the "development and expression of one's intellect, interests, and personality") have been proposed as bases for opening the records.[69] The privacy argument is more often used to protect the natural parents from embarrassing intrusion. Special interest groups have lobbied on both sides of this issue.[70] In one unreported case, a 41-year-old psychotherapy patient was successful in obtaining parental information after the therapist testified that such knowledge would aid treatment.[71]

A compromise proposal would require that a state department of health facilitate meetings between adoptees and natural parents by filing requests for such meetings over a period of 20 years. As soon as both parties (presuming the adoptee is at least 18 years old) have independently requested a meeting, the department must help them make contact.[72]

The dispute over access to adoption information does not directly affect the human services professional—most often social case workers in agencies—except as in the course of service or treatment identifying information about the natural parents comes to light. As a general rule, the professional should decline to disclose any information except on the express order of a court that will likely specify the nature and uses of the authorized communication.

NOTES

1. For example, Connecticut enacted a psychiatrist-patient statue explicitly giving the privilege to the patient by designating that ''a patient. . . has a privilege.'' (Conn. Gen. Stat., sec. 52–146a). This contrasts with traditional physician-patient statutes that provide that ''no physician shall be permitted to disclose. . .'' (e.g., Ill. Ann. Stat.,ch.51, sec.51). *See, In re* Lifschutz, 467 P.2d 557 (Cal. 1970) (psychiatrist has no independent claim of privilege).

2. Shah, S. A. Privileged communications, confidentiality, and privacy: Privileged communications, 1 *Professional Psychology* 56, 57 (1969)

3. Publication of private matters of non-public figures, even if truthful, is generally forbidden unless the matter is newsworthy and based on a record open to the public. Nelson, H. L. and Teeter, D. L. *Law of mass communications*. Mineola, NY: Foundation Press, 1969, pp. 155–169. Use of ''any electronic amplifying or recording device'' without the consent of all parties to a confidential communication is prohibited by Sec. 632, California Penal Code, and Sec. 900 et seq. of California Evidence Code. *See also,* Note, Anthropotelemetry: Dr. Schwitzgebel's machine. 80 *Harvard Law Review* 403 (Dec. 1966) (survey of legal issues related to psychological monitoring devices).

4. *E.g.,* American Psychiatric Assn., Position statement on the confidentiality of medical research records. 130 *American Journal of Psychiatry* 739 (June 1973), also the Association's Task Force report No. 9, ''Confidentiality and third parties,'' Washington, D.C.: APA, 1975; American Psychological Assn., Ethical standards of psychologists, ''Confidentiality'' (principle 6) (1972 rev.) (similar principle 5, 1977 rev.) American Personnel and Guidance Assn., Ethical standards, Sec. B (2) (1974); American School Counselor Assm., ''Privileged communication: an updated report'' (edited by J. D. Shafer) (1975) Some writers have asserted that such sanctions regarding unauthorized comment are ''weak and largely ineffective.'' Note, Functional overlap between the lawyer and other professionals: Its implications for the privileged communications doctrine, 71 *Yale Law Journal* 1226, 1256 (1962). ''While occupational groups usually

seek professional status with avowals of their concerns for the public welfare, once the privileged status has been attained, the professional groups typically manage to do rather well for themselves. . . . It has been suggested that professions do not differ very much from trade unions, except that professional groups tend to be more sanctimonious.'' Shah, S. A. *Tarasoff* and its implications: A broader perspective. *Monitor* (American Psychological Assn.) (Feb. 1977). *See also* Zitrin and Klein, H. Can psychiatry police itself effectively? The experience of one district branch. 133 *American Journal of Psychiatry* 653 (1976).

5. Wigmore, J. H. *Evidence in trials at common law*. Vol. 8 (McNaughton Revision). Boston: Little, Brown, 1961, p. 2285. Dean Wigmore apparently opposed the extension of privilege to mental health professionals. *Cf.,* Wigmore at p.2286, and 71 *Yale Law Journal, supra* note 4 at 1257.

6. Kuhlmann, F. L. Communications to clergymen—When are they privileged? 2 *Mental Health Digest* 44 (1970); also 22 A.L.R.2d 1152.

7. A summary of statutes for all states is in Ferster, E. Z. Statutory summary of physician-patient privileged communication laws. In R. C. Allen, E. Z. Ferster, and Rubin J. G. (Eds.) *Readings in law and psychiatry*. Baltimore: The Johns Hopkins Press, 1975 ed., pp. 239–249. (Privilege status should be verified by reference to current supplements of code sections cited therein.)

8. *Rules of evidence for the United States District Courts and Magistrates,* Rule 5-04. *But see*, notes 44 and 45 *infra*.

9. Privileged communication statutes for school personnel exist in Delaware, Idaho, Indiana, Maine, Maryland, Michigan, Montana, Nevada, North Carolina, North Dakota, Oklahoma, Oregon, Pennsylvania, South Carolina, South Dakota, and Washington. *Cf.* Shafer, *supra* note 4. Possibly the broadest protection is in a Michigan statute (sec. 617.85): ''No teacher, guidance officer, school executive or other professional person engaged in character building in the public school or any other educational institution including any clerical worker of such schools and institutions, who maintains records of students' behavior or has such records in his custody, or who receives in confidence communications from students or other juveniles, shall be allowed in any proceedings, civil or criminal, in any court of this state, to disclose any information obtained by him from such records or such communications nor to produce such records or transcripts thereof. . . .''

10. Alfred v. State, 554 P. 2d 411 (Alas. 1976) (privilege refused, however, for a social worker, counselor, or a psychology associate). Some social workers' communications have privilege in New York and in California. *See*, 50 A.L.R. 3d 563; and Comment, Underprivileged communications: Extention of the psychotherapist-patient privilege to patients of psychiatric social workers. 61 *California Law Review* 1050 (1973).

11. Wigmore, *supra* note 5, at 532–535. Other professionals, in a number of states, who have succeeded in obtaining special privilege include journalists, accountants, ''confidential'' clerks or stenographers, and radio/television newscasters. Academic researchers may also have some protection in civil, but not criminal, cases. In an unpublished case, a federal district court judge declined to order two university researchers to produce notes of interviews involving specifications of environmental equipment, *as reported in* Scholar's right to protect sources upheld in court. 12 *The Chronicle of Higher Education*

3 (June 21, 1976) (no official opinion rendered because case was settled out of court, but judge presented a written commentary).

12. Cranford v. Cranford, 170 S. E. 2d 844 (C.A. Ga. 1969)(Statutory confidentiality between psychologist and client not found to include daily appontment book, bank deposits from patients, etc.).

13. Shah, *supra* note 2, at 61, citing Kansas statute. *See also*, Ritt v. Ritt, 98 N.J. Sup. Ct. 590, 238 A. 2d 196 (1967) (physician specializing in psychiatry held *not* within purview of statute entitling a licensed psychologist to privilege of communications comparable to that afforded attorney-client).

14. *Statement of Ethics for Psychiatrists*, American Medical Assn., Section 9 (protect welfare); *Ethical Standards for Psychologists*, Principle 6 (a) (imminent danger).

15. Moore, R. A. Ethics in the practice of psychiatry—Origins, functions, and models. 135 *American Journal of Psychiatry* 157, 161 (Feb. 1978).

16. Family Educational Rights and Privacy Act, 20 U.S.C. 1232g(b) (1).

17. 529 P.2d 553 (Cal. 1974), *vac., reheard in bank, & aff'd.* 131 Cal. Rptr. 14, 551 P.2d 334 (1976). A similar case is that of Charles J. Whitman who fatally shot 17 people from a University of Texas belltower in 1966 and who had a few months earlier, according the the notes of a university psychiatrist, made reference to ''going up on the tower with a deer rifle and start shooting people.''

18. Id. at 345. For a bizarre case of multiple murder-suicide (including photos of monster-figure models created by a patient of lay psychotherapist preceding violent act), *see* Usher, A. The case of the disembowelled doll—A multiple murder.7 *Medicine, Science, and the Law* 211 (1977).

19. Motion and brief, amicus curae, in support of petition for rehearing, Tarasoff v. Regents of the University of California, S. F. No. 23042, Super. Ct. No. 405694. In the Supreme Court of the State of California, January 7, 1975. (Amici petitioners included the American Psychiatric Assn., California State Psychological Assn., National Assn. of Social Workers, and California Hospital Assn.)

20. This is a useful, authoritative document for direct or cross-examination of expert witnesses in involuntary commitment cases, especially where dangerousness must be proved beyond a reasonable doubt. *Cf.*, ''strict proof'' cases such as State of Oregon v. O'Neill, 545 P.2d 97 (Ore. Sup. Ct. 1976); People v. Burnick, 535 P.2d 352 (Sup. Ct. Cal. 1975) *See also*, A. A. Stone, *Mental health and law: A system in transition.* Rockville, Md.: Center for Studies of Crime and Delinquency, N.I.M.H. 1975, Ch. 2.

21. *Tarasoff*, 551 P. 2d at 345.

22. Bellah v. Greenson, 1 Civ. No. 39770 (Cal. Oct. 5, 1977)*as reported* in 2 *Mental Disability Law Reporter* 176 (Sept. /Dec. 1977).

23. Roth, L. H. and Meisel, A. Dangerousness, confidentiality, and the duty to warn. 134 *American Journal of Psychiatry* 508, 510 (May 1977). For commentary supporting, *see* Note, Untangling Tarasoff: Tarasoff versus the Regents of the University of California, 29 *Hastings Law Journal* 179 (Sept. 1977). A law review article of particular importance, because it was cited favorably in the majority opinion of the rehearing, is Fleming, J. G. and Maximov, B. The patient or his victim: The therapist's dilemma. 62 *California Law Review* 1025 (1974).

24. Stone, A. A. The *Tarasoff* decisions: Suing psychotherapists to safeguard society. 90 *Harvard Law Review* 358, 377–78 (1976). Regarding the hampering of psychotherapy,

the court asserted that such predictions are "entirely speculative," and observed that counsel for the psychiatrist in *In re Lifschutz, infra* note 45, forecast a similar harm that did not occur. Tarasoff, 551 P. 2d 346, nt. 12.

25. Stone, *id.* at 365. Quoting Fleming and Maximov, *supra* note 23, the *Tarasoff* majority concluded,". . . the ultimate question of resolving the tension between the conflicting interests of patient and potential victim is one of social policy, not professional expertise." 551 P.2d 345.

26. Although a duty to warn Ms. Tarasoff was breached, the defendant psychiatrist and his staff were protected from civil suit by statutory immunity for persons authorized to recommend confinement. 551 P. 2d 351.

27. "The privileged quality of communications between husband and wife and between any professional person and his patient or his client, except that between attorney and client, is hereby abrogated in situations involving known or suspected child abuse, sexual abuse or neglect." Education Commission of the States, *Child abuse and neglect: Model legislation for the states.* Denver, 1976, Report No. 71, sec. IX, p. 30. Connecticut School Code, sec. 10-154a makes reporting (without identification of particular student) of drug abuse mandatory. Both criminal and civil immunity for school personnel is provided.

28. Researchers so authorized "may not be compelled in any federal, state or local civil, criminal, administrative, legislative, or other proceedings to identify such individuals." DHEW, Protection of identity—research subjects, 42 CFR Part 2a, 44 *Federal Register* 20382 (Apr. 4, 1979). *Similarly,* LEAA, 28 CFR Part 22, sec. 524 (a).

29. Shah, *supra* note 2, at 64; *also* 44 A.L.R.3d 24.

30. Roberts v. Supreme Court of Butte County, 9 Cal. 3rd 330, 508 p. 2d 309 (1973).

31. Gibson v. Virginia, 219 S. E.2d 845 (1975) (statements of criminal defendants during compulsory interview not protected).

32. Rappaport, J. R. Psychiatrist as an amicus curiae, in *1972 Annual.* Baltimore, Md.: Medical Trial Technique Quarterly Publication, 1972, p. 301.

33. How voluntary and valid the consent might be is another issue. One study found that 100 percent of 1962 patients in four community mental health clinics signed release-of-information forms upon request, but the frequency dropped to as low as 20 percent when told that they would not have to sign in order to receive service. Rosen, C. E. Why clients relinquish their rights to privacy under sign-away pressures. 8 *Professional Psychology* 17 (Feb. 1977).

34. According to R. L. Sadoff (Informed consent, confidentiality and privilege in psychiatry: Practical applications. 2 *The Bulletin of the American Academy of Psychiatry and the Law* 101, 104 (1974), the most appropriate recipient of the information is not necessarily the intended victim as implied in *Tarasoff*, but might be the police or others who would restrain the patient while at the same time preserving the confidential relationship. ". . .If a patient tells a doctor in confidence that he has brought a time bomb into the hospital and hidden it under the bed of one of the other patients, it is a strange doctor indeed who would feel that this professional confidence should not be violated." Menninger, K., Mayman, M., and Pruyser, P. W. *A manual for psychiatric case study, 2nd edition.* New York: Grune & Stratton (1962), p. 1937. A situation is known to one of the authors wherein two commercial airline pilots are presently in private treatment for suicidal tendencies, without the knowledge of the employee airlines.

35. Foster, L. M. Group psychotherapy: A pool of legal witnesses? 25 *International Journal of Group Psychotherapy* 50 (1975); Morrison, J. K., Frederico, M. and Rosenthal, H. J. Contracting confidentiality in group psychotherapy. 7 *Journal of Forensic Psychology* 1 (Dec. 1975); Cross, W. Privileged communication between participants in group psychotherapy. 1970 *Law and Social Order* 191 (1970).

36. W. C. Driscoll (Ed.) 5 *Newsletter of the American Psychology-Law Society* 1 (1972).

37. Wichansky v. Wichansky, 126 N. J. Super. 156 A. 2nd (Chancery Div.,Nov.15 1973) as reported in, 7 *Newsletter of the American Psychology-Law Society* 7 (March 1974).

38. Shah, *supra* note 2, at 66, citing Colorado Statute (amendment of July 1, 1967), sec. 16. But some courts may not interpret the privilege to extend this far in common law, *see* Alfred v. State, 554 P.2d 411 (Alas. 1976).

39. *Cf., supra* note 1.

40. Morrison, *supra* note 35; Schwitzgebel, R. K. A contractual model for the protection of the rights of insitutionalized mental patients. 30 *American Psychologist* 815 (1975).

41. Doe v. Roe, 178 *New York Law Journal* 13 (Nov. 25, 1977). The court noted that the damages could be increased if more than the 230 copies of the book sold at the time were distributed.

42. *Id*. at 13.

43. Rule 501, Federal Rules of Evidence, as amended by P. L. 93–595, *U. S. Statutes at Large* (1975). An exception to this rule exists when citizens of different states (i.e., having "diversity of citizenship") come into federal court. Then state statutes will be controlling. *See generally,* Meyer, R. G. and Smith, S. R. a crisis in group therapy. 32 *American Psychologist* 638 (1977).

44. The situation can be modestly described as a gigantic can of worms. Either common law or various state statutes may be applicable in a given case, depending on the residence of the contesting parties. Furthermore, there was a federal judicial recommendation favoring a broad privilege which was subsequently ignored when Congress adopted Rule 501. The *proposed* Rule 5-04(a) (3) of *Rules of evidence for the U. S. Districts Courts and Magistrates* (1974) stated: "Communication is 'confidential' if not intended to be disclosed to third persons other than those present to further the interest of the patient in the consultation, examination, or interview, or persons reasonably necessary for the transmission of the communication, or persons who are participating in the diagnosis and treatment under the direction of the psychotherapist, including members of the patient's family." For extensive background and recommended statutory changes, *see* the 650-page report of the Privacy Protection Study Commission, *Personal privacy in an information society*. Washington, D. C.: U. S. Govt. Printing Office, 1977.

45. *In re* Lifschutz, 85 Cal. Rptr. 829, 467 P.2d 557 (Cal. 1970). A federal court of appeals has upheld the constitutionality of a statute effectuating a waiver of the psychotherapist-patient privilege when a litigating patient puts his mental condition at issue. Ceasar v. Mountanos, No. 74–2271 (9th cir., Sept. 13, 1976) as reported in 1 *Mental disability Law Reporter* 200 (Nov./Dec. 1976).

46. Existing federal data protection statutes include: 5 U.S.C.A. 551, 552 ("Freedom of Information Act"), 13 U.S.C.A. 8, 9 ("Census Data"), 21 U.S.C.A. 1175 ("Drug Abuse Data"), 42 U.S.C.A. 2000e-8 ("Equal Employment Opportunity Proceedings"), P.L. 93–579 (Privacy Act of 1974), P.L. 93–380 (the "Buckley Amendment"), and 45 C.F.R. 46 (DHEW Research with Human Subjects). States such as Texas, Oregon, New

Mexico, and Washington have statutes modelled after federal statutes. For comprehensive survey, *see* Carroll, J. D. Confidentiality of social science research sources and data. The Russell Sage Foundation, the American Political Science Assn., Project Progress Report, 1975; *and also,* National Academy of Sciences, *Protecting individual privacy in evaluation research.* Washington, D. C.: Author, 1975.

47. Schwitzgebel, R. K. Confidentiality of research information in public health studies. 6 *Harvard Legal Commentary* 187, 192–193 (1969). In 1969, 11 states had broadly-stated confidentiality statutes; at least five other states protected information of a specific type (e.g., veneral disease, air pollution).

48. Law Enforcement Assistance Administration, U. S. Dept. of Justice, Confidentiality of research information. Washington, D. C.: Author, 1978 (see 28 *Code of Federal Regulations,* part 22).

49. DHEW, Confidentiality of alcohol and drug abuse records: General provisions, sec. 2.52. 40 *Federal Register* 27802 (1975). *See* People v. Newman, 345 N.Y.S. 2d 502 (Ct. App. 1973),*cert. denied* 414 U. S. 1163 (1974).

50. N.I.H. Guide for Grants and Contracts, Vol. 4, No. 5 (June 9, 1975), pp. 6–7; HEW Regulations, 45 C.F.R. Part 5. The leading case opening up research documents is: Washington Research Project, Inc. v. Dept. of Health, Education, and Welfare, 366 F. Supp. 929 (D. C. 1973) (funded research using drugs to control behavior of school children not confidential).

51. Two sources of practical procedural information are a brochure, ''The Privacy Act: How it effects you,'' and a ''FOIA Litigation Handbook,'' both available from the Project on National Security and Civil Liberties, 122 Maryland Avenue N. E., Washington, D. C. 20002. *Also related,* Arnold, M. R. Who's going fishing in government files? 6 *Juris Doctor* 17 (1976). In many areas, the federal government has established Federal Information Centers under the U. S. General Services Administration that can often be reached on a toll-free line.

52. Martin, R. Litigation: Student records. 1 *Law and Behavior* 2 (Winter 1976).

53. 20 U.S.C. 1232g, (a) (4) (B) (iii). For interpretative background, *see* Goslin, D. A. *Guidelines for the collection, maintenance, and dissemination of pupil records* (report of the Conference on the Ethical and Legal Aspects of Sc ool Record Keeping), Hartford, Conn.: Russell Sage Foundation, 1970.

54. *Id.*

55. 20 U.S.C. 1232 g (b) (1) (I).

56. Grossman, M. Insurance reports as a threat to confidentiality, 128 *American Journal of Psychiatry* 96, 98 (1971).

57. *Id.* at 100.

58. Gaertner v. Michigan, 187 N. W. 2d 429 (Mich. 1971); Freeland, W. G. (chr.). *Report of the secretary's commission on medical malpractice.* DHEW publication No. 0873-88, Jan. 1973, p. 177; Bush v. Kallen, 302 A.2d 142 (App. Div. N. J. 1973); Hagman, D. G. The non-litigant patient's right to medical records: Medicine vs. law. 14 *Journal of Forensic Sciences* 352 (1969).

59. Freeland, *supra* note 58, at 76 and 177. *See also,* Hagman, *supra* note 58. In 1977, nine states had statutes allowing a rather broad right to inspect medical records. Illinois has an exceptionally liberal statute (Ill. Rev. Stat. chapt. 51. 5.1;23.5320) permitting a person to see his/her own medical record, including mental health records. For summary, *see*

Privacy Protection Study Commission, *Personal privacy in an information society.* Washington, D. C.: G.P.O., 1977, at 295.

60. Freeland, *supra* note 58, at 181.

61. New York Mental Hygiene Law, sec. 15.13 precludes both patients and former patients from direct access, but does permit access to a designated, licensed physician.

62. 514 F.2d 125 (2d Cir. 1975). *Confer* Gotkin, J. and P. G. *Too much anger, too many tears: A personal triump over psychiatry.* New York: Quadrangle, 1975.

63. Gotkin, 514 F.2d 130.

64. Hagman, supra note 58, at 360; Shah, *supra* note 2, at 161; Kelley, V. R. and Weston, H. B. Civil liberties in mental health facilities. 48 *Social Work* 53 (1974) (for record-keeping in social work); N.I.H., *supra* note 50 (for N.I.H. policy on distinctions in documents).

65. Martin, *supra* note 52, at 164.

66. A survey of 163 adoption agencies by the Child Welfare League estimated that in 1975, 3000 adult adoptees returned to agencies seeking information—40 percent wanted to meet their biological parents. Research Center, Child Welfare League of America, *The sealed adoption record controversy: Report of a survey of agency policy.* New York: Author, 1976. *See generally,* Note, the adoptee's right to know his natural heritage. 19 *New York Law Forum* (now *New York Law School Law Review*) 137 (1974); Note, The adult adoptee's constitutional right to know his origins. 48 *Southern California Law Review* 1196 (1975); Lifton, B. J. *Twice born: Memoirs of an adopted daughter.* New York: McGraw-Hill, 1975.

67. Va. Code sec. 63.1-236 (1973). *See* Klibanoff, E. B. Roots: An adoptee's quest. 28 *Harvard Law School Bulletin* 34 (Spring 1977).

68. Child Welfare League of America, *Standards for adoption service.* New York: Author, 1968 rev., sec. 4.12-15.

69. *Southern California Law Review, supra* note 66, at 1210.

70. *Pro*: Adoptees' Liberty Movement Association (ALMA), P.O. Box 154, Washington Bridge Station, New York, NY 10033, organized by Florence L. Fisher of New York City, author of *The search for Anna Fisher.* New York: Arthur Fields, 1973; Adoption Research Project (Reuben Pannor, director), P. O. Box 49809, Los Angeles, CA 90049. *Con:* Child Welfare League of America, and National Council of Adoptive Parents Organizations, as cited in Kiester, E., Jr. Should we unlock the adoption files? 52 *Today's Health* 54, 59 (1974). The most extreme position argues that potential harm to the natural parents by the child is not justified at all when the alternative could have been abortion.

71. Outagamie County, Wisconsin, case involving Kenneth Kubitz represented by the Wisconsin Civil Liberties Union, as reported in "Adoptees fight to know who they are," *Civil Liberties* No. 308 (Sept. 1975), p. 7. The National ACLU has no official policy, leaving the decision to local affiliates.

72. As stated by Rena Uviller, Director of the ACLU Juvenile Rights Project, reported in *Civil Liberties, id.*

13

Licensing, Unauthorized Practice, And Fees

LICENSING OR CERTIFICATION

The licensing or certification of practitioners is typically initiated by an organized group of persons already practicing the craft who assert that the public should be protected against the harmful practices of others who wish to render a similar service. This expressed concern for public welfare can also have economic benefit because licensing or certification can increase the group's prestige and simultaneously decrease competition by reducing the number of persons legally able to render the service. The subsequent increased cost of the service can be considered "in the public interest" if the burden of higher prices is less than the social harm that would occur in the absence of such licensing.[1]

The authority to regulate professions is vested in the "police powers" of the states for the purpose of preserving public health, safety, morals, or welfare. Presumably there must be a clear relationship between the activities of the profession and public safety. Certification and licensing of health professionals, including psychiatrists and psychologists, has been held to fall within the scope of such police power and to serve a legitimate public purpose.[2] Among other regulated professionals are nurses, clinical social workers, physicians, chiropractors, marriage and family counselors, psychiatric technicians, and physical therapists.[3] All 48 states, plus the District of Columbia and eight provinces of Canada, have had statutes regulating the practice of psychology or the title "psychologist."[4] A person who practices psychology in a research laboratory, university, or state or federal agency is explicitly exempt from licensure in many states. is not usually and specifically protected by statute. Any licenced physician could technically represent him/herself as a "psychiatrist" even though they had no training in that specialty. However, because psychiatrists are usually assumed to be physicians, a person without a recognized M.D. (or in some states a D.O. degree) who used such a title would likely be ordered to cease and desist from representing him/herself as a person practicing a medical specialty.[5]

A *licensing* statute regulates professional practice and function by prohibiting unqualified persons from engaging in such practice. The wording of psychology statutes typically describes the licensed activities in a very broad manner to include the "application of principles, methods, or procedures of understanding, predicting, or influencing behavior, such as the principles pertaining to learning, conditioning, perception, motivation, thinking, emotions or interpersonal relationships. . . . "[6] By contrast, a *certification* or *registration* statute limits the use of a title (e.g., "psychologist," "attorney at law," "registered social worker"). It may or may not contain a definition of practice, and it does not prohibit other persons from performing similar professional functions—for example, a clergyman doing social work, or an attorney doing marriage counseling.

Licensing or certifying statutes typically specify the qualifications of practitioners in four areas: personal characteristics, formal education, internship requirements, and performance on written and/or oral examinations.

- Personal characteristics usually include a mandatory minimum age and a vague requirement of "good moral character."[7] Sometimes specific disqualifying acts (such as fraud, drug use, or sex offenses) are listed. For example, deceptive conduct such as referring to oneself as "doctor" prior to getting the degree or falsifying attendance at professionally related classes falls within those professional qualifications of honesty and integrity which licensing is to regulate.[8] Other acts of presumed misconduct such as homosexual behavior or furnishing an alcoholic beverage to a minor are variously interpreted by courts.[9] The trend of judicial opinion seems to favor a "rational connection test"—namely, that before conduct can be classified as immorally disqualifying, the questionable conduct must relate to one's fitness to continue in his/her profession.[10]
- Statutory requirements uniformly conform to what the profession itself has agreed upon as its "entry level professional degree"—for example, M. A. or Ed. M. for school psychologists and family counselors, M.S.W. for social work, M. D. for medicine, Ph.D. for psychology, and LL.B. or J. D. for law.[11] Persons who have been practicing a profession for a substantial number of years prior to licensing are usually granted an educational

exemption (''grandfather/mother'' statutory exemption) to avoid depriving them of an economic interest.[12]

● One or two years of supervised professional post-graduate experience is typically required for licensure in psychology. (See summary of state statutes in Appendix LL.) Although, as a medical speciality, no training or experience beyond that of a medical license may be legally required for psychiatry,[13] the American Board of Psychiatry and Neurology has voluntary but rigorous requirements of three years of accredited psychiatric training and two years post-residency experience.[14] Approximately forty percent of the practicing psychiatrists in the U. S. are board-certified. Only two percent of Ph.D. psychologists are diplomats of the similar voluntary certification body for psychologists (i.e., the American Board of Professional Psychology). Generally unlicensed specialities, such as marriage and family counselors, include in their model legislation a two or three year post-degree supervised experience.[15]

● State licensing or certification boards are usually given wide discretion in examining the applicant for theoretical and applied knowledge and for utilization of relevant techniques within the scope of the prescribed area of practice. Because licensing is presumably designed to protect the general public, some attempt is often made to assess the candidate's readiness to assume responsibilities commensurate with independent private practice. Virtually all examinations have a written section, usually of essay type, involving analysis of technically and ethically challenging ''case studies,'' occasionally supplemented by oral interview or a practical demonstration of skill. Professional diplomate standards promulgated by professional boards, such as the American Board of Psychiatry and Neurology[16] or the American Board of Professional Psychology, are usually more rigorous than those of state licensing boards, and are almost always accepted in lieu of a state examination, if the applicant meets other specific requirements of the state where s/he intends to practice.

UNAUTHORIZED PRACTICE

Among the most controversial professional practices which licensing laws try to regulate is that of ''psychotherapy.'' One legal authority has defined psychotherapy as:

A method or system of alleviating or curing certain forms of disease, particularly diseases of the nervous system or such as are traceable to nervous disorders by suggestion, persuasion, encouragement, the inspiration of hope or confidence, the discouragement of morbid memories, associations, or beliefs, and other similar means addressed to the mental state of the patient, without (or sometimes in conjunction with) the administration of drugs or other physical remedies.[17]

Psychotherapy has been claimed as a legitimate part of the practice of psychiatry, psychology, child guidance, social work, and nursing.[18] And as previously indicated, medical licenses are usually rather broadly construed to include the treatment of mental as well as physical afflictions.[19] Persons without medical, psychological, or other appropriate training occasionally engage in psychotherapeutic practice by the subterfuge of renaming the activity.[20]

What professional reputations or functions constitute unauthorized psychological practice depend in part upon the wording of restrictive licensing statutes in the practioner's own state. "Medical practice" or "social work" may be narrowly or broadly defined. Certain practices, for example, are unanimously agreed in the United States to be medical in nature: psychosurgery, drug prescription, and electroshock therapy. Persons who are not licensed physicians may not legally perform these activities, nor may a licensed physician delegate these activities to a person without medical training.[21] Conversely, "psychosocial counseling" with a normal person and use of the term may be explicitly beyond the scope of medical practice.[22]

However, what lies clearly outside the scope of "psychological practice" is more ambigious. The American Psychological Association's Committee on State Legislation has suggested the following definition of the practice of psychology for regulatory legislation:

> The practice of psychology within the meaning of this act is defined as, but not limited to, the rendering to individuals, groups, organizations, institutions, or to the public any service involving the application of principles, methods and procedures of understanding, predicting, and influencing behavior, such as principles pertaining to learning, perception, motivation, thinking, emotions, mind-body relationships, interpersonal relationships, and inter-group relationships such as methods and procedures including but not restricted to: interviewing, consulting, the constructing, and/or adminstering, and/or interpreting of tests of mental abilities, aptitudes, interests, opinions, attitudes, emotions, motivations, personality characteristics, and psychophysiological characteristics; the assessment or diagnosis and treatment of emotional, and/or mental, and/or nervous disorder or dysfunction, and/or group dysfunction; psychotherapy; behavior modification; behavior therapy; bio-feedback techniques; hypnosis; marriage, education, and vocational counseling; personnel selection, counseling, and management; evaluation, planning, and consulting for effective work and learning situations, social relationships, organizational development, group dynamics; and the resolution of interpersonal. inter-group, and social conflicts.[23]

Various professions that might be logically related to a profession are often mentioned as being specifically excluded from the prohibitions applying to the general public. For example, psychologists, but not nurses, may be exempted the prohibition of rendering marital counseling; master's level school psychologists but not social workers may be excluded from laws prohibiting the administration of psychological tests.[24] This has tended to result in a hierarchy of professional practice: psychiatric social workers may not be paid for rendering psychological services unless supervised by a licensed psychologist; a clinical psychologist may not render an opinion regarding work-related emotional disability unless supervised by a licensed physician.[25] Conversely, a lower-prestige profession may not be able to prevent higher-prestige professions from performing services it is licensed to perform. For example, the Board of Marriage Counselors of Nevada (a state that certifies marriage and family counselors) requested that four psychologists and one psychiatrist cease and desist from listing themselves under the heading "Marriage and Family Counselors" in the yellow pages of the Las Vegas telephone directory. A subsequent appeal to the state Attorneys General's Office resulted in a ruling that because "counseling" is defined by statute as part of the practice of psychology, the listing could remain.[26] In the absence of a state regulatory agency for personnel and guidance counseling, such counselors may be permitted to practice "psychology" under laws governing such practice.[27]

In certain limited circumstances, a psychiatric social worker or clinical psychologist may assume the directorship of a mental health service, admit and discharge patients from the hospital, and perform related duties;[28] but the rationale and effect of such a broadening of the scope of professional authority is a matter of active debate.[29] As a rule, the boundaries of unauthorized practice in a given jurisdiction will depend on judicial interpretation of the wording of relevant statutes. Under a proposed model statute, persons conducting themselves in such a manner as to lead a reasonable person to believe by implication that they are, or function as, psychologists may be subject to the jurisdiction of a state Board of Psychology Examiners even though they may use terms such as "educational analyst" to describe themselves.[30] This conduct as a psychologist may be determined by factors such as membership in psychological organizations, engaging in psychological activities, and permitting other persons to act or believe that the person is a psychologist.

The *National Register of Health Service Providers in Psychology* lists psychologists, if they wish to be listed, who are licensed or certified by a state Board of Psychology Examiners (or its equivalent). Approximately 9000 providers are currently listed. The persons listed are to be able to practice psychology as an independent health service provider. The requirements include a doctorate degree from a regionally accredited educational institution and two years of supervised experience in health service (of which at least one year must be post-doctoral). These are very general requirements. Because of the diversity in training programs and the variability of licensing/certification requirements among the states, many psychological practitioners are interested in developing a national organization for monitoring the education and credentialing process.[31]

Although a psychologist may be properly licensed or certified, that fact does not necessarily allow the person to practice all aspects of psychology. Principle 2 of the *Ethical Standards of Psychologists* requires that "Psychologists recognize the boundaries of their competence and the limitations of their techniques, and only provide services, use techniques, or offer opinions as professionals that meet recognized standards."[32] If psychologists lack the required skill or knowledge to meet recognized standards of practice, they should obtain additional training. *Standards for Providers of Psychological Services* states that "Psychologists who wish to change their service specialty or to add an additional area of applied specialization must meet the same requirements with respect to subject matter and professional skills that apply to doctoral training in the new speciality."[33] This required training must be obtained under the auspicies of an accredited institution that offers a doctoral degree in the speciality. Attending workshops or participating in an internship or practicium is usually not adequate when prior training has not been in a relevant area.[34] The APA standards apply directly only to members of the American Psychological Association, not to all psychologists. The standards indicate, however, some general agreement, and the professional practice and licensing/certification codes of 30 states and the District of Columbia require compliance with the *Ethical Standards of Psychologists*.[35]

Federal law provides for the establishment of Professional Standards Review Organizations (PSROs) by HEW to monitor the utilization and quality of institutional services provided to beneficiaries of Medicare and other Social Security Act programs.[36] PSROs are organized by local medical groups. The involvement of nonphysician health practitioners in the development of standards for their own service is mandated in the administrative guidelines.[37] The potential impact of this assessment procedure on professional practice of psychologists and other practitioners is potentially great in terms of developing norms, utilizing research, and specifying service costs.[38] State psychological associations may also establish Professional Standards Review Committees (PSRCs) to settle issues about psychological services, fees, and other matters.[39] Patients, therapists, or third party payers may submit cases to the local PSRC when a satisfactory disposition of the matter has not been achieved by the parties directly involved.[40] (The parties may submit the case for review by using a "Request for Review" form available from the Office of Professional Affairs, American Psychological Association. See Appendix MM.)

Some professional organizations offer their members consultation or peer review services related to professional problems and standards. Particularly notable are the consultation services offered by the Association for the Advancement of Behavior Therapy which has provided evaluation, review, and (in a few cases) expert testimony for persons requesting it.[41] The service involves the assistance of psychiatrists, psychologists, and attorneys. It offers telephone or mail services free to members, and at cost to nonmembers. On-site reviews are provided at cost. The purpose is to improve practice and to help practitioners avoid professional, legal, and public-relations difficulties resulting from their practice.

In one widely publicized case involving the use of an alleged behavior therapy technique, a psychologist (who was not a behavior therapist) had his license revoked and was ordered to pay $170,000 in civil damages. This action was based on claims of injuries occurring from a "rage reduction" procedure during group therapy. Revocation of practitioners' licenses have also been supported by judicial action for gross negligence or for sexual intimacies with patients that resulted in emotional distress.[43] The procedures to be followed by the licensing board in examining applicants should be published in advance or follow state administrative regulations, and hearings (although not bound by the strict and technical rules of courtroom evidence or procedure) should be fair.[44] A practitioner whose license is being threatened by a complaining patient probably has the right to have the records submitted to the board, but should the board's decision be taken to court, both parties run the risk of losing some privacy.

An issue of recent concern has been the use of advertising by health services personnel. In 1978, the *Washington Post* initiated a weekly "Professional Directory" and announced that it was "now accepting advertising by psychologists, architects and C.P.A. 's as well as legal, medical and dental services." The Federal Trade Commisiion and the U. S. Office of Attorney General, supported by various consumer groups, have argued that ABA and AMA bans against advertising unfairly restrain trade and restrict commercial speech protected by the First Ammendment.[45] In response to such pressure, the American Psychological Association adopted standards regarding public statements that read, in part:

- Psychologists may list the following information: name, highest relevant academic degree earned from a regionally accredited institution, date, type and level of certification or licensure, diplomate status, APA membership status, address, telephone number, office hours, a brief listing of the type of psychological services offered, an appropriate presentation of fee information, foreign languages spoken, and policy with regard to third party payments.
- In announcing or advertising professional services, psychologists do not display any affiliations with an organization in a manner that falsely implies the sponsorship or certification of that organization.
- Psychologists do not participate for personal gain in commercial announcements or advertisements recommending to the general public the purchase or use of any proprietary or single-source product or service.
- As teachers, psychologists insure that statements in catalogs and course outlines are accurate and not misleading, particularly in terms of subject matter to be covered, bases for evaluation progress, and nature of course experience.
- Psychological services and products for the purpose of diagnosing, treating, or giving personal advice to particular individuals are provided only in the context of a professional relationship, and are not given by means of

public lectures or demonstrations, newspaper or magazine articles, radio or television programs, mail, or similar media.[46]

FEES AND INSURANCE

The reasonableness of fees charged by professionals is likely governed in individual cases by factors such as difficulty of the problem, time required, typical fees set by custom, results obtained in the case, and the ability to pay. In litigation where the professional is asked to serve as an expert witness, a daily or half-day rate rather than an hourly rate is usually charged (to absorb the uncertainties of preparation and court schedules), and a retainer for one-half of the expected amount prior to accepting the case is sometimes received. In contrast to some therapeutic endeavors, the professional in court should charge for his/her time. The fee should not be contingent upon the outcome of the case because, among other reasons, this can be used as evidence of bias in the testimony.

Although fee-setting is an intentional act on the part of the professional, an unconscionable fee is likely to be a breach of "good faith," rather than "fraud" (which is more dependent upon an intentional and contractual relationship). If, however, a practitioner agrees to render service and makes an implicit contractual arrangement but then provides a quality of service clearly below acceptable or customary professional standards (e.g., "acting out" feelings during "countertransference"), breach of contract may hold. In one such case, all fees paid over a two-year period were recovered by the plaintiff.[47]

Unless otherwise stated or implied, the fact that a practitioner undertakes to render service does not act as a guarantee of successful outcome.[48] In the absence of a contract to warrant a cure for schizophrenia, seven years of unorthodox and unsuccessful treatment at a cost to the patient of $55,000 was *not* held to constitute fraud. Psychiatric services are not "worthless" even when unsuccessful, but the practitioner might have the burden of proving that the fees conformed to customary or reasonable standards.[51] The following definitions of "usual," "customary," and "reasonable," as applied to practice and fees have been offered by the Board of Professional Affairs of the American Psychological Association:

> Usual—is defined as a practice in keeping with the individual psychologist's general modus operandi or, in terms of fees, the "usual" fee which is charged for a given service by an individual psychologist in his personal practice (i.e. "his own usual fee").
>
> Customary—is defined as that range of usual practices or fees provided or charged by psychologists of similar training and experience for the same service within a given specified geopgraphic or social-economic area.
>
> Reasonable—is defined as a practice or fee which meets the above two criteria

or, in the opinion of the responsible PSRC, is justifiable in the special circumstances of the specific case in question.[52]

The standards appear to be rather flexible for individuals and institutions. In a rather extreme case, a state hospital was permitted to collect for 44 years of hospitalization after the patient (who was confined on an indeterminate sentence for murder) inherited an estate.[53]

So-called "minimum" fee schedules for various professional services are now generally viewed as an unfair restraint of competition,[54] but insurance reimbursement schedules may be used as a reference. In 1976, a typical psychiatric fee for individual treatment was $50 per hour (or $760 per incident)[55]; the modal fee for psychologists was $40.[56] Third-party payers should be charged the same as private parties. Section 7 of the AMA *Principles of Medical Ethics* states: "In the practice of medicine a physician should limit the source of his professional income to medical services actually rendered by him, or under his supervision, to his patients."[57] Double billing, kickbacks, and unnecessary referrals are also forbidden.[58]

Insurance for some types of psychological service is provided by approximately 30 commercial carriers and more than 20 prepaid health service organizations or employee benefit plans.[59] Approximately 25 percent of psychotherapy patients have insurance coverage.[60] Twenty-seven states and the District of Columbia have enacted "freedom of choice" laws that recognize psychological services for insurance reimbursement. Insurance carriers must provide reimbursement for the service performed by a licensed or certified psychologist if the insurance contract covers this service, and the service lies within the scope of psychological practice authorized by the state's licensing or certification law.[61]

Insurance companies obviously need information regarding the disorder treated. At the same time there is a need to protect the privacy of the client as well as the client's right to information. These complex requirements have resulted in the widespread use of code numbers such as "301.1, DSM-II" which refers to "manic-depressive reaction, depressive type" in the official nomenclature of the *Diagnostic and Statistical Manual of Mental Disorders,* 2nd edition, of the American Psychiatric Association. Insurance carriers are familiar with these diagnostic categories, and a practitioner is usually permitted to insert a code number where a diagnostic description is required on the insurance form. Unfortunately, except for organic disorders, these categories appear to have relatively little reliability or prognostic value.[62] Certain social security and other federal government benefit programs such as workmen's compensation generally allow benefits to be paid if the claimant is unable to work as a result of emotional problems or if there is a work-related emotional disturbance. The trend is away from the traditional requirement that the injury be a result of some "physical impact."[63] Payment under private insurance programs will depend on the provisions of individual policies. The American Psychological Association is presently studying methods for achieving professional self-regulation and accountability in health insurance programs, in particular with the federal Civilian Health and Medical Program of the Uniformed Services (CHAMPUS) that covers approximately eight million people.

Malpractice insurance is a matter of concern to many practitioners. The public has become more sophisticated and claims-conscious; practitioners are generally more active and nontraditional in style; and the legal profession faces a labor surplus. A base-rate for claims is difficult to establish because there is a waiting period of four to seven years before trial in the largest cities and because both state liability laws and insurance policy provisions may change during that time. Generally the rate appears quite low. Even an invalid claim, however, may result in substantial legal fees. In successful cases, the damages sought are approximately fifty times greater than damages eventually recovered. Lawyers' contingency fees in malpractice cases range between twenty to forty percent.

Between 1946 and 1964, twenty-eight psychiatric cases reportedly reached appellate courts; and between 1964 and 1974, only two suits against psychologists were not settled out of court.[64] Approximately 50 claims per year are currently received by the insurance carriers for the American Psychiatric Association and approximately 25 claims per year for the American Psychological Association.

Improper commitment is the largest single type of claim against psychiatrists. This is followed by disputes regarding release or failure to release (i.e., subpoenas) confidential information, fees, and drug or ECT reactions. The most successful claims against psychologists have involved sexual relations and physical injury. These situations have subsequently been excluded from the insurance policy carried by most psychologists.[65] There have, apparently, been fewer claims against psychiatrists for sexual relations with patients, and that situation has not been specifically excluded by the American Psychiatric Association carrier. As with any insurance, the purchaser should note carefully the policy provisions. For example, "punitive" damages usually fall outside the coverage provided by professional liability policies. Two other important exclusions are (1) duties assumed by the insured under contract or agreement, and (2) actions taken as an executive officer of a hospital, laboratory, or business enterprise.[66] One means of limiting personal liability, but not professional liability, is to establish a professional service corporation either as an individual or in cooperation with other practitioners.[67]

NOTES

1. *See generally* Freidson, E. *Profession of Medicine: A Study of the Sociology of Applied Knowledge.* New York: Dodd, Mead & Co., 1970; and Slovenko, R. *Psychiatry and the Law.* Boston: Little, Brown 1973, p. 457. Arguments against licensing have been based on the 14th Amendment guarantee of freedom of association. According to Slovenko (p. 462), the State of Georgia had at one time a statute forbidding authorities from interfering with quacks. According to one commentator, "the evidence overwhelmingly supports the conclusion that licensing maintains a structure that is in the self-interest of the service giver and in opposition to the public interest," Gross, S. J. The myth of

professional licensing. 33 *American Psychologist* 1009 (Nov. 1978). For this and government economy reasons, South Dakota and Florida in 1979 became the first states to deregulate psychological practice.

2. Annotation, Dr. Thomas A. Pitts, et al. v. State Board of Examiners of Psychologists, 81 A.L.R.2d 787, 788 [222 Md. 224, 160 Atl. 2d 200 (1960)].

3. U. S. Department of Health, Education, and Welfare. *State licensing of health occupations*. Public Health Service Publ. No. 1758, Washington, D. C.: Government Printing Office, 1967.

4. Steering Committee of Education and Credentialing, *Education and credentialing in psychology*. Washington, D. C.: American Psychological Assn., 1978.

5. Slovenko, *supra* note 1, at 465. The most common confusion occurs when a foreign-trained medically unlicensed physician holding an M.B. or M.D. degree uses the title "psychiatrist." The number of foreign-trained graduates is in medicine 20 percent generally and above 75 percent in psychiatric residencies in state hospital systems. Torrey, E. F. and Taylor, R. Cheap labor from poor nations. 130 *The American Journal of Psychiatry* 428 (1973).

6. Shapiro, A. E., Dörken, H., Rodgers, D. A., and Wiggins, J. G. The legislative process. In H. Dörken and Associates (Eds.) *The professional psychologist today*. San Francisco: Jossey-Bass, 1976, p. 230. Exclusions from such a sweeping prohibition are often equally generous to forestall what might be serious and legitimate challenges by other professions. Some of the six states that currently have marriage counselor license laws specifically permit any professionally recognized lawyer, physician, minister, social worker, or psychologist to practice marriage counseling. In addition to representatives of these professions, the 1978 Los Angeles yellow pages included under "Marriage and Family Counselors" two wedding chapels and several ambiguous listings for sex consultants such as "National Busibody Services, Inc."

7. Curiously, lack of good moral character is grounds, according to California statute, for denying a license to hearing-aid dispensers, veterinarians, chiropractors, physicians, and psychologists but *not* to registered nurses, psychiatric technicians, marriage and family counselors, or social workers.

8. Packer v. Board of Medical Examiners, 112 Cal. Rptr. 76 (App. 1974). Obvious fraud would involve the practice of medicine by a Ph.D., *see* The two Dr. Polatins. 91 *Newsweek* (Apr. 17, 1978) p. 51.

9. Morrison v. State Board of Education, 1 Cal. 3d 214, 461 P.2d 375 (en banc 1969) (homosexual behavior not disqualifying for teacher); Pettit v. State Board of Education, 10Cal. 3d 29, 109 Cal. Rptr. 665 (1973)(revocation of teaching credential for sex acts in club with men other than husband); Lorenz v. Board of Medical Examiners, 298 P. 2d 537 (Cal. 1956) (physician furnishing alcoholic beverage to minor not disqualified); *contra* McLaughlin v. Board of Medical Examiners, 35 Cal. App. 3d 1010, 111 Cal. Rptr. 353 (1973) (physicain's probation, with mandatory psychiatric treatment, for homosexuality affirmed; cogent dissenting opinion by presiding judge, P. J. Kaus).

10. Mindel v. U. S. Civil Service Commission, 312 F. Supp. 485, 487 (D.C. 1970); Packer v. Board of Medical Examiners, 112 Cal. Rptr. 76 (App. 1974). *See also* Application of Ronwin, 555P.2d 315 (Ariz. 1976) (applicant denied admission to Bar as mentally unable to engage in practice of law due to "personality deficiencies"—i.e., derogatory untrue public accusations).

11. In recent years (starting with small, unaccredited institutions) most law schools have, without altering curriculum or length of study, changed the entry degree from LL.B. (Bachelor of Laws) to J.D. (Juris Doctor). This is similar to the practice of American medical schools which award a doctorate rather than a baccalaureate degree as the first professional degree, in contrast to the English tradition where the basic entry degree is M. B. (Bachelor of Medicine); an M. D. Degree is reserved for study requiring research and dissertation. Earned higher degrees in law include Master of Laws (LL.M. or M.L.), Doctor of Laws (LL.D.), and Doctor of Juridical Science (J.S.D. or S.J.D.). A person with a J.D. is not called ''doctor'' according to professional tradition. Social work has *lowered* its entry degree for private practitioners from D.S.W. (Doctor of Social Work) to the traditional M.S.W. (Master of Social Work).

12. Berger v. Board of Psychological Examiners, 521 F.2d 1056 (D.D.C. 1975) Whittle v. State Board of Examiners of Psychologist, 483 P.2d 328 (Okla. 1971).

13. ''Despite an elaborate regulatory facade, the practice of psychiatry requires nothing more than a medical license. No special skills are required, and no evidence of training in psychiatry is mandated.'' VanHoose, W. H. and Kotter, J. A. *Ethical and legal issues in counseling and psychotherapy.* San Francisco: Jossey-Bass, 1977. *See also* Harris, M. Tort liability of the psychotherapist. 8 *University of San Francisco Law Review* 405, 406-7 (Winter 1973).

14. *See generally* the annual report of the ABPN *in*, for example, 135 *American Journal of Psychiatry* 1302 (Oct. 1978).

15. American Association of Marriage and Family Counselors, *Marriage and family counseling model bill.* Claremont, CA: author, 1978. Six states (California, Georgia, Michigan, Nevada, New Jersey, and Utah) presently license this specialty.*See also* Lewis, H. Standards in social work: Implications for practice and education, 3 *Clinical Social Work Journal* 211 (1975).

16. For a detailed description, including sample multiple choice questions, of the American Board of Psychiatry and Neurology exam, *see* M. T., Peterson, M. H. and Davis, J. A. *Psychiatry*, 3rd edition. Flushing, N.Y. Medical Examination Publ. Co., 1976, pp. 457-487.

17. Black, H. C. *Black's law dictionary.* St. Paul, Minn.: West Publishing Co., 1968, p. 1392.

18. Cf., *e.g.,* Huckins, W. C. *Ethical and legal considerations in guidance.* Boston: Houghton-Mifflin, 1968, pp. 46–48; (no author), Models for licensing registration. 15 *National Association of Social Workers' News* 3 (May 1970); Stachyra, M. Nurses, psychotherapy, and the law. 7 *Perspectives in Psychiatric Care* 200 (1969).

19. Metreger, J. Legal limitations in the practice of psychology. 5 *Illinois Continuing Legal Education* 85, 88 (April 1967).

20. ''In Michigan, it is now expedient to apply another term to the same procedure. Instead of describing person-problem-type counseling as 'therapeutic,' it is characterized as an educative process.'' Huckins, *supra* note 18, at 47. For critical comment on viewing encounter groups as ''educative'' rather than ''therapeutic,'' *see* Crawshaw, R. How sensitive is sensitivity training? 126 *American Journal of Psychiatry* 868 (Dec. 1969).

21. State of California v. Eckley, 33 Cal. App. 3d 91 (Cal. App. 1973) (prescribing Valium without medical license). *See also,* Pisani, J. R. Acupuncture: Practice of medicine? 38 *Albany Law Review* 633 (1974).

22. According to NASW model licensing bill, sec. 9053, *supra* note 18, certain specific professions may "render clinical social work services . . . as long as they do not . . . use the word 'psychosocial' in their description of services." *Cf.* Zuckerman, L. T. and Savedra, R. A. *Professional licensing legislation in the U. S. with an emphasis on social work statutes in California.* Venice, Calif.: (privately printed), 1972 (Library of Congress No. 72-90505).

23. Committee on State Legislation, American Pyschological Assn., *A model for state legislation regulating the practice of psychology: 1977.* Unpublished paper, APA, 1977.

24. Shapiro, *supra* note 6, at p. 230; *contra* note 3.

25. Malican v. Blue Shield of Western New York, 364 N.Y.S.2d 691 (NYC Ct. 1975) (services of social worker reimbursable); Bilbrey v. Industrial Commission, 556 P.2d 27 (Ariz. 1976) (psychologist's opinion not "medical diagnosis).

26. *Reported in* Psychologist's counsel bests marriage counselors, 9 *Psychotherapy Bulletin* 23 (Fall 1976).

27. Traweek v. Alabama Board of Examiners in Psychology, Cir. Ct., 10 Judicial Cir. of Alabama Equity Div. (Jefferson County), Case NO. 198-073 (1976) (counselor training acceptable); Coxe v. Mississippi State Board of Psychology Examiners, Chancery Ct. of Harrison County, Complaint No. 4013 (1976).

28. "Any qualified health professional may command or exercise administrative direction of a military health care facility. . .without regard to the officer's basic health profession." Memorandum from Secretary of Defense to Secretaries of the Military on the subject of Staff and Command Assignments of Health Professionals, May 1, 1973, as cited in Dörken, *supra* note 6, p. 37, 168.

29. For a judicious statement generally reflecting advantages of psychiatric supervision (e.g., medical training, diversity of potential treatment methods, legal capacity to hospitalize), *see* Position statement on psychiatrist's relationship with nonmedical mental health professionals. 130 *The American Journal of Psychiatry* 389 (Mar. 1973). A stronger opinion can be found in Masor, N. *The new psychiatry,* New York: Philosophical Library, 1959, pp.5–6: "He [psychologist] is the mechanic without tools, the chauffeur without a car, the magician without his magic wand. His trademark is exactly similar to that of the orthodox psychiatrist, and being powerless to use any of the latter's additional medical modalities, zealously guards his tangential role in medicine. . .often using the title 'Dr.' as a prefix to his name and rarely the more explicit Ph.D. as a suffix, as though he is ashamed to admit the true identity of his title. . . . The psychologist is a hamstrung, pathetic individual who somewhere along the line missed the opportunity to study medicine and adapted a more pragmatic approach to his desired medical identity, with less obstacles." Opinions abound. Are there any data regarding efficacy of training beyond the use of organic therapies where where at least some aspects of traditional medical training seem obviously essential?

30. Committee on State Legislation, supra note 23, at 4.

31. Steering Committee on Education and Credentialing, *supra* note 4. For a view that argues against increased standardization in the training of psychologists, *see* Matarazzo, J. D. Higher education, professional accreditation, and licensure. 32 *American Psychologist* 856 (1977).

32. American Psychological Assn., *Ethical standards of psychologists* (1977 rev.) Washington, D. C.: author, 1977.

33. American Psychological Assn., *Standards for providers of psychological services.* Washington, D. C.: author, 1977, standard 1.7, p.6. *See also* American Psychological Assn., *Policy on training for psychologists wishing to change their specialty.* Washington, D. C.: author, 1976.

34. Interpretation of standard 1.7, id. at 6.

35. Alabama, Arkansas, Connecticut, Delaware, District of Columbia, Georgia, Idaho, Illinois, Indiana, Iowa, Kansas, Kentucky, Maine, Maryland, Massachusetts, Michigan, Minnesota, Mississippi, Montana, Nebraska, New Jersey, North Carolina, Oklahoma, Oregon, South Carolina, South Dakota, Tennessee, Texas, Utah, West Virginia. Six states pattern their code of ethics after that of the APA: Colorado, Hawaii, Missouri, New Mexico, Pennsylvania, and Wisconsin. Source: *Brief of the American Psychological Association as amicus curiae,* Detroit Edison v. National Labor Relations Board, U. S. Supreme Court, October term, 1977, at 21–22.

36. U. S. Department of Health, Education, and Welfare, Office of Professional Standards Review, *PSRO program manual.* Washington, D. C.: HEW, 1974.

37. PSRO Program Manual, supra note 36, at sec. 907.18.

38. McMillan, J. Peer review and professional standards for psychologist rendering personal health services. 5 *Professional Psychology* 51 (1974). American Psychological Assn., *PSRO handbook for psychology.* Washington, D. C.: author, 1975.

39. Committee on Professional Standards Review of the Board of Professional Affairs, American Psychological Assn., *PSRC procedures manual.* Washington, D. C.: author, 1975, p. 2.

40. Id. at 9.

41. Assoc. for the Advancement of Behavior Therapy, Professional consultation and peer review services. 420 Lexington ave., N.Y. 10017.

42. Abraham v. Zaslow, 1 Civil No. 33219 (Super. Ct. No. 245862), Cal. Ct. App. (1st Dist.) (Feb. 2, 1975).

43. Morra v. State Board of Examiners of Psychologists, 510 P.2d 614 (Kan. 1973) (psychologist's license revoked for sexual intimacies); Cooper v. Board of Medical Examiners, 123 Cal. Rptr. 563 (App. 1975) (psychologist's license revoked for sexual intimacy and furnishing dangerous drugs); Bernstein v. Board of Medical Examiners, 22 Cal. Rptr. 419 (App. 1962) (revocation of psychiatrist's license for heterosexual intercourse with 16-year-old patient); Bd. of Educ. v. Calderon, 35 Cal. App. 3d 480 (1974) (job dismissal of teacher upheld after acquittal on homosexual charge). The medical license of Martin Sheppard, author of *"The Love Treatment* and of *Games Analysts Play*, was revoked by the New York State Board of Regents for alleged sex with patients, as reported in *New York Times*, Dec. 17, 1977, p. 29. License revoked by California Psychology Examining Committee for UCLA Ph.D., Betty Eisner, for alleged "gross negligence" involving stimulant and anesthetic drugs, carbon dioxide gas, involuntary restraints. Timnick, L. Psychologist loses license for "negligence." *Los Angeles Times*, Dec. 22, 1978, Pt. II, p. 1.

44. Appelant v. State Board of Examiners of Psychologists, No. 46748 (1971) (syllabus by the Supreme Court of the State of Kansas) (hearing rules); Kizzar and Hagedorn v. Oklahoma State Board of Examiners of Psychologist, Distr. Ct. of Oklahoma County, Consolidated cases No 303 & 304 (1974) (must publish cutoff scores for written exam);

State of Ohio v. Cook, Cleveland Municipal Ct. (Cuyahoga County), 75 CRB 11478 (1975) (procedural irregularity permits counselor to practice).

45. Bates v. State Bar of Arizona, 97 Sup. Ct. 2691 (1976). Whitman, D. Advertising by professionals, 16 *American Business Law Journal* 39 (Spr. 1978); Camby, W. C. and Gellhorn, E. Physician advertising: The First Amendment and the Sherman Act. 1978 *Duke Law Journal* 543 (May 1978).

46. American Psychological Association, Rewording of Principle 4: Public statements of the Ethical Standards, as approved by the Council of Representatives. Washington, D. C.: Author (Jan. 1979).

47. Anclote Manor Foundation v. Wilkinson, 263 S.2d 256 (Fla. Dist. Ct. App. 1972) (psychiatrist's charges of $28,628 recovered for breach of contract for promising, then failing, to marry patient who subsequently committed suicide).

48. Note, Professional negligence. 121 *University of Pennsylvania Law Review* 628, 650 (1973).

49. Hammer v. Rosen, 198 N.Y.S.2d 803, 165 N.E.2d 756 (N.Y. Ct. App. 1960).

50. Olinde v. Seghers, 208 So. 657 (La. 1973) ($35 per hour not excessive and psychiatrist may collect from spouse).

51. Culver v. Jackson, 194 S.E.2d 585 (Ga. 1973) (burden of reasonableness placed on psychiatrist rendering bills). *Cf.* also American Psychological Association, *Standards for providers of psychological services*. Washington, D.C.: APA, 1974.

52. Committee on State Legislation, *supra* note 23, at p. 1.

53. Cox v. State, 439 S.W.2d 267 (Tenn. 1969).

54. Note, A critical analysis of bar associations' minimum fee schedules. 85 *Harvard Law Review* 971 (March 1972); *compare*, Morin, V. F. *How to make money practicing law*. Los Angeles: Ivar Publishing Co., 1970. When the Fairfax County (Virginia) Bar Association abandoned the minimum fee schedule, property title rates reportedly fell by almost 50 percent. Discount lawyers? 85 *Newsweek* (June 30, 1975) p. 39.

55. Goldensohn, S.S. Cost, utilization, and utilization review of mental health services in a prepaid group practice plan. 134 *American Journal of Psychiatry* 1222, 1224 (Nov. 1977).

56. Mills, D. H. & Wellner, A.M. Hourly fees for individual service by psychologists. *Register Report*, No. 12, (July 1978), p. 3.

57. The principles of medical ethics with annotations especially applicable to psychiatry. 130 *American Journal of Psychiatry*, 1058, 1061 (1973).

58. *Cf. e.g.*, various *New York Times* newspaper accounts: "Doctor gets 6 months" (jail for false Medicaid claims), Dec. 23, 1976, p. 27; "Psychiatrist indicted for stealing $500,000 in Medicaid payments" (e.g., billing for 45-min. sessions lasting five-to-ten min.). June 11, 1977, pt. II, p. 22.

59. Dörken, *supra* note 6, at p. 15.

60. Fee survey highlights. 4 *Psychotherapy Economics* 3 (special report, 1977).

61. Direct recognition legislation, 13 *Division 25 Recorder* (American Psychological Assn.) 4 (Winter 1978).

62. Tarter, R. Reliability of psychiatric diagnosis. 36 *Diseases of the Nervous System* 30 (1975).

63. Branham v. Gardner, 383 F.2d 614 (Cal. App. 1967) (no objective clinical evidence

required); Carter v. General Motors, 106 N.W.2d 105 (Mich. 1960) (psychosis developed from emotional pressure of production line compensable until recovered); *contra* Wolfe v. Sibley, Lindsay & Curr Co., 354 N.Y.S.2d 470 (N.Y. App. Div. 1974) (compensation nonpayable for mental injury precipitated solely by mental cause—seeing suicide of work supervisor).

64. Scattered data can be found in: Bellamy, W. A. Psychiatric malpractice. In S. Arieti (Ed.) *American handvook of psychiatry,* vol. 3, New York: Basic Books, 1966, p. 621 (1946-64 psychiatric appellate cases); White, A. E. and Gross, R. B. Professional liability insurance and the psychologist. 6 *Professional Psychology* 267 (Aug. 1975) (two court cases as reported by Jury Verdict Research, Inc.); News item, 6 *Behavior Today* 4 (March 8, 1976) (45 malpractice claims against psychologists in 1974–76); Trent, C. L. Psychiatric malpractice insurance and its problems. In W. E. Barton and C. L. Sanborn (Eds.) *Law and the mental health professions.* New York: International Universities Press, 1978 (number and type of psychiatric claims).

65. Exclusions contained in Central Mutual Insurance Co. and in American Home Assurance Co. policies. *Cf. generally,* White and Gross, *supra* note 62.

66. For limits which may exist in malpractice insurance, *see* Trent, C. L. and Wohl, W. P. Professional liability insurance and the American psychiatrist. 132 *American Journal of Psychiatry* 1312, 1313 (Dec. 1975).

67 Burker, W. J. and Zaloom, B. J. Blueprint for professional service corporations. New York: Dun. & Bradstreet, 1970. *See also* Internal Revenue Service regulations sec. 301.7701.2 (h) (4).

CHAPTER 14

The Expert Witness

Pavlov might have been the ideal expert witness in the case of *Burlington Mills Corp.* v. *Hagood.*[1] According to the court record, the facts of the case are these:

> On March 23, 1939, Ms. Hagood, 20 years of age and a regular employee of a textile company, was working at a machine approximately 15 feet away from an electric motor which was being repaired. Unexpectedly, a loose wire in the motor short circuited causing an explosive blue flash and a sound resembling a gun shot. Ms. Hagood saw the flash and fainted. But as she was falling backward, she was caught by a co-worker.
>
> She worked for the next week or so without incident. However, while at work on April 13, "She looked up and suddenly saw the employee who had caught her when she fell on March 23. She thereupon fainted and fell, and has not returned to work since."[2]

Three physicians testified to the effect that, although there was no overt physical injury, "There was a direct causal relation between the electric flash and the irritated condition of her nervous system."[3] On the strength of this unanimous expert opinion, the court affirmed her disability and ordered her to be paid the full amount of her claim—six dollars per week.[4]

Seldom is there such unanimous agreement among mental health expert witnesses in matters upon which they are called to testify. The contradictory opinion of experts in famous criminal trials such as those of Sam Shepphard, Sirhan Sirhan, and Patty Hearst has been widely publicized. The reason for such discrepancy lies, in part, in the complexity and ambiguity of the issues experts are asked to comment about.

The basic goal in any testimony is to obtain useful and relevant information to aid the court in making a legal decision. Usually, a lay witness can testify only to *events* that s/he has actually seen or heard first-hand. *Opinions and inferences* are not admissible.[5] In contrast, the opinions and inferences of an expert witness which are "within the scope of his special training, skill and experience to interpret"[6] are accepted into evidence in court. In a criminal case, for example, the expert may be expected to describe and explain "how the development, adaptations, and function of [the] defendant's behavioral processes may have influenced his conduct."[7] In civil commitment hearings, the expert has a similar duty to explain the development and manifestations of the alleged mental illness and also probably to make a prediction about the individual's "dangerousness" to self or others. Merely stating a conclusion (e.g., the individual suffers from schizophrenia) is not sufficient.[8] Presumably, the reason experts are used is to help the court to understand and evaluate evidence or to determine a fact at issue.[9] The expert is *not* a decision-maker or a determiner of what is a "fact" in the legal sense. There are many complex rules of procedure and evidence to be followed to determine legally valid facts.

WHO MAY SERVE AS AN EXPERT WITNESS?

Almost anyone can serve as an expert witness if s/he is professionally acquainted with, skilled, or trained in some science, art, or trade, and thereby has knowledge or experience in matters not generally familiar to the public.[10] In matters of mental disease or defect which bear upon legal decisions of criminal responsibility, civil commitment, competency to stand trial, and so forth, psychiatrists or other medical practitioners are usually the primary expert witnesses. In cases of actual or suspected physical trauma, a requirement that the witness have a license to practice medicine has been a traditional and logical rule of court procedure.[11] Furthermore, if one accepts the view that deviant behavior is often a result of "mental illness" which is, in turn, a manifestation of at least some degree of physiological malfunction, then medical training would seem to be a very useful and necessary qualification.

Whether other professionals are qualified to testify as expert witnesses in matters of possible mental illness or defect is a topic of considerable debate.[12] Cases can be found wherein courts have accepted the opinion of psychologists, sociologists, social workers, and hypnotists.[13] Perhaps the most unusual and successful use of a hypnotist was a case in which a young woman collected damages for becoming a nymphomaniac following a cable car accident. Extensive detail of the trial court proceedings has been published by the plaintiff's attorneys who introduced the hypnotist's testimony.[14] There has been growing acceptance of psychologists as expert witnesses in recent years.[15] Federal *criminal* courts have generally accepted psychologists, but federal *civil* courts have been inconsistent.[16]

One of the early cases that de-emphasized the necessity of medical training was *People* v. *Hawthorne*.[17] In *Hawthorne,* the trial court sustained the prosecution's objections to the fitness of a psychologist (Ph.D.) as a defense expert on insanity. The Michigan Supreme Court reversed, rejecting the argument that insanity is a medical matter about which *only* physicians can testify. The Court held that a psychologist's ability to detect insanity is not inferior to the physician's ability, if the latter's experience has not been so intensive as the former's. Relying indirectly on *Hawthorne,* a federal appeals court in *Jenkins* v. *United States*[18] held that the determination of a witness's qualifications to testify as to the presence or absence of mental disease or defect must depend on the nature and extent of the witness's knowledge. Determination of a witness's competence should not depend on his claim to the title of "psychologist" or "psychiatrist."[19] With rare exception, commitment certificates must be signed by a physician. Hence, by implication, courts have assigned diminished importance to the testimony of nonmedical experts in matters of mental disability.

The specific qualifications needed by a psychologist to satisfy the requirements of expert witness vary from jurisdiction to jurisdiction. In one case, the conviction of an accused murderer was reversed in part because a prosecution psychologist lacked the following qualifications: a Ph.D. degree, at least five years of postgraduate training in clinical psychology, and one year of internship at an American Psychological Association-approved mental hospital.[20] Licensing or certification seems to be an important factor in obtaining expert status; however, case law suggests that licensing is only one factor and perhaps not the controlling one.[21] Another obvious factor is the nature of the question before the court. For example, in cases involving the least restrictive alternative to hospitalization, a social worker might have very useful specialized knowledge.[22] In cases dealing with trademark infringement or the accuracy of eye-witness testimony, a research psychologist might be the expert of choice.[23] The best-known early treatise on the topic of eye-witnesses is that of Hugo Munsterberg.[24]

WHAT MAY THE EXPERT GIVE AN OPINION ABOUT?

Behavioral scientists may be asked to give opinion regarding child custody, copyright or trademark infringement, opinion sampling, drug addiction, sex offenses, perceptual acuity, impact of media programming, employment testing procedures, testamentary capacity (e.g., being of "sound mind" when making a will), etc.[25] There are, however, opinions which are not to be expressed by the expert— that is, those that are beyond the professional competency of the expert, and those that state a conclusion which is a legal matter to be decided by the judge or jury. For example, witnesses are not permitted to state whether an alleged crime was actually a "product" of some hypothesized mental defect or disease. This is viewed as a crucial legal issue, not a psychiatric or psychological issue.[26] In some jurisdictions, nonmedical experts may be restricted to simply presenting the results of tests or to inferring that a person was suffering a mental defect or disease at the time of an alleged crime. Only a psychiatrist is permitted to testify to the ultimate issue in the area of mental disease (i.e., whether the person was actually "insane"). In other jurisdictions, once a medical or nonmedical witness is qualified, s/he can testify to the ultimate issue of insanity or criminal responsibility.[27] Many witnesses only reluctantly accept this responsibility which might properly remain the burden of the court.

One of the most difficult assessments asked of expert witnesses is the prediction of "dangerousness." The concept has emerged as an important issue in civil and criminal commitment procedures.[28] Unfortunately, the adequacy of criteria and techniques used to predict dangerousness is highly suspect,[29] and there is considerable evidence that many nonviolent persons are falsely predicted as violence-prone.[30] It is relatively rare that a prospective expert witness has much expertise in predicting dangerousness. A motion to qualify the witness may be challenged on this ground, or, at minimum, the matter can be raised during cross-examination.[31] One study of 257 felony defendants over a three-year period concluded that the accuracy of psychiatrists in predicting violence was no greater than chance, and that "psychiatric testimony to the court in regards to applying the dangerousness standard currently should not be considered expert."[32]

In view of such difficulties of prediction, psychologists and others "should be exceedingly cautious in offering predictions of criminal behavior for use in imprisoning or releasing individual offenders. If a psychologist decides that it is appropriate in a given case to provide a prediction of criminal behaviors, she should clearly specify: (a) the acts being predicted; (b) the estimated probability that these acts will occur during a given time period; and (c) the factors on which the predictive judgment is based."[33]

How sure of his/her findings should the expert be? Somewhere between a "mere guess" and "absolute certainty" lie the varying standards that courts expect. Some courts have required an intermediate standard of "reasonable probability" which has been defined as "that standard of persuasion that is in quality sufficient to generate the belief that the tendered hypothesis is, in all human likelihood, the fact."[34] In admitting testimony of cause-effect relationships, courts may require that the witness state that the alleged events did in fact produce the effect;[35] other courts may permit proof that the alleged events might, could, or would have caused the effect.[36] Courts do not require categorical "yes" or "no" answers if such answers are contrary to the witness's belief.[37] Some courts allow experts to testify in their own professional vocabulary (e.g., "significant difference," "role model," "discriminative stimulus") before translating the concepts into terms understandable to a lay jury.[38] It should be noted that the trial judge has wide discretionary powers as to who will be qualified on what matters according to relevant rules of evidence, if any, within a given jurisdiction.

TESTIFYING

The courtroom is a place best reserved for those who are brave, adventuresome, and nimble-witted. Behavioral experts are usually asked to provide evidence in what lawyers euphemistically term ''difficult cases.''[39] The structure of inquiry in law is quite different from that in behavioral science. The adversary process places a different expectation upon attorneys than upon mental health professionals. ''Psychologists who interpret the science of psychology or the services of psychology to the general public accept the obligation to present the material fairly and accurately, avoiding misrepresentation through sensationalism, exaggeration, or superficiality.''[40] The attorney has a different task. ''The lawyer should represent a client zealously within the bounds of the law. . . . The advocate may urge any permissible construction of the law favorable to his client, without regard to his professional opinion as to the likelihood that the construction will ultimately prevail.''[41] The frustration of some attorneys at the equivocation of expert witnesses was strongly stated in the following summary statement to the jury in a tort case: ''You couldn't get him [the psychiatric witness] to say the sun was shining outside or that it was night time. I believe truthfully that if I brought a corpse in front of Dr. _____ and said, 'Doctor, is he dead?' he would say yes and no, and he wouldn't be too sure even then unless there was an autopsy and he saw it cut up.''[42] The legal system is required to make difficult decisions under considerable time pressure, and cannot wait for the results of long-term research.

Under courtroom stress and unusual publicity, even experienced and well-qualified practitioners may be led to use methods or draw conclusions that appear questionable to some observers. Some of the work of experts in the Sirhan Sirhan trial, for example, received bad press. A defense psychologist admitted under cross-examination to having lifted passages out of a psychiatric casebook; a court-appointed psychiatrist assertedly gave Sirhan six ounces of whisky over an 18-minute period to simulate conditions on the night of the homicide, (although Sirhan had had only three drinks over a two-to-three hour period), and a prosecution psychiatrist, when reportedly confronted with an earlier evaluation in which he claimed that Sirhan was too mentally ill to premeditate murder, attempted to make the distinction between a ''psychotic person'' and a person ''clinically psychotic.'' This witness also reportedly submitted a bill of $10,811 to the state for his services.[43]

Pretrial Preparation

The expert may be offered the opportunity to testify by the court or by counsel for either the plaintiff or the defendant. Some court systems have established panels of psychiatric and psychological experts upon whom they routinely call on a fixed fee-per-case basis. In federal courts, the expert will be informed of his/her duties by the court at a conference in which both parties may participate. In routine criminal cases, a range of five to ten hours is normally spent in preparation. The expert will inform both parties of the findings before testifying in court.

Often in criminal cases, no provision is made by the court for restricting the distribution of information obtained during these examinations, and thus some information damaging to the defendant's case may find its way to the prosecution. Although the prosecutor may not be able to use this information during the trial s/he may nevertheless find it useful in building a case against the defendant. Hence, interview or information is sometimes used to the defendant's disadvantage in ways the person did not expect.[44] It would seem fair and legally appropriate to inform the defendant of the potential uses of the information gained from the tests and interviews. The expert may use information collected from hospital reports, psychological tests, and interviews. Because there have been instances of mistaken identity, the practitioner should make sure that it is actually the assigned client who is examined and not someone else. The practitioner should not leave the room while the test is being taken, or allow the test to be administered by an assistant. As an expert witness, the practitioner must be able to prove the source of the answers and avoid hints by a cross-examiner that someone unduly influenced the answers.

Attorneys may also question the expert about the effects of stress upon the defendant's answers and possible distortions (deliberate or unintentional) due to the pending trial. A question might also be raised with regard to the standardization of the test relative to the cultural background of the defendant, his physical status, and the possibility that the results were influenced by drugs. The expert should be familiar with standard reviews of the relevant literature and with interdisciplinary law-psychiatry publications. For example, an expert conducting an examination for competency to stand trial should have a general knowledge of the criminal justice system, adequate interpersonal interviewing skills to elicit legally relevant data from defendants who are mentally disabled, knowledge of the legal criteria of competency, and a professional status that will enhance the creditability of his/her testimony.[45]

If the expert is not court-appointed, but instead selected by one of the contesting parties, a conference should be arranged with the attorney at least several days in advance of the trial in order to define goals and to generate a list of questions to be used during direct examination. The questions should be predominantly open-ended and build cumulatively toward a goal. It may help if the expert draws up a tentative question list for the attorney's consideration. A fee should be established and may be paid after the expert has prepared his/her testimony but before actual court appearance (to avoid the implication that the fee is contingent upon "saying the right thing"). On the other hand, there is nothing unethical about being paid for one's *time,* as in any other case. Hours in court may be billed. On the day of scheduled testimony, the expert should expect a wait of one or two hours, or even until the next day, due to court scheduling problems.

Cross Examination

To the novice, verbatim transcripts of the cross-examination of expert witnesses read something like a combination of true-life horror stories and science fiction novels.[46] The cross examination may begin with:

> "Good morning, doctor. I see you are here on behalf of an accused killer (or 'your fellow psychologists') again. How are you today?"

or with:

> "Doctor, were you paid to perform your examination? [Yes] How much? [$35 an hour.] How many hours did you spend in all? [20 hours.] That's $700, isn't it doctor? [Yes] And in your opinion the patient was insane on the night of January 26, 1975? [Yes] That's all, doctor."[47]

One expert witness reported that, as a tactic to harass him, he was asked to administer all 566 Minnesota Multiphasic Personality Inventory items to himself, item by item, out loud on the witness stand. Following each item he was to tell the court which, if any, of his responses to the items indicated that he was mentally ill.[48]

Generally, textbooks are not admitted as direct evidence in court because the text has a "hearsay" quality to it inasmuch as the author cannot be questioned.[49] In most states however, a textbook can be used to challenge the creditablity of an expert witness, particularly if the witness acknowledges the authoritativeness of the text. Therefore, one strategy of the witness can be to deny, or at least narrow the scope, of the writer's agreed-upon competence.[50]

The following strategies may also help the expert cope with cross examination.[51]

> *Be prepared* to defend your specific theories, methods, and conclusions. The most likely attack will not be upon your conclusions per se but upon the scientific adequacy of the method used to arrive at your conclusions.[52]

> *Be honest,* at least to the extent that you avoid performing awkward or contrived professional acts. If something sounds sour or phoney, do not do it. Including some necessary evidence against your position may actually enhance your credibility.

> *Admit weaknesses,* when such exist, directly, simply, and without great elaboration. Don't stammer and appear defeated. If the attorney presents a damaging bit of data, you can use the "push-pull" technique—pull in the same direction as s/he is pushing by perhaps responding with enthusiasm, "Oh my

gracious, yes!'' Thus you may transform the emotional aspect of the exchange to your advantage.

   Talk in personally meaningful terms and make eye contact with the jury, judge, and others in the courtroom. Most people have some resentment of ''experts,'' but the jury will identify more with you than the judge or the lawyers. Avoid arrogance. Also avoid falling into the trap of engaging in esoteric conversation with the attorney. Most people get quickly bored (and consequently mildly angered) by technical jargon. Except during cross-examination, when you have a prepared and important point to make, do not talk too much. Two or three sentences will usually do.

   Listen carefully to the wording of the questions. Often the attorney will be imprecise in forming the question. This will give you increased options for answering. Sometimes you can rephrase the question, asking if that is what s/he meant (again gaining an edge in the exchange). If the question cannot be reasonably answered by a requested ''yes'' or ''no'' reply, say so.

   Take time to think. Some attorneys will use a staccato, machine-gun pace in asking questions hoping to elicit rapid and ill-conceived replies from the witness. Pause, look away, give serious thought, then answer. It is natural to be anxious, but it may help to remember that you and your methods are not on trial.

Pre-sentencing Reports

The input of experts may also come *after* a defendant has been found, or pleaded, guilty. A pre-sentencing report is submitted to the court by probation authorities as a means of aiding the court in fitting the sentence to the needs of a particular situation.[53] The report contains information on the background and character of the defendant.[54]

   Although the defendant has no direct involvement in the preparation, content, or form of the report, it is entirely proper to have persons (including expert authorities) communicate with the probation department as to the defendant's good character, for instance.[55] When the report's psychiatric exam is incomplete, the court may vacate the sentence and order a complete exam.[56] Trial courts may permit inspection of the pre-sentencing report, but there is no violation of ''due process'' if the court denies requests for such inspection.[57]

   Under optimal conditions, the role of the expert witness is a difficult one by the very nature of the issues involved. The complex realities of practice are, by definition, something less than the abstract professional ideals we wish to actualize. In some unfortunate situations, the expert's testimony may be but one factor in a long chain of questionable and fortuitous events of the legal process (e.g., being asked by the prosecution to testify in a sodomy case wherein the alleged crime occurred on a date ''which the prosecutor picked by throwing darts at a wall calendar'').[58] If nothing else, the use of expert witnesses is a convenient social ritual that permits the court to distribute the burden of making extremely difficult decisions with inadequate or irreconcilably contradictory evidence.

NOTES

1. 13 S.E.2d 291 (Va. 1941).
2. Id. at 292.
3. Id. at 293.
4. In tort law, some form of ''impact'' has traditionally been required to assure that mental injury is not feigned, although this requirement is being loosened. Most worker's compensation statutes have not had this requirement, but regard the consequences themselves as sufficient proof. Prosser, W. L. *Handbook of the law of torts,* 4th ed. St. Paul, Minn.: West Publishing Co., 1971, pp. 328–333. *Compare* Blinder, M. Defense of claim of psychic trauma and psychiatric disability. 12 *Forum* 934 (Summer 1977).
5. Cook, C. M. The role and rights of the expert witness. 9 *Journal of Forensic Sciences* 456, 459 (Oct. 1964). One major exception is an inference rationally based on the lay witness's perception such as estimates of distance, speed, size, or time.
6. *Id.* at 459–460.
7. Washington v. United States, 390 F.2d 444, 457 (D.C. Cir. 1967) (appendix, ''Instruction to expert witness in case involving the 'insanity defense' '').
8. Carter v. United States, 252 F.2d 608, 617 (D.C. Cir. 1957).
9. Federal Rules of Criminal Procedure, 18 U.S.C.A., Rule 702, may be interpreted as requiring that expert testimony merely be *helpful* to the jury in order to be admissible.
10. Black, H. C. *Black's law dictionary.* St. Paul, Minn.: West Publishing Co., 1968, p. 689; Bratt, et al. v. Western Airlines, 155 F.2d 850, 853–854 (10th Cir. 1946).
11. In psychiatric matters, the physician need not have psychiatric training. Some psychiatrists have asserted that medical education *per se* is irrelevant to their practice. Mariner, A. S. A critical look at professional education in the mental health field. 22 *American Psychologist* 271 (1967).
12. Annotation, Qualification of nonmedical psychologist to testify as to mental condition or competency, 78 A.L.R.2d 919; Levine, E. R. Psychologist as expert witness in ''psychiatric questions,'' 20 *Cleveland State Law Review* 379 (May 1971). A lower court judge commented about a psychologist whom he did not permit to testify: ''Here is a man that comes in, glib of tongue, hasn't had a day's medical training at all, and he is going to qualify as an expert on insanity, when a part of the mental condition of legal insanity, as we know it in California, is a medical proposition; and I would like to see the Supreme Court tell me I am wrong.'' The California Supreme Court *did* tell him he was wrong. *Cf.,* People v. Davis, 62 Cal. 2d 791, 402 P.2d 142 (1965).
13. *See generally,* 78 A.L.R.2d 919. Social worker testimony rejected in Patton v. Armstrong, 6 Ill. App. 2d 991, 286 N.E.2d 351 (1972), but see, Bell, C. & Mlyniec, W. Preparing for a neglect proceeding: A guide for the social worker. 26 *Juvenile Justice* 29 (Nov. 1975).
14. Lewis, M. E. and Sadoff, R. L. Psychic injuries. *Courtroom medicine,* vol. 12. New York: Matthew Bender, 1975.

15. "Courts are ready to learn and to use it [psychologists' testimony], whenever the psychologists produce it, any method which the latter themselves are agreed is sound, accurate, and practical." Wigmore, J. H. *Evidence in trials at common law,* vol. 3. Boston: Little, Brown, 1961, p. 390. Rollins v. Commonwealth of Virginia, 207 Va. 575, 153 S.E.2d 622 (1966); State v. Holt, 37 S.W. 2646 (Tenn. 1969); Jones v. Williams, 246 A.2d 356 (Pa. 1968); People v. Davis, 44 Cal. Rptr. 454 (Cal. 1965) (failure to allow psychologist to testify on some aspects of insanity constitutes reversible error).

16. United States v. Riggelman, 411 F.2d 1190 (4th Cir. 1969) (testimony accepted in criminal case; Williams v. United States, 312 F.2d 862 (D.C. Cir. 1962) (exclusion of testimony harmless error); United States v. Brawner, 471 F.2d 969 (D.C. Cir. 1972) (testimony related to criminal responsibility accepted): Annotation, Expert evidence— pain, 11 A.L.R.3d 1249 (testimony on pain usually limited to medical witnesses).

17. People v. Hawthorne 291 N.W. 205 (Mich. 1940).

18. Jenkins v. United States, 307 F.2d 637 (D.C. Cir. 1962 en banc). The American Psychiatric Association filed an amicus curiae brief arguing against admission of psychological testimony.

19. *Id.* at 640. *Accord,* People v. Davis, 62 Cal. 2d 791, 402 P.2d 142, 148 (1965): "A medical degree is not the *sine qua non* to qualify one to testify in the area of mental functioning."

20. State of New Mexico v. Padilla, 66 N.M. 289, 347 P.2d 312 (1959); *see also,* Note, Psychologist as expert witness, 18 *Defense Law Journal* 303, 309 (1969); *contra In re* Masters, 216 Minn. 553, 13 N.W.2d 487 (1944) (permitting a witness who had been employed by the state for eight years but with only an M.A. degree to testify).

21. Many physicians, especially on hospital staffs, may be foreign-trained; and if not fully licensed, might or might not be excluded. In *State v. Jones,* 95 Ariz. 230, 388 P.2d 806 (1964) the court upheld prosecution's use of an unlicensed physician in a rape case. *Cf. also,* Note, The psychologist as an expert witness. 15 *Kansas Law Review* 88 (1966).

22. Social worker qualification is suggested in Schwartz, S. J. and Stern, D. *A trial manual for civil commitment.* Boston: Mental Health Legal Advisors Committee, 1977, Chapt. VI, as reprinted in 1 *Mental Disability Law Reporter* 397 (March–Apr. 1977).

23. An early book dealing with trademark infringement is Burt, H. E. *Legal psychology.* New York: Prentice-Hall, 1931. *See generally,* Buckhout, R. Expert testimony. 3 *Social Action and the Law* 41 (1976) for a list of case decisions on both sides. United States v. Brown, 501 F.2d 146 (9th Cir. 1974) (psychological testimony on eyewitness excluded).

24. *On the witness stand.* New York: Clark Boardman, 1949 (reprint of original 1908 edition).

25. Harriford v. Harriford, 336 S.W.2d 113 (Mo. App. 1960) (divorce); Texas Employees Insurance Association v. Steadman, 415 S.W.2d 211 (Tex. Civ. App. 1967) (psychological testing for "brain damage"); Coca Cola Company v. Chero-Cola Company, 273 F. 755 (D.C. Cir. 1921) (trademark dispute); Brown v. Godfrey, 200 Kan. 568, 438 P.2d 117 (1968) (reflexes in auto accident); U.S. v. Palladino, 475 P.2d 65 (1st Cir. 1973) ("prurient interests" in obscenity case); Sandow v. Weyerhaeuser Co., 449 P.2d 426 (Ore. 1969) (suicidal tendencies).

26. Wasbington v. U.S., 390 F.2d 444 (D.C. Cir. 1967); R. V. Chard, 56 Cr. App. R. 268 (1971) as cited in Note, Inadmissibility of doctor's opinion. 13 *Medicine, Science, and*

the Law 145 (1973) (appeal court upheld refusal to allow psychiatrist to give evidence on intent-to-commit-murder of an "ordinary man" who was not suffering mental illness).

27. People v. Felton, 325 N.E.2d 400 (3rd App. Ill. 1975) (qualifying only psychiatrists). *Contra*, "A clinical psychologist meeting stringent requirements may qualify as an expert witness on all aspects of mental illness and dangerousness." Schwartz and Stern, *supra* note 22 at 396, n. 180; State v. Williams, 361 A.2d 122 (Md. Ct. App. 1976) (psychologist may testify regarding factual findings but not diagnosis of defective delinquent).

28. Stone, A. A. *Mental health and law: A system in transition*. Rockville, Md.: Center for Studies of Crime and Delinquency, NIMH, 1975, ch. 2 ("dangerousness").

29. "Our criteria for predicting who will commit a dangerous act are totally inadequate." Halleck, S. *Psychiatry and the dilemmas of crime*. Berkeley: University of California Press, 1971, p. 348; *see generally,* Stone, *supra* note 28, for opinion and data; Ennis, B. J. and Litwach, T. R. Psychiatry and the presumption of expertise: Flipping coins in the courtroom. 62 *California Law Review* 693 (May 1974); Steadman, H. J. and Keveles, G. The community adjustment and criminal activity of the Baxtrom patients: 1966–1970. 129 *American Journal of Psychiatry* 304 (1972); Schwitzgebel, R. K. Professional accountability in the treatment and release of dangerous persons. In B. D. Sales (Ed.) *Perspectives in law and psychology I: The criminal justice system*. New York: Plenum, 1977 pp. 139–149. "Prediction of potential dangerous behavior is presently highly inaccurate. Studies have shown that psychiatrists often are no more reliable than others who may be called upon to make the difficult prediction." *HEW News* ADAMAH Press Release on "Symposium on Dangerousness and Mentally Disturbed Persons," August 8, 1974, p. 1.

30. Wenk, E. A., Robison, J. O., and Smith, G. W. Can violence be predicted? 18 *Crime and Delinquency* 393 (1972) (criminal offender studies showing between 86–99 percent false positive predictions). *See* Stone, *supra* note 28.

31. "Generally physicians or psychiatrists do not have specific training to diagnose or predict dangerous behavior." [Nor do any other professionals.] Gallup v. Alden, Appellate Div. Western Dist., No. 149, 1976 Mass. Adv. Sheet 113, as cited in Schwartz & Stern, *supra* n. 22 at 390, ftnt. 136.

32. Steadman, H. J. and Cocozza J. J. A natural experiment in the psychiatric prediction of dangerousness. Unpublished paper (Mental Hygene Research Unit, New York State Dept. of Mental Hygene, Albany, N.Y.) 1976, at p. 11.

33. Task Force on the Role of Psychology in the Criminal Justice System, American Psychological Association, *Report of the Task Force on the Role of Psychology in the Criminal Justice System*. Recommendation 9. Washington, D.C.: (author), 1978, p. 24.

34. Conrad, E. C. The expert and legal certainty, 9 *Journal of Forensic Sciences* 445, 449 (Oct. 1964); Grimes v. Goodlett and Adams, 345 S.W.2d 47 (Ky. 1961); Falconer v. Proto Tool Co., 19 App. Div. 2d 926, 244 N.Y.S.2d 52 (1963).

35. Beezer v. Baltimore & Ohio R. Co., 107 F. Supp. 361 (1952), *aff'd.* 203 F.2d 954 (3rd Cir. 1953).

36. Healy v. Nordous, 40 Ill. App. 2d 230, 188 N.E.2d 227 (1963); DeNucci v. Navajo Freight Lines Inc., 297 N.Y.S.2d 164 (App. Div. 1969).

37. Cook, C. M. The role and rights of the expert witness. 9 *Journal of Forensic Sciences* 456, 457 (Oct. 1964).

38. Nash, M. M. Psychological testimony on its own in court. 6 *American Psychology-Law Society Newsletter* 11 (March 1973).

39. "Let's face facts, they aren't difficult cases at all, they are impossible cases, dirty cases, cases loaded with such emotionality that any attempt to get at anything near what may be rationally regarded as factual is impossible." Kaplan, R. G. Frustrations of an expert witness, 1972 (mimeo. paper by author, P. O. Box 2411, La Jolla, Ca. 92037).

40. American Psychological Association, *Ethical standards of psychologists,* Principle 4(f). Washington, D.C.: (author), 1977 rev.

41. American Bar Association, *Code of professional responsibility,* Principle 24c. Chicago: (author), 1973.

42. Lewis, *supra* note 14, at p. 383. For a thoughtful discussion of the adversary process (largely positive), see Slovenko, R. Psychiatric expert testimony and the adversary system, *Psychiatry and Law.* Boston: Little, Brown, 1973, pp. 18–39.

43. Note, The kiss of death—a psychiatrist testifying. 18 *Current Medicine for Attorneys* 15, 17–18, quoting Robitscher, J. Psychiatry 1969, *Medical World News,* Special Issue 1969; Test case, 73 *Newsweek* 94 (April 7, 1969). For psychologist's complete Rorschach protocol, *see* Appendix E in Kaiser, R. B. *RFK must die.* New York: Dutton, 1970.

44. A client may not usually demand the presence of legal counsel to protect against self-incrimination during expert examination or other "noncritical" stages of commitment proceedings or competency determinations. Thornton v. Corcoran, 407 F. 2d 695 (D.C. Cir. 1969); People v. Clark, 77 Cal. Rptr. 50 (1969). Now there is a tendency to permit counsel to be present during pretrial examination if requested by the person to be examined. A legal counsel has the right, when consulting with an accused person as a client, to be accompanied by a psychiatrist, psychologist, hypnotist, or similar practitioner. 72 A.L.R.2d 1120.

45. McGarry, et al. *Competency to stand trial and mental illness.* Washington, D.C.: NIMH, Center for Studies of Crime and Delinquency, U.S. Government Printing Office, 1973, p. 63. If a psychiatrist (or other practitioner) testifies as to the mental condition of a person s/he has *not* interviewed, three criteria must be met: (1) the psychiatrist must have observed the person in the jail or courtroom or both, (2) must have exceptional expertise and experience in the particular area involved (e.g., criminal competency) and (3) must be thoroughly familar with the case history or record of the person. Note, Inadequacies of physical examination by psychiatrist. 17 *Current Medicine for Attorneys* 28, 29 (Nov. 1970).

46. A standard reference source, with sample questions aimed at impugning the creditability of psychiatric and psychological witnesses, is Ziskin, J. *Coping with psychological and psychiatric testimony.* Los Angeles: Behavior and Science Books, 1973, pp. 208–277; excerpts are reprinted in 1 *Mental Disability Law Reporter* 165 (Sept.–Oct. 1976) aimed at excluding psychiatric testimony on dangerousness and showing that medical training is irrelevant to commitment decisions. *See also,* Schwartz & Stern, *supra* note 22 at 389 for procedural suggestions to be used by patients' advocate. Practitioner-oriented guides, with sample dialog, include Sadoff, R. L. *Forensic psychiatry: A practical guide.* Springfield, Ill.: Charles C Thomas, 1975; Brodsky, S. L. The mental health professional on the witness stand: A survival guide. In B. D. Sales (Ed.) *Psychology in the legal process,* New York: Spectrum, 1977, pp. 269–276. An extended verbatim cross-examination appears in R. C. Allen, E. Z. Ferster, and J. G. Rubin (Eds.) *Readings in law and psychiatry,* 2d ed. Baltimore: The Johns Hopkins Univ. Press, 1975, pp. 165–180. For detailed suggestions regarding standard courtroom procedure, as well as examples of testimony, see classic volume by Liebenson, H. A. and Wepman, J. M. *The psychologist as a witness.* Mundelein, Ill.: Callaghan, 1964.

47. Kaplan, supra note 39 at 3.
48. Personal communication of R. Langston, as reported by Poythress, N.C. Mental health expert testimony: Current problems. 5 *The Journal of Psychiatry and Law* 201, 218 (1977) (a general review of problems of law-mental health interaction in the courtroom).
49. Perr, I. N. Cross examination of the psychiatrist, Using publications. 5 *Bulletin of the American Academy of Psychiatry and the Law* 327, 328 (1977).
50. *Id.* at 328–330.
51. Brodsky, *supra* note 46, at pp. 2–4.
52. Note, Cross examination of specialists: Collateral attack of psychiatrists, 18 *Current Medicine for Attorneys* 15, 19 (Feb. 1970). Standard ploy: ask the witness how long s/he spent examining the client, then how long the witness spends with the *average nonlegal* client.
53. Federal Rules of Criminal Procedure, 18 U.S.C.A., Rule 32; People v. Amor, 202 N.W.2d 486 (Mich. App. 1972) (supporting court's requirement for background information).
54. Information in the pre-sentencing report typically includes (among other data) vital statistics, psychiatric history, nature of early home life, grades and achievement test scores, I.Q., dependability, antisocial behavior, willingness to refrain from future criminal activity, and general mood. Bailey, F. L. & Rothblatt, H. B. *Handling narcotic and drug cases.* San Francisco: Bancroft, Whitney Co., 1972, sec. 380.
55. Federal Rules of Criminal Procedure, 18 U.S.C.A., Rule 32(c); Bailey, *supra* note 54, at sec. 381.
56. People v. Drake, 290 N.Y.S.2d 629 (App. Div. 1968) (incomplete psychiatric report of rape offender stating that offender was incapable of understanding the charges, but without information on sexual proclivities).
57. Federal Rules of Criminal Procedure, 18 U.S.C.A., Rule 32(c); Cook v. Willingham, 400 F.2d 885 (10th Cir. 1968).
58. People v. Blakesley, 102 Cal. Rptr. 885, 888, n. 12 (Cal. App. 1972).

CHAPTER 15

Malpractice

The traditional ethic of the marketplace is "Let the buyer beware." In 1374, the first civil malpractice action on record was brought before an English court. It alleged that the plaintiff's hand had been maimed by the inept treatment of a physician. There is now general acceptance of the proposition that when the general public has need of a service (e.g. from engineers, physicians, accountants), but cannot be reasonably expected to have the knowledge to evaluate the quality of such service, the public must, of necessity, rely upon the representations and skill of those persons offering such service. This reliance places a duty upon the practitioner to act with reasonable care and skill.

The basic concept underlying malpractice is that of negligence. *Negligence* is conduct "which falls below the standard established by law for the protection of others against unreasonably great risk of harm."[1] In most situations, negligence is simply a carelessness on the part of the practitioner that makes him unaware of the harmful results which can follow from his action or lack of action. There is no intent to cause harm. There is merely the probability of injury, apparent from the facts of the situation, such that an "average reasonal man"[2] or practitioner would anticipate the injury and guard against it.

When an injury occurs because of negligence on the part of the practitioner, there seems to be particularly good reason to give the injured person some type of remedy. Thus, a tort action for malpractice is the means society has provided to give an injured party an opportunity for monetary compensation. *Malpractice* is the negligent (or otherwise improper) performance, by a professional person, of the duties that are incumbent upon him/her by reason of a professional relationship with a patient or client.[3] There must be an expressed or implied professional relationship at the time of the negligent behavior, and the burden of proving negligence rests with the plaintiff. A case illustrating this point occurred when a defendant psychologist, hired by a divorced mother, wrote a letter to her attorney recommending that the father of the child should be restricted in the number of visits. The psychologist had interviewed the child but not the plaintiff father. The court held that there was no malpractice based on negligent diagnosis because the father was not a patient, and therefore the psychologist owed no duty to him.[4]

The most frequent causes of malpractice actions against psychotherapists are:

1. Faulty or negligent rendering of services
2. Wrongful commitment
3. Slander and libel
4. Negligence leading to suicide
5. Birth control and abortion counseling
6. Electroshock or drug therapy
7. Sex or other "sensuous" therapies
8. Illegal search or violation of privacy
9. Nude encounter groups
10. Failure to properly supervise a disturbed client.[5]

Some of these matters will be raised in this chapter; others have been discussed previously in Chapters 1, 5, and 12.

NEGLIGENCE

Four elements are necessary to establish a course of action: a *duty* on the part of the practitioner, a *breach* of that duty, *actual loss* or injury, and a *causal relationship* between the breach of duty and the resultant injury.[6]

Duty

Professional individuals are required not only to exercise reasonable care in what they do, but to possess a "standard minimum of special knowledge and ability."[7] Standards for performance can be generated by custom, by statute, or by rules of practice of professional organizations. Custom is learned, presumably, in the course of training and internship. In most cases, custom is the primary means of establishing a standard of care in malpractice.[8] Traditionally, practitioners were expected to meet the standards of practice in the same or similar localities, but this "locality rule" is being abandoned, and general professional standards are being applied.[9]

Practitioners who claim to be specialists are held to higher standards than the usual practitioner.[10] "Even in jurisdictions which have not adopted a national standard for all malpractice issues, . . . specialists are required to exercise that degree of care and skill expected of a reasonably competent practitioner in his specialty acting in the same or similar circumstances."[11] No special training or skill is necessary to make the practitioner liable under the specialist's standard—the practitioner's own claim of skill is sufficient.

Psychiatrists are held to a higher standard than general medical practitioners when they are dealing with mental or behavioral problems. In *Christy* v. *Salitermann*,[12] a psychiatrist dismissed a patient from a hospital by telephone without seeing him. Heavy sedation was prescribed for use at home. Neither the patient or his family was warned about the powerful effects of the medication. During the night of his release, the heavily sedated patient set himself on fire with a cigarette, and was seriously burned. The court found the psychiatrist negligent for failing to evaluate the patient more carefully prior to discharge and for neglecting to warn the patient about the drug. The court did not apply the locality rule but instead held the psychiatrist responsible for meeting the national standards for the psychiatric specialty.

Violation of a statute is often a criminal offense, but sometimes a statute's primary purpose is to establish a standard for civil liability if the intent of the legislation was essentially to protect the class of individuals harmed.[13] Statutes and administrative regulations have been used in this manner to regulate methadone prescriptions by physicians.[14]

If a client reasonably believes that a practitioner has met the profession's requirements for licensing, then he may rightfully assume that the service he will receive conforms to the profession's standards.[15] In *Stone* v. *Procter*,[16] a psychiatrist administered a series of electroshock treatments to a patient who complained of severe pains in his lower back following the first treatment. Although some treatment was given for the pain, no X rays were taken to determine the possible cause of the pain. Despite the symptoms, the duration and intensity of electroshock treatment was increased. The court held that American Psychiatric Association "Standards of Electroshock Treatment" could be used as evidence of malpractice against this practitioner who was familiar with these standards and was a Fellow of the APA.

It should be noted that a practitioner does not have to conform perfectly to all published statutes, regulations, and professional codes to avoid liability. Reasonable modifications or deviations are permitted based on the particular circumstances of the case. Experts often disagree as to the best course of treatment, especially in psychotherapy. The "minimum common skill" of practitioners "in good professional standing" is the threshold criterion.[17] This criterion, in the opinion of experts or others, may be quite low or ambiguous. For example, it may be a common, but harmless, practice for psychiatric aides to sleep or doze at night instead of watching patients.[18] Can any implications be justifiably drawn about the quality of psychiatric care when an unlicensed clinical psychologist, posing as a psychiatrist at a state hospital, went undetected and "looked pretty good on the job" according to administrators?[19] One writer has asserted that prescribing psychoactive drugs without performing a medical examination and blood tests is a "dangerous practice," despite the relative rarity of such procedures among psychiatric practitioners.[20]

Practitioners are not required to conform their practices to the dominant or majority view in the profession, but their practice should generally be acceptable to a "respectable minority" or school within the profession. If not, then their practices might be characterized as experimental in nature, and clients or patients should be so informed.

The usual manner of determining what customary and acceptable practice is called for in a particular case is to use expert testimony (rather than textbooks, professional codes, etc.). In certain trial situations, the defendant practitioner himself may be called to the stand, qualified as an expert, and questioned as an adverse witness. In this way, a standard of care may be established from the defendant's own statements, and no "locality rule" limitation can be appealed to by the defense.

In areas of nonexpertise, a professional will be held only to a standard expected of a layman. Thus, an attorney who is not an expert in human psychology can be excused for failure to detect mental incompetence in a client,[21] and a school counselor may not be liable for failing to recognize suicide potential in a counselee.[22] In this latter case, a student committed suicide 40 days after counseling was terminated at the suggestion of the director of student personnel services of a state college. The student's parents charged that the director of the counseling and testing center for "personal, vocational, educational and other problems" should have recognized the emotional condition of the student. The Wisconsin Supreme Court affirmed the trial court's reasoning to the effect that: "To hold that a teacher who has no training, education, or experience in medical fields is required to recognize in a student a condition the diagnosis of which is in a specialized and technical medical field, would require a duty beyond reason."[23]

BREACH OF DUTY

Obviously, only where a standard of care can be established can a breach occur. Proving psychotherapeutic malpractice is quite difficult. Minimal standards of acceptable practice are poorly defined, the number of different "schools" or "respected minorities" is large, records are sparse or shielded by statutory claims of privileged communication, the client does not wish to have details of his personal life revealed, and so forth. Insurance company statistics estimate that the number of psychiatric malpractice claims is approximately one claim per 100 psychiatrists per year, and approximately 0.5 claim per 100 psychologists per year.[24] Most claims are settled out of court or dismissed by the court.[25] As mentioned earlier, the large majority of cases involve the negligent administration of electroconvulsive shock or drugs, problems of commitment or release from hospitals, and restraint or supervision of dangerous patients.[26] Psychologists and other mental health professionals are normally not responsible for decisions in these aspects of treatment, and hence have diminished liability; although a claim might be asserted against them for any involvement.[27] Areas of more probable claims against nonmedical therapists involve misdiagnosis, psychic trauma during encounter groups, failure to consult or refer to a specialist, injury from physical contact during psychotherapy, sexual relations, undue influence, violation of confidentiality, and fees charged.[28] ("Breach of contract" or an "intentional tort," rather than malpractice, may be a more relevant basis for some claims in such situations. These theories are mentioned briefly later in this chapter.) A survey of cases is presented below to illustrate these problem areas, although the claims asserted by the plaintiff were often not sustained.

Misdiagnosis. Suits have been successfully initiated for failure to recognize the suicide potential of a patient or counselee,[29] making a diagnosis without a first-hand examination,[30] and the failure to examine a patient for homicidal tendencies and follow-up by prescribing requested drugs.[31] Courts are generally concerned that examinations be conducted carefully, and negligent diagnoses (e.g., mistaking a physical disorder for an hysterical paralysis) have resulted in liability.[32] In *O'Neil* v. *State,*[33] a physician at a state hospital failed to discover a newly admitted patient's addiction to barbiturates although the patient mentioned taking a barbiturate and exhibited signs of barbiturate poisoning. Furthermore, the physician did not attempt to obtain medical records of the patient prior admission to the same hospital which would have shown that the symptoms were the result of drug abuse. The patient died within four days. In making an evaluation, care should also be taken to avoid relying upon hearsay in reaching conclusions. Statements by others about the client may be based on misunderstanding or hostility.[34]

Good faith or intention alone is not sufficient to avoid liability if a negligent assessment harms the patient or others. There is, however, some room for honest error. In discussing the "open door" philosophy of residential treatment facilities, a federal district court determined that "a physician is not an insurer of a successful cure; he may decide which of two or more approved methods to use in treating a patient, and will not be liable for honest mistakes or errors of judgment so long as he was exercising a reasonable degree of care and skill."[35] Or more succinctly: "Risks must be taken with mental patients, otherwise the case is left as hopeless."[36] Also, the practitioner's judgment is to be evaluated in view of the reasonable foreseeability of events at the time, not in the view provided by hindsight.

Encounter Groups/Sensitivity Training. Data regarding the rate of traumatic effects of encounter groups are fragmentary and contradictory. Reported "casualty" rates range from 0.1 to 9 percent.[37] Presumably, malpractice suits for physical and emotional injury have led to the establishment of standards for use of sensitivity group methods, and for recognition of competently trained group leaders.[38] An important document establishing guidelines of practice for psychologists has been published by the American Psychological Association.[39] (See Appendix KK.)

Consultation or Referral. When continued treatment has not assisted a patient, then there may be a legal duty to seek outside consultation or to discontinue the case after making proper referral. Cases on this point are rare, however, and within the practitioner's own area of competence there certainly appears to be no need to consult at the outset of treatment.[40] A practitioner is not liable for abandonment if s/he fails or refuses to treat a patient, assuming s/he is unable to provide needed specialized treatment and refers the patient to a specialist or if the practitioner dismisses the patient after sufficient notice to the person to allow alternate treatment plans to be made.[41]

Physical Contact During Psychotherapy. Probably the most frequently cited case is *Hammer* v. *Rosen*.[42] Dr. John Rosen, a psychiatrist well-known for his innovative and controversial "direct analysis" with schizophrenics, treated the patient for a period of seven years at a cost of over $55,000. Prior to treatment by Dr. Rosen, she had received between 150 and 200 electroshock treatments. Dr. Rosen allegedly struck or beat her on several occasions which might have caused her some unnecessary pain and suffering. The Court of Appeals of New York held that "a malpractice cause should be submitted to the jury because the beatings made out a prima facie case of malpractice which, if uncontradicted and unexplained and credited by the jury, would require a verdict for the plaintiff."[43]

In another well-known case, a psychologist conducted a "rage reduction" session during which the plaintiff was held down on her back on the laps of some eight to 12 people sitting on a couch. She asserted that for "twelve hours . . . [she was] choked and tortured and beaten and couldn't get out of the situation."[44] After the session, she suffered from acute anxiety, bruises, vomiting, and temporary renal failure of both kidneys. The plaintiff had signed a release which indicated that she had knowledge of only a possibility of superficial bruising and flaking of skin and not of psychological damage or severe bruising. The appellate court upheld a judgment against the defendant psychologist on the basis of a failure to meet an adequate standard of care during treatment and the inability of the defense to show that the patient had knowingly assumed the risks involved.[45] Damages have also been recovered where mental hospital attendants beat a patient.[46] Particular care should be taken if the patient is not an adult to avoid violation of child abuse statutes.

Sexual Relations. There is little doubt that some therapists occasionally have sex with their patients,[47] and at least one psychiatrist has proposed sexual intimacy as a legitimate aspect of treatment.[48] A leading case of an actionable injury arising from a sexual relationship during psychotherapy is *Zipkin* v. *Freeman* wherein the court decided that tbe psychiatrist mishandled the "transference" phenomenon.[49] In another appellate-level case,[50] the plaintiff husband of the patient claimed that the psychiatrist used the pretext of treatment over a period of two years to induce his wife into a sexual relationship and eventual divorce. The appellate court affirmed the trial court's summary judgment in favor of the defendant psychiatrist on the grounds that the husband's claim was in fact for "alienation of affection" that state statutes had abolished as a legitimate cause of action.

In *Whitesell* v. *Green,*[51] a psychologist was found legally liable as a result of his intimacy with a patient's wife. The patient had consulted the psychologist for marital counseling and contended that the psychologist's relationship with his wife was a breach of professional responsibility. Intimate relations with a patient's wife is certainly not, at present, a conventional or expected method of dealing with marital problems.

In *Roy* v. *Hartogs,*[52] a psychiatrist allegedly "administered" sexual inter-course to a woman for over one year to cure her lesbianism. The patient claimed that she was coerced into having sexual relations because of his overpowering influence and her reasonable trust in his competency. The court remanded the matter to a jury, stating that because the plaintiff consulted the defendant about sexual problems, the treatment prescribed was not palpably unreasonable and thereby might induce a patient to submit to sexual relations. The trial court assessed $25,000 in punitive damages. A dissenting judge noted, however, that the patient was capable of giving consent and did not complain until after the relationship was terminated.[53] Although consent does not mitigate liability for malpractice, it may act as a defense against claim of deception, fraud, or battery.

Criminal complaints, rather than civil actions, may be brought under a variety of statutes. For example, a psychiatrist was convicted of statutory rape for having intercourse with a 16-year-old promiscuous female sent to him for treatment.[54] The use of sexual surrogate partners[55] allows the possibility that prostitution, pandering, adultery and related offenses may be charged by a prosecutor or district attorney. But because legitimate "medical" sex clinics would not normally frustrate the legislative intent of prostitution statutes (e.g., to prevent economic exploitation and the spread of venereal disease), "their personnel and patients should not suffer from these potential liabilities."[56]

Even if no criminal or civil charges are brought against a therapist for sexual relationships with patients, there is still the possibility of the revocation of his/her license to practice. In *Morra* v. *State Board of Examiners of Psychologists,*[57] the court upheld a finding by the licensing board that a psychologist had violated the code of ethics of the American Psychological Association because of sexual impro-prieties with two patients, and his license was revoked. In a contrary split decision, the Colorado Supreme Court affirmed the trial court's holding that a physician's license should not be revoked for recommending extra-marital intercourse for a female patient suffering a psychological disorder, and then himself participating in the prescribed treatment.[58] A critical factor may be the degree to which therapeutic and nontherapeutic goals remain distinct. "Occurences in which therapists and patients do become involved in a meaningful and mature relationship are frequent enough to reflect that such may not be pathological and harmful. Therapists and patients have married or otherwise have become reasonably involved in a non-therapeutic relationship. This is not to be confused in any manner, however, with sexual activity entered into in the guise of therapy. If a personalized relationship develops, then alternative modes of therapy and referral elsewhere should be considered."[59]

Undue Influence. During therapy, the therapist may, without intention or conscious manipulation, become the object of hostile or affectionate responses. The affectionate responses may bring subsequent allegations of undue influence and unprofessional opportunism. These are most likely to involve estates left by older persons,[60] claims of alienation of affection by spouses,[61] and child enticement.[62] The essence of the concept of undue influence is that the fiduciary relationship has been violated by the dominant party who takes unfair advantage of the subservient party. Mental patients may be particularly susceptible to unfair suggestions or pressures because of irrational thought patterns. The majority of American courts will honor the transfer of property unless there has been some overt activity to procure such transfer by the therapist.[63]

   With respect to the counseling of youth, there is little or no risk in talking. But suggesting alternate courses of action to a minor (rather than merely supporting the minor's own plans) increases the probability of an allegation of undue influence. The greatest risk of civil action by aggrieved parents arises when the professional undertakes affirmative interference with parental control by giving financial support, providing alternate housing, or concealing the youngster's whereabouts.[64]

Violation of Confidentiality. A balance of competing duties is involved here: (1) the protection of the client's privileged communications, and (2) the reasonable expectation of third parties to be warned of potential dangers. As a general rule, a client's condition should not be disclosed unless necessary to protect the safety of others. When it can be reasonably foreseen that such disclosure will cause harm to the client, the matter should be discussed with the client in advance and, if necessary, efforts to restrain should be undertaken.[65]

Liability for Suicide or Homicide. In English common law, suicide was a felony; attempted suicide was a misdemeanor; and one who encouraged another was guilty of murder.[66] At the present time, the laws are ambiguous and conflicting. Both the person who attempts suicide and the practitioner rendering treatment *may* be subject to criminal and civil sanctions. Although a few states have in the past upheld convictions for attempted suicide,[67] most states have formulated rules specifically exempting suicide or attempted suicide from criminal offenses.[68] The trend is to remove criminal penalties, due in part to a plethora of logical entanglements.[69]

That a mental health practitioner may be civilly liable for the suicide of his/her patient is widely acknowledged at present, but the necessary conditions for attaching such liability are ambiguous. People are normally held responsible for their own acts. Hence, the courts are reluctant to find one person at fault for the behavior of another. Suicide is apparently one of a number of exceptions (e.g., parent-child relationships, and persons officially acting as agents) wherein "diminished capacity," "mental illness," "irresistible impulse," or a similar concept is used to shift some responsibility from the patient to the therapist.[70]

In conformity with the general rules of malpractice, the practitioner or hospital can be held to a standard of due care but is not an insurer that suicide will be prevented.[71] The following three factors determine professional liability:

Foreseeability of a Patient's Suicide Attempt. The degree to which a suicide attempt is foreseeable varies and is almost always subject to speculation or subjective judgment. If, for example, a docile or cheerful patient runs away from a hospital and subsequently dies of exposure or jumps off a boat, the institution would probably not be liable.[72] Similarly, a practitioner who failed to recognize the suicide potential of a violent or homicidal person might not be liable.[73] Even when a patient has received extensive evaluation and treatment prior to release, the therapist may not be liable for an error in assessment of future dangerousness to self and others, due to the difficulty of predicting dangerousness.[74]

Attempted suicide and hoarding of pills at home for the purpose of attempting suicide has not been sufficient to create liability after the patient was placed on a semi-open ward.[75] The courts have traditionally hesitated to intrude upon matters of professional opinion. If, however, a patient has been actively suicidal on a ward or a teenage training school resident is physically punished and left alone, then liability may be found because an unfortunate result is reasonably foreseeable.[76]

Reasonableness of Professional Judgment in Directing a Course of Treatment. The failure to exercise proper precaution, when it is recognized that the patient is a threat to himself, is lack of "due care."[77] The more obvious and severe the patient's suicidal tendencies, the greater the potential liability for not following through on some preventative measures. In a mild or "hidden" case, a simple error of professional judgment may absolve the practitioner. In a severely depressed patient, some requirement of hospitalization, drug therapy and/or general observation might be expected (although the particular choice of treatment would be a matter of option). For an actively suicidal person, placement in a high security hospital ward with removal of glass or other potentially destructive objects may be viewed as a reasonable standard of care.[78] In the past, a few cases indicated that the required standard of care of a suicidal patient was "close observation, restriction, and restraint," but "this standard of care has fallen into complete disrepute in modern hospitals as being antitherapeutic and so aggravating of feelings of worthlessness as to possibly provoke suicidal acts."[79]

Dependability with which Directions are Carried Out. Once a course of treatment has been undertaken, then a duty is imposed on the practitioner to act without negligence. If a known high suicide risk patient should be placed on the second floor of a hospital near an open window, then ordinary or common-sense negligence would seem to make a hospital logically liable regardless of ambiguities of psychological treatment strategies or claims of "open door" policy, etc.[80] In jurisdictions where suicide is not a crime, constitutional safeguards of individual liberty might be broadly interpreted to restrain a third party from preventing self-destruction.[81] It would seem that the claim to such a right, if it exists at all, could only be asserted if the treatment restraints were excessive or more than temporary.

The duty a practitioner has in a given case may extend beyond that of rehabilitation of the patient. If the patient poses a danger to others, the practitioner may be required to warn those endangered or at least to follow a treatment plan if one has been authorized by a court. A psychiatrist, probation officer, and private psychiatric institute were found negligently liable for the death of a young woman slain by a mental patient after he had been put on out-patient status despite a court probation order "that he continue to receive treatment at and remain confined in the psychiatric institute until released by the Court."[82] The appeals court rejected the defense contention that transfer from daily supervision as a day-care patient (which was approved by the court) to twice-a-week group therapy as an out-patient was a normal treatment progression requiring no court approval. (The patient lived alone, and medication was not effectively monitored.)

There is, apparently, no duty to warn relatives of a potentially suicidal patient. In declining to extend *Tarasoff*,[83] an appellate court ruled that a psychiatrist was not liable to the parents of a patient who had suicidal tendencies for not disclosing such tendencies to the parents.[84] The court in this case noted that *Tarasoff* did not require disclosure of a confidence in instances of *self-inflicted* harm, and further, that the therapist's failure to commit the patient or restrain her from committing suicide did not render him liable.

ACTUAL LOSS OR INJURY

Proof of damage is an essential element in proving malpractice. Nominal damages, to technically vindicate a civil right, cannot be awarded to the plaintiff where no actual harm has occurred.[85] This is in contrast to intentional torts (e.g., battery) where nominal damages can be awarded for an offensive act even without injury.

Causal Connection Between Negligent Act and the Injury

The plaintiff has the burden of showing a reasonably close connection between the practitioner's conduct and the resulting injury. This connection is commonly referred to as "proximate cause."[86] Because the "natural" course of an individual's psychological disturbance—without the alleged malpractice—is difficult to state with a reasonable degree of certainty, the fact that a psychological injury has occurred due to the application or omission of some procedure is almost impossible to prove.[87] "Proximate cause" is most easily shown when the alleged negligence prompted the patient to sustain or inflict tangible physical injuries on himself or others.[88] Even then, the nature or circumstances of the injury must have been foreseeable.[89]

REMEDIES

An injured party may seek remedy through civil action, a criminal complaint, or professional disciplinary action. The usual burden in a civil action rests with the plaintiff to show that an alternate course of treatment would have prevented the alleged injury. Because of the difficulty of this proof, the plaintiff may invoke the doctrine of *res ipsa loquitur* ("the fact speaks for itself") which may meet the burden of proof. A situation, on the face of it, may appear so harmful, that a presumption or inference of negligence is established, thus requiring the practitioner to come up with a convincing explanation for the injury.[90] Usually, however, psychiatric patients have not been permitted this liberal method of proof.[91] Contributory negligence on the part of the patient may not be sufficient to block a claim,[92] but generally a defense to malpractice is quite strong due to the (a) relatively unreliable standards of diagnosis and treatment of psychological disorders, (b) difficulty of establishing proximate cause, (c) reluctance of expert witnesses, and (d) governmental immunities.[93] In some situations, a public employee will be liable for proximately caused negligent injuries, and the state agency must pay the judgment—but only if the practitioner is licensed in one of the healing arts (including psychology).[94] This distinction may be very important in determining the size of an award which could be collected, the lawyer's potential contingency fee, and so forth.

There is some tendency away from attempts to prove "good faith" mistakes of malpractice. The intentional tort actions of breach of warranty, assault and battery, libel, false imprisonment[95] offer alternative possibilities. The tactical advantage of intentional torts for the plaintiff is that expert testimony, foreseeability of injury, or actual damage are not always required in proof.

Under contract theory, the plaintiff will look for some implied or express promise which has been breached. In the absence of such warranty, the practitioner will not be liable for an honest mistake of judgment, where the proper course of treatment is open to reasonable doubt.[96] As a rule, a contract is not constitutionally valid if it, in advance, exempts the practitioner from claims of negligence. For example, a hospital may not require all patients to sign a contract as a condition of admission that they will not sue the hospital or hold any of its employees liable for negligence.[97] In states which have statutory provisions for professional corporations, members are not held liable for torts of an associate, as is the case in a professional association or partnership.[98]

Conformity to established standards of professional conduct are often considered an implicit term in a contract between a professional and his/her client.[99] If a professional does not act in a manner consistent with these standards, his/her failure to perform all or part of what was promised may allow compensatory damages sufficient to put the client in a position as good as he would have been in had the professional performed up to standard. (Punitive damages are not allowed in a breach of contract.)[100]

Both client and practitioner may want to consider the possibility of preventing malpractice litigation by agreeing to binding arbitration prior to treatment and as part of a private contract.[101]

One writer summarized the malpractice situation as follows: "While psychotherapists have been inventive and daring in the choice of treatment, so too have attorneys in choosing theories of liability."[102] Although good intentions alone are not sufficient to avoid malpractice liability, the probability of a successful claim is small.[103]

NOTES

1. *Restatement of the Law, Second, Torts.* Philadelphia: American Law Institute, 1967, sec. 282.
2. This mythical individual, "the average, reasonable man," offers great opportunities for forensic psychometricians (if such exist). Courts have held that this man will know the law of gravity, his own physical size, principles of balance and leverage, dangers of firearms, normal habits of children, that alcoholic beverages are intoxicating, and so forth. (*cf.*, Prosser, W. L. *The law of torts,* 4th ed. St. Paul, Minn.: West Publishing Co., 1971, pp. 158–159 and generally ch. 5). "[T]his excellent but odious character stands like a monument in our Court of Justice, vainly appealing to his fellow citizens to order their lives after his own example. . . . In all that mass of authority which bears on this branch of law, there is no single mention of a reasonable woman." Herbert, A. P. *Misleading cases in common law.* London: Methuen Press, 1930, pp. 12–16, cited in Prosser, *id.* at 150. The practitioner is usually held to a higher standard of care than the average, reasonable man or woman.
3. *Cochran's law lexicon,* 5th ed. Cincinnati, Ohio: W. H. Andersen Co., 1973, p. 189.
4. Chatman v. Millis, 517 S.W.2d 504 (Ark. 1975).
5. Adapted from Van Hoose, W. H. and Kottler, J. A. *Ethical and legal issues in counseling and psychotherapy.* San Francisco: Jossey-Bass, 1977, p. 98.

6. Prosser, *supra* note 2, at 143. *See also,* Dawidoff, D. J. *The malpractice of psychiatrists: Malpractice in psychoanalysis, psychotherapy and psychiatry.* Springfield, Ill.: Charles C Thomas, 1973.

7. Prosser, *supra* note 2, at 161.

8. Note, An evaluation of changes in the medical standards of care. 23 *Vanderbilt Law Review* 729 (1970).

9. Duckworth, G. F. Torts: Medical malpractice: Expert testimony as affected by the "locality rule," 26 *Oklahoma Law Review* 296 (1973). *See,* for example, Morgan v. Sheppard, 188 N.E.2d 808, 816 (Ohio App. 1963) (liability for death of postsurgical patient despite local custom of prescription by telephone).

10. *E.g.* Kronke v. Danielson, 499 P.2d 156 (Ariz. 1972).

11. Robbins v. Footer, 553 F.2d 123, 129 (D.C. Cir. 1977).

12. 179 N.W.2d 288 (Minn. 1970).

13. Prosser, *supra* note 2, at 191; Rosenfeld v. Coleman, Pa. D.& C.2d 635, 645 (1959) (psychiatrist's violation ov Anti-Narcotics Act may be considered evidence of negligence).

14. Blinder v. California, 101 Cal. Rptr. 635 (1972).

15. Note, Professional negligence. 121 *University of Pennsylvania Law Review* 628 (1973); Note, The use of "Codes" of private professional societies to prove malpractice. 16 *Current Medicine for Attorneys* 29 (1969).

16. 259 N.C. 633, 131 S.E.2d 297 (1963); Tarshis, C.B. Liability for psychotherapy. 30 *Faculty of Law Review* 75 (1972).

17. Prosser, *supra* note 2, at 163.

18. Auditors make spot-check of psychiatric centers. *New York Times.* June 26, 1977, p. 14.

19. See case of Carmi Bar-Ilan, graduate of Hebrew University and the University of Michigan in psychology, who practiced more than one year as staff psychiatrist, *in* The two Dr. Polatins, 91 *Newsweek* 51 (Apr. 17, 1978). Psychiatrist David Viscott reportedly charged that "about 20 to 30 percent of the psychiatrists practicing in this country today are quacks who're doing their patients more harm than good." 50 *National Inquirer* 29 (Oct. 7, 1975). The charge was not empirically substantiated. The quality of service of psychologists, social workers, probation officers and others might be equally or even more suspect.

20. Appleton, W. S. Psychotherapist prescribing a drug in his office. 16 *Medical Trial Technique Quarterly* 33, 35 (1969); Note, An evaluation of changes in the medical standards of care, 23 *Vanderbilt Law Review* 729 (1970).

21. Everett v. Downing, 298 Ky. 195, 182 S.W.2d 232 (1944).

22. Bogust v. Iverson, 10 Wis. 2d 129, 102 N.W.2d 1003 (1960).

23. *Id.* at 1007. What if the defendant was a licensed school psychologist, marriage and family counselor, or a social worker at a suicide prevention center? Is estimation of suicide potential (or proneness to violence, drug addiction, fire-setting, rape) exclusively or partly the expected function of medically-trained professionals? The American Personnel and Guidance Association and the National Education Association prepared briefs on behalf of this successful defendant, thus supporting suicide assessment as a medical procedure.

24. Trent, C. L. Psychiatric malpractice insurance and its problems: An overview. In W. E.

Barton and C. J. Sanborn (Eds.) *Law and the mental health professions*. New York: International Universities Press, 1978, pp. 101–113. News item: Malpractice insurance carrier receiving approximately 25 cases per year for psychologists between 1974 and 1976, as reported in 6 *Behavior Today* 4 (March 8, 1976).

25. Slawson, P. F. Psychiatric malpractice: A regional incidence study, 126 *American Journal of Psychiatry* 1302, 1303 (1970).

26. Trent, *supra* note 24, and Chapter 13 at notes 64 and 65. Also, Louisell, D. and Williams, H. *Trial of medical malpractice cases,* 2d ed. Albany, NY: Mathew Bender, 1971 supplement, Appendix A.

27. Merchants National Bank & Trust Co. v. U.S., 272 F. Supp. 409 (D.N.D. 1967) ($200,000 judgment against a psychologist and two psychiatrists for failing to warn employer of danger resulting in subsequent injury to a third party).

28. *See* Harris, M. Tort liability of the psychotherapist. 8 *University of San Francisco Law Review* 405, 412 (Winter 1973).

29. Brogust v. Iverson, 102 N.W.2d 1003 (1960). Baker v. U.S., 226 F. Supp. 129 (S.D. Iowa 1964), *aff'd* 343 F.2d 222 (8th Cir. 1965).

30. Daniels v. Finney, 262 S.W.2d 431 (Tex. Civ. App. 1953).

31. McCord v. State, Nos. 43404–07 (N.Y. Ct. Cl., Feb. 7, 1968) and 43405–07 (Aug. 21, 1969).

32. Brown v. Moore, 247 F.2d 711 (3rd Cir. 1957). *See also* DiGiovanni v. Pessel, 250 A.2d 756 (N.J. 1968); Beckham v. Cline, 10 So.2d 419 (Fla. 1942).

33. 323 N.Y.S.2d 56 (Ct. Cl. 1971).

34. Kleber v. Stevens, 241 N.Y.S.2d 497 (Sup. Ct. 1963) (vindictive husband).

35. Johnson v. United States, 409 F.Supp. 1283, 1292 (M.D. Fla. 1976); Rosario v. State, 305 N.Y.S. 574 (Supr. Ct. App. Div. N.Y. 1969) (several years of hospitalization due to wrong professional judgment). *See generally* Note, Liability of mental hospitals for acts of their patients on the open door policy. 57 *Virginia Law Review* 156 (1965).

36. Eanes v. United States, 407 F.2d 823, 829 (4th Cir. 1969).

37. Gibb, J. R. The effects of human relations training. In A. E. Bergin and S. L. Garfield (Eds.) *Handbook of psychotherapy and behavior change*. New York: Wiley, 1971, p. 856 ("The evidence is clear that the reputed dangers of sensitivity training are greatly exaggerated.") National Training Laboratory, News Release, as reported in Black, K. W. *Beyond words*. New York: Russell Sage Foundation, 1972, p. 219 (25 serious psychiatric incidents out of 11,000 participants in 22 years of summer programs; eight incidents out of 3000 participants in 13 years of industrial programs—0.2 to 0.3 percent rate). Ross, W. D., Kligfeld, M., Witman, R. W. Psychiatrists, patients and sensitivity groups, 25 *Archives of General Psychiatry* 178 (1971) (questionnaire to psychiatrists showed that 0.66 percent of 2900 group participants became acutely ill). *Contra:* Lieberman, M., Yalom, I., and Mills, M. *Encounter groups: First facts*. New York: Basic Books, 1973, as excerpted in 6 *Psychology Today* 69, 74 (1973) (9 percent "casualty rate" in 179 encounter group participants compared to zero rate in control group; "damage rate" of 19 percent, including negative changes and casualties, twice as large as overall negative impact of traditional psychotherapies). *See generally,* Hartley, D., Roback, H. B., and Abramowitz, S. I. Deterioration effects in encounter groups. 31 *American Psychologist* 247 (March 1976) (survey of literature).

38. *Standards for the use of laboratory methods in NTL institutional programs.*

Washington, D.C.: National Training Lab, 1969; APA Task Force on Recent Developments in the Use of Small Groups, *Encounter groups and psychiatry*. Washington, D.C.: American Psychiatric Assn., 1970; American Psychological Assn., *infra,* note 39; Note, Standards of care in administration of nontraditional psychotherapy. 7 *Univ. of California—Davis Law Review* 56 (1974).

39. American Psychological Association, Guidelines for psychologists conducting growth groups, 28 *American Psychologist* 933 (1973).

40. Landau v. Werner (QB March 7, 1961; 105 Solicitor's Journal 1008 [C.A. 1961]) (English court awarded £6,000 to plaintiff suggesting that at the moment when the psychiatrist had "fallen in love" with the plaintiff patient, he should have withdrawn from treatment and made referral); Gasperini v. Mangenelli, 196 Misc. 547, 92 N.Y.S.2d 575 (Sup. Ct. 1949) (psychiatrist need not call in consulting psychiatrist upon commencing treatment); *cf.* Dawidoff, *supra* note 6, at 74.

41. Brandt v. Grubin, 329 A.2d 82 (Super. Ct. N.J. 1974).

42. 7 App. Div. 2d 216, 181 N.Y.S.2d 805, *modified* 7 N.Y.2d 376, 165 N.E.2d 756 (1960). For a general treatment rationale, *see* Rosen, J. N. *Direct analysis.* New York: Grune, 1953.

43. Hammer v. Rosen, *supra* note 42, at 757.

44. Abraham v. Zaslow. 1 Civil 33219, Sup. Ct. No. 245862, 1st Distr., Cal. App. (Feb. 2, 1975) at p. 3.

45. *Id.* at 11, 13. Tape recordings of the session made by the psychologist were used during trial but the plaintiff did not testify due to her inability to "withstand the strain of testifying or discussing her condition with a stranger" according to her psychiatrist. *Id.* at 5.

46. Davis v. N.Y., 332 N.Y.S.2d 569 (N.Y. 1972) (15-year-old boy died after beating by two attendants). Traver v. Feinstein, 331 N.Y.S.2d 150 (App. Div. 1972) (dismissal of employee who struck and choked retarded patients). Intentional torts and criminal charges may also be actionable in such cases.

47. A survey involving 114 psychiatrists found that 5 percent of those responding had reportedly engaged in sexual intercourse (with one and usually no more than five patients). Kardener, S. H., Fuller, M. and Mensh, I. N. A survey of physician's attitudes and practices regarding erotic and nonerotic contact with patients. 130 *American Journal of Psychiatry* 1077, 1079–1080 (Oct. 1973). *Also,* Doe v. Roe, 165 *New York Law Journal,* No. 93, p. 19 (May 14, 1971) (former therapist sought to prevent adoption of a patient's child whom he fathered).

48. Shepard, M. The love treatment: Sexual intimacy between patients and psychotherapist. New York: Peter H. Wyden, 1971. *Cf. also,* Dahlberg, C. C. Sexual contact between patient and therapist. *Contemporary Psychoanalysis* (Spring 1970).

49. 436 S.W.2d 753, 761 (Mo. 1968) *en banc.* One expert witness in this case stated that "A psychiatrist should no more take an overnight trip with a patient than shoot her. . . ."

50. Nicholson v. Han, 12 Mich. App. 35, 162 N.W.2d 313 (1968). *Cf.,* Annot., Civil liability of doctor or psychologist for having sexual relations with patients, 33 A.L.R.2d 1393.

51. Whitesell v. Green, Hawaii Dist. Ct., Honolulu, Docket No. 38745 (Nov. 19, 1973).

52. Roy v. Hartogs, 366 N.Y.S.2d 297 (N.Y.C. Civ. Ct. 1975). *See also* Freeman, L and

Roy, J. *Betrayal*. New York: Stein & Day, 1976; "Love thy analyst," 105 *Time* 76 (March 24, 1975).

53. 381 N.Y.S.2d 587, 591 (Sup. Ct. App. Term 1976). Although the defendant psychiatrist presented evidence of a physical disability that would have prevented sexual intercourse, a later court asserted that the defendant had "prescribed and personally administered multiple, repetitive doses of *"fornicatus Hartogus"* to the patient. Hartogs v. Employers Ins., 89 Misc.2d 468 (N.Y. Sup. Ct. 1977).

54. People v. Burnstein, 340 P.2d 299 (Ct. App. Cal. 1939).

55. Partners were used in 41 cases by Johnson and Masters for single male patients. Johnson, V. E. and Masters, W. H. *Human sexual inadequacy*. New York: Norton (New American Library), 1971, p. 147.

56. Leroy, D. H. The potential criminal liability of human sex clinics. 16 *St. Louis University Law Journal* 586, 599.

57. Morra v. State Board of Examiners of Psychologists, 510 P.2d 614 (Kan. 1973).

58. Colorado State Board of Medical Examiners v. Weiler, 402 P.2d 606 (Col. 1965). Do therapists make themselves equally available to physically unattractive patients when paid for therapy? What about female therapists and male patients? Or same-sex relationships when harmlessly desired by the patient? Dawidoff, *supra* note 6, at 92 commented: "What the court in *Landau v. Werner (supra* note 40) may be telling us is that the intimacies of the psychiatrist/patient relationship may be all right so long as the patient remains the initiator."

59. Perr, I. N. Legal aspects of sexual therapies. 3 *The Journal of Legal Medicine* 33, 38 (1975).

60. Kurt Eissler reported that a suit was brought against him by relatives of a patient who left him, at her death and while in treatment, a substantial estate. Eissler, K. *The psychiatrist and the dying patient*. New York: International Universities Press, 1955, p. 150f. *See also, In re* Faulks' Will, 246 Wis. 319, 17 N.W.2d 423 (1945) (legacy left to young physician); *In re* Pitt's Estate, 88 Ariz. 312, 356 P.2d 408 (1960) (estate left to lawyer).

61. Nicholson v. Han, 12 Mich. App. 35, 162 N.W.2d 313 (1968).

62. McEntee v. N. Y. Foundling Hospital, 21 Misc. 2d 903, 194 N.Y.S.2d 2969 (Sup. Ct. 1954) (child placement agency prevented natural mother from seeing child).

63. Shaffer, T. L. Undue influence, confidential relationships, and the psychology of transference, 45 *Notre Dame Lawyer* 197, 235 (1969–70). A minority rule raises a presumption of undue influence in every case of a confidential relationship, and thereby shifts the burden of proof to the professional. *Id.*, also *In re* Wood's Estate, 374 Mich. 278, 132 N.W.2d 35 (1965).

64. Note, Counseling the counselors: Legal implications of counseling minors without parental consent. 31 *Maryland Law Review* 335, 353 (1971). Apparently most courts are refusing to impose liability even on physicians who prescribe contraceptive services to minors without parental consent. *Id.*

65. Berry v. Moench, 8 Utah 2d 191, 331 P.2d 814 (1958) (psychiatrist held liable for disclosing his diagnosis of psychopathic personality of a former patient to the family physician and parents of the patient's fiancée); Furniss v. Fitchett (1958) New Zealand Law Reports 396 (Sup. Ct.) (psychiatrist held liable for sending unauthorized report of patient's condition to her husband used later in a legal action); *compare* Clark v. Geraci,

208 N.Y.S.2d 564 (N.Y. 1960) (action dismissed against psychiatrist for revealing to an employer that a patient was an alcoholic when patient initiated the request); Merchants National Bank and Trust Company v. U.S., 272 F. Supp. 409 (D.N.D. 1967) (duty to warn employer of dangerous propensities); Tarasoff v. Regents of University of California, 108 Cal. Rptr. 878 (Cal. 1972) (duty to warn potential third-party victim).

66. In a famous English case, two persons encouraged each other to drown themselves, and both plunged into the water by mutual agreement, whereupon one was drowned while the other was saved. The survivor was found guilty of the murder of the deceased. Rex v. Dyson, Russ & Ry. 523, 168 Eng. Rep. 930 (1823), cited in Perkins, R. M. *Criminal law,* 2d ed. Mineola, N.Y.: The Foundation Press, 1969, p. 83.

67. New Jersey v. LaFayette, 117 N.J.L. 442, 188 Atl. 918 (C.P. Camden County 1937); North Carolina v. Willis, 225 N.C.473, 121 N.E.2d 854 (1961); *see also,* Wallace v. Indiana, 232 Ind. 700, 116 N.E.2d 100 (1953); Prudential Insurance Co. of New York v. Petril, 43 F. Supp. 768, 771 (E.D. Pa. 1942). For general reference *see* Schulman, R. E. Suicide and suicide prevention: A legal analysis, 54 *American Bar Association Journal* 855 (1968).

68. *E.g.,* Iowa v. Campbell, 217 Iowa 848, 251 N.W. 717 (1933); Maine Rev. Stat. Ann., title 17, sec. 251 (1964); Vermont Stat. Ann., title 13, sec. 9 (1953).

69. If, for example, a felony is ''any crime punishable by death or imprisonment in the state prison,'' the deceased cannot be so punished and the person who attempted suicide (if an honest effort) might readily accept the death sentence. At common law, the decedant's estate was given to the State, but this punishes the survivors more than the decedant. Furthermore, some jurisdictions require that the accused in order to stand trial must *not* suffer from a ''mental disease or disorder.''

70. Slawson, P. F., Flinn, D. E., and Schwartz, D. A. Legal responsibility for suicide, 48 *The Psychiatric Quarterly* 50, 60 (1974).

71. Dawidoff, D. J., *supra* note 6, at 132.

72. Dahlberg v. Jones, 232 Wis. 6, 285 N.W. 841 (1939) (exposure); Dalton v. State, 308 N.Y.S.2d 441 (Sup. Ct. of N.Y. App. 1970) (jump from ferry boat).

73. Hernandez v. Baruch, 232 A.2d 661 (1967), 244 A.2d 109 (N.J. Sup. Ct. 1968).

74. Johnson v. United States, 409 F. Supp. 1283 (M.D. Fla. 1976).

75. Katz v. State, 46 Misc. 2d 61, 258 N.Y.S.2d 912 (Ct. Cl. 1965).

76. Hunt v. King County, 481 P.2d 593 (Wash. App. 1971) (hospital patient); McBride v. State, 52 Misc. 2d 880, 277 N.Y.S.2d 80 (Ct. Cl. 1967) *aff'd on other grounds,* 30 App. Div. 1025, 294 N.Y.S.2d 265 (1968) (training school resident).

77. Collins v. State, 32 App. Div. 2d 898, 258 N.Y.S.2d 938 (1965).

78. Robitscher, J. The depresssed patient and physician responsibility, 72 *Pennsylvania Medicine* 87 (Nov. 1969); *also* Schwartz, V. E. Civil liability for causing suicide, 24 *Vanderbilt Law Review* 217, 252–254 (1971).

79. Perr, I. N. Suicide responsibility of hospitals and psychiatrists. 9 *Cleveland-Marshall Law Review* 427, 439–40 (1960). Perr, I. N. Suicide and civil litigation. 19 *Journal of Forensic Sciences* 261 (1974).

80. Meier v. Ross General Hospital, 69 Cal. 2d 420, 445 P.2d 519 (1968); Schwartz, *supra* note 78, at 251.

81. Bellah v. Greenson, 1 Civ. No. 39770 (Cal. Oct. 5, 1977), *as reported in* 2 *Mental Disability Law Reporter* 176 (Sept/Dec. 1977) (no duty to actively restrain outpatient).

The suicide crisis is "often a matter of only minutes or hours at the most. . . . Of those who attempted suicide and failed, only 10 percent killed themselves later." Summary of report by Seiden, R. *Suicide: Preventable death,* in "Newsline," 8 *Psychology Today* 138 (Dec. 1974).

82. Semler v. Wadeson, No. 74–2345/2346 (4th Cir. Feb. 27, 1976) as reported in 1 *Mental Disability Law Reporter* 29 (July-Aug. 1976) ($25,000 judgment for breach of duty to comply with court order).

83. Tarasoff v. Regents of the University of California, 131 Cal. Rptr 13 (1976).

84. Bellah, *supra* note 81.

85. Prosser, *supra* note 2, at 143.

86. Much good material exists here for psychological debates—that is, what is a "reasonably close connection"? The majority of cases say that if a person is injured, becomes insane, and commits suicide without any obvious intervening force, the defendant will be liable. If, however, the person is injured, does *not* become insane but his life becomes unbearable, then his voluntary choice of suicide is "an abnormal thing which supercedes the defendant's liability." Prosser, *supra* note 2, at 280–281.

87. *E.g.,* Eisele v. Malone, 2 App. Div. 2d 550, 157 N.Y.S.2d 155 (1957) (plaintiff's claim dismissed that hospital was negligent for not having X ray facilities available to diagnose injury following shock therapy because such lack not shown "directly related to and causative of plaintiff's condition"). *Similarly,* Milano v. State, 44 Misc. 2d 290, 253 N.Y.S.2d 662 (Ct. Cl. 1964) (failure to administer Rorschach test).

88. Rothblatt, H. B. & Leroy, D. H. Avoiding psychiatric malpractice. 9 *California Western Law Review* 260, 264 (Winter 1973); for example, Underwood v. U.S., 356 F.2d 92 (5th Cir. 1966) (mentally ill airman released to duty and given permission to draw pistol and ammunition with which he killed his former wife); White v. U.S., 317 F.2d 13 (4th Cir. 1963) (hospital held liable for death by self-inflicted wounds of suicidal patient).

89. Hunt v. King County, 481 P.2d 593 (Wash. App. 1971) (hospital held liable for reasonably foreseeable jump from unbarred window of acutely psychotic suicidal patient); *compare,* Dunn v. State, 29 N.Y.2d 313, 327 N.Y.S.2d 622, 277 N.E.2d 647 (1971) (hospital not held liable when an escaped patient, being chased in a stolen vehicle by police, killed the driver of another vehicle).

90. Meier v. Ross General Hospital, 69 Cal. 2d 420, 445 P.2d 519, 71 Cal. Rptr. 903, *vacating* 67 Cal. Rptr. 471 (Dist. Ct. App. 1968) (reversed for plaintiff on grounds that *res ipsa loquitur* should not be foreclosed even if deceased patient voluntarily committed suicide due to hospital's negligence).

91. Rothblatt, H. B. & Leroy, D. H., *supra* note 88, at 264.

92. *Id.*

93. *E.g.,* Hernandez v. California, 11 Cal. App. 3d 895, 900, 90 Cal. Rptr. 205, 209 (1970) (immunity from action of ex-hospital patient who killed his mother); Cawthon v. Coffer, 264 So. 2d 873 (Fla. 1972) (court-appointed psychiatrist held immune against claim of cursory examination without psychometric evaluation of committed mental patient).

94. *E.g.,* Cal. Govt. Code 854.8.

95. Stowers v. Wolodsko, 191 N.W.2d 355 (Mich. 1971) ($40,000 damage awarded against psychiatrist on grounds of false imprisonment and assault and battery for forcibly preventing temporarily committed patient from calling relatives or attorney).

96. Prosser, *supra* note 2, at 162.

97. Tunkel v. Regents of the University of California, 383 P.2d 441 (Cal. 1963).

98. *E.g.,* Pa. Stat. Annot. title 15, sec. 2901–14 (Supp. 1972); Calif. Bus. & Professions Code, sec. 2996.6 (West's 1971).

99. *University of Pennsylvania Law Review, supra* note 15, at 679; Farnsworth, E. A. Implied warranties of quality in non-sales cases. 57 *Columbia Law Review* 653 (1957); Dawidoff, *supra* note 6, at 11–18 (implied contract and fiduciary relationship). Doe v. San Francisco Unified School District, No. 653–312 (Super. Ct. Cal., filed Oct. 31, 1973) (suit against school and teachers claiming they breached duty to instruct because plaintiff's son graduated high school but unable to read and get a job); *In re* H., 66 Misc. 2d 1097, 323 N.Y.S.2d 302 (Family Ct., Westchester Co. 1971) (lack of progress of son in special education program due to poor instruction).

100. Except perhaps where defendant acted maliciously and damaged plaintiff's character. Simpson, L. P. *Law of contracts,* 2d ed. St. Paul: West Publishing Co., 1965, p. 394.

101. *See generally,* Henderson, S. D. Arbitration and medical services: Securing the promise to arbitrate malpractice. 28 *The Arbitration Journal* 14 (March 1973).

102. Harris, M. Tort liability of the psychotherapist. 8 *University of San Francisco Law Review* 405, 411 (1973–74).

103. Slawson, P. F. and Flinn, D. E. Hospital liability for suicide: A regional survey. 5 *The Bulletin of the American Academy of Psychiatry and the Law* 29, 32 (1977) (over a five year period, 27 psychiatric facilities reported 49 suicides with only four out of 10 litigations going to court).

16

Litigation: Actions, Defenses, and Remedies

In July 1964, *Fact* magazine sent a questionaire to 12,356 psychiatrists asking:

> Do you believe Barry Goldwater is psychologically fit to serve as President of the United States?
>
> [ ] No   [ ] Yes

A cover letter referred to Senator Goldwater's "two nervous breakdowns"—a "fact" subsequently refuted, based only on two previous magazine articles by Alvin Toffler.[1] Despite a prior warning to the magazine from the American Psychiatric Association,[2] numerous edited letters from the 2417 respondents were published along with demeaning cartoons. For example: "In my opinion, the personality weakness that forces Goldwater to extreme opinions would make him a dangerous President.—Harrington V. Ingham, M.D., Assoc. Professor of Psychiatry, U.C.L.A."[3] The results of the poll were evaluated only by the magazine's editor, Ralph Ginsburg, who "had taken two college courses in psychology and had read various books on the subject."[4]

Goldwater filed a libel and slander suit charging that Ginsburg had maliciously published falsehoods. According to case law in New York State, a false accusation of "insanity, mental imbalance, or mental disease" is libelous.[5] Goldwater was awarded one dollar in compensatory damages and $75,000 in punitive damages. ("Compensatory" damages are designed to remunerate an individual for expenses incurred, lost wages, irrestorable bodily injury. "Punitive" or "exemplary" damages punish the defendant for misconduct.[6])

This notorious, though unusual, case illustrates one of several causes of action that an injured party may assert to effect a remedy. This chapter will summarize three classes of legal action—constitutional violations, torts, and breaches of contract—and the defenses that can be raised against these actions. Although the readers should already recognize much of the terminology and many of the cases, the present chapter focuses on the procedures and theories of litigation rather than on mental conditions or techniques. Litigation is the ultimate means by which the law applies sanctions in to change the behavior of citizens.

CONSTITUTIONAL VIOLATIONS

Wrongful Confinement

There are relatively few remedies that may be sought by a person involuntarily committed to a mental health facility. Freedom from such compulsory detention is the most direct and logical remedy. The United States Constitution (Article 1, section 9) guarantees the privilege of the Writ of Habeas Corpus to any person who has been restrained of his liberty. The writ provides the only rapid and common procedural alternative to mandatory detention or treatment. Furthermore, habeas corpus is the appropriate remedy if the *fact* or *duration* (rather than conditions) of confinement is challenged; that is, if (a) the proceedings leading to commitment (either civil or criminal) were improper and/or (b) in civil commitment cases, hospitalization is no longer warranted because either the patient is no longer mentally ill or the mental illness does not require hospitalization. Habeas corpus is a civil action in which the petitioner carries the burden of proof.[7]

Most efforts at redressing grievance via writs prepared by the petitioner himself are not successful, but such efforts may be a means of gaining prestige among fellow residents. A 1971 survey in Arizona State Prison showed that only three percent of the inmates had received a high school diploma.[8]

Upon satisfactory completion of an "Application for Writ of Habeas Corpus" (see Appendix D) by the detained person or his representative, a judge will order that a writ be served upon the detaining institution and will set a date for an inquiry as to whether or not the detention procedure was lawful. If there has been noncompliance with or irregularities in the commitment proceedings, the patient will be released. If the writ is denied, such denial should be accomplished by a statement of the reasons for the denial.[9] Placement in a particular ward of a hospital may also be challenged by habeas corpus.[10] Although habeas corpus is an appropriate remedy during confinement, upon release habeas corpus may not be applicable because the lack of confinement could be seen to make the issue moot.

If a person has exhausted all administrative remedies (e.g., an institutional grievance committee) and has been unsuccessful in obtaining a Writ of Habeas Corpus from a state court,[11] then he may petition a federal district court.[12] The court has the option of doing more than merely ruling on confinement. It may order that certain rights of the petitioner be respected, or order a transfer to another institution.[13] The well-known case of *Rouse* v. *Cameron*[14] resulted from a petition for habeas corpus, with the Court specifying conditions necessary for the continued confinement of the patient.

Compulsory psychiatric treatment involves such a "massive curtailment of liberty" that medical judgment alone that a person is mentally ill and treatable does not justify confinement.[15] Also required is a social or legal judgment, probably based on some recent overt act or threat, that the person is dangerous to himself or others (or likely to harm himself or others).[16] Relying upon the Ninth Amendment ("the enumeration in the Constitution, of certain rights, shall not be construed to deny or disparage others retained by the people") and the Fourteenth Amendment's "due process" clause, several state commitment statutes have been found unconstitutionally vague.[17]

When the *conditions* (rather than the fact or duration) of institutionalization violate fundamental rights, at least two remedies may be pursued: private initiative such as publicizing alleged unfair practices, and civil action under Section 1983 of the Federal Civil Rights Act.[18] The former remedy is necessarily limited in scope and of questionable effectiveness. The latter remedy is probably more effective for detained individuals.[19] A person may bring suit under Section 1983 if an individual acting in concert with a state government[20] appears to have caused the deprivation of a privilege, right, or immunity secured by Congress or the Constitution.

This type of federal civil suit usually seeks damages from those perpetrating wrongful procedures and practices, or petitions for injunctive and declaratory relief from such procedures and practices.[21] Where the alleged violation is physical harm or the intentional infliction of mental distress, money damages may be sought from each individual (not from an agency or department)[22] who had personally participated in the violation. A court injunction may be sought when a continuing practice is believed unconstitutional, and when there is, among other requirements, a danger of (a) recurrent violations and (b) greater and more substantial harm to the plaintiff than to the defendant or to society if the injunction is not granted.[23] Unlike damage claims, injunctions may be sought against superior administrative officers, whether or not the officers have personally authorized the acts of their staff.[24]

It is highly desirable, but unnecessary, to have legal counsel to bring a Section 1983 suit. The appropriate papers (e.g., summons and complaint, affidavits, memo of law, In Forma Pauperis papers, and request for appointment of counsel) in proper form with a sufficient number of copies must be sent to the U.S. District Court where the claim originates.[25] Under certain conditions of serious and immediate harm which would prevent the plaintiff from continuing the Section 1983 suit, a temporary restraining order can be sought by filing a "Temporary Restraining

Order'' and an "Order to Show Cause for a Preliminary Injunction,'' plus an affidavit detailing potential harm, in addition to the usual Section 1983 papers. A "Writ of Mandamus" (an order requiring a person or corporation to do some act necessary to fulfill a duty) might be requested, but such is seldom issued when the party is merely exercising professional discretion.[26] The formal complexity of these actions prevents many patients, prisoners, and students from redress; hence, institutional ombudsmen are now being required for some institutions in some jurisdictions.[27]

Substantive Violations of Various Amendments

Appeals are often made to the federal courts for alleged violations of constitutional protections. Often the appeals are speculative, broad, and unsuccessful. This situation should not necessarily be viewed as a criticism of a judicial system which often displays a certain amount of creativity in decision-making and which places high value on giving citizens "their day (or week) in court." The customary review process should be distinguished from relatively rare instances where the process of litigation is undertaken with the ulterior motive to coerce some behavior from the defendant unrelated to the claim—for example, undertaking an incompetency hearing against an elderly person as a means of extorting property or a change in their will. The "abuse of process" is itself a tort. Note, however, that when a litigant does nothing more than engage in the legal proceedings themselves and there is no external act or threat, this is *not* an abuse of process even if done with ill-will or bad intentions.[28]

Not every injury or wrong involves a constitutional issue. Nonetheless, a substantial, though diverse, body of constitutional law related to mental disability is slowly developing. For example, two federal appellate courts have held that involuntary administration of psychotropic medication to a patient over objections violated the First Amendment (freedom of worship, speech, press, assembly).[29] Experimental psychosurgery has been limited in some cases on the rationale that a person's mental processes, the communication of ideas, and the generation of ideas, come within the ambit of the First Amendment.[30]

The Fifth Amendment (privilege against self-incrimination) has been used to argue against compulsory psychiatric exams[31] or the use of polygraph tests as trial evidence.[32] The Fifth Amendment is also the basis of privileged communication between patient and therapist (with certain exceptions, such as when the patient introduces his mental condition as an element of his claim or defense).[33]

The Eighth Amendment (prohibition of cruel and unusual punishment) was violated when nonconsenting mental patients were administered apomorphine[34] and when harassment and excessive isolation were inflicted upon incarcerated juveniles.[35] But in some situations the compulsory treatment of narcotics addicts or convicts has not been prohibited.[36]

The First, Fourth, Fifth, and Ninth amendments have been combined to develop a doctrine of privacy as a matter of civil right (rather than as a common-law tort). Some commentators have urged that this doctrine be extended to cover psychological testing,[37] but case law precedent is very limited.[38] The right of privacy, though recognized at the state level in many jurisdictions, has not been interpreted so broadly as to invalidate compulsory institutionalization of the mentally ill.[39]

The Thirteenth Amendment (prohibition of involuntary servitude), combined with the Fourteenth Amendment (due process), has resulted in several landmark decisions involving token economies, minimum wage, and the general living conditions of institutionalized persons. In *Clonce* v. *Richardson*[40] severe deprivation of physical comforts as a motivational technique was prohibited without consent of the participants. The well-known *Wyatt*[41] case had the benefit of numerous organizations (such as the American Orthopsychiatric Association, American Psychological Association, American Civil Liberties Union) serving as *amici* to specify living and treatment standards. Understandably, other courts may not have the opportunity to promulgate such extensive standards. The Fourteenth Amendment was the primary basis on which the court in *Jones* v. *Robinson*[42] prevented the summary transfer of mental patients (for violating hospital rules) to maximum security facilities without at least the procedural protection of one impartial observer if there was a disputed issue of fact.

TORTS

''Broadly speaking, a tort is a civil wrong, other than breach of contract, for which the court will provide a remedy in the form of an action for damages.''[43] An action in tort usually seeks compensation for losses suffered by a private individual because of the socially unreasonable conduct of others. Three elements of a tort are: (a) existence of a legal duty from the defendant to the plaintiff, (b) breach of that duty, and (c) damages as a potential remedy.[44]

Intentional Interference

False Imprisonment. One method of redressing tortious harms is action asserting false imprisonment.[45] A casual or insufficient examination by institutional personnel,[46] or failure to provide adequate treatment after commitment,[47] may support such a charge. Probably, the plaintiff does not have to prove that defendants acted in bad faith or maliciously, but only establish that the patient was not dangerous and received only custodial care, all of which was known to the defendants. Some states have statutes that require periodic examinations *after* civil commitment, presumably to insure that the patient's stay at the institution will be kept at a minimum. Failure to conduct such an exam and to provide relevant information regarding treatment progress to administrators, courts, and perhaps to the patient himself, may be actionable[48] on the theory of false imprisonment, negligence, or other grounds.[49]

A trial court awarded punitive money damages against a university when a student, who had borrowed $1300, was committed to a mental ward overnight after she notified the dean of her intention to leave school.[50] The false imprisonment charge was later reversed by an appellate court but the charge of abuse of due process (under a state statute permitting temporary detention of persons who demonstrate symptoms of dangerous mental illness) was sustained.

Battery. The unconsented touching of a person gives rise to a legal action in tort even though that touching, as in treatment, is for the welfare of the patient and actually benefits the patient. The touching must have been an external manifestation of the actor's will, and while it may include the intent to inflict a harmful or offensive touching, "the gist of the action for battery is not the hostile intent of the defendant, but rather the absence of consent to the contact on the part of the plaintiff."[51] If the person consents to the touching, then there is no battery.

Under what circumstances, if any, the use of aversion therapy, organic therapy, or research methods constitutes a battery is unclear. A physical examination, an X ray, or the injection of a drug is a touching which requires consent. Research procedures that involve electroshock, biofeedback, and physical punishment might also constitute battery if without consent.[52] To be legally effective, such consent must be, among other requirements, informed. Consent is never absolute or unlimited in scope. For example, a researcher who obtained consent but failed to inform a subject of a substantial potential risk, would have obtained, at best, limited consent. To sustain an action in such a case, the plaintiff must show that an injury occurred as a result of the touching, and show also that "there is a causal relation between the failure to disclose and the specific injury that resulted from the occurrence of an undisclosed risk."[53]

Infliction of Mental Distress. An increasingly recognized tort is that of infliction of mental distress. The 1947 *Restatement of Torts* of the American Law Institute (section 46) advised: "One who, without a privilege to do so, intentionally causes severe emotional distress to another is liable (a) for such emotional distress, and (b) for bodily harm resulting from it."[54] The majority of cases require physical consequences, as well as severe mental distress, not mental injury alone.[55] If undue stress is produced by a particular treatment, then duress may be considered to have occurred when consent was originally obtained from the patient should the patient be prohibited from withdrawing from treatment. "Relatively few cases have dealt with the problem of consent given under duress. . . . There are odd cases which have held that duress is a tort in itself; but much more commonly it is held merely to invalidate the consent given, and so permit any other tort action (e.g., infliction of mental distress, battery, or false imprisonment) which would arise if there were no consent."[56]

Defamation. Defamation is a derogatory communication to a third party that injures a person's reputation. The law regarding oral or written defamation is plagued with anomalies and absurdities, but generally defamation is construed as being something more than impulsive name-calling.[57] It must involve some charge that disgraces the person socially—for example, asserting that a person was raped, was responsible for a suicide, is a "queer," "rotten egg," or "drunkard";[58] or publishing a novel (using an individual's real name and address) that depicts her as "a killer, a pestilence, a person who feasts on blood, a person of immoral sexual appetites and habits."[59]

Greater restraint may be expected of professionals than laymen, especially when mere opinion is asserted as a fact. And even a truthful disclosure of a fact, in a professional relationship, may result in a judgment for libel,[60] although truth is ordinarily an adequate defense. Professional disagreement exists as to whether the name of a researcher who admits to falsifying data should be published to the relevant research community.[61]

A practitioner also has the option of filing a libel suit against individuals who defame his/her character and thereby cause a loss of professional livelihood. Of possible interest to research psychologists is a libel suit filed against Senator William Proxmire by Ronald Hutchinson, former director of research at Kalamazoo (Michigan) State Hospital and a recipient of Senator's Proxmire's "Golden Fleece of the Month" award for April 1975 for research on aggression in rats, monkeys, and humans.[62] The Senate voted to pay Proxmire's legal expenses for this suit, which prompted Senator Goldwater to say that Proxmire should win his own "golden fleece" award for soaking the taxpayer. Proxmire lost a Supreme Court appeal.

A counter-suit might also be filed if a patient has made a frivolous claim merely for the purpose of harassing the practitioner.[63] Barring extremely exceptional circumstances, however, counter-claims are very rarely successful because the practitioner must prove malice on the part of the original plaintiff and also overcome the presumption that legal claims are normally brought in good faith.

Invasion of Privacy. An act may be a wrongful invasion of privacy if it has resulted in a serious and unreasonable invasion, and there has been the requisite intent to do so. An invasion of privacy does not necessarily require public disclosure of private facts. "One who intentionally intrudes, physically or otherwise, upon the solitude or seclusion of another, or his private affairs or concerns, is subject to liability to the other for invasion of his privacy if the intrusion would be highly offensive to a reasonable man."[64] The intrusion may occur by use of electronic equipment,[65] opening personal mail, examining private bank accounts,[66] and so forth. A defendant-researcher would not be liable under the *Restatement* rule for the examination of *public* records or for observations normally made in a public place.[67] Any observation of behavior in public places would probably not be an invasion of privacy.[68]

Misrepresentation (Deceit). A willful misstatement, including fraudulent assurances of little or no risk or of "secret" cures, could constitute the tort of misrepresentation.[69] One plaintiff, for example, suffered a fractured arm during ECT. The complaint alleged that the psychiatrist had advised the plaintiff "that the treatments as given by him were perfectly safe."[70] The court ruled for the plaintiff, holding that the statements of the psychiatrist could be properly construed as misrepresentation and a warranty. Such intentional misstatements would be unprofessional conduct and would certainly support revocation of a license, even if no harm occurred.

The failure to disclose risk (in contrast to a positive assertion of no risk), or the misrepresentation of risk, may also be the basis of successful malpractice action. However the only hazards a researcher can be expected to explain are those that can be reasonably foreseen. "Those risks which are not in fact inherent in a procedure are beyond the scope of the requirements of informal consent."[71]

In cases of tacit or careless nondisclosure, particularly where one has a duty to give warning and a tangible injury results, an action for negligent misrepresentation would probably be recognized.[72] Although it is generally true that nondisclosure of material facts is not actionable at common law, the exceptions have gone far toward becoming the rule. One such exception, found by some courts, may be applicable to a doctor-patient relationship. When certain allegedly misrepresented facts were exclusively in the control of one party, failure to disclose them is equivalent to active concealment.[73] An accused person may, for example, rely on promises of treatment and rehabilitation in choosing to plead not guilty by reason of insanity rather than receive a moderate criminal sentence. Failure of an examining physician to disclose a hopeless prognosis would certainly seem to be a failure to disclose a material fact. Another situation might involve the preparation of a purposefully complicated research consent form so that potential participants will not understand the risks involved.

Negligence

"Negligence" is a failure to conform to standards of conduct recognized by law for the protection of others against unreasonable risks. "Psychological or psychiatric negligence" (malpractice) may be defined as an act or omission by a practitioner in the treatment of a patient that is inconsistent with the reasonable care and skill usually exercised by practitioners of good standing of the same school or system of practice in the nation.[74] Malpractice differs from conventional negligence theory in two respects: There is a special doctor-patient relationship involved, and proof is required of a breach of a standard of care. (The doctrine of negligence is more fully discussed in Chapter 15.)

The courts have usually considered a practitioner's failure to inform a patient of material facts a form of negligence supporting an action in malpractice.[75] If a plaintiff asserts that his consent was inadequate because the defendant failed to advise him sufficiently of the hazards involved,[76] the plaintiff must offer expert evidence to show "what disclosure of risks incident to a proposed treatment should be made in a particular situation."[77] If the plaintiff alleges that post-treatment care was inadequate (e.g., allowing patient to walk down stairs unattended after shock treatment),[78] he must be able to show that the psychiatrist or institution failed to exercise *reasonable* care in observing and/or restraining him.[79]

A patient who has been injured during treatment, but who cannot detail the exact circumstances of the injury nor prove intent on the part of the defendant, might invoke *res ipsa loquitur* in an attempt to prove negligence. A possible application of this doctrine to psychiatric techniques would be a situation in which serious injury such as a spinal fracture resulted during ECT therapy because of the failure to administer a muscle relaxant.[80] *Res ipsa loquitur* has not been used frequently in malpractice cases. Its application appears to be increasing, however, especially when the injury arises from a situation in which danger is readily apparent to a layman—for example a phobia of death and hospitals after having been mistakenly pronounced dead and taken to a funeral parlor for embalming.[81]

Negligence may also be the basis of a legal action concerning the product liability of behavioral devices. The area of product liability is presently undergoing rapid change. Therefore, the present summary is tentative and provides only a very general orientation to this area.[82]

The manufacturer and seller have a duty not to provide defective products. If they are negligent or willfully attempt to defraud, they may be liable to not only the immediate purchaser but also to any user, because no direct interaction ("privity of contract") is required. The manufacturer and seller are held to a standard of reasonable, due care. This care usually includes adherence to applicable statutory standards. Additionally, failure to follow FDA regulations may be used to help demonstrate negligence.[83] The fact, however, that only one of a class of items might have caused injury may not be sufficient to prove a degree of negligence suitable for liability.

The manufacturer owes a duty to exercise reasonable care not only in the construction of the device but also in the inspection of it for obvious or latent defects. Similarly, the seller may be responsible for inspecting it for obvious defects.[84] Of course, a manufacturer cannot guarantee indefinite performance. The purchaser has a duty to follow reasonable directions. Both purchaser and user bear some responsibility for inspection and replacement. When a businessman arrives late at the office because the alarm clock upon which he usually relies fails to function, he does not normally have a cause of action against the manufacturer. Nonetheless, in matters of critical medical or psychological importance, additional consideration should be given to the development of internal warning systems, redundant circuits, and easily inspectable and replaceable components.

The manufacturer and seller are not liable for defects for the device resulting from damage to it beyond reasonable use or after it has left the scope of their control.[85] The seller might wish to limit the use of such products to specifically trained persons. For example, biofeedback devices might be available only to licensed or otherwise qualified therapists.

A frequently attempted but rarely successful source of money damages for negligence from institution officials is action under the Federal Tort Claims Act.[86] The Act "makes the United States liable under the local law of the place where the tort occurs, for the negligent or wrongful acts or omissions of federal employees within the scope of their employment 'in the same manner and to the same extent as a private individual under like circumstances.' "[87] But the Act provides a number of broad exclusions, including "any claim arising out of assault, battery, false imprisonment, false arrest, malicious prosecution, abuse of process, libel, slander, misrepresentation, deceit, or interference with contract rights."[88]

Nonetheless, governmental entities have been found liable for culpable negligence and have been required to pay damages.[89] The tort action may be based primarily on the negligence of the institution, mental health professional, or assistants.[90] In *Wright* v. *State*,[91] the plaintiff, who was involuntarily confined because of the likelihood of self-injury, was hurt when he jumped from a second-story window of the mental hospital. The state's compelling interest and justification for his involuntary confinement was presumably protection from harm to himself. The state negligently failed to provide this protection.

A noteworthy case of negligence on the part of a state agency is *Whitree* v. *State*.[92] Whitree pleaded guilty to third-degree assault and was placed on probation (maximum term for the offense: three years). Whitree violated probation and was found incompetent to stand trial on the new charge. He was sent to a state hospital where he was confined nearly *11 years longer* than he would have been under the maximum criminal sentence.[93] The court found that if Whitree had been treated with medical and psychiatric care consonant with prevailing medical standards, he would have been released many years earlier. The primary theory relied upon by the court in awarding damages of $300,000 appears to be malpractice:[94] "The damages recoverable in malpractice are for personal injuries, including the pain and suffering which naturally flowed from the tortious act."[95]

The action of negligence has also been used in another area of professional practice, that of confidential communication. On rare occasions, unauthorized transmission of a confidential communication has resulted in a claim asserting negligence. A professional's "carelessness in divulging professional confidences in such a manner as to cause injury to his patient" may sustain such a claim.[96]

BREACH OF CONTRACT

Formal contracts are seldom used by private practitioners, although many institutions routinely ask persons entering the institution to sign an agreement holding the person to an appropriate standard of conduct or limiting the liability of the institution. For example, private schools have often used a breach of contract as a means of dismissal for "misconduct."[97] Conversely, and less successfully, students have sometimes claimed that the school has not fulfilled its promise of adequate instruction.[98]

Therapeutic contracts which state the objectives of treatment, nature and duration of treatment, criteria for assessment, and fee arrangements are more clearly actionable for breach but may also prevent litigation by clarifying in advance mutual rights and duties.[99] Implied contracts may exist where participation in a program must be voluntary (e.g., federally funded methadone programs)[100] because the program manager has a duty to obtain agreement and consent in advance. The information presented to prospective participants could be construed as an offer in ordinary contract law.

If an assertion is made that a product or a course of treatment is suitable for a specified purpose, then the seller or practitioner may have made a warranty. Assuming that an implied or express contract was made, a breach of warranty may be viewed as a breach of contract. The plaintiff does not need to show negligence, only that the product or treatment was not suitable for its intended purposes.[101] As previously noted, nonnegligent but injurious electroshock treatments were held to be a breach of warranty when a promise of no risk was made.[102]

DEFENSES

An obvious first consideration for practitioners involves the degree to which immunity of state agencies or officials can be asserted. Governmental agencies have traditionally been held by the courts to be immune from liability on the theory that the state is sovereign and cannot be sued without its consent. Most actions are likely to be grounded on Section 1983 (Civil Rights Act); hence state agency defendants are liable only for injunctive and declaratory relief. As a consequence, hospital administrators and state officials may be named as *individuals* in their official capacities as defendants.

The majority of states have statutes specifically limiting liability of state agencies for torts and specifying the procedure by which an aggrieved person may make a claim.[103] For example, most jurisdictions provide both civil and criminal immunity to any institution, hospital, or person (other than relative or friend) who renders services or opinions *during the commitment proceedings*—in a few cases even when the diagnosis was made with malice or was grossly negligent (e.g., based on a three-minute conversation in a parking lot).[104] Technically, the court, and not the examining physicians or witnesses, commits the patient; therefore, in most cases complaints are not sustained.[105] Furthermore, most physicians when serving as an examiner are given an official cloak of immunity, by case law or by specific statute.[106]

Traditional immunity appears to be eroding.[107] In a split decision, a U.S. court of appeals overturned the ruling of a district court which had held that the officers and supervising psychiatrist of a state mental hospital were immune from suit in light of the need for "effective administration of the state's program for mental defectives and the effect that the fear of constant and vexatious suits may have upon persons charged with its administration."[108] A U.S. district court held that "where the action and/or the statute under which the action is taken are unconstitutional, the individual officer is, for jurisdictional purposes, stripped of his representative character and thus has no jurisdictional immunity."[109] This rationale allows for damages as well as injunctive relief.

Thus, the Eleventh Amendment does not appear to bar an award of damages against a state hospital official in his personal capacity if his action or the statute under which his action was taken was unconstitutional. There are two other conditions which may weaken the general protection against liability: lack of a "probable cause" for the commitment and failure to act in "good faith." In *O'Connor* v. *Donaldson,* the Supreme Court held that the superintendent of a state hospital was personally liable for monetary damages for violating a patient's constitutional right of liberty only if the superintendent "knew or should have known that the action he took within his sphere of official responsibility would violate the constitutional rights of [Donaldson], or if he took the action with malicious intention. . . ."[110]

To effectively limit possible liability, a practitioner should be prepared to prove "good faith"—for example, if a commitment examiner can truthfully answer "yes" to the first set of questions which follow, and "no" to the second set, then he most likely has acted in good faith and can defend himself against litigation:[111]

YES	NO
1. When listing behavior described by others, did I indicate the informant?	1. Am I related to the patient by blood, marriage, or business association?
2. Have I made an exact copy of my own statements as I wrote them on the commitment paper?	2. Am I on the payroll of the receiving hospital?
3. Have I been in practice the minimum time required by law?	3. Did I put any words in the patient's mouth which I did not actually hear him utter?
4. Did I have any chance to interview the patient alone?	4. Did I describe, as my own observation, behavior which I did not personally observe?
5. Did I actually do the required physical examination?	5. Was the patient under the influence of heavy sedation when I examined him?
6. Is the date on the commitment paper correct?	6. Have I accepted an unusually large fee for this commitment? [An excessive fee may appear to be a bribe from an eager petitioner.]

Demonstration of good faith and lack of malice on the part of the defendant physicians or hospital can mitigate damages awarded to the plaintiff patient but does not negate the charge.[112] Therefore, it would be prudent for examiners to obtain duplicate examination forms, fill out two complete copies, and retain the unsigned copy. As an additional protection against a claim that the examination was superficial, the examiner's file should be more complete than the typically brief forms he submits to the courts. Filed data should include physical and neurologic findings, psychological test data, family information, and samples of the patient's verbal and nonverbal behavior.[113]

Finally, a defense may allege that committed patients, due to their mental incapacities, lack the legal status to sue. The hospital defendant, however, "must raise this issue by specific negative averment, which shall include such supporting particulars as are peculiarly within the pleaders' knowledge."[114] That is, the burden of proof of incapacity rests with the defendants—a patient does not lose the right to sue merely because s/he has been committed.[115]

With regard to prisons, a number of cases have held that prison officials have no special immunity from liability in damage suit.[116] Liability is intended to be satisfied entirely out of the individual's pocket.[117] Superior officials who took no part in the actual mistreatment may even be held liable for damages by virtue of their positions of responsibility.[118] Some courts, before assessing liability to a higher official, have required "that the official either (a) participated in, directed or encouraged the misconduct, or (b) took some other wrongful *action* which helped cause the misconduct."[119] Other defenses to allegations of injury may assert that the force used to keep a prisoner in custody was necessary and that the injury resulted from the prisoner's own wrongful or negligent acts.[120] Punitive damages may not be allowed to stand if (a) the official's improper conduct reflects no pattern of such behavior by himself or by other officials, (b) the deterrent impact of the punitive award would be minimal, and (c) the official's attempts to meet requirements were frustrated by lack of resources.[121]

With respect to "due process" allegations that are raised, a demonstration of a compelling state interest may provide an adequate defense for public institutions.[122] It is thought that such a demonstration in regard to testing procedures, for instance, could be made by showing that (a) the tests utilized were accurate, (b) testing was a reasonable method of discovering the emotionally unstable who in turn constituted a significant threat to the efficiency of the federal service, and (c) alternative methods to testing were not available.[123]

Similarly, in situations of substantial discipline or loss of privileges, whether by a governmental entity or by private parties, the trend of case law appears to require some advance written notice (perhaps a 24-hour minimum), an opportunity for the resident to reply to charges (probably before a hearing board), and a reasonable investigation into the relevant facts.[124] Adherence to these elements of due process may provide a partial defense. Officials are *not* required, however, to promulgate and adhere to rules and regulations of a trial-like nature (e.g., cross-examination of accusers, right to counsel) in matters of discipline or confinement.[125]

Another constitutional right which must be especially safeguarded in matters of discipline and confinement is freedom from involuntary servitude. Allegations of violations of this right occur most frequently with regard to token economy programs. A specific factual defense for token economies might be predicated on the common observation that such arrangements "merely replicated the contingencies which are operative, legal, and ethical in the 'real world,' such as charges for meals and sleeping quarters."[126] A conservative legal approach to any behavior modification program would see that the procedures are instituted within a generally humane psychological and physical environment, that participants have given voluntary informed consent, that qualified professionals have authority and responsibility for supervision of the program, and that individual problem-oriented treatment plans and records are developed.

The primary defense to both tort actions and Section 1983 actions is securing, in advance of treatment or therapy, legally adequate consent. (See Chapter 11 for a more complete discussion of the elements of "consent.") Consent, even if legally adequate, does not automatically provide a defense for acts which are criminal such as battery or embezzlement. However, even "treatment" of little or no value almost always lacks the necessary element of criminal intention on the part of the practitioner; hence, the adequacy of express (or implied) consent becomes the central issue. Temporary restraint of a supposedly mentally disabled person would not constitute false imprisonment unless the plaintiff could prove malicious intention.[127]

When a treatment is successful and it results in no injuries, the courts have been reluctant to allow technical tort claims even when the consent was incomplete.[128] One extreme case[129] allowed parents to consent to insulin shock therapy for their 34-year-old son who had *not* been declared incompetent. In another case,[130] a circuit court dispensed with the requirement of *any* informed consent by the patient where there was evidence that information about risks would substantially worsen the patient's psychological state. The more esoteric and experimental a treatment happens to be, obviously the greater the assumed requirement of explanation and weighing of cost/benefits for and by the patient. Tape-recording the consent process may have evidentiary value, or at least the consent form can include a clause that states, in effect, that the signer understand the contents of the document and sign voluntarily.

If a patient waives a right or some other assumed protection, caution must be exercised to assure that such a waiver was understood and voluntary. If the patient assumes (correctly or incorrectly) that the waiver must be given to shorten institutionalization, then the consent may be tainted with duress.

If the action is for defamation, the strongest defense is a complete one: that all information revealed was true or merely the expression of strong opinion.[131] A weaker defense may be based on "qualified privilege": that an untrue and defamatory statement of another was "made without improper motive in circumstances in which there was a legal or moral duty to make it, and that the statement was made to some person who had a corresponding interest or duty to receive it."[132] Perhaps the only feasible defense against an allegation of negligence or breach of contract in this situation is a proof that alleged violations occurred while acting in "good faith." For example, a psychotherapist could define the limits of confidentiality to her patient at the outset of treatment and give "only pertinent information that cannot be of embarrassment or harm to other people or to the patient if not relevant to the case at hand."[133] The therapist may also argue that there was implied consent by the client, that the information was already generally public, and that the public interest outweighed the plaintiff's right to privacy. Note, finally, that the plaintiff will have the difficult task of translating the alleged injury into monetary damages.

In previous chapters, the use of contracts for therapy or research was recommended as a means of clarifying mutual expectation of the persons involved. Assumed limits of liability can be clarified, although the degree to which a court might enforce such limits is uncertain. For example, if a therapist contracts with a patient or his/her family to prevent suicide, then presumably s/he ought to be allowed to use the force necessary to conduct his/her treatment and be held liable under the contract. Conversely, if the therapist chooses to use no coercion or restraint and clearly makes no promise to prevent suicidal acts, then the therapist ought not to be held liable. Similarly, assuming a complete understanding and no unequal bargaining, a research contract involving scientifically and morally acceptable research could probably stand against a claim of trespass and invasion of privacy. It is doubtful, however, that research or therapy contracts could serve as a release for claims based on negligence.[134] The usual reason that contracts are found unenforceable is that there was unequal bargaining power, that that agreement is overly general, or that it is "contrary to public policy" (which means about anything the court wants it to mean).

It can be argued that there is a general public benefit to psychological and psychiatric interventions. Furthermore, just as some well-accepted medical or dental procedures involve pain, so social rehabilitation may involve noxious elements. Although it would be socially repugnant and technically unnecessary to apply intense electrical shock to a psychotic child to correct a trivial behavior such as messy eating habits, failure to use electrical shock to suppress serious self-destruction in the same child might be considered professional misfeasance because the technique has been demonstrated effective with such problems.[135] Extracting a retarded patient's teeth or tying her in a laundry bag to prevent biting and ruminating is more cruel than necessary. In contrast, the prevention of ruminative vomiting by aversive conditioning may not be.[136] Social custom, as well as some case law, supports the notion that punishment graduated to "fit the crime" is a natural and expected consequence or retribution for rule violation.[137] One strategy to protect the

defendant during litigation concerning alleged abusive treatment is to have
documented evidence that the aversive procedures conformed to widely accepted or
customary standards of practice. Such standards have been developed by various
organizations (see Chapter 4).

A certain amount of frivolous litigation is obviously undertaken by patients
who are angry and perhaps see an opportunity for economic gain. Successful,
publicized countersuits might restrain these unreasonable impositions. A
nonpsychiatric case involved Harriett Nathan who injured her finger while playing
tennis. Radiologist Leonard Berlin failed to diagnosis a small fracture that was later
seen on another X ray. Mrs. Nathan's husband, a lawyer, helped her to bring a
malpractice suit for $250,000 against the radiologist, the hospital, and the or-
thopedic surgeon who had treated her. The treatment received by Mrs. Nathan for
her finger was the same as that normally given for a fracture. Dr. Berlin reportedly
countersued Mrs. Nathan and her husband on the grounds that they had brought suit
against him "without reasonable cause," and he also sued the two lawyers who
assisted the Nathans for filing the suit without proper investigation. After only
fifteen minutes of deliberation, a jury awarded Dr. Berlin $8000 in damages, thus
fining both the Nathans and their lawyers.[138]

One legal commentator has called the lawyer in psychiatric malpractice the
"healing hammer." This is because, in his opinion, a wrong "needs to be nailed to
the wrongdoer and the victim made whole."[139] Treatment by hammer has unfortunately characterized too much of the recent, and probably desirable, expansion of
patient rights. Litigation is only one—and not necessarily the best—way of resolving disputes or of applying negative consequences to wayward practitioners. State
licensing boards and employers can also apply formal or informal sanctions (or
rewards). Professional screening panels that hear initial complaints and render advisory opinions are alternate sources of conflict resolution. Several states have established by statute a system of "medical claim conciliation panels" to review tort
claims against health providers.[140] The law is not merely a static list of rules. It
is the ever-shifting verbal expression of compromise between long-term and short-
term personal and public interests.

NOTES

1. The case summarized here is reported in detail in Goldwater v. Ginzburg, 414 F.2d 324
(2d Cir. 1969). Toffler's assertions appeared in *Pageant* magazine, December 1959 at
p. 57 and in *Good Housekeeping* magazine, May 1964 at p. 62.
2. A letter to *Fact* magazine, dated August 3, 1964, over the signature of Dr. Walter E.
Barton, APA Medical Director, stated in part: ". . . Should you decide to publish the
results of a purported 'survey' of psychiatric opinion on the question you have posed,
the Association will take all possible measures to disavow its validity." Goldwater v.
Ginzburg, *supra* note 1, at p. 334.

3. 1 *Fact* 20 (Sept.–Oct. 1964).

4. Goldwater, *supra* note 1, at p. 332.

5. Cases cited in *Goldwater* at p. 338: Bishop v. New York Times Co., 233 N.Y. 446, 135 N.E. 845 (1922); Brunstein v. Almansi, 79 N.Y.S.2d 802 (Sup. Ct. Nassau Co. 1947).

6. Although the award of damages often makes news, two less spectacular judicial remedies are more common and possibly more effective in resolving disputes equitably: "declaratory relief" (a determination of the rights and obligations of the parties in a contested matter) and "preventative relief" (an injunction prohibiting the defendant from engaging in certain activities that infringe upon the plaintiff's interests).

7. 28 USCA 2254 as interpreted in Dillon v. Downs, 401 F. Supp. 1240 (D.C. Va. 1975). *In re* Ballay, 482 F.2d 648, 652 (D.C. Cir. 1973), held that as to sufficiency of proof required of defendant institutions, the criminal standard ("beyond reasonable doubt") rather than the civil standard ("preponderance of evidence") should be used.

8. Cleary, D. Patient writ-writer. 130 *American Journal of Psychiatry* 320 (March 1973).

9. Tatem v. United States, 275 F.2d 894, 896 (D.C. Cir. 1960).

10. Covington v. Harris, 419 F. 2d 617 (D.C. Cir. 1969). The rigbt to treatment and revocation of a conditional release was tested by habeas corpus in Darnell v. Cameron, 348 F.2d 64 (D.C. Cir. 1965).

11. *E.g.,* as outlined in Administrative Procedures Act, 5 United States Code, sec. 552 et seq.

12. 28 United States Code, sections 2241–2243, 2254(b) (1970).

13. United States v. Carey, 143 F.2d 445, 447 (9th Cir. 1944). A more traditional or strict interpretation would, however, permit only a ruling on confinement, not on the nature of treatment within the institution.

14. Rouse v. Cameron, 373 F.2d 451 (D.C. Cir. 1966).

15. Humphrey v. Cady, 405 U.S. 504, 509 (1972).

16. *Id.:* Doremus v. Farrell, 407 F. Supp. 509 (D. Nebr. 1975). For survey of state commitment criteria, *see* Schwitzgebel, R. K. Survey of state civil commitment statutes, In A. L. McGarry, R. K. Schwitzgebel, P. D. Lipsitt and D. Lelos, *Civil commitment and social policy.* Washington, D.C.: Center for Studies of Crime and Delinquency, NIMH, 1979.

17. Doremus, *id.;* Kendall v. True, 391 F. Supp. 413 (W.D. Ky. 1975); Commonwealth ex rel. Finken v. Roop, 339 A.2d 764 (Pa. Super. Ct. 1975). By including a "dangerousness" clause, the Oregon Supreme Court upheld the constitutionality of its commitment statute but determined that "the commitment decision . . . ultimately must be a legal judgment by a court rather than a medical diagnosis by examining experts." State of Oregon v. O'Neill, 545 P.2d 97, 103 (Ore. 1976).

18. Federal Civil Rights Statute, 42 U.S.C.A. section 1983 (1970) (R. S. section 1979), ch. 22: "Every person who, under color of any statute, ordinance, regulation, custom, or usage of any State or Territory, subjects, or causes to be subjected, any citizen of the United States or other person within the jurisdiction thereof to the deprivation of any rights, privileges, or immunities secured by the Constitution and laws, shall be liable to the party injured in an action at law, suit in equity, or other proper proceeding for redress."

19. It should be noted that institutional officials may not attempt to punish inmates who take legal action or help other inmates with legal problems. Landman v. Royster, 333 F.

Supp. 621 (E.D. Va. 1971); U.S. *ex rel.* Cleggett v. Pate, 229 F. Supp. 818 (N.D. Ill. 1964); Seller v. Beto, 345 F. Supp. 499 (S.D. Texas 1972).

20. The right to sue prison officials was confirmed in Cooper v. Pate, 378 U.S. 546 (1964).
21. There is no requirement that other remedies be sought prior to filing an action under the civil rights act. Jacob, B. R. Prison discipline and inmate rights. 5 *Harvard Civil Rights-Civil Liberties Law Review* 227, 257 (1970). The Supreme Court has held that where *conditions* of confinement are being challenged by seeking money damages, an action can be brought in federal court under the Civil Rights Act by a prisoner (and presumably also by a civilly committed mental patient) *without* prior exhaustion of state remedies. Preiser v. Rodriguez, 411 U.S. 475, 93 S. Ct. 1827 (1973).
22. Monroe v. Pape, 365 U.S. 167, 187–192 (1961).
23. Clutchette v. Procunier, 328 F. Supp. 767 (N.D. Calif. 1971) (disciplinary rules at San Quentin).
24. Wiltsie v. Department of Corrections, 406 F.2d 515 (1968).
25. A useful source of procedural information is Prison Law Collective, *The jailhouse lawyer's manual*. San Francisco: Brian Glick and the Prison Law Collective, 1973, but note the differences often occur from one jurisdiction to another. Check with the Clerk of the U.S. District Court, and from a law library or other source obtain a copy of *Local rules of practice*.
26. Saunders v. Virginia Polytechnic Instit., 307 F. Supp. 326, *rev.* 417 F.2d 1127 (4th Cir. 1969). University of Miami v. Vilitana, 184 So. 2d 701 (Fla. App. 1966); Kaelin v. University of Pittsburgh, 421 Pa. 220, *cert. denied,* 385 U.S. 837 (1966); Strank v. Mercy Hospital, 383 Pa. 54, 117 A.2d 697 (1955) (a court of common pleas can grant specific equitable remedies).
27. Patient representation or advocacy statutorily established by Calif. Wel. & Inst. Code sec. 5350; Fla. Stat. sec. 394.459; Ga. Code sec. 88–502.19; Ill. Stat. ch. 91.5 sec. 9-6. *Also* Morales v. Turman, 383 F. Supp. (E.D. Texas 1974) (rights and duties of ombudsmen).
28. Prosser, W. L. *Handbook of the law of torts,* 4th ed. St. Paul: West Publishing Co., 1971, pp. 856–857.
29. Scott v. Plante, 532 F.2d 939 (3rd Cir. 1976); Winters v. Miller, 446 F.2d 65 (2d Cir.), *cert. den.* 404 U.S. 985 (1971).
30. Kaimowitz v. Dept. of Mental Health, civ. act. No. 73–19434–AW (Wayne Co., Mich. Cir. Ct., July 10, 1973) quoted in 2 *Prison Law Reporter* 433, 477 (1973). *Similarly,* Wyatt v. Aderholt, 503 F.2d 1305 (5th Cir. 1974).
31. McNeil v. Dir., Patuxent Institution, 407 U.S. 245 (1972).
32. Hearings before Subcommittee on Government Operations, House of Representatives, *The use of polygraphs and similar devices by federal agencies.* Washington, D.C.: U.S. Govt. Printing Office, 1974, pp. 7–48.
33. *Rules of evidence for the U.S. District Courts and Magistrates,* Rule sec. 5-04.
34. Mackey v. Procunier, 477 F.2d 877 (9th Cir. 1973).
35. Morales v. Turman, 383 F. Supp. 53 (E.D. Texas 1974).
36. In re Spadafora, 54 Misc. 2d 123, 281 N.Y.S.2d 923 (Sup. Ct. 1967); Haynes v. Harris, 344 F.2d 463 (8th Cir. 1965).
37. *E.g.,* Emerson, C. D. Nine justices in search of a doctrine. 64 *Michigan Law Review* 219, 231–234 (1965).

38. Merriken v. Cressman, 364 F. Supp. 913 (E.D. Pa. 1973) (school's personality test violated privacy of *family* relationships when there was inadequate consent and confidentiality safeguards).

39. State of Oregon v. O'Neill, 545 P.2d 97, 102 (1976): [The state] may legitimately intrude on the privacy of an unfortunate individual if he is a 'mentally ill' person. . . . ''

40. 379 F. Supp. 338 (W.D. Mo. 1974).

41. Wyatt v. Stickney, 325 F. Supp. 781 (M.D. Ala. 1971), *reinforced in* 334 F. Supp. 1341 (M.D. Ala. 1971), 344 F. Supp. 373 (M.D. Ala. 1972), *aff'd. sub nom* Wyatt v. Aderholt, 503 F.2d 1305 (5th Cir. 1974).

42. 440 F.2d 249 (D.C. Cir. 1971).

43. Prosser, W. L. *Handbook of the law of torts,* 4th ed. St. Paul, Minn.: West Publishing Co., 1971, p. 165.

44. *Id*. at 4–7.

45. *See., e.g.,* Geddes v. Daughters of Charity of St. Vincent De Paul, Inc., 348 F.2d 144 (5th Cir. 1965) (jury should decide issue of false imprisonment); Whitree, 56 Misc. 2d at 708, 290 N.Y.S.2d at 502. A county government has been found liable in a false imprisonment case. Sullivan v. County of Los Angeles, 117 Cal. Rptr. 241, 527 P.2d 865 (Cal. Sup. 1974).

46. Bacon v. Bacon, 76 Miss. 468, 24 So. 968 (1899) (casual examination); Beckham v. Cline, 151 Fla. 481, 10 So. 2d 419 (1942) (no examination).

47. O'Connor v. Donaldson, 95 S. Ct. 2486 (1975). *See generally,* Schwitzgebel, R. K. The right to effective treatment. 62 *California Law Review* 936 (1974).

48. The plaintiff has the burden of showing that his incarceration was, in fact, false (i.e., that illness and/or danger did not exist at the time of his examination)—not an easy task because this is likely to require, among other things, the expert testimony of at least one psychiatrist on the patient's behalf.

49. People *ex. rel.* Stutz v. Conboy, 59 Misc. 2d 791, 300 N.Y.S.2d 453 (Sup. Ct. 1969) (information to the patient). *See generally,* Schwitzgebel, R. K. Right to treatment for the mentally disabled: The need for realistic standards and objective criteria. 8 *Harvard Civil Rights-Civil Liberties Law Review* 533 (1973); Schwitzgebel, R. K. Implementing a right to effective treatment. 1 *Law and Psychology Review* 117 (1975).

50. Maniaci v. Marquette Univ., 148 N.W. 168 (Wisc. 1971).

51. Prosser, *supra* note 43, at 36.

52. Wilson v. Lehman, 379 S.W.2d 478 (1964) (shock therapy); *contra,* Anonymous v. State of New York, 236 N.Y.S.2d 88 (Sup. Ct. App. 1963) (shock therapy not an assault or battery).

53. Friedman, P. R. Legal regulation of applied behavior analysis in mental institutions and prisons. 17 *Arizona Law Review* 39, 53 (1975). *Cf. generally,* Waltz, J. R. and Scheuneman, T. W. Informed consent to therapy. 64 *Northwestern University Law Review* 628 (sections also reprinted in Katz, J. *Experimentation with human beings.* New York: Russell Sage Foundation, 1972, pp. 579, 605).

54. Section 46 was cited and used as a rationale in State Rubbish Collectors' Assn. v. Siliznoff, 38 Cal. 2d 330, 240 P.2d 282 (Sup. Ct. Cal. 1952). The *Restatement* explanation of section 46 (retained in comment "k" of the *2nd Restatement):* "The interest in freedom from severe emotional distress is regarded as of sufficient importance to require others to refrain from conduct intended to invade it. Such conduct is tortious. . . .''

Quoted in Prosser, W. L. and Wade, J. W. *Cases and material on torts,* 5th ed. Mineola, New York: The Foundation Press, 1971, p. 66.

55. Wolfe v. Sibley, Lindsay & Curr Co., et al., 354 N.Y.S.2d 470 (App. 1974) (workman's compensation not cover psychiatric treatment for person seeing another's suicide). *See* Prosser & Wade, *supra* note 54, at 68, for other illustrative cases. *Also* Note, Recovery for nervous injury resulting from mental stimulation under workmens compensation. 53 *Chicago–Kent Law Review* 731 (1977).

56. Prosser, supra note 43, at 106. See Neibuhr v. Gage, 99 Minn. 149, 109 N.W. 1 (1906) (duress a "form of fraud").

57. Prosser, *supra* note 43, chap. 19; Nelson, H. L. and Teeter, D. L. *Law of mass communication.* Mineola, N.Y.: The Foundation Press, 1969, chap. 3.

58. Prosser, *supra* note 43, at 740.

59. "Not a vampire—woman sues," *Los Angeles Times,* Pt. 1, p. 29 (Jl. 21, 1978). The book includes direct questioning of her sanity by one of the characters: "That old broad is a nut. I mean a real nut. . . . Isn't there some legal definition of all this shit that would make her insane?" Randolphe, A. *The vampire tapes.* New York: Berkley Publishing Corp., 1977, p. 218.

60. Berry v. Moench, 8 Utah 2d 191, 331 P.2d 814 (1958) (charge of libel sustained against psychiatrist for disclosing suicide in family and stating his patient was a psychopathic personality in a letter that subsequently caused patient's wife to be disinherited).

61. "Researcher found cheating at psi lab," 106 *Science News* 100 (Aug. 17, 1974). (accused person's name published at p. 101).

62. Reported in 7 *Behavior Today* 4 (Apr. 26, 1976).

63. Jankelson v. Cisel, 473 P.2d 202 (Wash. 1970) (dentist recovered damages from dissatisfied patient). *Also see* Two Kentucky doctors win record countersuit award. 19 *Medical World News* 17 (Nov. 13, 1978) (two lawyers ordered to pay $50,000 for malicious prosecution).

64. *Restatement of the Law, Second, Torts* (Tentative draft No. 13). Philadelphia: American Law Institute, 1967, p. 103 (section 652B).

65. Hamberger v. Eastman, 106 N.H. 107, 206 A.2d 239 (landlord held liable for microphone placed in tenants' bedroom).

66. *Restatement, supra* note 64, at 103, comment on section "b."

67. *Id.* at 115, comment on section "c."

68. Schwartz v. Thiele, 51 Cal. Rptr. 767 (Ct. App. 1966) (parking lot conversation).

69. *See generally,* Prosser, *supra* note 43, at 683–731. *See also,* Minnesota State Board of Medical Examiners v. Schmidt, 292 N.W. 255 (Minn. 1940) (licensed physician diagnosing by mail and using placebos "energized" by machine of his own invention).

70. Johnston v. Rodis, 151 F. Supp. 345 (D.C. Cir. 1957), *rev'd* 251 F.2d 917, 918 (D.C. Cir. 1958).

71. Holder, A. R. *Medical malpractice law.* New York: Wiley & Sons, 1975, p. 232. *See* Yeates v. Harms, 401 P.2d 659 (Kan. 1965); Woods v. Brumlop, 71 N.M. 222, 377 P.2d 520 (1962).

72. Prosser, *supra* note 43, at 694–699.

73. Harper, F. V. and James, F. *The law of torts.* Boston: Little, Brown, 1957, p. 558.

74. Prosser, *supra* note 43, at 143.

75. Salgo v. Leland Stanford Board of Trustees, 317 P.2d 170 (Cal. 1957); Sisler v. Jackson, 450 P.2d 903 (Okla. 1969).

76. Mitchell v. Robinson, 334 S.W.2d 11 (Mo. 1960) (failure to warn patient of risks of insulin and electroconvulsive shock therapies).

77. Aiken v. Clary, 396 S.W.2d 668, 674 (Mo. 1965).

78. Brown v. Moore, 247 F.2d 711 (1957) (patient fell down stairs, broke his neck, and died).

79. *See* Constant v. Howe, 436 S.W.2d 115 (Texas 1968), *rev.* Howe v. Citizens Memorial Hospital, 426 S.W.2d 882 (Texas Civ. App. 1968).

80. Wilkerson v. Vesey, 295 A.2d 676 (R.I. 1972); Holder, *supra* note 71, at 167. *Res ipsa loquitur* not found in ECT injuries: Constant v. Howe, 436 S.W.2d 398 (Pa. 1968).

81. Cordray v. Cruz and Timken-Mercy Hospital, Stark County, Ohio, case No. 72–800 PI, Agreed settlement judgment entry, Ct. Common Pleas (Nov. 13, 1974).

82. Excerpted in large part from Schwitzgebel, R. K. Ethical and legal aspects of behavioral instrumentation. In R. L. Schwitzgebel and R. K. Schwitzgebel (Eds.) *Psychotechnology*. New York: Holt Rinehart & Winston, 1973, 267–283.

83. Orthopedic Equipment Co., Inc. v. Eutsler, 276 F.2d 455, 79 A.L.R.2d 390 (1960). A discussion of FDA regulations can be found in Schwitzgebel, R. K. Federal regulation of psychological devices: An example of medical-political drift. In B. D. Sales (Ed.) *Psychology in the legal process*. New York: Spectrum, 1977, 215–221.

84. Cases differ as to duty of a distributor or seller to inspect for defects. A duty was imposed in Sinatra v. National X-ray Products Corp., 26 N.J. 546, 141 A.2d 28 (1958). A physician may be found liable for malpractice for failing to exercise reasonable care in discovering a defect in a device. Cohran v. Harper, 115 Ga. App.2d. 277, 154 S.E.2d 461 (1967).

85. Helene Curtis Industries, Inc. v. Pruitt, 385 F.2d 841 (5th Cir. 1958) (no liability for misuse of product).

86. Federal Tort Claims Act, 28 U.S.C.A. sec. 1346(b), 2674.

87. Prosser, *supra* note 43, at 972.

88. Section 2680(h).

89. Logue v. U.S., 354 F. Supp. 322, *rev.* 459 F.2d 408 (S.D. Texas, 1971) (culpable negligence). *See also,* Cox v. Heckler, 218 F. Supp. 749 (E.D. Pa. 1963). *Contra,* Fahey v. United States, 152 F. Supp. 535 (S.D.N.Y. 1957) (no liability for refusal to commit mental patient).

90. "It appears generally that the care required of a hospital includes giving such care to a patient as the hospital knew, or in the exercise of reasonable care, should have known was required." Baker v. U.S., 226 F. Supp. 129 (S.D. Iowa, 1964), as quoted in R. C. Allen, E. Z. Ferster, and J. G. Rubin (Eds.) *Readings in law and psychiatry*. Baltimore: Johns Hopkins Press, 1968, p. 298.

91. Wright v. State, 31 App. Div. 2d 421, 300 N.Y.S.2d 153 (4th Dep't. 1969).

92. Whitree v. State, 56 Misc. 2d 693, 290 N.Y.S.2d 486 (Ct. Cl. 1968).

93. Whitree, *id.* at 697, 290 N.Y.S.2d at 491.

94. This was the primary theory presented to the court by Whitree's attorneys. Personal communication, Aaron J. Broder, July 17, 1972. Negligence was mentioned in the court's opinion. 56 Misc. 2d at 710, 290 N.Y.S. 2d at 504. Upon agreement not to appeal, the case was eventually settled for $200,000.

95. Whitree, 56 Misc. 2d at 708, 290 N.Y.S.2d at 502.

96. A physician disclosing a psychiatric diagnosis to a spouse—Fox, R. G. Professional confidences and the psychologist. 3 *University of Tasmania Law Review* 30 (1968)

reporting Furniss v. Fitchett, New Zealand Supreme Court, N.Z.L.E. 396 (1958). *See also,* 34 *New Zealand Law Journal* 65.

97. Carr v. St. John's University, 17 App. Div. 2d 632, 231 N.Y.S.2d 410, *rev.* 34 Misc. 2d 319, *aff'd mem,* 187 N.E.2d 18, 235 N.Y.S.2d 834 (1962); Anthony v. Syracuse University, 231 N.Y.S. 435, 224 App. Div. 487 (1928).

98. Doe v. San Francisco Unified School Dist., No. 653–312 (Super. Ct. Cal. filed Oct. 31, 1973) (high school graduation without reading ability necessary to obtain job); *In re* H., N.Y.S.2d 302 (Family Ct., Westchester County 1971) (poor instruction in special education class).

99. Ayllon, T. and Skuban, W. Accountability in psychotherapy: A test case. 4 *Journal of Behavior Therapy and Experimental Psychiatry* 19 (1973); Schwitzgebel, R. K. A contractual model for the protection of the rights of institutionalized mental patients. 30 *American Psychologist* 815 (1975). There appears to be a gradual shift in the traditional therapist-patient relationship from that of implied fiduciary to quasi-contract. Hoffman, B. D. and Dunn, R. C. Guaranteeing the right to treatment. 6 *Psychiatric Annals* 258 (June 1976).

100. *E.g.,* 21 C.F.R. 130.44, 37 Fed. Reg. 242 d (3) (Dec. 14, 1972).

101. *See generally,* Prosser, *supra* note 43, at 650–662. Intended or reasonably anticipated use of products may be aided by behavioral research, *see* Note, Use of behavioral research in products liability litigation. 2 *Hofstra Law Review* 777 (Summer 1974).

102. Johnson, *supra* note 70.

103. For a useful summary of statutes and relevant cases, *see* Commission on Correctional Facilities and Services and the Young Lawyers Section, Liability in correctional volunteer programs: Planning for potential problems. Chicago: National Volunteer Parole Aide Program, American Bar Association, 1975, pp. 11–24.

104. Schwartz v. Thiele, 51 Cal Rptr 767 (Ct. App. 1966). For other cases of wrongful commitment in which the examining physician was not held liable, *see* summary in Bellamy, W.A. Psychiatric malpractice, in S. Arieti (Ed.) *American handbook of psychiatry,* vol. 3 New York: Basic Books, 1966, p. 621.

105. Morris v. University of Texas, 348 S.W.2d 644 (1961). Numerous states have statutes granting immunity, for example, "to any health officer or his employee when there is reasonable cause for believing the application is for the best interest of the person." Calif. Welfare & Institutions Code, section 6610.3. *See also,* Employees v. Missouri, 411 U.S. 279 (1973) (barring relief under Fair Labor Standards Act from a nonconsenting state under 11th amendment). Note, Guaranteed treatment for the committed mental patient: The troubled enforcement of an elusive right. 32 *Maryland Law Review* 41, 54 (1972). In right-to-treatment cases where the patient refuses treatment, such refusal may be viewed as an affirmative defense to the obligation for treatment placed upon the defendant institution. The trial judge, in O'Connor v. Donaldson, instructed the jury not to award damages for any period of confinement during which Donaldson, a Christian Scientist, had declined treatment (including medication). O'Connor v. Donaldson, 95 S. Ct. 2486, 2490 n. 4 (1975).

106. Downs v. Department of Public Welfare, 368 F. Supp. 454 (E.D. Pa. 1973). This was also the protection which shielded the staff involved in Tarasoff v. Regents of the University of California, 131 Cal. Rptr. 14, 551 P.2d 334 (1976).

107. Francis v. Lyman, 216 F.2d 583 (1st Cir. 1954); *see generally,* Note, The doctrine of

official immunity under the Civil Rights Act. 68 *Harvard Law Review* 1229 (1955).

108. Jobson v. Henne, 355 F.2d 129, 134 (2d Cir. 1966).
109. Downs v. Department of Public Welfare, 368 F. Supp. 454, 462 (E.D. Pa. 1973).
110. O'Connor v. Donaldson, 95 S. Ct. 2486, n. 58 (1975).
111. Davidson, H. A. The commitment procedures and their legal implications. In S. Arieti (Ed.) *Handbook of psychiatry,* vol. 2. New York: Basic Books, 1959, pp. 1921–1922.
112. Miroz v. Kippell, 158 Wis. 557, 149 N.W. 375, 377 (1914). *Contra,* O'Connor, *supra* note 110. For theory of monetary remedy without, as yet, judicial support, see Frankel, L. H., Preventative restraints and just compensation. 78 *Yale Law Journal* 229 (1968).
113. Davidson, *supra* note 111, at 1904, 1922.
114. Downs v. Department of Public Welfare, 368 F. Supp. 454 (E.D. Pa. 1973).
115. *See* Ferleger, D. (Mental Patient Civil Liberties Project), Loosing the chains: In-hospital civil liberties of mental patients. Reprinted in 13 *Santa Clara Lawyer* 447 (1973), interpreting Winters v. Miller, 446 F.2d 65 (2d Cir. 1971); *accord* Wyatt, 344 F. Supp. 373, 379 (M.D. Ala. 1972).
116. Sostre v. McGinnis, 442 F.2d 178 (2d Cir. 1971); Wright v. McMann, 460 F.2d 126 (2d Cir. 1972); Roberts v. Williams, 302 F. Supp. 972 (D. Miss. 1969).
117. Sostre v. McGinnis, 442 F.2d 178 (2d Cir. 1971).
118. Wright v. McMann, 460 F.2d 126 (2d Cir. 1972).
119. Prison Law Collective, *supra* note 25, at 13, reporting on cases in the Ninth Circuit Court of Appeals.
120. L. R. Frumer and M. I. Friedman (Eds.) *Personal injury: Actions, defenses, damages,* vol. 5. Albany, New York: Matthew Bender, 1965, p. 607.
121. Sostre v. McGinnis, 442 F.2d 178 (2d Cir. 1971) (no behavior pattern or impact); Terri Lee Halderman et al. v. Pennhurst State School and Hospital, C.A. No. 74–1345 (E.D. Pa. Dec. 23, 1977) *as reported in* 2 *Mental Disability Law Reporter* 210 (Sept.–Dec. 1977).
122. "... Where there is a significant encroachment upon personal liberty, the State may prevail only upon showing a subordinating interest which is compelling." Bates v. Little Rock, 361 U.S. 516, 524 (1960).
123. Creech, W. A. Psychological testing and constitutional rights. 1966 *Duke Law Journal* 322, 368 (1966), interpreting Williams v. Zuckert, 371 U.S. 531 (1963), 83 S. Ct. 403 (1963).
124. Wright v. McMann, 460 F.2d 126 (2d Cir. 1972); Clutchette v. Procunier, 497 F.2d 809 (1974).
125. Wright v. McMann, 460 F. 2d 126 (2d Cir. 1972); Wolff v. McDonnell, 14 U.S. 39, 94 S. Ct. 2963 (1974).
126. Braun, S. H. Ethical issues in behavior modification. Arizona State Hospital (Phoenix, Arizona), Social Learning Division, 1974, p. 9 (mimeo.).
127. Morris v. Univ. of Texas, 348 S.W.2d 644 (Tex. Civ. App. 1961) (plaintiff unable to prove necessary intention).
128. See exceptions in Federal Tort Claims Act, *supra* note 86.
129. Anonymous v. State of New York, 236 N.Y.S.2d 88 (Ct. App. 1963).
130. Lester v. Aetna Casualty & Surety Co., 240 F.2d 676 (5th Cir. 1957). A minority view is that consent is implied when the patient does not object or resist. Wilson v. Lehman, 399 S.W.2d 478 (Ky. 1964).

131. Prosser, *supra* note 43, at pp. 796–799; Emmett v. Eastern Dispensary & Casualty Hospital, 396 F.2d 931 (D.C. Cir. 1967); *contra,* Berry v. Moench, 331 P.2d 814 (Utah 1958) (truth not adequate defense for physician reporting psychopathy of patient). King v. Memalasalno, 555 P.2d 442 (Ore. 1976) (controversy regarding DSMO for retardates not libelous).

132. Fox, R. G. Professional confidences and the psychologist. 3 *University of Tasmania Law Review* 30, 31–32 (1968); *cf. also:* "Libel and slander" in 53 C.J.S., sec. 120: "A communication to the relatives of a party defamed (when made on request or in the discharge of a duty, social, moral or legal) is qualifiedly privileged."

133. Sadoff, R. L. Informed consent, confidentiality, and privacy in psychiatry: Practical applications. 2 *The Bulletin of the American Academy of Psychiatry and Law* 1, 14 (1974).

134. Ladimer, I. Ethical aspects of medical research on human beings. In I. Ladimer and R. W. Newman (Eds.) *Clinical investigation in medicine: Legal, ethical and moral aspects.* Boston: Boston University Law-Medicine Research Institute, 1963, p. 207.

135. Cahoon, D. D. Use of aversive stimuli in behavior modification. In M. R. Jones (Ed.) *Miami symposium in the prediction of behavior.* Coral Gables, Fla.: University of Miami Press (1968), pp. 77–145.

136. Buddenhage, R. G. Until electric shocks are legal. 9 *Mental Retardation* 48 (December 1971).

137. Sostre v. McGinnis, 442 F.2d 178 (2d Cir. 1971).

138. "Berlin's victory," 107 *Time* 65 (June 14, 1976).

139. Sauer, J. G. Psychiatric malpractice—A survey. 2 *Washburn Law* Journal 461 (1972).

140. E.g., Medical Professional Liability Act, Hawaii Act 219, sec. 2.11 (1976). For report of mixed results using such panels in Massachusetts, Missouri, and Pennsylvania, *see* 20 *Medical World News* 23 (Apr. 16, 1979). A novel arrangement for reducing *defense* legal fees is to make amount contingent on expected savings— *see* 20 *Medical World News* 55 (Apr. 2, 1979).

APPENDIXES

APPENDIX A

Finding The Law

Where you begin your search to find relevant law depends on where you are. That is, your approach will be determined by whether you have a *topic, statute, case,* or *regulation* already in hand.

TOPIC

If you have only a topic or word, several legal encyclopedias may be useful. *American Jurisprudence* or *Corpus Juris Secondum* are the most general and popular. (Always check the pocket parts at the back of *any* reference volume for more recent information.) *West's Dicennial Digest* and *West's General Digest* are also topically indexed with extensive annotations from state and federal cases. Another valuable source for case law, topically arranged, is the *American Law Reports.* Almost all states have similar and separate digests, e.g., *Massachusetts' Digest Annotated, Indiana Dicennial Digest, Callaghan's Wisconsin Digest.* The standard source for locating relevant law review articles on a topic is the *Index to Legal Periodicals* which is similar in function to *Index Medicus* or *Psychological Abstracts.*

STATUTE

Current federal statutory law is contained in *United States Codes* or *United States Codes Annotated* (includes relevant court cases). *United States Statutes at Large* presents all the laws passed by Congress in sequence. *Shephard's Acts and Cases by Proper Names* is helpful if you only know a statute by a popular title, such as the "Freedom of Information Act."

CASES

Thousands of appellate-level judicial decisions are printed in volumes of "Reports" or "Reporters." This is, however, only a small fraction of all court cases because the decisions of "lower courts" or "courts of original jurisdiction" are rarely included. (See Fig. A.1.)

The title or case name designates the parties, such as *Donaldson* v. *O'Connor*. This plaintiff-defendant order is usually kept. However, in some courts, the order is reversed on appeal when the defendant has lost. Thus it is wise to look in case indexes under both names. A citation or "cite" to a case takes the following form:

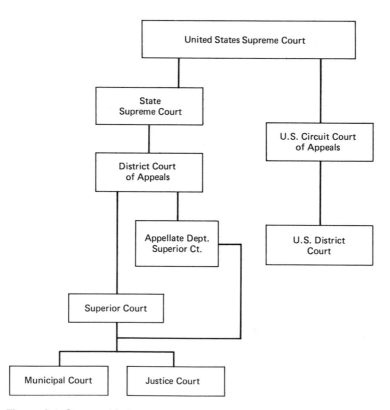

Figure A.1. State and federal court system.

O'Connor v. *Donaldson*, 95 S.Ct. 2486 (1975). This series of items includes the case name, volume number, abbreviated title of the publication ("S.Ct." for *Supreme Court Reporter*), page number where the case begins, and the year of the decision.

Often a cite will have more than one reference, indicating that the text of the same case is reported in several different publications. A U.S. Supreme Court decision may be found in the *United States Supreme Court Reports* (U.S.), *Supreme Court Reporter* (S. Ct.) or *Lawyers' Edition of the Supreme Court Reports* (L. Ed.). Federal Circuit Court decisions are reported in the *Federal Reporter* (F.) and Federal District Court decisions in the *Federal Supplement* (F. Supp.). The decisions of the highest court of every state (and often lower courts) are published in a regional or state reporter: Atlantic (A.), California (Cal.), New York Supplement (N.Y.S.), Northeastern (N.E.), Northwestern (N.W.), Pacific (P.), Southeastern (S.E.), Southwestern (S.W.), and Southern (S.).

ADMINISTRATIVE REGULATIONS

Federal administrative law such as promulgated by HEW is published in the *Federal Register* or in a more limited annual edition under the title *Code of Federal Regulations* (CFR) which incorporates the rules that are actually in force at the end of a calendar year. Both of these serial publications have cumulative indexes. Within a given state, the advisory opinion of the chief law officer may be useful where case law or statute law is ambiguous or nonexistent on a particular matter (e.g., definition of "psychotherapy"). These opinions are usually published as "Attorney General's opinions."

Any serious search for relevant case law must use a citator. This is typically referred to as "Shephardizing" a case because the volumes universally used to find related cases are published by Shephard's Citations, Inc. The citators serve as a master index that indicates all previous and subsequent cases in the reporter system that have cited a particular case as authority. Its function is similar to that of the *Science Citation Index* for scientific publications. Instructions for using Shephard's citators are explained at the front of each volume. A separate citator is published for each federal and regional reporter. Specialized abstracting services issue periodic summaries of legal developments in criminal law, mental health law, and so forth. For more detailed directions for using law materials, consult specialized volumes such as M. O. Price & H. Bitner's *Effective Legal Research* (Little, Brown & Co.) or M. Cohen's *Legal Research in a Nutshell* (West Publishing Co.).

APPENDIX B

Glossary of Legal Terms*

Acceptance An unqualified assent to the act or proposal of another person of an offer to make a contract.

Action A proceeding brought to enforce any right.

Affidavit A written statement of fact signed and sworn before a person authorized to administer an oath (e.g., a notary public).

Amicus curiae A friend of the court. Also a person who has no right to appear in a suit but is allowed to introduce argument, authority, or evidence to protect his/her interests.

Appellant The party who takes an appeal from one court or jurisdiction to another.

Appellee The party in a cause against whom an appeal is taken; that is, the party who has an interest adverse to setting aside or reversing the judgment.

Brief A written document prepared by an attorney addressed to the court summarizing facts and arguments in support of a litigant's position.

Case law The aggregate of reported cases forming a body of jurisprudence, or the law of a particular subject as evidenced or formed by the adjudged cases, in distinction to statutes and other sources of law.

Certiorari The name of a writ of review or inquiry. Certiorari is an appellate proceeding for re-examination of action of inferior tribunal or as auxiliary process to enable appellate court to obtain further information in pending case. In case citations, the history of the case may indicate *cert. granted* or *cert. denied*.

Civil A term referring to an individual's relation to fellow citizens (in contrast to his/her relation to the State).

Common law A system of legal principles that does not derive its authority from statutory

---

*For definitions not included here, a convenient reference source is any recent edition of *Cochran's Law Lexicon* (published by W.H. Anderson Company). This dictionary contains a list of abbreviations found in reporters and law books and also the ABA's "Code of Professional Responsibility" for lawyers.

law but from general usage and custom (particularly old English law) as evidenced by decisions of courts.

Consideration   The promise or performance by the other party that the promisor demands as the price of his/her promise.

Contract   A binding agreement based on the genuine assent of the parties, made for a lawful object, between competent parties, in the form required by the law, and generally supported by consideration.

Cross examination   The questioning of a witness during a trial or deposition by the party opposing those who originally asked him/her to testify.

Damages   A sum of money recovered to redress or make amends for the legal wrong on injury done.

Defendant   The person against whom an action is made for relief or recovery.

Dictum   An expression of opinion contained in the decision of a court on some matter related to the subject of the decision itself. It does not have the force of a decision but may be cited in later legal arguments on issues on which the dictum bears directly.

Direct examination   The initial question of a witness by the party who originally called him/her to testify.

Due process of law   Law in its regular course of administration through courts of justice. . . . Due process of law implies the right of a person affected thereby to be present before the tribunal that pronounces judgment upon the question of life, liberty, or property, in its most comprehensive sense to be heard, by testimony or otherwise, and to have the right of controverting, by proof, every material fact that bears on the question of right in the matter involved.

Duty   An obligation or responsibility to perform or refrain from performing an act that may arise from the relationship between the particular parties.

Enjoin   To command that some particular action shall or shall not be performed.

Equity   A system of law and courts emphasizing ''fairness'' that developed separate from, and as a complement to, common law.

Exemplary damages   An award of money given over and above that required to compensate the victim for loss where the wrong committed was done with malice. It is intended to act as a form of punishment and to provide an ''example'' for others.

Felony   A crime more serious or harmful than a misdemeanor, and usually punishable by death or long-term imprisonment.

Fiduciary   Describing relationships of high trust and confidence. Guardians, trustees, executors, administrators, and the like are fiduciaries.

Guardian *ad Litem*   One who is appointed by the court to protect the interests of a minor in a lawsuit. He/she is empowered to act in the child's behalf until the case is concluded.

Habeas corpus (literally, ''You have the body'')   A writ or order requiring that the officer who has custody of a prisoner bring him/her before the court to determine if the prisoner is lawfully detained.

Hearsay   Evidence that is not based on the personal, first-hand knowledge of the witness.

In bank (en banc)   A term applied to court proceedings heard by all the court officers as a group, in contrast to the proceedings before one judge and a jury.

In loco parentis (literally, ''in place of parents'')   A party acting legally in behalf of the parents.

In re   In the matter of (The typical method of assigning a name to a case where there are no adversary parties.)

Infra   Below, following.

Intent   A state of mind (inferred from a person's actions) showing purpose or determination to act in a certain manner.

Jurisdiction   The authority a court has to decide a case; the geographical area in which it has authority.

Malfeasance   Unlawful conduct; acts that are expressly prohibited.

Mandamus   A writ or order of a superior court to a lower court or to a governmental body commanding that a certain act be performed or not performed.

Misdemeanor   An unlawful act not as serious as a felony; typically punishable by a fine or short-term imprisonment.

Misfeasance   The improper performance of an act the person has a right or duty to perform.

Moot   A topic for debate—often abstract in nature in which there are no specific, real-life facts to be determined or arguments settled.

Motion   An application to the court requesting that a particular order be given.

Parens patriae   In the United States, the State, as a sovereign—referring to the sovereign power of guardianship over persons under disability; such as minors, and insane, and incompetent persons.

Plaintiff   A person who initiates an action.

Pleading   The process in which alternate and opposing written statements are presented by the contesting parties for the purpose of focusing on a particular issue.

Prima facie evidence   A fact presumed to be true as a matter of initial appearance and logic.

Privilege   An advantage or exemption, beyond those commonly held by citizens, to perform or not perform an act.

Proximate cause   An event that, in an unbroken and ordinary chain of events, produces an injury.

Putative   Reputed or supposed.

Remand   To send back. The sending the case back to the same court out of which it came, for purpose of having some action on it there (e.g., when a prisoner is brought before a judge on habeas corpus, for the purpose of obtaining liberty, the judge hears the case, and either discharges him or remands him/her).

Remedy   The means by which a right is enforced or the violation of a right is prevented, redressed, or compensated. Strictly speaking, "remedy," is no part of the action, but is the result thereof, the object for which the action is presented, the end to which all the litigation is directed.

Respondent   The party who makes an answer to a charge or the party who contends against an appeal.

Right   A power or claim, legally enforced, inherent in one person that may make demands on another.

Statute   An act of the legislature, in contrast to unwritten or common law.

Stipulation   An agreement between opposing parties that a particular fact or principle of law is true and applicable.

Sub nom   In the name of. (Often used when the original name of a case must be changed because of a change in parties.)

Subpoena   A process commanding a witness to appear and give testimony in court.

Subpoena duces tecum   A process commanding that a witness produce a particular document or record.

Supra   Before, above.

Tort   A private injury or wrong arising from a breach of a duty created by law.

Undue influence   Wrongful persuasion of a person thereby causing him/her to do what would not normally be done.

Uniform laws   A body of written laws approved by the National Conference of Commissioners of Uniform State Laws.

Warrant   A document directing a public officer to perform an act (e.g., make a search).

Waive   To forego a legal right.

Appendix C

Appendix C

Type of Hospitalization

State	Emergency Alone	Emergency With MD	Judicial Alone	Judicial With MD	Voluntary Alone	Voluntary With MD	Significant Terminology	State Law Reference and Year Enacted
Arizona				X			Evaluation Independent evaluator Certified psychologist	Arizona Revised Statutes 36-501 through 36-550, 1974
California	X			X			Evaluation Qualified professional Psychologist	Division 5, Community Mental Health Services, Part 1 (Lanterman-Petris-Short Act), 1970; Register 76, #5, 1976
Colorado	X		X[a]				Professional person Certified psychologist	Colorado Revised Statutes, Vol. II, 1973
Idaho			X[b]				Designated examiner Clinical psychologist	Idaho Code, Title 66, State Charitable Institutions, 1974
Iowa				X[c]			Qualified mental health professional Certified psychologist	Code of Iowa, Chapter 229, Hospitalization of Mentally Ill Persons, 1976
Kentucky		X[d]					Qualified mental health professional Psychologist	Kentucky Revised Statutes Chapter 202A, 1976
Maine	X		X[b]				Licensed psychologist	Maine Statutes, Chapter 191, 1973
Minnesota				X[d]	X		Examiner, health officer Consulting psychologist	Minnesota Statutes, Chapter 253A, 1971
Mississippi				X[d]			Psychologist	Mississippi Laws, 1975, Chapter 492
Montana			X		X		Professional person	Revised Codes of Montana, Chapter 12 Title 38, 1975

Type of Hospitalization

State	Emergency Alone	Emergency With MD	Judicial Alone	Judicial With MD	Voluntary Alone	Voluntary With MD	Significant Terminology	State Law Reference and Year Enacted
Nebraska			X[e]				Mental health professional; Clinical psychologist; Independent evaluation	Nebraska Mental Health Commitment Act, 93-1001 et seq. (RS Supp., 1976) 1977
Nevada				X[f]			Certified psychologist	Nevada Revised Statutes, Chapter 433A, 1975
North Dakota	X			X[c]	X		Mental health professional; Clinical psychologist	North Dakota Century Code, Chapter 25-03.1, Commitment Procedures, 1977
Ohio	X			X[g]			Licensed clinical psychologist, independent expert evaluation	Ohio Revised Code, Chapter 51, Section 5122.01-5122, 1976
Oklahoma				X[d]			Qualified examiner; Licensed clinical psychologist	Chapter 43A, Section 54(a), Oklahoma Statutes as amended by SB No. 240, 1977
Oregon				X[d]			Qualified mental health professional	Oregon Revised Statutes, Chapter 426, Title 35, 1974
Rhode Island	X[h]						Psychologist; Mental health professional	Rhode Island General Laws, Chapter 40.1-5, 1970
South Carolina				X[d]		X	Designated examiner	New and Revised Laws, South Carolina, 1975, Correspondence, Dr. Ackerman, CMH Services, 1975

		Qualified mental health professional	HB 573; Title 27, South Dakota Statutes, 1975
South Dakota	X[i]	Qualified mental health professional	HB 573; Title 27, South Dakota Statutes, 1975
Utah	X[d]	Designated examiner	Utah Code, Utah Mental Health Services Act, 1975
Virginia	X[j]	Clinical psychologist (licensed)	Code of Virginia, Title 37, Sections 37.1-63 through 37.1-70, 1974
Washington	X[d]	Mental health professional Professional person Psychologist	Washington Laws, Chapter 142, "Mentally Disordered Persons—Commitment Procedures", 1973
West Virginia	X[d]	Psychologist	MH Laws of West Virginia Including Act of the Legislature through 1974, Chapter 27, 1974
Wisconsin	X[d]	Licensed Psychologist	Wisconsin Statutes, Chapter 430, 1976.

[a] Screening and certification for extending commitment period. The initial commitment certification must be by a physician.

[b] Two examiners are required; either or both may be psychologists or physicians.

[c] A physician *may* consult with a mental health professional.

[d] Requires two physicians *or* one physician and one psychologist (or mental health professional) to conduct an examination.

[e] An evaluation and/or "predisposition investigation" by a physician *or* psychologist *may* be requested by a quasi-judicial, lay board that can also include a psychologist as a member.

[f] Court can require an examination by a multidisciplinary team *or* two more physicians *or* physicians *and* a psychologist.

[g] The court requires an examination by a psychiatrist *or* by a physician *and* psychologist.

[h] By a mental health professional *if* a physician is unavailable.

[i] A petition for commitment *must* have a certificate from a mental health professional *or* physician.

[j] One physician or one physician and a clinical psychologist.

Source: Reprinted with permission from Drude, K. P. Psychologists and civil commitment: Review of state statutes. 9 *Professional Psychology* 504 (August 1978).

305

D

Application for Habeas Corpus

_____ , Petitioner
(Name of patient)

v.

_____ , Respondent
(Name of institution's administrator),

    1. Petitioner is held in _____of _____ County,
                      (Institution's name)

_____ , of which respondent is the chief administrative officer.
(State)

    2. Petitioner does not know the cause for which s/he is being held, but is advised by respondent s/he is being held at the request of _____

                                                (Name of party making original
_____ on the claim that petitioner is _____
complaint)

_____ .
dangerous to self or others)

    3. Petitioner states that s/he is a citizen of the United States in that s/he was born in _____ , on _____ .
             (City, state)   (Date)

    4. The detention of the petitioner on the grounds as aforementioned is illegal and unconstitutional, and no other cause for detention appears or has been made known to petitioner.

Wherefore petitioner prays the court for its writ of habeas corpus, directing that s/he be brought before the court, and that s/he be discharged from custody on hearing.

_____
(Name of petitioner)

State of _____)
) ss.
County of _____)

_____ , petitioner, being first duly sworn, states
(Name of petitioner)
that the allegations of the foregoing application for habeas corpus are true.

_____
(Signature of petitioner)

Subscribed and sworn to before me this _____ day of _____ , 19____ .

_____
Notary Public

(If the person in custody is unable to be communicated with or unable to sign the document or have it notarized, another person may do so for him/her).

APPENDIX E

Checklist for Obtaining Consent for Treatment

- ☐ Is the client competent to consent?
- ☐ If the client is not competent, is there a logical representative to grant consent?
- ☐ Is there any reason to suspect that the representative is not competent to consent?
- ☐ Should more than one representative give consent? For example, if both parents of a minor child are available, both signatures should be obtained.
- ☐ If the client's representative(s) consent(s), does the client offer any protest?
- ☐ Does the explanation of information needed to get consent from a surrogate, who is not the client's parent, violate any rights of privacy of the client?
- ☐ Is consent given voluntarily and free of any institutional coercion?
- ☐ Is any threat implied if the client or his/her representative does not consent?
- ☐ Is there a clear invitation to participate? (i.e., the client must realize that s/he is being asked to do something different).
- ☐ Is there an explanation of the overall purpose of the activity and why s/he has been asked to participate?
- ☐ Is the procedure going to involve research or treatment or a combination of both?
- ☐ Is there an explanation of other appropriate alternative strategies for dealing the problem and an offer to implement any one of them chosen by the client?
- ☐ As much as possible, are the explanations of the innovative procedure, treat-

ment, and alternatives offered in writing in nontechnical and objective language?

☐ Is the client given the name of someone or some group who have experienced the procedure and could freely discuss its benefits and disadvantages? (If not actual contact, is the client at least given an article to read that argues both sides of the proposed approach?)

☐ Are steps explained to guarantee there will be a system for early detection, minimization, and correction of harms? Is there an explanation of how the client will be compensated, if at all, for any loss due to a harm suffered?

☐ Are procedures to preserve confidentiality explained, along with limitations? (i.e., types of data to be collected, length of retention, persons or agencies with access, publication plans).

☐ Are any material inducements being offered to participate in the program?

☐ Is there any explanation of how the client's progress will be evaluated?

☐ Is there a clear offer to answer any inquiries? (Sometimes the inquiries and their responses are written, or a tape recorder is used.)

☐ Is there a clear instruction that the client is free to withdraw his/her consent at any time without punishment? (There may be limitations if there is physical or mental danger to the person; if so, state such conditions.)

☐ Is there a notation of the time the information was given and the consent given? (At least 48 hours should be allowed if possible to give the person time to "think it over.")

☐ How is the consent acknowledged? (At minimum, the person should sign underneath a statement reading "I have read and understand the above explanation. A few correctly answered multiple choice questions would give even more manifest evidence of the person's understanding.)

☐ Is there a signature of an uninvolved third party who can serve as a witness to the consent process?

Source: Condensed and adapted from Martin, R. Consent—A negotiation for services. 1 *Law and Behavior* 1 7 (Fall 1976). Readers are encouraged to consult the original source for additional items and explanations.

APPENDIX F

Sample Contingency Contract for Therapy

1. Overview of problem and therapeutic program

The overall objective of this therapeutic program is to develop and stabilize Mike's behavior patterns so that he may be considered for admission to school this fall. In general, this will involve strengthening some requisite behaviors such as following commands from an adult, and eliminating others, such as the screaming and tantrumming that accompany most of his refusals to follow instructions.

Mike has a discouraging behavior history for most teachers to consider working with. Because his characteristic reaction to requests is to throw tantrums, he is considered "untestable" by standard psychological means. This does not necessarily mean that he cannot do the items on a test, but rather that he has little or no control over his own behavior. His uncooperativeness quickly discourages most people from making much of an effort to work with him. What is clearly needed is an intensive rehabilitation program designed to enable Mike to build patterns of self-control which would lead to the elimination or drastic reduction of his disruptive behavior. This, in turn, would open other possibilities for developing Mike's potential, that is, the avenues which are blocked by his unmanageable behavior.

The overall goal of this 8-week program will be the development of self-control with its reciprocal outcome of decreasing or eliminating tantrums and disruptive behaviors. Implementation of this program will require that the child and his trainer engage in such activities as trips to the zoo, museums, parks, movies, swimming pools, shopping centers, supermarkets, and so on as well as having lunch and snacks together. These settings are included to expose Mike to a maximal number of normal situations where expectations of a standard of conduct are imposed by the setting itself.

As much as possible, the techniques used in the day program will be designed with the ultimate objective of utilization in the home. An attempt will be made to see that procedures used in the program are transferred to home management at the termination of treatment. The therapist will give instructions weekly to the parents by phone to insure that efforts both at home and in rehabilitation do not conflict.

II. Behavioral objectives of therapy

1. The objective of the therapeutic program is to teach Mike to comply with between 80–100 per cent of the verbal commands given to him by an adult(s). Compliance will be defined as Mike's beginning to perform the behavior specified by the command within 15 sec after it has been stated and then completing the specified task.

2. In addition, we intend to eliminate or drastically reduce Mike's excessive screaming and tantrumming. The goal is not to tantrum more frequently than once out of 30 commands and for no longer than 1 min at a time.

3. Evaluation of treatment outcome: The decision as to the attainment of these specific objectives will rest upon Mike's performance during a 30 min test session to be conducted in a classroom situation. At this session the therapist, the parents, and an additional person will make 10 verbal requests each of Mike, for a total of 30 verbal requests. Mike must comply with 80–100 per cent of these requests for the program to be considered a success. In addition, he must have tantrummed not more than once, and for not more than 1 min. during this final evaluation.

III. Time and place of therapeutic intervention

1. The therapeutic program will start on _____ and terminate on _____ . Evaluation of the effectiveness of treatment will be held on or about the termination date of the therapeutic program.

2. Location: The meeting place will be at the _____ . Session activities, however, will involve time spent elsewhere, for example, having lunch, trips to shopping centers, amusements, and other special events. If the facility is not available, some other place agreeable can be designated as meeting and base center.

3. Days of training: Therapy sessions will be scheduled 5 days per week. The specific days may vary from week to week to comply with the objectives of the program. The family will be advised of the therapy schedule 1 week in advance.

4. Hours per day: Therapeutic sessions will be scheduled for 7 hr a day. Session time may be extended when therapeutically necessary as decided by the therapist.

5. Absences: There will be 4 notified absences allowed. The mother is expected to notify the therapist at least 1 hr before the scheduled therapy session. Any additional absences will require an additional fee of $10 per absence.

IV. Fees

Achievement of the behavioral objectives is expected to take 7 weeks of training from _____. This training will cost a total of _____. The monies will be disbursed in the following manner:

1. A check for ⅔ of the total amount will be given to the therapist at the beginning of therapy.

2. The balance of ⅓ will be paid to the therapist upon the achievement of the program objectives as specified above on about the date of termination of the program. In the event that the above objectives are not reached by this date, therapy will be discontinued and the balance will be forfeited by the therapist.

3. All expense incurred during training will be defrayed by the therapist. This will include admission to baseball games, the city zoo, swimming pools, and so on, as well as the cost of field trips, lunch, and snacks.

By my signature I do hereby attest that I have read the above proposal and agree to the conditions stated therein.

_____
(Parent)

_____
(Supervising Therapist)

_____
(Co-Therapist)

_____
Date

Source: Ayllon, T. & Skuban, W. Accountability in psychotherapy: A test case. *Journal of Behavior Therapy and Experimental Psychiatry* 19–29 (1973). Copyright, 1973 by Teodoro Ayllon.

APPENDIX G

Consumer/Therapist Contract

I. _____, agree to join with _____ each _____
from _____ until _____, at _____. During these
_____ we will direct our mutual efforts towards *three* goals:

1.

2.

3.

I agree to pay _____ $_____ per session for the use of his/her re-
sources, training and experience as a psychotherapist. This amount is payable
within _____.

If I am not satisfied with the progress made on these goals, I may
_____. In that event I am _____ required to pay for sessions
not met. However, if I miss a session without forewarning _____, I am
_____ financially responsible for that missed, exceptions to this arrangement
being unforseen and unavoidable accidents.

At the end of _____ sessions, _____ and I agree to renegotiate this contract. We include the possibility that the stated goals will have changed during the _____ period. I understand that this agreement does not guarantee that I will have attained those goals; however, it does constitute an offer on my part to pay _____ for access to her/his resources as a psychotherapist and his/her acceptance to apply all those resources as a psychotherapist in good faith.

I further stipulate that this agreement become a part of the medical record which is accessible to both parties at will, but to no other person without my written consent. The therapist will respect my right to maintain the confidentiality of any information communicated by me to the therapist during the course of therapy. In particular, the therapist will not publish, communicate or otherwise disclose, without my written consent, any such information which, if disclosed, would injure me in any way.

_____

Date: _____

SAMPLE COMPLETED CONSUMER/THERAPIST CONTRACT

I. *Mr. Client* agree to join with *Ms. Therapist* each Thursday afternoon from May 1, 1975, until June 5, 1975, at 3 P.M. until 3:50 p.m. During these six 50-minute sessions we will direct our mutual efforts towards three goals:

1. enabling me to fly in airplanes without fear
2. explaining to my satisfaction why I always lose my temper when I visit my parents
3. discussing whether it would be better for me to give up my full-time job and start working part-time

I agree to pay $30 per session for the use of her resources, training and experience as a psychotherapist. This amount is payable within 30 days of the session.

If I am not satisfied with the progress made on the goals here set forth, I may cancel any and all subsequent appointments for these sessions, provided that I give Ms. Therapist 3 days warning of my intention to cancel. In that event I am not required to pay for sessions not met. However, in the event that I miss a session without forewarning, I am financially responsible for that missed session. The one exception to this arrangement being unforseen and unavoidable accident or illness.

At the end of the six sessions Ms. Therapist and I agree to renegotiate this contract. We include the possibility that the stated goals will have changed during the six-week period. I understand that this agreement does not guarantee that I will have attained those goals; however, it does constitute an offer on my part to pay Ms. Therapist for access to her resources as a psychotherapist and her acceptance to apply all those resources as a psychotherapist in good faith.

I further stipulate that this agreement become a part of the medical record which is accessible to both parties at will, but to no other person without my written consent. The therapist will respect my right to maintain the confidentiality of any information communicated by me to the therapist during the course of therapy. In particular, the therapist will not publish, communicate or otherwise disclose, without my written consent, any such information which, if disclosed, would injure me in any way.

(Date)   (Name of client)   (Name of Professional)

Contract form and sample completed form reproduced from Adams, S. and Orgel, M. *Through the mental health maze: A consumer's guide to finding a psychotherapist, including a sample consumer/ therapist contract.* Copyright, Public Citizen's Health Research Group, Washington, D.C., 1975.

APPENDIX H

Intervention Contract

Name of Client: Name of Therapist:
    Address: Title:
    Phone: Organization:
                               Highest academic degree:
                               License:

1. I, the above named therapist, certify that I am (circle one) duly licensed to offer the services described below *or* under the supervision of _____ who is so licensed.

    (Name, address)

2. I have assessed the client's behavior change objective(s) in the following manner: _____

3. I propose to use the following intervention technique(s) in my effort to assist the client to achieve the above objective(s): _____

    a. This (these) technique(s) have been fully described in the following standard professional reference:_____

    b. The most recent comprehensive account of the clinical results achieved with this (these) technique(s) may be found in the following source(s):

316

4. It is expected that this (these) intervention technique(s) will have the following beneficial effects for the client by the dates specified:_____

5. It is also noted that this (these) intervention technique(s) may be associated with the following undesirable side effect(s): _____

6. Both the progress toward achieving the specified objectives and the potential side effects will be monitored continuously in the following manner(s): ____

_____   _____
(Date)   (Signature of Therapist)

A. I, the above named client, assert that I have discussed the above named objectives for the change of my behavior and that I consent to work toward the achievement of those objectives.

B. I further assert that I have discussed the above named intervention technique(s) with the therapist and that I consent to apply these techniques.

C. I further assert that I shall provide the above named data in order to determine the effectiveness of the use of the intervention technique(s).

D. I further assert that I shall provide the therapist with the following compensation for his or her efforts in my behalf: _____

E. I further assert that I have freely entered into this contract knowing the therapeutic objectives and both the positive and negative potential effects of the intervention technique(s).

F. I further assert that I have been assured of my right to terminate my participation in treatment at any time, for any reason, and without the need to offer an explanation.

G. I further specifically limit the above named therapist's use of any information which can in any way identify me to others unless I have offered my specific, written permission

_____   _____
(Date)   (Signature of Client)   (Signature of Witness)

Consent for Token Economy Project on Behalf of Incompetent Person

I, the undersigned, in my capacity as legal guardian, consent to have
_____ included in the Token Economy Program. I understand that this
(Name of patient)
program will involve earning tokens by appropriate behavior in order to pay for
privileges, meals, and living accommodations. I understand visiting privileges and
home leaves are encouraged; but such privileges will depend on the decision of the
staff, based on the need and behavior of the individual patient. Leaves may be
requested for one weekend per month (Friday evening to Sunday); visits for the
day on Saturday or Sunday.

I am aware that this program is directed toward either return home or family
care placement; and that, whenever, upon the decision of the Ward Team, it is
thought that such placement is appropriate, such plans will be made.

_____
(Signature of guardian)

_____
(Signature of patient, if available)

APPENDIX J

Guidelines for Psychologists Conducting Growth Groups[1]

The following guidelines are presented for the information and guidance of psychologists who conduct growth or encounter groups. They are not intended to substitute for or to supplant ethical practices for psychologists specified elsewhere.

The development of these guidelines was prompted by the concern of several units within the American Psychological Association that there be a set of operating principles for the use of psychologists active in such groups. The guidelines do not presume to specify or endorse any professional procedure or technique used in a group, but only to aid psychologists who offer groups to present themselves in a manner that is ethically sound and protective of the participant.

The present statement attempts to accommodate those suggestions from various psychologists in response to the draft statement published by the Board of Professional Affairs in the *APA Monitor* of December 1971 (Vol. 2, No. 12, p. 3). It is to be expected that these guidelines will be subject to modification as they are

[1]Approved for publication by the Board of Directors of the American Psychological Association on February 15, 1973. An ad hoc committee consisting of Donald H. Clark, Wilbert Edgerton, and John J. McMillan (Chair), the Board of Professional Affairs, and the Board of Directors were successively responsible for development of the statement in its final form.

Requests for reprints should be sent to Department of Professional Affairs, American Psychological Association, 1200 Seventeenth Street, N.W., Washington, D.C. 20036.

Source: Reprinted with permission from 28 *American Psychologist* 933 (Oct. 1973).

put to use, and also in the light of the evolution of new knowledge and practices in the utilization of growth groups.

1. Entering into a growth group experience should be on a voluntary basis; any form of coercion to participate is to be avoided.

2. The following information should be made available in writing to all prospective participants:

    (a)   An explicit statement of the purpose of the group;

    (b)   Types of techniques that may be employed;

    (c)   The education, training and experience of the leader or leaders;

    (d)   The fee and any additional expense that may be incurred;

    (e)   A statement as to whether or not a follow-up service is included in the fee;

    (f)   Goals of the group experience and techniques to be used;

    (g)   Amounts and kinds of responsibility to be assumed by the leader and by the participants. For example, (i) the degree to which a participant is free not to follow suggestions and prescriptions of the group leader and other group members; (ii) any restrictions on a participant's freedom to leave the group at any time; and,

    (h)   Issues of confidentiality.

3. A screening interview should be conducted by the group leader prior to the acceptance of any participant. It is the responsibility of the leader to screen out those individuals for whom he or she judges the group experience to be inappropriate. Should an interview not be possible, then other measures should be used to achieve the same results.

At the time of the screening interview, or at some other time prior to the beginning of the group, opportunity should be provided for leader-participant exploration of the terms of the contract as described in the information statement. This is to assure mutual understanding of the contract.

4. It is recognized that growth groups may be used for both educational and psychotherapeutic purposes. If the purpose is primarily educational, the leader assumes the usual professional and ethical obligations of an educator. If the purpose is therapeutic, the leader assumes the same professional and ethical responsibilities he or she would assume in individual or group psychotherapy, including before and after consultation with any other therapist who may be professionally involved with the participant. In both cases, the leader's own education, training, and experience should be commensurate with these responsibilities.

5. It is recognized that growth groups may be used for responsible research or exploration of human potential and may therefore involve the use of innovative and unusual techniques. While such professional exploration must be protected and encouraged, the welfare of the participant is of paramount importance. Therefore,

when an experience is clearly identified as "experimental," the leader should (*a*) make full disclosure of techniques to be used,(*b*) delineate the respective responsibilities of the leader and participant during the contract discussion phase prior to the official beginning of the group experience, and (*c*) evaluate and make public his or her findings.

K

Behavior Management Program Consent Form (For All Patients When Unusual or Intrusive Stimuli Are Used)

I, ＿＿＿＿＿＿, give my consent to participate in the therapy program described below which uses unusual or intrusive stimuli. I have read the description, and/or each part of the program was explained to me in detail by ＿＿＿＿＿. I understand what will happen to me during my program and that I can end my participation in it at any time.

My rights have been explained to me by ＿＿＿＿＿. I understand that as a part of this program I will be giving up my right(s) to ＿＿＿＿＿＿＿＿＿

＿＿＿＿＿＿＿＿＿＿＿＿＿＿＿＿＿＿＿＿＿＿＿＿＿＿＿＿＿＿＿＿＿＿＿

＿＿＿＿＿＿＿＿＿＿＿＿＿＿＿＿＿＿＿＿＿＿＿＿＿＿＿＿＿＿＿＿＿＿＿

＿＿＿＿＿＿＿＿＿＿＿＿＿＿＿＿＿＿＿＿＿＿＿＿＿＿＿＿＿＿＿＿＿＿＿

＿＿＿＿＿＿＿＿＿＿＿＿＿＿＿＿＿＿＿＿＿＿＿＿＿＿＿＿＿＿＿＿＿＿＿

The grievance procedure for protecting my rights has also been explained to me, and I understand that I may complain to ＿＿＿＿＿＿ if at any time I believe my rights have been inappropriately denied.

＿＿＿＿＿＿＿＿＿＿＿＿＿＿＿＿＿＿＿＿＿＿＿＿＿＿＿＿＿＿＿＿＿＿＿＿

(Client's signature)   (Date)

＿＿＿＿＿＿＿＿＿＿＿＿＿＿＿＿＿＿＿＿＿＿＿＿＿＿＿＿＿＿＿＿＿＿＿＿

(Guardian's signature)   (Date)
(If client is a minor or has been declared incompetent)

I, the undersigned, have witnessed the fact that the above described behavior management program has been fully explained to _____. The client indicated that he/she understands how the program will operate and realizes that he/she may terminate participation in the program at any time. The client's rights and the grievance procedure have also been explained to him/her, and the client indicated understanding of which rights he/she may be relinquishing during the course of the program. In light of this information, _____ voluntarily consented to participation in the program.

_____

(Name of Program Professional)   (Date)

Source: Division of Community Services, Department of Health and Social Services, State of Wisconsin, Revised Behavior Management Guidelines (July 1977). The guidelines also specify in detail the procedures to be followed by program staff to obtain consent. Copies may be obtained from the Coordinator of Client Advocacy, Division of Community Services, 1 W. Wilson St., Madison, Wis. 53702.

Information to Clients Regarding Confidentiality

WHO WE ARE

The psychological Services Center provides a variety of psychological services to individuals and their families. It is also a teaching, training, and research center supported by the Department of Psychology and the University.

Services are provided in part by the clinical faculty, but largely by advanced graduate students in clinical psychology who are supervised by clinical faculty.

TRAINING

Since we are a teaching-training center, permission is requested of our clients to record the interviews we have with them. However, no recording is ever done unless the client gives the permission to do so. In addition to providing a valuable therapeutic aid, recorded interviews serve as an important training and learning device, and they may on occasion be used for instructional and supervisory purposes. They are, however, never used outside this training situation.*

CONFIDENTIALITY

Clients may be assured that their contacts with the Center will remain confidential. There may be a rare exception to this policy such as if a client should express a serious intent to harm him/herself or someone else. In general, in order to safeguard client confidentiality we use the following procedures:

    1.   We will not acknowledge inquiries about clients. We will adhere to this policy even if the client requests us to release information unless we have had an opportunity to discuss the request with the client personally. Even after such a discussion, the Center reserves the right to limit the imparted information.

    2.   All clinical records are destroyed within 90 days after clients terminate their contacts witht the Center. If you do not wish the Center to destroy your clinical records, please discuss this with your counselor.

A WORD OF EXPLANATION

A brief explanation of the procedures regarding confidentiality may be desirable. Many individuals, agencies, and institutions in our society still incorrectly believe that individuals who seek help for personal problems are or were "ill," and they believe that it is permissible for them to inquire about "the illness." As examples of this belief, insurance companies or employers occasionally ask individuals if they ever have consulted anyone for a "mental health" problem. The way companies may interpret the information they receive from a former therapist or counselor might result in their adopting a negative attitude toward the job or insurance applicant. Other examples of this are applications for college admission, drivers' licenses, and so forth.

    It is for these reasons that the Center is most reluctant to release any information or to acknowledge a person's contacts with the Center.

    Your counselor will be pleased to discuss any questions you may have about this information or about the Center.

Source: Form used by Psychology Training Clinic, Department of Psychology, University of North Dakota, as reported by John O. Noll, Professor and Director of Clinical Training, 1978.
*One may want to add the condition: except for occasional presentation at a professional meeting where the identity of the client will be disguised.

APPENDIX M

Confidentiality Agreement in Group Sensitivity Training and Therapy

THIS AGREEMENT entered into this _____ day of _____, _____, is made by and between all participants in group sessions who sign below, including the group leader and by representation all of his/her assistants and employees associated with this training or therapy.

NOW THEREFORE, in consideration of our mutual participation in group sessions and in return for possible benefits from such participation and in consideration of and in return for similar promises by other participants, we agree that the presence of and all communications by the participants are confidential. We agree not to disclose this confidential information in any manner unless the participant providing the information expressly agrees to its disclosure or waives confidentiality by legal action.

More specifically but not exclusively:

1. We agree not to disclose the identity or likeness of any past, present, or future participant in these group sessions to any person who is not also a participant.

2. We realize that to discuss or otherwise reveal specific characteristics, behaviors, or problems of a participant, even though the name of the participant may not be used, may at times lead to the eventual discovery of the participant's identity. Therefore, we agree not to disclose such information and to avoid discussing a participant's behavior or problems in any manner which would even remotely risk revealing the identity of the participant.

3. We, as group members, agree not to photograph, videotape, film, or oth-

erwise record on any medium the appearance, behaviors, conversations, or any other characteristic or identifying mark, number, or possession of any participant unless express written permission is given by the participant. Nor will any articles, news stories, or books be written without the express, written consent of all participants mentioned therein.

4. We understand that in certain exceptional circumstances absolute confidentiality cannot be guaranteed. In rare circumstances, such as when a participant would present a serious danger of violence to others, disclosure of information may be legally required.

5. We recognize that the unlawful disclosure of confidential information may subject the person who so discloses to legal action. We agree that in the event of the breach of this agreement, we give the offended party the right to recover for injury to his/her reputation the minimum amount of $ _____ from each person who disclosed the information. Also, the offended party may recover additional damages for other harms which can be proven such as invasion of privacy, defamation of character, interference with economic or personal relations, and loss of livelihood.

6. This agreement may be changed, amended, or supplemented at any time or from time to time by the participants by a written instrument signed by each of them, but not otherwise.

IN WITNESS WHEREOF, we, the participants, have hereunto set our hands as of the date and year first above written in the presence of each other who have served as witnesses hereto.

(Signature of participant)	(Signature of participant)
(Signature of participant)	(Signature of participant)
(Signature of participant)	(Signature of participant)
(Signature of participant)	(Signature of participant)

(date)   (month)   (year)

APPENDIX **N**

Employee Confidentiality Agreement

As a condition of employment, I agree not to divulge to unauthorized persons any confidential information obtained from observations, conversations, correspondence, personal records, clinical materials, or any other sources. I will not publish or otherwise make public any confidential information such that the person involved will be identifiable or harmed, except as I may be legally required to do so. Violation of this agreement may subject me to civil penalties.

_____
(Employee signature)

_____
(Date)

_____
(Witness)

APPENDIX O

Request for Release of Information

TO:_____
(Organization/person name, address)

RE:_____ Birthdate: _____
(Client/patient)

The above named person has applied for services at/with _____
(institution/health professional)

We would appreciate receiving written information from you regarding events relevant to the services we may render. For example, a social history, case summary, or
court report would be useful to us in establishing an appropriate treatment program.

Would you please forward this information to me as soon as possible.

Thank you,

_____
(Health professional)

_____
(Title)

Date: _____

Encl: Signed authorization for release of information

P

Authorization for Release of Information[1]

RE: _____ Birthdate: _____
    (Client/patient)

This authorizes _____
          (Institution/social worker/psychologist/physician/etc.)

to release to _____
        (Organization/attorney/health professional/etc.)

the following information: _____

_____

Signed: _____
    (Client/patient)

Signed: _____
    (Parent or guardian, if applicable)

Witness: _____

Signed: _____
    (Health professional in charge of client/patient)

                                         Date: _____

[1](optional) The reverse side of this form may contain a summary of statutory law regarding release of information.

APPENDIX Q

Permission to Release Permanent School Record Information to Third Party

Dear Parent,
We have received a request from

_____

(name of requesting individual, agency, etc.)
for a copy of (access to) (*name of pupil*)'s school record.

Please indicate in the space below whether you are willing for us to comply with this request.

_____

(*Name of requesting party*) may have a copy of (access to) the following parts of (*name of pupil*)'s record:

☐ Official Administrative Record (name, address, birthdate, grade level completed, grades, class standing, attendance record)
☐ Standardized Achievement Test Scores
☐ Intelligence and Aptitude Test Scores
☐ Personality and Interest Test Scores
☐ Teacher and Counselor Observations and Ratings
☐ Record of Extracurricular Activities
☐ Family Background Data

_____   _____
Parent's signature   Date

Source: Guidelines for the collection, maintenance, and dissemination of pupil records. New York: Russell Sage Foundation, 1970, p. 42.

R

Permission to Use Film

AGREEMENT entered into this   day of   between Dr.
            (hereinafter referred to as the First Party) and
(hereinafter referred to as the Second Party).

WHEREAS, the First Party is desirous of using and exhibiting videotape, kinescope, motion pictures and/or photographs of the Second Party for the purpose of professional education, treatment and research, and

WHEREAS, the Second Party, in consideration of the premises, is desirous of endorsing and supporting the use of such videotape, kinescope, motion pictures and/or photographs for the purpose of professional education treatment and research,

NOW, THEREFORE, it is agreed by the parties hereto as follows:

1. In consideration of the mutual covenants contained herein the Second Party consents to the use of videotape, kinescope, motion pictures and/or photographs of himself heretofore made or hereinafter to be made by the First Party. Specifically the Second Party refers to videotape, kinescope, motion pictures and/or photographs of himself, alone or with others, taken in the office of the First Party during the course of individual and group treatment by the First Party.

2. The First Party agrees that the said videotape, kinescope, motion pictures and/or photographs will be used solely in the interest of the advancement of mental health programs and only for the purpose of professional education, treatment or research activities connected with such programs, and will not be used for any other purpose.

3.   The First Party agrees not to use or permit the use of the name of the Second Party in connection with any direct or indirect use or exhibition of such videotape, kinescope, motion pictures and/or photographs.

4.   The Second Party hereby agrees that he will never sue the First Party or the Estate of the First Party and will never attach the assets thereof and further agrees that this covenant may be pleaded as a defense to any action or proceeding which may be instituted by the Second Party against the First Party or his Estate.

IN WITNESS WHEREOF, the parties have duly executed this agreement the day and year first above written.

                           _____

                                        Psychiatrist

                           _____

                                           Patient

Possible additional clauses:

I agree that the First Party is to be the sole owner of all rights in and to the said videotape, kinescope, motion pictures and/or photographs for all purposes herein set forth.

I understand that I shall receive no financial compensation for the use of such videotape, kinescope, motion pictures or photographs.

Source: Fields, D. N. Legal implications and complications—Model forms for signed releases. In Berger, M. M., *Videotape techniques in psychiatric training and treatment.* New York: Brunner/Mazel, 1975, pp. 192–93. Copyright © 1975 by Milton M. Berger.

APPENDIX S

Release for Audiovisual Materials

I hereby give _____ the absolute right and permission to copyright and/or publish and/or display photographs, videotapes, autiotapes, or films of me, or in which I may be included in whole or in part, for public information purposes.

I understand and consent to the use of such materials, provided that my name or other readily identifiable information is not attached.

I hereby waive any right that I may have to inspect and/or approve the finished product or the informational copy that may be used in connection therewith, or the use to which it may be applied.

I hereby release discharge, and agree to save _____ from any liability by virtue of any blurring, distortion, alteration, optical illusion or use in composite form, whether intentional or otherwise, or in any processing tending toward the completion of the finished product.

_____
(Signature)

_____
(Date)

_____
(Parental signature if participant is a minor)

_____
(Witness)

APPENDIX T

Photo Release for Commercial Purposes

I hereby consent to the use and/or reproduction of pictures of me, the undersigned, by _____ who may use or be represented by trade names, for art, advertising and/or trade purposes in any publication, advertising media, photographic displays, etc. without limitation and/or reservation. Permission to publish and republish photographs of me, in whole or in part, in composite or edited form is granted without restriction and said photos may be used in conjunction with my own or a fictitious name, or reproductions thereof, in any media, art advertising, trade, editorial or for any other purpose, including printed matter of any kind, story form, or advertising, etc.

I hereby release, discharge and agree to save harmless _____ and any other trade or business names represented or used by him/her from any liability by virtue of blurring, distortion, alteration, optical illusion or use in composite form, in whole or in part, whether intential or otherwise, that may occur or be produced in the taking, processing, printing, reproduction of publication of said pictures of me.

I hereby warrant that I have every right to contract in my own name in the above regard. I state further that I have read the above release and authorization prior to its execution and that I am fully familiar with the contents herein.

Date:_____

Witness:_____

Name _____

Address _____

City _____

State _____ ZIP _____

Phone: _____

Photographer: _____

Address: _____

_____

PARENT OR GUARDIAN (To be signed if model is under 18 years of age):

_____

APPENDIX U

Summary of Standards for Use of Educational and Psychological Tests[1]

A test user should have a general knowledge of measurement principles and of the limitations of test interpretation.

A test user should know and understand the literature relevant to the tests s/he uses and the testing problems with which s/he deals.

One who has the responsibility for decisions about individuals or policies that are based on test results should have an understanding of psychological or educational measurement and of validation and other test research.

Test users should seek to avoid bias in test selection, administration, and interpretation; they should try to avoid even the appearance of discriminatory practice.

Institutional test users should establish procedures for periodic internal review of test use.

The choice or development of tests, test batteries, or other assessment procedures should be based on clearly formulated goals and hypotheses.

A test user should consider more than one variable for assessment and the assessment of any given variable by more than one method.

In choosing an existing test, a test user should relate its history of research and development to his/her intended use of the instrument.

In general a test user should try to choose or to develop an assessment technique in which "tester-effect" is minimized, or in which reliability of assessment across testers can be assured.

Test scores used for selection or other administrative decisions about an individual may not be useful for individual or program evaluation and vice versa.

337

A test user is expected to follow carefully the standardized procedures described in the manual for administering a test.

The test administrator is responsible for establishing conditions, consistent with the principle of standardization, that enable each examinee to do his best.

A test user is responsible for accuracy in scoring, checking, coding, or recording test results.

If specific cutting scores are to be used as a basis for decisions, a test user should have a rationale, justification, or explanation of the cutting scores adopted.

The test user shares with the test developer or distributor a responsibility for maintaining test security.

A test score should be interpreted as an estimate of performance under a given set of circumstances. It should not be interpreted as some absolute characteristic of the examinee or as something permanent and generalizable to all other circumstances.

Test scores should ordinarily be reported only to people who are qualified to interpret them. If scores are reported, they should be accompanied by explanations sufficient for the recipient to interpret them correctly.

The test user should recognize that estimates of reliability do not indicate criterion-related validity.

A test user should examine carefully the rationale and validity of computer-based interpretations of test scores.

In norm-referenced interpretations, a test user should interpret an obtained score with reference to sets of norms appropriate for the individual tested and for the intended use.

Any content-referenced interpretation should clearly indicate the domain to which one can generalize.

The test user should consider alternative interpretations of a given score.

The test user should be able to interpret test performance relative to other measures.

A test user should develop procedures for systematically eliminating from data files test-score information that has, because of the lapse of time, become obsolete.

Excerpted from: *Standards for Educational and Psychological Tests*. Washington, D.C.: American Psychological Association, 1974, pp. 56–73. Readers are urged to consult the full text of this publication, particularly revised editions that are periodically issued.

APPENDIX V

Ante-nuptial Agreement Waiving All Rights in the Property of the Other Party Except by Specific Bequest

THIS AGREEMENT made between [James White], residing at _____, City of _____, State of _____, and [Joan Brown], residing at _____, City of _____, State of _____,

WITNESSETH:

The parties are about to marry. In anticipation thereof they desire to fix and determine the rights and claims that will accrue to each of them in the property and the estate of the other by reason of the marriage, and to accept the provisions of this agreement in full discharge and satisfaction of such rights.

NOW, THEREFORE, in consideration of the premises, and of the mutual promises and undertakings below set forth, the parties agree:

1. Each party hereby waives, releases and relinquishes any and all claims and rights of every kind, nature or description that he or she may acquire by reason of the marriage in the other party's property or estate under the present or future laws of the state of [New York] or any other jurisdiction, including:

The right to elect to take against any present or future last will and testament or codicil of the other party;

(b) The right to take his or her intestate share in the other party's estate; and

(c) The right, if any, to act as administrator or administratrix of the other party's estate.

This provision is intended to and shall serve as a waiver and release of each party's right of election in accordance with the requirements of [Section 5-1.1 of the Estates, Powers and Trusts Law of the State of New York], and any law amendatory thereof or supplemental or similar thereto.

2. Nothing herein contained shall be deemed to constitute a waiver by either party of any bequest that the other party may choose to make to him or her by will or codicil. However, the parties acknowledge that no promises of any kind have been made by either of them to the other with respect to any such bequest.

3. Each party during his or her lifetime shall keep and retain sole ownership, control and enjoyment of all his or her property, real and personal, free and clear of any claim of the other.

4. Each party acknowledges that the other has made full disclosure of his or her means and resources; and that he or she is entering into this agreement freely, voluntarily and with full knowledge.

5. Each party shall upon the other's request take any and all steps, and execute, acknowledge and deliver to the other party any and all further instruments necessary or expedient to effectuate the purposes of this agreement.

6. This agreement contains the entire understanding of the parties. There are no representations, warranties, or promises other than those expressly set forth herein.

7. The consideration for this agreement is the marriage about to be solemnized.

8. This agreement shall enure to the benefit of, and shall be binding upon, the heirs, executors and administrators of the parties.

IN WITNESS WHEREOF the parties have hereunto set their hands and seals this _____ day of _____, 19__.

Witnessed by:

_____

As to [James White]

_____

As to [Joan Brown]

_____

[James White]

_____

[Joan Brown]

Source: Lindey, A. *Separation agreements and ante-nuptial contracts,* Vol. 2 New York: Matthew Bender, 1976, pp. 291–93 (original title changed). See this source for a variety of detailed forms.

Sample court-enforced property settlement agreements can be found in: Cain v. King, 313 F. Supp. 10 (D.C. La. 1970); and Cochran v. Cochran, 269 So. 2d 884 (Ala. 1970), *rev'd in part* 289 Ala. 615, 269 So. 2d 897 (1972); Robuck v. Robuck, 20 N.C. App. 374, 201 S.E.2d 557 (1974).

Complete typical separation agreements can be found in: Crosby v. Crosby, 188 Kan. 274, 362 P.2d 3 (1961); and Sorenson v. Sorenson, 119 N.W.2d 129 (Iowa 1963).

W

Contract for Joint Living Arrangement Without Marriage

This agreement is made between _____ and _____ for the purpose of specifying the rights and obligations of our joint living arrangement.

Article I. We choose of our own free will to live together outside the formal state regulations governing marriage and divorce, and we do not intend our relationship to be interpreted as a common law marriage. We further state that we each make this agreement in consideration of the agreement of the other, and that the provision of sexual services by either of us is not consideration for this contract. We further state that this agreement shall remain in full force and effect until such time as we separate or make a written and signed ammendment.

Article II. Neither party is obligated to provide financial or other material support to the other.

Article III. We agree that all income, however derived, and any accumulations of property traceable to that income, belongs absolutely to the person who earns or otherwise acquires the income. At the time of signing this contract, we have each prepared a list of major items of property that each of us owns. This list is marked as Exhibit 1 and is attached to this contract and by this reference is made a part of this contract. We will update this list as it becomes necessary. Any and all joint purchases shall be made under the terms of Article V.

Article IV. We agree that any gifts or inheritances that either party receives shall be the separate property of that person. Should a gift or inheritance be made to us jointly, we shall consider that we own it in equal shares unless otherwise specified by the donor. Each of us shall keep our own money in our own separate bank accounts. We shall not open joint bank or credit accounts. We agree to return any credit cards that are issued to both of us, and, further, not to make any purchases using the credit or credit cards of the other.

Article V. We may occasionally desire to pool our separate resources to purchase a specific item. Prior to the purchase of such an item, we will make a separate written agreement. These agreements shall be marked as Exhibit 2 and shall be attached to and incorporated in this agreement. As part of each joint purchase agreement, we shall include a clause providing for what happens to the property if we separate. If for any reason we fail to provide for the possibility of our separation, we agree to divide all jointly-owned property equally. If we cannot agree as to an equal division, we shall sell the jointly-owned property and equally divide all proceeds of the sale. If a selling price cannot be agreed upon, we shall jointly select a third party who will set the price.

Article VI. We agree to share equally all monthly household expenses. This includes food, incidental supplies necessary to home maintenance, rent and utilities, not including long distance telephone charges which shall be paid by the person making the call.

Article VII. We each agree to own, insure, and pay for the maintenance of our own motor vehicles. If at any time we wish to share ownership of a motor vehicle, we shall make a separate written agreement as to ownership under terms of Article V and shall have the fact of joint ownership recorded on the motor vehicle title slip.

Article VIII. Should we buy a house, investment property, or any other real property, we agree that a copy of a deed to the property and any and all supplementary contracts or agreements covering the property shall be marked as Exhibit 3 and attached to this contract and thereby incorporated. We futher agree that neither of us shall have any rights to, or financial interest in, any separate real property of the other, whether acquired before or after the signing of this contract, unless such interest is set forth in a written agreement signed by both parties to this contract.

Article IX. We realize that our power to contract with respect to children is limited by state law. With this knowledge, and in a spirit of cooperation and mutual respect, we wish to state the following as our agreement should we have children.

1) The father shall sign and have notarized a statement acknowledging that he is the father of our child(ren) within 10 days after birth;

2) Our children shall be given the following last name _____.

3) Because of the possbile trauma our separation might cause our child(ren), we shall each make a good faith effort to participate in a jointly-agreed upon program of counseling before separation;

4) If we separate, we shall do our best to see that our child(ren) has/have a good and healthful environment in which to grow up. Specifically we agree to the following:

a) We will do our best to see that our child(ren) maintain a close and loving relationship with each of us;

b) We will share in the upbringing of our child(ren) and, on the basis of our respective abilities to pay and the needs of the child(ren), in his/her or their support.

c) We will make a good faith effort to make all major decisions affecting the health and welfare of our child(ren) jointly;

d) Should circumstances dictate that our child(ren) should spend a greater portion of the year living with one of us than the other, the person who has actual physical custody shall be sensitive to the needs of the other to have generous rights of visitation and shall cooperate in all practical steps necessary to make visitation as easy as possible;

e) If after separation we have problems communication as to the best interest of our child(ren), we shall seek help in the form of a jointly-agreed upon program of counseling with the hope that we can work out our differences without having to take our problems to court;

f) At the death of either of us, our child(ren) shall be cared for and raised by the other whether or not we are living together at the time of the death.

Article X. We agree that either of us can end our agreement to live together at any time by simply ceasing to live with the other. If this is done, neither of us shall make claim upon the other for money or support, except as provided for by the terms of this agreement pertaining to the division of joint property (Articles V and VIII).

Article XI. We agree that from time to time this contract may be amended. All ammendments shall be in writing and shall be signed by both parties.

Article XII. We further agree that if any court finds any portion of this contract to be illegal or otherwise unenforceable, that the remainder of the contract is still valid and in full force.

Executed at _____

_____

(Date)   (Signature)

_____

(Date)   (Signature)

Authors' note: This contract is a slightly modified version of one appearing in: T. Ihara & R. Warner, *The Living Together Kit*. Berkeley, Calif.: Nolo Press, 1978. Readers are urged to consult this very readable and practical manual regarding buying a house, starting a family, getting a divorce, and so on. It can be obtained from Nolo Press, P.O. Box 544, Occidental, Calif. 95465.

APPENDIX X

Standard Arbitration Agreement to Submit Existing Disputes

We, the undersigned parties, hereby agree to submit to arbitration under the Commercial Arbitration Rules of the American Arbitration Association[1] the following controversy: (cite briefly). We further agree that the above controversy be submitted to (one)/(three) arbitrator(s) who (is/are): _____ .[2]

The decision of the (arbitrator)/(majority of arbitrators) shall be binding and conclusive upon the parties, and may be rendered in such a form that a judgment may be entered thereon by the Court having jurisdiction. We will faithfully observe this agreement, and abide by the arbitration decision. It is the desire of the parties that the hearings be prompt and a decision quickly rendered.

---

1 A copy of these Rules may be obtained from the American Arbitration Association, 140 West 51st Street, New York, NY 10020.

2 If three arbitrators are to be used, each party chooses one arbitrator, and these two then choose a third.

APPENDIX Y

Agreement to Submit Future Disputes to Arbitration (Short Form)

Any controversy or claim arising out of or relating to this contract or agreement shall be settled by arbitration in accordance with the Rules of the American Arbitration Association, and the judgment rendered by the arbitrator(s) shall be faithfully observed by the parties. The judgment rendered may also be entered in any Court having jurisdiction thereof.

Agreement to Submit Future Disputes to Arbitration (Long Form)

Any claim, dispute or misunderstanding arising out of or in connection with this agreement shall be arbitrated. Except as otherwise provided below, the arbitration shall be conducted by three arbitrators, each party designating one arbitrator and the two designees naming a third. The procedure shall be as follows:

(a) The aggrieved party shall name (her) (his) designee in a notice demanding arbitration.

(b) The other party shall name (her) (his) designee in writing within (five) days of receipt of the notice of demand.

(c) The two designees so named shall agree on the third arbitrator in writing within (five) days after the naming of the second arbitrator.

(d) Arbitration proceedings shall be conducted within (ten) days after the naming of the third arbitrator. The arbitrators shall make known their findings within (five) days after the close of the arbitration hearing.

(e) If the party on whom the demand for arbitration is served fails to name his/her designee as required under subdivision (b), the designee of the aggrieved party may, upon not less than (three) days' written notice to the other party, proceed with the arbitration as sole arbitrator; and his/her findings shall have the same force and effect as if made by a full board of three arbitrators.

(f) If the respective designees of the parties cannot agree upon a third arbitrator within (five) days, arbitration shall be conducted before three arbitrators appointed by the American Arbitration Association, and subject to the rules then obtaining of that Association.

(g) The cost of arbitration shall be borne as the finding directs.

(h) If arbitration is conducted before a board of three arbitrators, the decision of the majority of the board shall be controlling.

(i) Findings shall be binding on the parties, and shall be rendered in such a form that a judgment may be entered thereon in a Court of appropriate jurisdiction.

Source: Long form revised from Lindey, A. *Separation agreements and ante-nuptial contracts,* Vol. 1. New York: Matthew Bender, 1976, pp. 2–25. Chapter 29 of Lindey's book contains other sample forms, plus a summary of advantages and disadvantages of arbitration generally and in marriage and separation specifically (e.g., all issues can be arbitrated, but the courts are not likely to enforce child custody or visitation agreements).

APPENDIX Z

Guidelines for Constructing Research Consent Forms

A. Use nontechnical language and first-person when possible.

B. State the purpose and benefits of the research. Usually the research is not being done for the benefit of the subject but for information of potential future benefit to others. This broader social benefit should be made explicit. State terms of compensation, if any, to be paid to the subject.

C. Indicate risks, potential discomforts, and inconveniences (including, when appropriate, risks and benefits of alternative treatments).

D. Include a statement in which the subject affirms that s/he has received information about the benefits and risks of the research.

E. Provide assurance that refusal to participate will not prejudice the person's future standing as a patient, student, employee, and so forth. Similarly, assurance should be given that the person may withdraw at any time without prejudice unless his/her health or safety is in clear jeopardy.

F. Give the name, office address, and telephone number of the principal investigator or other responsible person who may be contacted for additional information, and concerns.

G. When applicable, have the consent form also signed by the legal guardian of persons under age 18 or persons mentally disabled. (Guardians may consent to experimental procedures for minors and for individuals judged incompetent, *if* there is some direct benefit to the subject. Where no potential, direct benefit occurs, the legal validity of a guardian's consent is questionable.)

H.   The principal investigator or person administering treatment, not a subordinate, should obtain the consent.

I.   If applicable, include a statement to the effect that some information gained during the research may have to be disclosed as required by law (e.g., instances of child abuse). Therefore, absolute confidentiality or privilege of communication cannot be assured, although a vigorous effort will be made to provide anonymity for the subject and to give identifying information only to persons s/he specifically authorizes.

J.   Some consent forms include a statement in which the subject releases the experimenter and the institution from any future claims of harm (i.e., an "exculpatory clause"). Federally funded research projects should *not* include such a clause because federal agencies, as a matter of policy, have maintained that a clause of this kind may unreasonably inhibit a subject from seeking legitimate remedies for injuries caused by the negligence of the experimenter.

K.   Indicate whether or not monetary compensation or medical/psychological treatment will be available, and the nature of such (e.g., only to extent of insurance coverage, acute medical only at specified facility, financial compensation for wages lost) for any research-related injury.

L.   The sample consent forms that follow in this section of the appendix are presented as illustrations of various intervention agreements. There is no intention to suggest that these are the best possible forms in a given circumstance or that they have legal effect and validity in a particular jurisdiction.

AA

Regulations for Biomedical and Behavioral Research Involving Prisoners

§46.301 Applicability

(a) The regulations in this subpart are applicable to all biomedical and behavioral research conducted or supported by the Department of Health, Education, and Welfare involving prisoners as subjects.

(b) Nothing in this subpart shall be construed as indicating that compliance with the procedures set forth herein will authorize research involving prisoners as subjects, to the extent such research is limited or barred by applicable State or local law.

(c) The requirements of this subpart are in addition to those imposed under the other subparts of this part.

§46.302 Purpose

Inasmuch as prisoners may be under constraints because of their incarceration which could affect their ability to make a truly voluntary and uncoerced decision whether or not to participate as subjects in research, it is the purpose of this subpart to provide additional safeguards for the protection of prisoners involved in activities to which this subpart is applicable.

§46.303 Definitions

As used in this subpart:

(a) "Secretary" means the Secretary of Health, Education, and Welfare and any other officer or employee of the Department of Health, Education, and Welfare to whom authority has been delegated.

(b) "DHEW" means the Department of Health, Education, and Welfare.

(c) "Prisoner" means any individual involuntarily confined or detained in a penal institution. The term is intended to encompass individuals sentenced to such an institution under a criminal or civil statute, individuals detained in other facilities by virtue of statutes or commitment procedures which provide alternatives to criminal prosecution or incarceration in a penal institution, and individuals detained pending arraignment, trial, or sentencing.

(d) "Minimal risk" is the probability and magnitude of physical or psychological harm that is normally encountered in the daily lives, or in the routine medical, dental, or psychological examination of healthy persons.

§46.304 Composition of Institutional Review Boards Where Prisoners Are Involved

In addition to satisfying the requirements in § 46.106 of this part, an Institutional Review Board, carrying out responsibilities under this part with respect to research covered by this subpart, shall also meet the following specific requirements:

(a) A majority of the Board (exclusive of prisoner members) shall have no association with the prison(s) involved, apart from their membership on the Board.

(b) At least one member of the Board shall be a prisoner, or a prisoner representative with appropriate background and experience to serve in that capacity, except that where a particular research project is reviewed by more than one Board only one Board need satisfy this requirement.

§ 46.305 Additional Duties of the Institutional Review Boards Where Prisoners Are Involved

(a) In addition to all other responsibilities prescribed for Institutional Review Boards under this part, the Board shall review research covered by this subpart and approve such research only if it finds that:

(1) The research under review represents one of the categories of research permissible under § 46.306(a)(2);

(2) Any possible advantages accruing to the prisoner through his or her participation in the research, when compared to the general living conditions, medical care, quality of food, amenities and opportunity for earnings in the prison, are not of such a magnitude that his or her ability to weigh the risks of the research against the value of such advantages in the limited choice environment of the prison is impaired;

(3) The risks involved in the research are commensurate with risks that would be accepted by nonprisoner volunteers;

(4) Procedures for the selection of subjects within the prison are fair to all prisoners and immune from arbitrary intervention by prison authorities or prisoners.

Unless the principal investigator provides to the Board justification in writing for following some other procedures, control subjects must be selected randomly from the group of available prisoners who meet the characteristics needed for that particular research project;

(5)   The information is presented in language which is understandable to the subject population;

(6)   Adequate assurance exists that parole boards will not take into account a prisoner's participation in the research in making decisions regarding parole, and each prisoner is clearly informed in advance that participation in the research will have no effect on his or her parole; and

(7)   Where the Board finds there may be a need for follow-up examination or care of participants after the end of their participation, adequate provision has been made for such examination or care, taking into account the varying lengths of individual prisoners' sentences, and for informing participants of this fact.

(b)   The Board shall carry out such other duties as may be assigned by the Secretary.

(c)   The institution shall certify to the Secretary, in such form and manner as the Secretary may require, that the duties of the Board under this section have been fulfilled.

§ 46.306 Permitted Research Involving Prisoners

(a)   Biomedical or behavioral research conducted or supported by DHEW may involve prisoners as subjects only if:

(1)   The institution responsible for the conduct of the research has certified to the Secretary that the Institutional Review Board has approved the research under § 46.305 of this subpart; and

(2)   In the judgment of the Secretary the proposed research involves solely the following:

(A)   Study of the possible causes, effects, and processes of incarceration, and of criminal behavior, provided that the study presents no more than minimal risk and no more than inconvenience to the subjects;

(B)   Study of prisons as institutional structures or of prisoners as incarcerated persons, provided that the study presents no more than minimal risk and no more than inconvenience to the subjects;

(C)   Research on conditions particularly affecting prisoners as a class (for example, vaccine trials and other research on hepatitis which is much more prevalent in prisons than elsewhere; and research on social and psychological problems such as alcoholism, drug addiction and sexual assaults) provided that the study may proceed only after the Secretary has consulted with appropriate experts including experts in penology medicine and ethics, and published notice, in the FEDERAL REGISTER, of his intent to approve such research; or

(d)   Research on practices, both innovative and accepted, which have the intent and reasonable probability of improving the health or well-being of the subject. In cases in which those studies require the assignment of prisoners in a manner consistent with protocols approved by the IRB to control groups which may not benefit from the research, the study may proceed only after the Secretary has consulted with appropriate experts, including experts in penology medicine and ethics, and published notice, in the FEDERAL REGISTER, of his intent to approve such research.

(b)   Except as provided in paragraph (a) of this section, biomedical or behavioral research conducted or supported by DHEW shall not involve prisoners as subjects.

Source: 43 *Federal Register* 53655 (Nov. 16, 1978)

APPENDIX BB

Proposed Rules on Research Involving Those Institutionalized as Mentally Disabled

§ 46.501 Applicability

(a)   The regulations in this subpart are applicable to all biomedical and behavioral research conducted or supported by the Department of health, Education, and Welfare involving as subjects individuals institutionalized as mentally disabled.

(b)   Nothing in this subpart shall be construed as indicating that compliance with the procedures set forth herein will in any way render inapplicable pertinent State or local laws bearing upon activities covered by this subpart.

(c)   The requirements of this subpart are in addition to those imposed under the other subparts of this part.

§ 46.502 Purpose

Individuals institutionalized as mentally disabled are confined in institutional settings in which their freedom and rights are potentially subject to limitation. In addition, because of their impairment they may be unable to comprehend sufficient information to give a truly informed consent. Also, in some cases they may be legally incompetent to consent to their own participation in research.

At the same time, so little is known about the factors that cause mental disability that efforts to prevent and treat such disabilities are in the primitive stages. There is widespread uncertainty regarding the nature of the disabilities, the proper

354

identification of persons who are disabled, the appropriate treatment of such persons, and the best approaches to their daily care. The need for research is clearly manifest. It is the purpose of this subpart to permit the conduct of responsible investigations while providing additional safeguards for those institutionalized as mentally disabled.

§ 46.503 Definitions

As used in this subpart:

(a)   "Secretary" means the Secretary of Health, Education, and Welfare and any other officer or employee of the Department of Health, Education, and Welfare to whom authority has been delegated.

(b)   "DHEW" means the Department of Health, Education, and Welfare.

(c)   "Mentally disabled" individuals includes those who are mentally ill, mentally retarded, emotionally disturbed, psychotic or senile, regardless of their legal status or the reason for their being institutionalized.

(d)   "Individuals institutionalized as mentally disabled" means individuals residing, whether by voluntary admission or involuntary confinement, in institutions for the care and treatment of the mentally disabled. Such individuals include but are not limited to patients in public or private mental hospitals, psychiatric patients in general hospitals, inpatients of community mental health centers, and mentally disabled individuals who reside in halfway houses or nursing homes.

(e)   "Children" are persons who have not attained the legal age of consent to general medical care as determined under the applicable law of the jurisdiction in which the research will be conducted.

(f)   "Parent" means a child's natural or adoptive parent.

(g)   "Legally authorized representative" means an individual or judicial or other body authorized under applicable law to consent on behalf of a prospective subject to such subject's participation in the particular activity or procedure. An official serving in an institutional capacity may not be considered a legally authorized representative for purposes of this subpart.

(h)   "Minimal risk" is the probability and magnitude of physical or psychological harm or discomfort that is normally encountered in the daily lives, or in the routine medical or psychological examination, of normal individuals.

(i)   "Assent" means a prospective subject's affirmative agreement to participate in research. Mere failure to object shall not, absent affirmative agreement, be construed as assent. Assent can only be given following an explanation, based on the types of information specified in § 46.103(c), appropriate to the level of understanding of the subject, in accordance with procedures established by the Institutional Review Board.

(j)   "Consent auditor" means a person appointed by the Institutional Review Board to ensure the adequacy of the consent process, particularly when there is a substantial question about the ability of a subject to consent or assent or when there is a significant degree of risk involved. Consent auditors are responsible only to the Board and should not be involved with the research, nor should they be employed by or otherwise associated with the institution conducting or sponsoring the research, or with the institution in which the subject resides. They should be persons familiar with the physical, psychological, and social needs of the class of prospective subjects as well as with their legal status.

(k) "Advocate" means an individual appointed by the Institutional Review Board to act in the best interests of the subject. The advocate will, although he or she is not appointed by a court, be construed to carry the fiduciary responsibilities of a guardian ad litem toward the person whose interests the advocate represents. No individual may serve as an advocate if the individual has any financial interest in, or other association with, the institution conducting or sponsoring the research, nor with the institution in which this research is conducted; nor, where the subject is the ward of a State or other agency, institution, or entity, may the advocate have any financial interest in, or other association with, that State, agency, institution, or entity. An advocate must be familiar with the physical, psychological, and social needs and the legal status of the class of individuals institutionalized as mentally disabled in the institution in which the research is conducted. [This definition will be retained in the final regulations if duties are assigned to "advocates."]

§ 46.504 Additional Duties of the Institutional Review Boards Where Individuals Institutionalized as Mentally Disabled Are Involved

(a)   In addition to all other responsibilities prescribed for Institutional Review Boards under this part, the Board shall review research covered by this subpart and approve such research only if it finds that:

(1)   The research methods are appropriate to the objectives of the research;

(2)   The competence of the investigator(s) and the quality of the research facility are sufficient for the conduct of the research;

(3)   Appropriate studies in nonhuman systems have been conducted prior to the involvement of human subjects;

(4)   There are good reasons to involve institutionalized individuals as subjects of the research. In reviewing proposals to involve institutionalized persons in research, the Board should evaluate the appropriateness of involving alternative, noninstitutionalized populations in the study instead of, or along with, the institutionalized individuals. Sometimes, the participation of alternative populations will not be possible or relevant, as when the research is designed to study problems or functions that have no parallel in free-living persons, (e.g., studies of the effects of institutionalization or studies related to persons, such as the profoundly retarded or severely handicapped, who are almost always found in residential facilities.)

(5)   Risk of harm or discomfort is minimized by using the safest procedures

consistent with sound research design and by using procedures performed for the diagnosis or treatment of the particular subject whenever possible;

(6)   Adequate provisions are made to protect the privacy of the subjects and to maintain confidentiality of data. For example, data may be disclosed to authorized personnel and used for authorized purposes only; data should be collected only if they are relevant and necessary for the purposes of the research and analysis; data should be maintained only as long as they are necessary to the research or to benefit the subjects; and all data should be maintained in accordance with fair information practices;

(7)   Selection of subjects among those institutionalized as mentally disabled will be equitable. Subjects in an institution should be selected so that the burdens of research do not fall disproportionately on those who are least able to consent or assent, nor should one group of patients be offered opportunities to participate in research from which they may derive benefit to the unfair exclusion of other equally suitable groups of patients.

(8)   Adequate provisions are made to assure that no prospective subject will be approached to participate in the research unless the health care professional who is responsible for the health care of the subject has determined that the invitation to participate in the research and the participation itself will not interfere with the health care of the subject;

(9)   The Board shall appoint a consent auditor to ensure the adequacy of the consent procedures when, in the opinion of the Board, such a person is considered necessary, e.g., when there is a substantial question about the ability of a subject to consent or to assent or when there is a significant degree of risk involved; and

[In the event the Department decides that there should be consent auditors for all projects, the above paragraph will be appropriately modified.]

(10)   The conditions of all applicable subsequent sections of this subpart are met.

(b)   The Board shall carry out such other duties as may be assigned by the Secretary.

(c)   The institution shall certify to the Secretary, in such manner as the Secretary may require, that the duties of the Board under this subpart have been fulfilled.

§ 46.505 Research Not Involving Greater than Minimal Risk

Biomedical or behavioral research that does not involve greater than minimal risk to subjects who are institutionalized as mentally disabled may be conducted or supported by DHEW provided the Institutional Review Board has determined that:

(a)   The conditions of § 46.504 are met; and

(b)   Adequate provisions are made to assure that no subject will participate in the research unless:

(1)   The subject gives informed consent to participation;

(2)   If the subject lacks the capacity to give informed consent, the research is relevant to the subject's condition, the subject assents or does not object to participation, and the subject's legally authorized representative consents to the subject's participation; or

(3)   If a subject, who lacks the capacity to give informed consent, objects to participation: (i) The research includes an intervention that holds out the prospect of direct benefit to the subject, or includes a monitoring procedure required for the well-being of the subject, (ii) the subject's legally authorized representative consents to the subject's participation, and (iii) the subject's participation is authorized by a court of competent jurisdiction.

[Consideration is being given to mandating that, in addition to the above requirements: (1) A "consent auditor" be appointed by the Institutional Review Board to ensure the adequacy of the consent process and determine whether each subject consents, or is incapable of consent but assents, or objects to participation, and (2) whenever the consent auditor determines that a subject is incapable of consenting, the subject may not participate without the authorization of an "advocate."]

§ 46.506 Research Involving Greater than Minimal Risk but Presenting the Prospect of Direct Benefit to the Individual Subjects

(a)   Biomedical or behavioral research in which more than minimal risk to subjects who are institutionalized as mentally disabled is presented by an intervention that holds out the prospect of direct benefit for the individual subjects, or by a monitoring procedure likely to contribute to the well-being of the subjects, may be conducted or supported provided the Institutional Review Board has determined that:

(1)   The conditions of section 46.504 are met;

(2)   The risk is justified by the prospect of benefit to the subjects;

(3)   The relation of the risk to anticipated benefit to subjects is at least as favorable as that presented by available alternative approaches;

(4)   Adequate provisions are made to assure that no adult will participate in the research unless:

(i)   The subject gives informed consent to participation;

(ii)   If the subject lacks the capacity to give informed consent, the subject assents to participation, and the subject's legally authorized representative consents to the subject's participation; or

(iii)   If a subject who lacks the capacity to give informed consent, does not assent, or objects to participation: (A) The intervention or monitoring procedure is only available in the context of the research, (B) the subject's legally authorized representative consents to the subject's participation, and (C) the subject's participation is authorized by a court of competent jurisdiction.

[Consideration is being given to mandating that, in addition to the above requirements: (1) A "consent auditor" be appointed by the Institutional Review Board to ensure the adequacy of the consent process and determine whether each subject consents, or is incapable of consent but assents, or objects to participation, and (2) whenever the consent auditor determines that a subject is incapable of consenting, the subject may not participate without the authorization of an "advocate."]

(5) Adequate provisions are made to assure that no child will participate in the research unless:

(i) The subject assents (if capable) and the subject's parent(s) or guardian(s) give permission, as provided in section 46.409 of this part; or

(ii) If the subject objects to participation, the intervention or monitoring procedure is available only in the context of the research, the subject's parent(s) or guardian(s) give permission, and the subject's participation is authorized by a court of competent jurisdiction.

(b) Where appropriate, the Institutional Review Board shall appoint a consent auditor to ensure the adequacy of the consent process and determine whether each subject consents, or is incapable of consent but assents, or objects to participation. [This paragraph will be deleted if a consent auditor is required in all cases.]

§ 46.507 Research Involving Greater than Minimal Risk and No Prospect of Direct Benefit to Individual Subjects, but Likely to Yield Generalizable Knowledge about the Subject's Disorder or Condition

(a) Biomedical or behavioral research in which more than minimal risk to subjects who are institutionalized as mentally disabled is presented by an intervention that does not hold out the prospect of direct benefit for the individual subjects, or by a monitoring procedure that is not likely to contribute to the well-being of the subjects, may be conducted or supported provided an Institutional Review Board has determined that:

(1) The conditions of section 46.504 are met;

(2) The risk represents a minor increase over minimal risk;

(3) The anticipated knowledge (i) is of vital importance for the understanding or amelioration of the type of disorder or condition of the subjects, or (ii) may reasonably be expected to benefit the subjects in the future;

(4) Adequate provisions are made to assure that no adult will participate in the research unless the following conditions are met:

(i) The subject gives informed consent to participation;

(ii) If the subject lacks the capacity to give informed consent, the subject assents to participation, and the subject's legally authorized representative consents to the subject's participation; or

(iii) If the subject lacks the capacity to assent but does not object, the subject's legally authorized representative and a court of competent jurisdiction consent to the subject's participation.

[The Department is considering the following additions to the above provisions:

In § 46.507(a)(B), with respect to subjects capable of consenting: (i) Adding the requirement that inclusion of each subject be approved by the Secretary based upon the advice of a panel of experts, or (ii) requiring the approval of an "advocate."

In § 46.507(a)(C), with respect to subjects incapable of assenting: (i) Prohibiting use of such subjects on the theory that there is no research which can be performed only with these subjects, (ii) requiring approval by the Secretary based upon the advice of a panel of experts, or (iii) requiring the approval of an "advocate."]

(5)   If the subject is a child, the requirements of §§ 46.407 and 409 of subpart D (relating to research involving children) are satisfied.

(b)   No subject may be involved in the research over his or her objection.

(c)   The Institutional Review Board shall appoint a consent auditor to ensure the adequacy of the consent process and determine whether each subject consents, or is incapable of consenting but assents, or is incapable of assenting but does not object, or objects to participation. [This paragraph will be deleted if a consent auditor is required for all research covered by this subpart.]

§ 46.508 Research Not Otherwise Approvable Which Presents an Opportunity to Understand, Prevent, or Alleviate a Serious Problem Affecting the Health or Welfare of Individuals Institutionalized as Mentally Disabled

Biomedical or behavioral research that the Institutional Review Board does not believe meets the requirements of §§ 46.505, 46.506, or 46.507 may nevertheless be conducted or supported by DHEW provided:

(a)   The Institutional Review Board has determined the following:

(1)   The conditions of § 46.504 are met; and

(2)   The research presents a reasonable opportunity to further the understanding, prevention, or alleviation of a serious problem affecting the health or welfare of individuals institutionalized as mentally disabled; and

(b)   The Secretary, after consultation with a panel of experts in pertinent disciplines (e.g., science, medicine, education, ethics, law) and following opportunity for public review and comment, has determined either (1) that the research in fact satisfies the conditions of §§ 46.505, 46.506, or § 46.507, as applicable, or (2) the following:

(i)   The research presents a reasonable opportunity to further the understanding, prevention, or alleviation of a serious problem affecting the health or welfare of individuals institutionalized as mentally disabled;

(ii)   The conduct of the research will be in accord with basic ethical principles of beneficence, justice, and respect for persons, that should underlie the conduct of research involving human subjects; and

(iii)   Adequate provisions are made for obtaining consent of those subjects capable of giving fully informed consent, the assent of other subjects and the consent of their legally authorized representatives, and, where appropriate, the authorization of a court of competent jurisdiction [and if §§ 46.505, 46.506, 46.507 require an advocate, the authorization of that advocate].

Source: 43 *Federal Register* 53954 (Nov. 17, 1978)

APPENDIX CC

Proposed Rules Regarding Protection of Human Subjects; Research Involving Children

§ 46.401 Applicability

(a)   These regulations apply to all biomedical and behavioral research conducted or supported by the Department of Health, Education, and Welfare involving children as subjects.

(b)   Compliance with these procedures will in no way render inapplicable pertinent State or local laws bearing upon activities covered by this subpart.

(c)   These requirements are in addition to those imposed under the other subparts of this part.

§ 46.402 Purpose

Children are normally legally incapable of consenting to their own participation in biomedical or behavioral research and may also be unable to comprehend fully the consequences and risks which might be involved in such participation. This subpart provides additional safeguards for the protection of children involved in biomedical and behavioral research.

§ 46.403 Definitions

As used in this subpart:

(a)   "Secretary" means the Secretary of Health, Education, and Welfare and any other officer or employee of the Department of Health, Education, and Welfare to whom authority has been delegated.

(b) "DHEW" means the Department of Health, Education, and Welfare.

(c) "Children" are persons who have not attained the legal age of consent to general medical care as determined under the applicable law of the jurisdiction in which the research will be conducted.

(d) "Research" means a formal investigation designed to develop or contribute to generalizable knowledge in such fields as human biology and medicine and in the behavioral sciences including psychology, educational psychology, and sociology.

(e) "Advocate" means an individual appointed by the Board, or through procedures approved by the Board, to act in the best interests of the child. The advocate will, although he or she is not appointed by a court, be construed to carry the fiduciary responsibilities of a guardian ad litem toward the children whose interests the advocate represents. No individual may serve as an advocate if the individual has any financial interest in, or other association with, the institution conducting or sponsoring the research; nor, where the subject is the ward of a State or other agency, institution, or entity, may the advocate have any financial interest in, or other association with, that State, agency, institution, or entity.

(f) "Assent" means a child's affirmative agreement to participate in research. Mere failure to object should not, absent affirmative agreement, be construed as consent. Assent can only be given following an explanation, based on the types of information specified in § 46.103(c) of this part, appropriate to the level of understanding of the child, in accordance with procedures established by the Institutional Review Board.

(g) "Permission" means the agreement of parent(s) or guardian to the participation of their child or ward in research. Permission can only be given following an explanation including the information specified in § 46.103(c) of this part.

(h) "Parent" means a child's biological or adoptive parent.

(i) "Guardian" means an individual who is authorized under applicable State or local law to consent on behalf of a child to general medical care for the child.

(j) "Minimal risk" is the probability and magnitude of physical or psychological harm that is normally encountered in the daily lives, or in the routine medical, dental, or psychological examination of healthy children.

§ 46.404 Additional Duties of an Institutional Review Board Where Children Are Involved

(a) In addition to all other responsibilities under this part, each Institutional Review Board (Board) shall review research covered by this subpart. It may approve the research only if it finds that:

(1) The research methods are appropriate to the aims of the research;

(2)   The competence of the investigator(s) and the quality of the research facility are sufficient for the conduct of the research;

(3)   Where appropriate, studies have been conducted first on animals and adult humans, and then on older children before involving very young children;

(4)   Risks are minimized by using the safest procedures consistent with sound research design and by using procedures performed for the examination, diagnosis, or treatment of the particular subject whenever appropriate and feasible;

(5)   Adequate provisions are made to protect the privacy of children and their parents, and to maintain the confidentiality of data. For example, data may be disclosed to authorized personnel and used for authorized purposes only; data should be collected only if they are relevant and necessary for the purposes of the research and analysis; data should be maintained only as long as they are necessary to the research or to benefit the children; and all data should be maintained in accordance with fair information practices;

(6)   The criteria for subject selection are appropriate for the research aims and will permit the selection of subjects in an equitable manner, avoiding overuse of any one group of children based solely upon administrative convenience or availability of a population;

(7)   Where appropriate, adequate provisions are made for involving a parent, guardian, or advocate in the conduct or monitoring of the research, for example, in situations in which the Board finds the subjects to be incapable of assenting and the research involves more than minimal risk or more than minimal discomfort to these subjects;

(8)   Adequate provisions are made for monitoring solicitation of assent and permission, as, for example, through participation by Board members or by advocate in the actual solicitation process, either for all subjects or for a sampling of subjects; and

(9)   The conditions of all applicable subsequent sections of this subpart are met.

(b)   The Board shall carry out such other duties as may be assigned by the Secretary.

(c)   The institution sponsoring the Board shall certify to the Secretary, in such manner as the Secretary may require, that the duties of the Board under this subpart have been fulfilled.

§ 46.405 Research Not Involving Greater than Minimal Risk

DHEW may conduct or support research that does not involve greater than minimal risk to children if the Board finds that:

(a)   The conditions of §46.404 are met; and

(b)   Adequate provisions are made for soliciting the assent of the children and the permission of their parents or guardians, as set forth in § 46.409.

§ 46.406 Research Involving Greater than Minimal Risk but Presenting the Prospect of Direct Benefit to the Individual Subjects

DHEW may conduct or support research in which the Board finds that more than minimal risk to children is presented by an intervention or procedure that holds out the prospect of direct benefit for the individual subject, or by a monitoring procedure that is likely to contribute to the subject's well-being, if the Board finds that:

(a) The risk is justified by the anticipated benefit to the subjects;

(b) The relation of the anticipated benefit to the risk is at least as favorable to the subjects as that presented by available alternative approaches;

(c) The conditions of Section 46.404 are met; and

(d) Adequate provisions are made for soliciting the assent of the children and permission of their parents or guardians, as set forth in § 46.409.

§ 46.407 Research Involving Greater than Minimal Risk and No Prospect of Direct Benefit to Individual Subjects, but Likely to Yield Generalized Knowledge about the Subjects' Disorder or Condition

DHEW may conduct or support research in which the Board finds that more than minimal risk to children is presented by an intervention or procedure that does not hold out the prospect of direct benefit for the individual subject, or by a monitoring procedure which is not likely to contribute to the well-being of the subject, if the Board finds that:

(a) The risk represents a minor increase over minimal risk;

(b) The intervention or procedure presents experiences to subjects that are reasonably commensurate with those inherent in their actual or expected medical, dental, psychological, social, or educational situations;

(c) The intervention or procedure is likely to yield generalizable knowledge about the subjects' disorder or condition which is of vital importance for the understanding or amelioration of the subjects' disorder or condition;

(d) The conditions of § 46.404 are met; and

(e) Adequate provisions are made for assent of the children and permission of their parents or guardians, as set forth in section 46.409.

§ 46.408 Research Not Otherwise Approvable Which Presents an Opportunity to Understand, Prevent, or Alleviate a Serious Problem Affecting the Health or Welfare of Children

DHEW may conduct or support research that the Board does not believe meets the requirements of §§ 46.405, 46.406, or 46.407 if:

(a) The Board finds that: (1) The conditions of § 46.404 are met; and (2) the research presents a reasonable opportunity to futher the understanding, prevention, or alleviation of a serious problem affecting the health or welfare of children; and

(b)   The Secretary, after consultation with a panel of experts in pertinent disciplines (e.g., science, medicine, education, ethics, law) and following opportunity for public review and comment, has determined either: (1) That the research in fact satisfies the conditions of §§ 46.405, 46.406, or 46.407, as applicable, or (2) the following:

(i)   The research presents a reasonable opportunity to further the understanding, prevention, or alleviation of a serious problem affecting the health or welfare of children;

(ii)   The research will be conducted in accordance with the basic ethical principles;

(iii)   Adequate provisions are made for soliciting the assent of children and the permission of their parents or guardians, as set forth in section 46.409.

§ 46.409 Requirements for Permission by Parents or Guardians and for Assent by Children

(a)   In addition to the determinations required under other applicable sections of this subpart, the Board shall determine that adequate provisions are made for soliciting the assent of the children, when in the judgment of the Board the children are capable of doing so. In determining whether children are capable of assenting, the Board shall take into account the ages and maturity of the children involved. This judgment may be made for all children under a particular research protocol, or on a more individualized basis, as the Board deems appropriate. If the Board determines the child is so incapacitated that he or she cannot reasonably be consulted or that the intervention or procedure involved in the research holds out a prospect of direct benefit that is important to the health or well-being of the child and is available only in the context of the research, the assent of the child need not be obtained. If the Board determines that a child is so incapacitated, and the child is not under the guardianship of a parent, then permission of both the guardian and a subject advocate must be obtained.

(b)   Where the Board determines under paragraph (a) that the child's assent need not be obtained, it shall also determine whether a advocate should be appointed for the child, taking into account such factors as, for example, whether there are likely to be financial or other pressures on the parents or guardian which could affect their ability to consider solely the interests of the child in deciding whether to consent to the child's participation in the research. The role of the advocate would be to advise the Board, parents, and investigators of any concerns the advocate may have about the child's participation in the research.

(c)   In addition to the determinations required under other applicable sections of this subpart, the Board shall determine that adequate provisions are made for soliciting the permission of each child's parent(s) or guardian. Where parental permission is to be obtained, the Board may find that the permission of one parent is sufficient for research to be conducted under § 46.405 or 46.406, but in doing so the

Board must consider such factors as the nature of the research and the age, maturity, status, and condition of the subjects. Where research is covered by §§ 46.407 and 46.408 and permission is to be obtained from parents, both parents must give their permission unless one parent is deceased, unknown, incompetent, or not reasonably available, or the child belongs to a single-parent family (i.e., when only one parent has legal responsibility for the care and custody of the child).

(d)   If the Board determines that a research protocol is designed for conditions or for a subject population for which parental or guardian permission is not a reasonable requirement to protect the subjects (e.g., neglected or abused children); it may waive the consent requirements in subpart A of this part and paragraph (c) of this section, provided an appropriate mechanism for protecting the children who will participate as subjects in the research is substituted, and provided further that the waiver is not inconsistent with State or local law. The choice of an appropriate mechanism would depend upon the nature and purpose of the activities described in the protocol, the risk and anticipated benefit to the research subjects, and their age, maturity, status, and condition.

(e)   The Institutional Review Board shall determine that permission by parents or guardians will be documented in accordance with the requirements of § 46.110 of this part.

(f)   When the Institutional Review Board determines that assent is required, it shall also determine how assent must be documented.

§ 46.410 Wards

(a)   Children who are wards of the State or any other agency, institution, or entity can be included in research approved under § 46.407 or 46.408 only if such research is:

(1)   Related to their status as wards; or

(2)   Conducted in schools, camps, or similar group settings in which the majority of children involved as subjects are not wards.

(b)   If the research is approved under paragraph (a) of this section, the Board shall require appointment of an advocate for each child, in addition to any other individual acting as guardian or in loco parentis for the child. The advocate will act in the best interests of the child, and will have the same opportunities to intercede normally provided parents. One individual may serve as advocate for more than one child. No individual may serve as an advocate if the individual has any financial interest in, or other association with, either the guardian organization or any institution responsible for the research.

(c)   If a child who is a ward objects to participation in the research, but the child's assent is not required under § 46.409, the child may be included as a subject only with the approval of both the child's guardian and the advocate for the child.

Source: 43 Federal Register 31792 (July 21, 1978).

DD

Consent and Agreement for Participation in Research

IDENTIFICATION

Name of research director:
Name of research organization:
   Address:
Name of the research participant:
   Address:
Name of auditor-witness:
   Address:
Title of the research project:

Date: Time: A.M.
                   A.M.

Phone number:

Phone number:

Phone number:

DESCRIPTION OF RESEARCH PROCEDURES

(Include the nature and purpose of the research, basic procedures, and the possible material or significant benefits and risks)

STATEMENT OF CONSENT AND AGREEMENT

     I, _____ hereby request permission to participate in the research described above and related incidental procedures. The nature and purpose of this research and the possible material or significant benefits and risks have been explained to me so that I understand them.

I am freely requesting participation without duress or coercion in exchange for expected benefits for me or for others. I understand that I may withdraw my consent at any time I wish without penalty or prejudice and may stop participating as soon thereafter as it is safe to do so. If I am being paid for my participation in this research, I may collect my entire fee at any time I choose to withdraw from the research.

If I am not satisfied with my participation, I will immediately inform the research director. I may also inform _____
(Name of advisory group member)
©o _____ who is a member of an independent advisory group in-
(Phone number and/or address)
terested in the opinions and welfare of research participants. I acknowledge that no guarantee or assurance has been made as to the results of my participation.

If I want any additional information, have any questions, or have any reservations I may now mention them to the people present or write them in the space below:

ANY ADDITIONAL UNDERSTANDINGS OR AGREEMENTS (note 1)

AUTHORIZING SIGNATURES (notes 2, 3)

All matters and issues mentioned above have been discussed to my satisfaction and agreement. My signature indicates that I have read and understood all of the above.

_____
(Signature of the research participant)

_____
(Signature of the research director or the signature, printed name, and address of an authorized agent of the research director)

ATTESTATION

I attest that the nature and purpose of this research, its procedures, and its benefits and risks were fully explained to the applicant in my presence. I am convinced of the applicant's complete understanding, competence and willingness to participate in the research. I am confident that no duress or undue influence of any kind was present in these proceedings.

_____
(Signature of the auditor-witness)

- Note 1 (optional clauses)

Assumption of Risk   I realize that not all potential benefits or risks of research (personal, social, or physical risls) can be known ahead of time even when research is properly or well conducted. A major purpose of research is to find answers or to develop new knowledge. As a part of my contribution and participation in this research, I freely assume as my own these unknown or unexpected risks as well as the known risks described above.

I understand that the harm or danger from some of these risks may be very severe. I also realize that I may withdraw from participation, as mentioned above, whenever I feel that the potential risks might outweigh the benefits for me.

Release from Liability I understand that the research investigator is legally liable for the obviously negligent conduct of this research or for any acts intentionally done to harm me. I also understand that harm may occur in the absence of any clearly negligent or intentionally harmful act. Therefore, in return for being accepted as a research participant, I release the research investigator from all liability and waive all my rights and claims against him (or her) except those claims arising directly from clearly negligent or intentionally harmful acts by him (or her). This release from liability and waiver is made by me for myself, my heirs, and any person who might claim through me or on my behalf. It applies not only to the research investigator but also to his assistants and agents and to the research institution and its employees. It is understood that these persons, as well as the research investigator, remain liable for clearly negligent or intentionally harmful acts.

Consent to Recording and Photographs For the purpose of advancing knowledge, I consent to the taking and use of audio recordings, motion pictures, video tapes, or other pictorial representations of me appropriate for scientific, rehabilitative, or educational purposes. It is specifically understood that in any publication or use I shall not be identified by name.

   (If the identity of the person is not to be provided, the following sentence may
   be substituted for the last sentence above.)

I understand that I shall in no way be identified by name or otherwise, and that every reasonable effort will be made to preserve my anonymity and to conceal my identity.

- Note 2 (optional additional signature of legal guardians)

   Because _____ is under the age of 18 years and/or is incompetent to
      (Name of research participant)
give valid consent, I, _____ am also signing this agreement.
         (Name of legal guardian)

_____

(Signature of legal guardian)

- Note 3 (optional additional signature of attending physician)

  I understand that my patient _____ has agreed to participate in a study
                             (Name of research participant)

of _____ to be conducted by _____. I am aware of the purpose,
(Brief description of research)   (Name of principal investigator)

design, and plan of this study and agree with the procedures to be performed with
my patient.

_____
(Signature of physician)

_____
(Date)

EE

Consent to Act as a Research Participant

- I hereby agree to have _____ and/or _____ perform the following procedures on me for experimental purposes:
- These procedures will be done in _____ and will take the following amount of time:
- The purpose of performing these procedures is:
- I understand that the procedures described above involve the following possible risks and/or discomforts:
  and that they have the following possible benefits:
- I understand that there are alternative procedures that could be used for my diagnosis or therapy. These are:
  These alternatives have the following risks and benefits:
- This information was explained to me by _____. I understand that s/he will answer any questions I may have concerning this investigation or the procedures at any time. I may reach him/her at _____.
- I understand that my participation in any study is entirely voluntary and that I may decline to enter this study or may withdraw from it at any time without jeopardy to my further treatment. I understand that the investigator may drop me from the study as long as it is not detrimental to me.
- I understand that in case of physical injury, I _____ entitled to monetary
  (am/am not)

compensation and that I _____ receive medical treatment, as has been ex-
            (will/will not)
plained to me.

● I understand that my payment for participation in this research is $ _____. If I
do not complete the study, I will receive a minimum of $ _____ or _____
percent if I participate longer than _____.

_____

(Staff member/witness)   (Participant)

                                       _____
                                       (Date)

APPENDIX FF

Consent by a Minor to Participate in a Research Project

- I, _____, state that I _____ over eighteen (18) years of age and
  (am/am not)
wish to participate in a program of research being conducted by _____.
- I understand that the primary purpose of the proposed research is to ____
_____.
- The project involves the following procedures: _____
_____.
- I understand that, as with any research study, there may be some personal
risks involved, both anticipated and unanticipated, such as _____
_____.
Professionally trained personnel will take reasonable precautions to reduce risk and
prevent harm.
- All information collected will be treated as confidential. Reasonable precautions will be taken to safeguard the confidentiality of information and to prevent
the disclosure and misuse of this information. Subjects will be given a code number
so that their names do not appear on records obtaining information. A code list
which matches names and code numbers will be kept separately in a locked file
available only to the principal investigator or his legal designee.
- I realize that absolute confidentiality cannot be guaranteed, because in
extreme situations (such as those involving clear and imminent danger to others or
court orders) access to information by others may be legally required. I will be

374

asked for permission, before information is disclosed to my parents. If significant problems are found during clinical evaluations, either I or my parents will be informed.

● I understand that I am free to withdraw my consent and to discontinue my participation in the project or activity at any time without any negative consequences to me or to my parents by the research personnel.

● If at any time I feel that the risks of this study outweigh the benefits, I will request changes in my participation in the study or terminate my participation. I accept the risks involved with a full understanding that it is for the possible benefit of myself or the advance of knowledge in the interest of humanity. If I want an evaluation without participating in the study, I may request it on an individual basis from _____ or other medical facilities, at a cost ranging approximately $ _____ to _____.

● I understand that in the event of physical injury resulting from research procedures, medical treatment will be made available as provided by the hospital insurance and liability coverage.

● I have had the study described to me to my complete satisfaction and I have been allowed to read a summary of the project and the institutional review board certification. I have also had the opportunity to ask questions and if I have any additional questions or concerns, I may ask them now or write them in the space below.

I authorize, in conformity with existing institutional regulations, _____ to keep, preserve, publish, use, or dispose of the information and results of this research.

THE STUDY HAS BEEN FULLY EXPLAINED TO ME AND I HAVE CAREFULLY READ AND UNDERSTOOD THE AGREEMENT, THEREFORE I FREELY AND VOLUNTARILY CONSENT AND AGREE TO PARTICIPATE IN THIS STUDY.

Subject's name_____

Subject's signature _____

Witness signature _____

Date _____

Source: Adapted from; Use of Human Subjects in Research. Institutional Review Board. The Graduate College, University of Illinois (Urbana-Champaign), 1976.

APPENDIX GG

Parental Consent for a Minor's Participation in Research

We, parents or guardians of the above minor volunteer, agree to the participation of the above minor in the research project set out above. We have been informed of the need for the research, the benefits to be derived from it, and the risks involved and that we may withdraw him/her from participation at any time. We have also been informed that the research can best be conducted with a subject population including minors because of the nature of the research.

(Strike out A or B).

A)   Being aware of the value of the participation of minors in this research project and further being aware that this procedure will not benefit the minor here involved personally, we consent to the minor's participation.

B)   Being aware of the value of the participation of minors in this research project and being informed that the procedures may also benefit the above-named minor personally in the following way _____

_____

_____

_____

_____

we consent to the minor's participation.

Signature of staff member

Witness to explanation
  (not to signature)

Date

Signature of parents or guardians

Signature of parents or guardians

HH

Consent Form Coversheet and Verification by Researcher

The following standardized cover sheet might be used for consent forms:

     Participation in a research project is always voluntary. If you do not want to participate, just tell the researcher. If you do not want to participate, you can still get medical treatment that is not experimental. If you decide to participate, you are still free to withdraw at any time. Please do not feel compelled to participate.

     You should discuss the research procedure with the researcher. You should not sign the consent form until you are sure you understand exactly what is going to be done, what risks there might be, and what other kinds of medical treatment you can have.

     You will be given this cover sheet and the consent form at least 24 hours before the research is to begin. During this 24 hours you should carefully think about the research project, and ask the researcher any questions you might have. Please do not sign the consent form until the end of the 24 hours.

     Your signature below means that you have received and understood this cover sheet.

                                          _____

                                   (Subject's signature)   (Date)

The following standardized acknowledgment might be placed below the subject's signature on each consent form:

I personally have discussed the research procedure, the risks involved and the available treatment alternatives with the research subject whose name appears on this form, and am satisfied that the subject understands these areas and is voluntarily consenting to participate in this research project.

_____
(Researcher's signature)   (Date)

Source: Proposed changes for obtaining consent from experimental subjects. 1 *Law and Human Behavior,* 403,414–415 (1977).

APPENDIX ‖

Acknowledgment of Grant Support from U.S. Department of Health, Education, and Welfare*

This study was supported by DHEW _____ grant No. _____, awarded by
(research/training)
the _____ of the Public Health Service.
(institute/division/center)

*To be used as a footnote on the first page of a published article or in the acknowledgments section of a book. Prior program approval is not required. Published or unpublished surveys or questionnaires must include a positive statement clearly stating that the contents are in no way the responsibility of the awarding agency.

APPENDIX JJ

Consent to Participation in Training and Demonstration (HYPNOSIS)

I _____ voluntarily consent to participate in training and demonstration procedures which may involve hypnosis. I have been fully informed and understand the nature and purpose of my participation. From my participation, I hope to obtain a better understanding of hypnosis and to contribute to increased understanding of hypnosis by others.

I will not be deliberately embarrassed or asked to perform illegal acts. Instead, efforts will be made to enhance my self esteem and well being. I will remain aware of all the hypnotic procedures as they are conducted. I understand that I may end my participation at any time I wish without any adverse academic or social consequences. My participation is not required as a part of my classwork.

Although potential harm from the hypnotic procedures to be used is not very likely, I understand that not all psychological, social, or physical risks from hypnosis can be known ahead of time. I freely assume all such risks of participation.

If I want additional information, have any questions, or have any reservations, I may now mention them to the instructor or write them in the space below:

I have been informed, I understand, and I willingly consent to and request participation. In consideration of my being accepted for participation, and for other good and valuable consideration, I, acting for myself, my heirs, personal representatives, my estimate and my assigns, do hereby release _____

(name of institution and of hypnotist)

his/her colleagues, assistants, and all other participating in these procedures from all liability of any kind or character, including claims and suits in law or equity for damage or any injury however severe which may result to me or to my property from my participation.

IN WITNESS WHEREOF I hereunto set my hand and affix my seal this _____ day of _____, 19_.

_____
(Signature of applicant)

APPENDIX KK

Standards for Providers of Psychological Services

DEFINITIONS

Providers of psychological services refers to the following persons:

A. Professional psychologists. Professional psychologists have a doctoral degree from a regionally accredited university or professional school in a program that is primarily psychological and appropriate training and experience in the area of service offered.

B. All other persons who offer psychological services under the supervision of a professional psychologist.

Psychological services refers to one or more of the following:

A. Evaluation, diagnosis, and assessment of the functioning of individuals and groups in a variety of settings and activities.

B. Interventions to facilitate the functioning of individuals and groups. Such interventions may include psychological counseling, psychotherapy, and process consultation.

C. Consultation relating to A and B above.

D. Program development services in the areas of A, B, and C above.

E. Supervision of psychological services.

A psychological service unit is the functional unit through which psychological services are provided:

A. A psychological service unit is a unit that provides predominantly psychological services and is composed of one or more professional psychologists and supporting staff.

B. A psychological service unit may operate as a professional service or as a functional or geographic component of a larger governmental, educational, correction, health, training, industrial, or commercial organizational unit.

C. A psychologist providing professional services in a multioccupational setting is regarded as a psychological service unit.

D. A psychological service unit also may be an individual or group of individuals in a private practice or a psychological consulting firm.

User includes:

A. Direct users or recipients of psychological services.

B. Public and private institutions, facilities, or organizations receiving psychological services.

C. Third-party purchasers—those who pay for the delivery of services but who are not the recipients of services.

Sanctioners refers to those users and nonusers who have a legitimate concern with the accessibility, timeliness, efficacy, and standards of quality attending the provision of psychological services. In addition to the users, sanctioners may include members of the user's family, the court, the probation officer, the school administrator, the employer, the union representative, the facility director, etc. Another class of sanctioners is represented by various governmental, peer review, and accreditation bodies concerned with the assurance of quality.

STANDARD 1. PROVIDERS

    1.1   Each psychological service unit offering psychological services shall have available at least one professional psychologist and as many more professional psychologists as are necessary to assure the quality of services offered.

    1.2   Providers of psychological services who do not meet the requirements for the professional psychologist shall be supervised by a professional psychologist who shall assume professional responsibility and accountability for the services provided. The level and extent of supervision may vary from task to task so long as the supervising psychologist retains a sufficiently close supervisory relationship to meet this standard.

    1.3   Wherever a psychological service unit exists, a professional psychologist shall be responsible for planning, directing, and reviewing the provision of psychological services.

1.4   When functioning as part of an organizational setting, professional psychologists shall bring their background and skills to bear whenever appropriate upon the goals of the organization by participating in the planning and development of overall services.[11]

1.5   Psychologists shall maintain current knowledge of scientific and professional developments that are directly related to the services they render.

1.6   Psychologists shall limit their practice to their demonstrated areas of professional competence.

1.7   Psychologists who wish to change their service specialty or to add an additional area of applied specialization must meet the same requirements with respect to subject matter and professional skills that apply to doctoral training in the new specialty.

STANDARD 2. PROGRAMS

2.1   Composition and organization of a psychological service unit:

2.1.1   The composition and programs of a psychological service unit shall be responsive to the needs of the persons or settings served.

2.1.2   A description of the organization of the psychological service unit and its lines of responsibility and accountability for the delivery of psychological services shall be available in written form to staff of the unit and to users and sanctioners upon request.

2.1.3   A psychological service unit shall include sufficient numbers of professional and support personnel to achieve its goals, objectives, and purposes.

2.2   Policies:

2.2.1   When the psychological service unit is composed of more than one person wherein a supervisory relationship exists or is a component of a larger organization, a written statement of its objectives and scope of services shall be developed and maintained.

2.2.2   All providers within a psychological service unit shall support the legal and civil rights of the user.

2.2.3   All providers within a psychological service unit shall be familiar with and adhere to the American Psychological Association's Ethical Standards of Psychologists, Psychology as a Profession, Standards for Educational and Psychological Tests, and other official policy statements relevant to standards for professional services issued by the Association.

2.2.4   All providers within a psychological service unit shall conform to relevant statutes established by federal, state, and local governments.

2.2.5 All providers within a psychological service unit shall, where appropriate, inform themselves about and use the network of human services in their communities in order to link users with relevant services and resources.

2.2.6 In the delivery of psychological services, the providers shall maintain a continuing cooperative relationship with colleagues and co-workers whenever in the best interest of the user.

2.3 Procedures:

2.3.1 Where appropriate, each psychological service unit shall be guided by a set of procedural guidelines for the delivery of psychological services. If appropriate to the setting, these guidelines shall be in written form.

2.3.2 Providers shall develop a plan appropriate to the provider's professional strategy of practice and to the problems presented by the user.

2.3.3 There shall be a mutually acceptable understanding between the provider and user or responsible agent regarding the delivery of service.

2.3.4 Accurate, current, and pertinent documentation shall be made of essential psychological services provided.

2.3.5 Providers of psychological services shall establish a system to protect confidentiality of their records.

STANDARD 3. ACCOUNTABILITY

3.1 Psychologists' professional activity shall be primarily guided by the principle of promoting human welfare.

3.2 Psychologists shall pursue their activities as members of an independent, autonomous profession.

3.3 There shall be periodic, systematic, and effective evaluations of psychological services.

3.4 Psychologists are accountable for all aspects of the services they provide and shall be responsive to those concerned with these services.

STANDARD 4. ENVIRONMENT

4.1 Providers of psychological services shall promote the development in the service setting of a physical, organizational, and social environment that facilitates optimal human functioning.

Source: Excerpted from American Psychological Association. Standards for providers of Psychological services. Washington, D.C.: Author, 1977. Readers are urged to read entire publication for interpretations of the standards and reference notes.

LL

Psychology Licensing (L) or Certification (C) Laws

		Year of Original Approval	Coverage	Educational Requirement	Experience: Post Degree	Experience: Supervised	Experience: TOTAL EXP.	ABPP Accepted?	Examination Mandatory?	Continuing Education (renw.) Req'd.?	Renewal	Examining Board: Psych. Members	Examining Board: Public Members	Examining Board: Terms
Alabama	(L)	1963	Practice of Psychologists	Doctorate	—	—	0	yes	yes	no	2 yrs.	5	—	5
Alaska	(L)	1967	Practice of Psychology:					yes	yes	no	1 yr.	3	0	3
			—Psychologist	Doctorate	1	1	1		yes					
			—Psychological Associate	Masters	—	1	3		yes					
Arizona	(C)	1965	Psychologist	Doctorate	—	—	0	—	yes	no	1 yr.	5	0	8
Arkansas	(L)	1955	Psychologist	Doctorate	—	—	1	—	yes	no	1 yr.	5	0	5
			Psychological Examiner	Masters	—	—	0		yes					
California	(L)	1957	Psychologist	Doctorate	1	2	2	yes	yes	yes	1 yr.	5	3	4
	(C)	1969	Psychological Assistant		—	—	—		yes		2 yrs.			
Colorado	(L)	1961	Psychology	Doctorate	2	2	2	yes	yes	yes	1 yr.	5	0	5
Connecticut	(L)	1945	Psychologist	Doctorate	—	—	1	yes	yes	no	1 yr.	5	0	5
Delaware	(L)	1962	Practice of Psychology	Doctorate	2	2	2	yes	yes	no	1 yr.	5	0	3
Dist. of Col.	(L)	1971	Practice of Psychology	Doctorate	2	—	2	yes	yes	no	1 yr.	5	0	3
Georgia	(L)	1951	Pract. of Applied Psych.	Doctorate	—	—	1	yes	yes	no	2 yrs.	5	0	5
Hawaii	(L)	1967	Practice of Psychology	Doctorate	—	1	1	—	yes	no	2 yrs.	5	2	2
Idaho	(L)	1963	Practice of Psychology	Doctorate	—	—	2	—	yes	no	1 yr.	3	0	3
Illinois	(C)	1963	Psychologist	Doctorate	—	—	2	—	yes	no	2 yrs.	5	0	5

388

State		Year	Title	Degree							Period			
Indiana	(C)	1969	Psychologist in Private Practice	Doctorate	3	—	3	yes	yes	no	2 yrs.	5	0	3
			Psychologist	Doctorate	—	—	3	yes	yes	no	2 yrs.			
Iowa	(L)	1974	Practice of Psychology	Doctorate	1	1	1	yes	yes	no	1 yr.	5	2	3
			Pract. of Associate Psychology (Indep.)											
Kansas	(C)	1967	Psychologist	Masters	—	2	5		yes	yes	2 yrs.	7	0	3
Kentucky	(L)	1948	Practice of Psychology (Certificand)	Doctorate	1	2	2	—	no	no	3 yrs.	5	0	4
			(contin.)	Masters	—	1	1		yes	no	3 yrs.			
Louisiana	(C)	1964	Psychologist	Doctorate	2	2	2	yes	yes	no	1 yr.	5	0	3
Maine	(L)	1953	Psychologist	Doctorate	—	2	2	—	yes	no	2 yrs.	5	1	5
			Psychologist Examiner	Masters	1	1	1	—	yes	no	2 yrs.			
Maryland	(C)	1957	Psychologist	Doctorate	1	1	2	yes	yes	yes	1 yr.	5	0	3
Massachusetts	(L)	1971	Psychologist	Doctorate	1	2	2	yes	yes	no	2 yrs.	5	0	5
Michigan	(C)	1959	Consulting Psychologist	Doctorate	4	1	5	yes	waiv.	no	1 yr.	7	0	—
			Psychologist	Doctorate	1	1	1	—	waiv.	no	1 yr.			
			Psychologist Examiner or Technician	Masters	—	1	1	—	—	waiv.	1 yr.			
Minnesota	(L)	1973	Consulting Psychologist	Doctorate	2	—	2	yes	yes	yes	2 yrs.	11	4	4
			Psychologist	Masters	2	1	2	—	yes	yes	2 yrs.			
Mississippi	(C)	1966	Psychologist	Doctorate	1	—	1	yes	yes	no	1 yr.	5	0	3
Missouri	(L)	1977	Psychologist	Doctorate	—	1	1	—	yes	no	2 yrs.	5	0	5
				Masters	—	—	3	—	yes	no	2 yrs.			
Montana	(L)	1971	Practice of Psychology	Doctorate	1	—	2	yes	yes	no	1 yr.	3	0	3
Nebraska	(L)	1967	Practice of Psychology	Doctorate	—	—	0	—	yes	no	1 yr.	5	0	5
Nevada	(L)	1963	Practice of Psychology	Doctorate	1	—	1	—	yes	yes	2 yrs.	5	0	4
New Hampshire	(C)	1957	Psychologist	Doctorate	1	2	2	yes	yes	no	1 yr.	3	0	3
			Associate Psychologist	Masters							1 yr.			
New Jersey	(L)	1966	Practice of Professional Psychological Services	Doctorate	1	2	2	yes	yes	no	2 yrs.	8	1	3
New Mexico	(C)	1963	Psychologist	Doctorate	2	—	2	yes	yes	yes	1 yr.	5	0	3

389

State		Year of Original Approval	Coverage	Educational Requirement	Experience: Post Degree	Supervised	TOTAL EXP.	ABPP Accepted?	Examination Mandatory?	Continuing Education Req'l. (renw.)	Renewal	Examining Board: Psych. Members	Public Members	Terms
New York	(C)	1956	Psychologist	Doctorate	—	2	2	yes	yes	no	2 yrs.	11	0	5
North Carolina	(L)	1967	Practicing Psychologist	Doctorate	2	2	2	yes	yes	no	1 yr.	5	0	3
			Psychological Examiner	Masters	—	—	0	—	yes	no	1 yr.			
North Dakota	(L)	1967	Psychologist	Doctorate	—	—	0	yes	yes	yes	1 yr.	5	0	3
Ohio	(L)	1972	Practice of Psychology	Doctorate	1	2	2	yes	yes	no	2 yrs.	6	1	5
	(L)	1972	Pract. of School Psych.	Masters	3	4	4	—	yes	no	2 yrs.			
Oklahoma	(L)	1965	Practice of Psychology	Doctorate	—	—	2	—	yes	no	1 yr.	5	0	3
Oregon	(L)	1973	Practice of Psychology	Doctorate	—	2	2	—	yes	no	1 yr.	7	2	3
			Psychologist Associate	Masters	—	3	—	—	yes	yes	1 yr.			
Pennsylvania	(L)	1972	Practice of Psychology	Doctorate	3	1	2	yes	yes	no	2 yrs.	7	0	3
Rhode Island	(C)	1969	Consulting Psychologist	Masters	4	2	4	—	yes	no	2 yrs.	3	0	3
			Academic Psychologist	Doctorate	1	2	2	yes	yes	no	1 yr.			
South Carolina	(L)	1968	Practice of Psychology	Doctorate	1	2	2	yes	yes	no	1 yr.	7	0	5
			Psychologist Associate	Masters	—	—	0	yes	waiv.	no	2 yrs.			
Tennesse	(L)	1953	Psychologist	Doctorate	—	1	1	yes	yes	yes	2 yrs.	5	0	5
			Psychological Examiner	Masters	—	—	0	yes	yes	no	perm.			

Texas	(L)	1969	Psychologist	Doctorate	1	1	2	yes	waiv.	no	1 yr.	6	0	6
			Psychological Associate	Masters	—	—	0		no	no	1 yr.			
Utah	(L)	1959	Practice of Psychologist	Doctorate	1	1	2	—	yes	yes	1 yr.	5	0	5
Vermont	(L)	1976	Practicing Psychologist	Doctorate	2	2	3	yes	yes	yes	2 yrs.	3	2	5
			Psychological Associate	Masters	3	3	4		yes	yes	2 yrs.			
Virginia	(L)	1966	Clinical Psychologist	Doctorate	2	2	2	yes	yes	yes	—	5	0	5
		1966	Psychologist	Doctorate	2	2	2	yes	yes	no	2 yrs.			
		1976	School Psychologist	Masters	4	2	4	n.a.	yes	no	2 yrs.			
Washington	(L)	1955	Psychologist	Doctorate	1	—	1	yes	yes	no	1 yr.	5	0	3
West Virginia	(L)	1970	Practice of Psychology	Doctorate	1	1	1	yes	yes	no	2 yrs.	5	0	3
				Masters	5	5	5		yes	no	2 yrs.			
Wisconsin	(L)	1969	Practice of Psychology	Doctorate	1	1	1	yes	yes	no	1 yr.	4	1	3
Wyoming	(C)	1965	Psychologist	Doctorate	—	—	0	yes	yes	no		5	0	3
CANADA														
Alberta	(C)	1960	Psychologist	Masters	—	—	0	—	no	no		8	0	1
British Columbia	(C)	1977	Registered Psychologist	Doctorate	—	1	1	—	no	no		5	2	2
Manitoba	(C)	1966	Psychologist	Doctorate	—	—	0	—	yes	—		7	0	2
New Brunswick	(C)	1967	Psychologist	Doctorate	—	—	1	—	yes	no		5	0	1
Nova Scotia—P.E.I.														
Ontario	(C)	1960	Psychologist	Doctorate	1	1	1	—	yes	no	perm.	5	0	5
Quebec	(C)	1962	Psychologist	Doctorate	—	—	0	—	no	no		8	0	1
				Masters	—	—	0							
Saskatchewan	(C)	1962	Registered Psychologist	Doctorate	—	—	0	no	no	—		5	0	2

Source: Compiled by the American Psychological Association Office of Professional Affairs, May 1978; reprinted with permission. Due to recent statutory changes in some states, the reader is cautioned that some inaccuracies may exist in this table.

APPENDIX MM

Professional Standards Review Committee

REQUEST FOR REVIEW

1. Request for review submitted by: (check one)

   A. Psychologist   ( )
   B. Third Party Reimbursement Organization   ( )
   C. Insured—or Insured Patient   ( )

2. Reason for submission to Review Committee _____

_____

3. Patient's Name _____ Age _____ Sex _____
   Address_____

   Relationship to Insured _____
4. Type of Service Rendered (in detail, including complication, if any)

_____

_____

_____

_____

_____

5. Fee(s) charge for these services $ _____

6. Treatment period _____

7. Action to date with respect to settlement of case _____
_____

8. Any additional information (attach copies of the questioned billing or claim forms) _____
_____
_____

9. Psychologist's supporting comments _____
_____
_____

10. Psychologist's Name _____
Address _____
Phone No. _____

11. Type of Insurance Coverage _____
_____

Address _____
Phone No. _____

BY: _____
     (Name)   (Title)

DATE: _____

PROFESSIONAL STANDARDS REVIEW COMMITTEE
CASE SUMMARY

1. Name of Professional Standards Review Committee person reporting _____
_____

Address _____

Phone _____ State _____

2. Who initiated the complaint:
   (a) Patient _____
   (b) Psychologist _____
   (c) Third Party Payor _____

3. What issues were involved:
   (a) Fees _____
   (b) Utilization _____
   (c) Appropriateness _____

    (d) Quality of Care _____
    (e) Qualifications of the prac-
        titioner _____
    (f) Other _____

4. How did the review committee handle
    these?
    (a) Physical meeting _____
    (b) Mail _____
    (c) Phone _____

5. Of the _____ members on the review committee, how many participated in
    the decision? _____

6. List any complications as far as the review committee was concerned:
    (a) Nature of case _____
    (b) Procedures _____

7. Date of Submission _____
    Date of Disposition _____

8. What was the disposition? _____
    Was decision by committee unanimous _____ Yes _____ No _____ If not,
    what was the vote? Favoring majority decision _____ Opposed majority
    decision _____ Abstentions _____

9. Was the decision accepted? _____
10. What guiding principles do you think helped you make a decision?_____
    _____

11. Did the parties turn to other agencies such as the courts, ethics committee, or
    other boards? _____

12. If this case is unusual or complex, please explain further on the reverse side.

Return to: Department of Professional Affairs
             AMERICAN PSYCHOLOGICAL ASSOCIATION
             1200 Seventeenth Street, N.W.
             Washington, D.C. 20036

Source: Committee on Professional Standards Review of the Board of Professional Affairs, *Procedures Manual.* American Psychological Assn., 1975.

NN

Competency to Stand Trial Assessment Instrument

COMPETENCY TO STAND TRIAL ASSESSMENT INSTRUMENT

			Degree of Incapacity			
	Total	Severe	Moderate	Mild	None	Unratable
1. Appraisal of available legal defenses	1	2	3	4	5	6
2. Unmanageable behavior	1	2	3	4	5	6
3. Quality of relating to attorney	1	2	3	4	5	6
4. Planning of legal strategy, including guilty plea to lesser charges where pertinent	1	2	3	4	5	6
5. Appraisal of role of:	1	2	3	4	5	6
a. Defense counsel	1	2	3	4	5	6
b. Prosecuting attorney	1	2	3	4	5	6
c. Judge	1	2	3	4	5	6

		1	2	3	4	5	6
d.	Jury	1	2	3	4	5	6
e.	Defendant	1	2	3	4	5	6
f.	Witnesses	1	2	3	4	5	6
6.	Understanding of court procedure	1	2	3	4	5	6
7.	Appreciation of charges	1	2	3	4	5	6
8.	Appreciation of range and nature of possible penalties	1	2	3	4	5	6
9.	Appraisal of likely outcome	1	2	3	4	5	6
10.	Capacity to disclose to attorney available pertinent facts surrounding the offense including the defendant's movements, timing, mental state, and actions at the time of the offense	1	2	3	4	5	6
11.	Capacity to realistically challenge prosecution witnesses	1	2	3	4	5	6
12.	Capacity to testify relevantly	1	2	3	4	5	6
13.	Self-defeating v. self-serving motivation (legal sense)	1	2	3	4	5	6

Examinee _____   Examiner _____

Date _____

BRIEF DEFINITIONS

1. *Appraisal of available legal defenses:* This item calls for an assessment of the accused's awareness of his possible legal defenses and how consistent these are with the reality of his particular circumstances.

2. *Unmanageable behavior:* This item calls for an assessment of the appropriateness of the current motor and verbal behavior of the defendant and the degree to which this behavior would disrupt the conduct of a trial. Inappropriate or disruptive behavior must arise from a substantial degree of mental illness or mental retardation.

3. *Quality of relating to attorney:* This item calls for an assessment of the interpersonal capacity of the accused to relate to the average attorney. Involved are the ability to trust and to communicate relevantly.

4. *Planning of Legal stragegy including guilty pleas to lesser charges where pertinent:* This item calls for an assessment of the degree to which the accused can understand, participate, and cooperate with his counsel in planning a strategy for the defense which is consistent with the reality of his circumstances.

    5. *Appraisal of role of:*   a. Defense counsel
                                       b. Prosecuting attorney
                                       c. Judge
                                       d. Jury
                                       e. Defendant
                                       f. Witnesses

This set of items calls for a minimal understanding of the adversary process by the accused. The accused should be able to identify prosecuting attorney and prosecution witnesses as foe, defense counsel as friend, the judge as neutral, and the jury as the determiners of guilt or innocence.

    6. *Understanding of court procedure:* This item calls for an assessment of the degree to which the defendant understands the basic sequence of events in a trial and their import for him; e.g., the different purposes of direct and cross examination.

    7. *Appreciation of charges:* This item calls for an assessment of the accused's understanding of the charges against him and, to a lesser extent, the seriousness of the charges.

    8. *Appreciation of range and nature of possible penalties:* This item calls for an assessment of the accused's concrete understanding and appreciation of the conditions and restrictions which could be imposed on him and their possible duration.

    9. *Appraisal of likely outcome:* This item calls for an assessment of how realistically the accused perceives the likely outcome and the degree to which impaired understanding contributes to a less adequate or inadequate participation in his defense. Without adequate information on the part of the examiner regarding the facts and circumstances of the alleged offense, this item would be unratable.

    10. *Capacity to disclose to attorney available pertinent facts surrounding the offense including the defendant's movements, timing, mental state, and actions at the time of the offense:* This item calls for an assessment of the accused's capacity to give a basically consistent, rational, and relevant account of the motivational and external facts. Complex factors can enter into this determination. These include intelligence, memory, and honesty. The difficult area of the validity of amnesia may be involved and may prove unresolvable for the examining clinician. It is important to be aware that there may be a disparity between what an accused is willing to share with a clinician as opposed to what he will share with his attorney, the latter being the more important.

    11. *Capacity to realistically challenge prosecution witnesses:* This item calls for an assessment of the accused's capacity to recognize distortions in prosecution testimony. Relevant factors include attentiveness and memory. In addition, there is an element of initiative in that if false testimony is given, the degree of activism with which the defendant will apprise his attorney of inaccuracies, is of importance.

    12. *Capacity to testify relevantly:* This item calls for an assessment of the

accused's ability to testify with coherence, relevance, and independence of judgment.

13. *Self-defeating v. self-serving motivation (legal sense):* This item calls for an assessment of the accused's motivation to adequately protect himself and appropriately utilize legal safeguards to this end. It is recognized that accused persons may appropriately be motivated to seek expiation and appropriate punishment in their trials. At issue here is the pathological seeking of punishment and the deliberate failure by the accused to avail himself of appropriate legal protections. Passivity or indifference do not justify low scores on this item. Actively self-destructive manipulation of the legal process arising from mental pathology does justify low scores.

Source: Laboratory of Community Psychiatry (Harvard Medical School), *Competency to stand trial.* Rockville, Md.: Center for Studies of Crime and Delinquency, 1973, pp. 100–102.

Appendix 00

A Selected List of U.S. Organizations and Agencies

Academy of Psychologists in Marital Counseling, 123 Gregory Avenue, West Orange, NJ 07052

Adoptees Liberty Movement Association (ALMA), P.O. Box 154, Washington Bridge Station, New York, NY 10033

Alcohol and Drug Problems Association of North America, 1101 15th Street, NW, Washington, DC 20005

American Academy of Child Psychiatry, 1800 R Street, NW, Suite 904, Washington, DC 20009

American Academy of Psychiatry and the Law, University of Pittsburgh School of Law, Pittsburgh, PA 15260

American Academy of Psychotherapists, 1040 Woodcock Road, Suite 241, Orlando, FL 32803

American Arbitration Association, 140 West 51st Street, New York, NY 10020

American Association for the Abolition of Involuntary Mental Hospitalization Inc., 301 Sedgewick Drive, Syracuse, NY 13202

American Association for Social Psychiatry, 2323 Oak Park Lane, Santa Barbara, CA 93105

American Association of Marriage and Family Counselors, 225 Yale Avenue, Claremont, CA 91711

American Association of Professional Hypnologists, 460 Market Street, Suite 301, Williamsport, PA 17701

American Association of Psychiatric Services for Children, 1701 18th Street, NW, Washington, DC 20009

399

American Association of Sex Educators and Counselors, 5010 Wisconsin Avenue, NW, Suite 304, Washington, DC 20016

American Association of Suicidology, 2151 Berkeley Way, Berkeley, CA 94704

American Association of Volunteer Services Coordinators, 18 South Michigan Avenue, Chicago, IL 60603

American Association on Mental Deficiency, 5101 Connecticut Avenue, NW, Washington, DC 20015

American Bar Association, Commission on the Mentally Disabled, 1705 DeSales Street, NW, Washington, DC 20036

American Board of Clinical Hypnosis, 353 West 57th Street, New York, NY 10019

American Board of Professional Psychology in Hypnosis, 17 John Dave's Lane, Huntington, NY 11743

American Board of Professional Psychology, Inc., 185 Broad Street East, Rochester, NY 14604

American Board of Psychiatry and Neurology, 1603 Orrington Avenue, Evanston, IL 60201

American College of Neuropsychiatrists, 27 East 62nd Street, New York, NY 10021

American Correctional Association, 4321 Hartwick Road, Suite L208, College Park, MD 20740

American Corrective Therapy Association, 1222 South Ridgeland Avenue, Berwyn, IL 60402

American Group Psychotherapy Association, Inc., 1865 Broadway, New York, NY 10023

American Hospital Association, Psychiatric Services Section, 840 North Lake Shore Drive, Chicago, IL 60611

American Humane Association, Children's Division, P. O. Box 1266, Denver, CO 80201

American Law Institute, 4025 Chestnut Street, Philadelphia, PA 19104

American Medical Association, 535 North Dearborn Street, Chicago, IL 60610

American Nurses' Association, 2420 Pershing Road, Kansas City, MO 64108

American Orthopsychiatric Association, 1775 Broadway, New York, NY 10019

American Personnel and Guidance Association, 1607 New Hampshire Avenue, NW, Washington, DC 20009

American Polygraph Association, 315 Nolan Bldg., Louisville, KY 40205

American Psychiatric Association, 1700 18th Street, NW, Washington, DC 20009

American Psychoanalytic Association, 1 East 57th Street, New York, NY 10021

American Psychological Association, 1200 17th Street, NW, Washington, DC 20036

American Psychology-Law Society, c/o Gwendolyn L. Gerber, Department of Psychology, John Jay College of Criminal Justice, 445 West 59th Street, New York, NY 10019

American Society of Clinical Hypnosis, 800 Washington Avenue, SE, Minneapolis, MN 55414

American Society of Group Psychotherapy and Psychodrama, 259 Wolcott Avenue, Beacon, NY 12508

American Sociological Association, 1722 N Street, NW, Washington, DC 20036

Association for Advancement of Behavior Therapy, 420 Lexington Ave., New York, NY 10017

Association for the Advancement of Psychoanalysis, 329 East 62nd Street, New York, NY 10021

Association for the Advancement of Psychotherapy, 114 East 78th Street, New York, NY 10021

Association for Humanistic Psychology, 325 9th Street, San Francisco, CA 94103

Association for Psychiatric Treatment of Offenders, 162-17 73rd Street, Flushing, NY 11366

Association of Existential Psychology and Psychiatry, 815 Park Avenue, New York, NY 10021

Association of Family Conciliation Courts, 10015 S.W. Terwilliger Blvd., Portland, OR 97219

Association of Medical Superintendents of Mental Hospitals, P. O. Box 500, Osawatomie, KS 66064

Association of Mental Health Administrators, 2901 Lafayette Avenue, Lansing, MI 48906

Bio-Feedback Research Society, Veterans Administration Hospital, 200 Springs Road, Bedford, MA 01730

Bureau of Social Science Research, Inc., Legal Services Program, 1990 M Street, NW, Washington, DC 20036

Child Welfare League of America, 67 Irving Place, New York, NY 10003

Children's Defense Fund, 1520 New Hampshire Avenue, NW, Washington, DC 20036

Citizens Commission on Human Rights, Church of Scientology, 835 South West Lake Avenue, Los Angeles, CA 90057

Conference for the Advancement of Private Practice in Social Work, 55 East Washington Avenue, Room 2304, Chicago IL 60602

Conference of Conciliation Courts, Los Angeles Conciliation Court, Room 241, 111 North Hill Street, Los Angeles, CA 90012

Coordinating Council for Handicapped Children, 407 South Dearborn, Room 1070, Chicago, IL 60605

Council for the Advancement of the Psychological Professions and Sciences, 1725 Eye Street, NW Suite 606, Washington, DC 20006

Council for Exceptional Children, 1411 South Jefferson Davis Highway, Arlington, VA 22202

Council for the National Register of Health Service Providers in Psychology, 1200 17th Street, NW, Suite 403, Washington, DC 20036

Crime Victims Compensation Board, 875 Central Avenue, Albany, NY 12206

Family Service, 445 East 23 St. New York, NY 10010

Gerontological Society, 1 Dupont Circle, Suite 520, Washington, DC 20036

Group for the Advancement of Psychiatry, Western Psychiatric Institute, 3811 Ohara Street, Pittsburgh, PA 15213

International Association for Suicide Prevention, 1041 South Menlo Avenue, Los Angeles, CA 90006

International Association of Voice Identification, 730 Michigan National Tower, Lansing, MI 48933

International Society of Stress Analysts, Burlington, VT 05401

International Transactional Analysis Association, 3155 College Avenue, Berkeley, CA 94705

Lambda Legal Defense & Education Fund, 22 E. 40th St., New York, NY 10016

Law and Society Association, University of Denver, College of Law, 200 W. 14th Avenue, Denver, CO 80204

Legislative Services Branch, Office of Program Planning, National Institute of Mental Health, 5600 Fishers Lane, Rockville, MD 20852

Lesbian Mothers' National Defense Fund, 1941 Division Street, Enumclaw, WA 98002

Mental Health Association, 3260 Wilson Blvd., Arlington, VA 22201

National Association for Retarded Children, 2709 Avenue E, East, Arlington, TX 76112

National Association of Coordinators of State Programs for the Mentally Retarded, 2001 Jefferson Davis Highway, Suite 802, Arlington, VA 22202

National Association of Human Services Technologies, 1127 11th Street, Main Floor, Sacramento, CA 95814

National Association of Private Psychiatric Hospitals, 353 Broad Avenue, Leonia, NJ 07605

National Association of School Psychologists, College of Education, University of Akron, Akron, OH 44304

National Association of Social Workers, 1425 H. Street, NW, Suite 600, Washington, DC 20005

National Clearinghouse for Legal Services, Northwestern University School of Law, 710 North Lake Shore Drive, Chicago, IL 60611

National Committee for Sexual Civil Liberties, 1800 N. Highland Ave., Hollywood, CA. 90028

National Conference of Lawyers and Social Workers, 2 Park Avenue, Room 2310, New York, NY 10016

National Consumer Center for Legal Services, 1750 New York Avenue, NW, Washington, DC 20006

National Council of Juvenile Court Judges, P. O. Box 8978, University of Nevada, Reno, NV 89507

National Council of Senior Citizens, 1511 K Street, NW, Washington, DC 20005

National Council on Community Mental Health Centers, 2233 Wisconsin Ave. NW., Washington, D.C. 20037

National Council on the Aging, 1828 L Street, NW, Washington, DC 20036

National Council on Family Relations, 1219 University Avenue SW, Minneapolis, MN 55414

National Education Association, 1201 16th Street, NW, Washington, DC 20036

National Federation of Clinical Social Workers, c/o Wright Williamson, 7979 Old Georgetown Road, Suite 312, Bethesda, MD 20014

National Organization on Legal Problems of Education, 825 Western, Topeka, KS 66606

Network Against Psychiatric Assault (NAPA), 629 Sutter Street, San Francisco, CA 94102

Office for Protection from Research Risks, National Institute of Health, HEW, 5600 Fishers Lane, Rockville, MD 20852

President's Commission on Mental Health, Room 121, Old Executive Office Building, Washington, DC 20500

Public Citizen's Health Research Group, 2000 P Street, NW, Washington, DC 20036

Recovery, Inc., 116 South Michigan Avenue, Chicago, IL 60614

School Records Task Force, HEW, Room 5660, 330 Independence Avenue, SW, Washington, DC 20201

Sex Information and Education Council of the United States, 1855 Broadway, New York, NY 10023

Sex Law Information Office, 3701 Wilshire Boulevard, Suite 700, Los Angeles, CA 90010

Society for Autistic Children, 169 Tampa Ave., Albany, NY 12208

Society for Clinical and Experimental Hypnosis, 140 West End Avenue, New York, NY 10023

Society for the Right to Die, Inc., 250 W. 57th St. New York, NY 10019

Technical Advisory Service for Attorneys, 428 Pennsylvania Avenue, Ft. Washington, PA 19034

The Compassionate Friends, P.O. Box 3247, Hialeah, FL 33013

The Freedom of Information Clearinghouse, P. O. Box 19367, Washington, DC 20036

Case Index

Author Index

Subject Index